# Communications
# in Computer and Information Science

**2960**

Series Editors

Gang Li, *School of Information Technology, Deakin University, Burwood, VIC, Australia*

Joaquim Filipe, *Polytechnic Institute of Setúbal, Setúbal, Portugal*

Zhiwei Xu, *Chinese Academy of Sciences, Beijing, China*

**Rationale**

The CCIS series is devoted to the publication of proceedings of computer science conferences. Its aim is to efficiently disseminate original research results in informatics in printed and electronic form. While the focus is on publication of peer-reviewed full papers presenting mature work, inclusion of reviewed short papers reporting on work in progress is welcome, too. Besides globally relevant meetings with internationally representative program committees guaranteeing a strict peer-reviewing and paper selection process, conferences run by societies or of high regional or national relevance are also considered for publication.

**Topics**

The topical scope of CCIS spans the entire spectrum of informatics ranging from foundational topics in the theory of computing to information and communications science and technology and a broad variety of interdisciplinary application fields.

**Information for Volume Editors and Authors**

Publication in CCIS is free of charge. No royalties are paid, however, we offer registered conference participants temporary free access to the online version of the conference proceedings on SpringerLink (http://link.springer.com) by means of an http referrer from the conference website and/or a number of complimentary printed copies, as specified in the official acceptance email of the event.

CCIS proceedings can be published in time for distribution at conferences or as postproceedings, and delivered in the form of printed books and/or electronically as USBs and/or e-content licenses for accessing proceedings at SpringerLink. Furthermore, CCIS proceedings are included in the CCIS electronic book series hosted in the SpringerLink digital library at http://link.springer.com/bookseries/7899. Conferences publishing in CCIS are allowed to use our online conference service (Meteor) for managing the whole proceedings lifecycle (from submission and reviewing to preparing for publication) free of charge.

**Publication process**

The language of publication is exclusively English. Authors publishing in CCIS have to sign the Springer CCIS copyright transfer form, however, they are free to use their material published in CCIS for substantially changed, more elaborate subsequent publications elsewhere. For the preparation of the camera-ready papers/files, authors have to strictly adhere to the Springer CCIS Authors' Instructions and are strongly encouraged to use the CCIS LaTeX style files or templates.

**Abstracting/Indexing**

CCIS is abstracted/indexed in DBLP, Google Scholar, EI-Compendex, Mathematical Reviews, SCImago, Scopus. CCIS volumes are also submitted for the inclusion in ISI Proceedings.

**How to start**

To start the evaluation of your proposal for inclusion in the CCIS series, please send an e-mail to ccis@springer.com

Safaa O. Al-Mamory · Ali Al-Sherbaz ·
George S. Oreku · Ahmed S. Albahri ·
Eman S. Alshamery
Editors

# Innovations of Intelligent Informatics, Networking, and Cybersecurity

Third International Conference, 3INC 2025
Babylon, Iraq, December 15–16, 2025
Proceedings

*Editors*
Safaa O. Al-Mamory
University of Babylon
Hillah, Iraq

Ali Al-Sherbaz
University of Cambridge
Cambridge, UK

George S. Oreku
Open University of Tanzania
Dar es salaam, Tanzania

Ahmed S. Albahri
University of Information Technology
and Communications
Baghdad, Iraq

Eman S. Alshamery
University of Babylon
Hillah, Iraq

ISSN 1865-0929        ISSN 1865-0937  (electronic)
Communications in Computer and Information Science
ISBN 978-3-032-24238-9        ISBN 978-3-032-24239-6  (eBook)
https://doi.org/10.1007/978-3-032-24239-6



This Springer imprint is published by the registered company Springer Nature Switzerland AG
The registered company address is: Gewerbestrasse 11, 6330 Cham, Switzerland

If disposing of this product, please recycle the paper.

# Preface

The 3rd International Conference on Innovations of Intelligent Informatics, Networking, and Cybersecurity (3INC 2025), held in Babel, Iraq, on December 15-16, 2025, was hosted and organized by the College of Information Technology at the University of Babylon. It was an international conference focusing on specific topics in Intelligent Informatics, Information Networking, and Cybersecurity.

One of the 3INC 2025 conference aims was to enhance the development of scientific research in Iraq. This was done by establishing a meeting for advance discussion of the accepted papers for evolving applications of computer methodologies to be used to understand cognition in the conference research fields. Hence, researchers and participants were invited to submit their high-quality research in such fields. The conference brought together researchers and experts to share novel outcomes and practical findings.

There were 62 local and international submitted manuscripts, from which 4 papers were screened out for various reasons such as out of scope or unqualified manuscripts. Only 17 (with about 29% as an acceptance rate) manuscripts were accepted from the remaining 58 short and long papers. The double-blind peer-review process by professional reviewers was rigorous to ensure selection of the best-quality manuscripts, with each manuscript being reviewed by at least three reviewers. The accepted manuscripts were distributed into three groups encompassing Security and Privacy, Networks, and Computing Methodologies.

The high-quality program would not have been possible without the effort and expertise of the Program Committee Chairs. Our great gratitude goes to the conference Committee members and all reviewers for their valuable feedback and time, during the reviewing process. All submissions were reviewed within the reviewing period and this should be greatly admired. It is expected that the accepted papers in this volume will inspire readers and researchers and open the door for further research. It is hoped that the readers will find much of interest in these proceedings.

December 2025

Safaa O. Al-Mamory
Ali Al-Sherbaz
George Oreku
Ahmed S. Albahri
Eman S. Alshamery

# Organization

## General Chair

Wesam S. Bhaya        University of Babylon, Iraq

## Program Committee Chairs

| | |
|---|---|
| Safaa O. Al-Mamory | University of Babylon, Iraq |
| Ali Al-Sherbaz | University of Cambridge, UK |
| George Oreku | Open University of Tanzania, Tanzania |
| Ahmed S. Albahri | University of Information Technology and Communications, Iraq |
| Eman S. Alshamery | University of Babylon, Iraq |

## Program Committee Members

| | |
|---|---|
| Abdelnaser Omran | Bright Star University, Libya |
| Ahmad Al Smadi | Zarqa University, Jordan |
| Ahmed Al-Ajeli | University of Babylon, Iraq |
| Ahmed Al-Azawei | University of Babylon, Iraq |
| Ahmed Hussein Ali | Al-Iraqia University, Iraq |
| Ahmed J. Hintaw | University of Karbala, Iraq |
| Ahmed M. Abdulkadium | Al-Qasim Green University, Iraq |
| Ahmed Mahdi Al-Salih | University of Babylon, Iraq |
| Ahmed Saad Hussein | University of Information Technology and Communications, Iraq |
| Aini Syuhada Md Zain | Universiti Malaysia Perlis, Malaysia |
| Akhil Mittal | UltraViolet Cyber, USA |
| Alaa H. Jarah | University of Babylon, Iraq |
| Alaa Fareed Abdulateef | Universiti Utara Malaysia, Malaysia |
| Alaa Shawqi Jaber | University of Babylon, Iraq |
| Alaa Yaseen Taqa | University of Mosul, Iraq |
| Aladdin A. Alsharify | University of Babylon, Iraq |
| Alejandro Zunino | ISISTAN, National University of Central Buenos Aires & CONICET, Argentina |
| Alharith A. Abdullah | University of Babylon, Iraq |

| | |
|---|---|
| Ali Al-Bayatti | De Montfort University, UK |
| Ali Al-Sherbaz | University of Cambridge, UK |
| Ali Jaddoa | Canterbury Christ Church University, UK |
| Ali Kadhum M. Al-Qurabat | University of Babylon, Iraq |
| Ali N. Al-Shuwaili | University of Information Technology and Communications, Iraq |
| Ali Saeed Alowayr | Al Baha University, Saudi Arabia |
| Ali Saleem Haleem | Al-Mustaqbal University College, Iraq |
| Ameer A. Alshamery | University of Babylon, Iraq |
| Ameer Kadhim Hadi | University of Babylon, Iraq |
| Amera I. Melhum | Duhok University, Iraq |
| Amera W. Al-Funjan | University of Babylon, Iraq |
| Anas M. Al-Shabndar | University of Information Technology and Communications, Iraq |
| Angela Amphawan | Sunway University, Malaysia |
| Ashraf AbdelRaouf | Misr International University, Egypt |
| Asraa A. Abd Al-Ameer | University of Karbala, Iraq |
| Assad H. Thary Al-Ghrairi | Al-Nahrain University, Iraq |
| Athraa Jani | Al-Nahrain University, Iraq |
| Aws Zuheer Yonis | Ninevah University, Iraq |
| Balqees Talal Hasan | Ninevah University, Iraq |
| Baydaa Sadeq | University of Baghdad, Iraq |
| Daniela Litan | Hyperion University, Romania |
| Elham M. T. A. Alsaadi | University of Karbala, Iraq |
| Emad Ahmed Mohammed | Northern Technical University, Iraq |
| Eman S. Alshamery | University of Babylon, Iraq |
| Fryal Jassim Abd Al-Razaq | University of Babylon, Iraq |
| G. Vijay Kumar | Osmania University, India |
| Hadab Khalid Obayes | University of Babylon, Iraq |
| Haider M. Al-Mashhadi | University of Basrah, Iraq |
| Hanaa Mohsin Ali | University of Babylon, Iraq |
| Haneen Ahmed | University of Baghdad, Iraq |
| Hasan Abdulameer | University of Babylon, Iraq |
| Hasan S. M. Al-Khaffaf | University of Duhok, Iraq |
| Hasanain Ali Al Essa | University of Babylon, Iraq |
| Hassan H. Alrehamy | University of Babylon, Iraq |
| Haydar Al-Tamimi | University of Technology, Baghdad, Iraq |
| Hayder Faeq Alhashimi | University of Malaya, Malaysia |
| Hayder Kadhim Zghair | University of Babylon, Iraq |
| Hiba Ameer Jabir | University of Babylon, Iraq |
| Hiba Mohammed Al-Khafaji | University of Babylon, Iraq |
| Hilal Mohammed Yousif Albayatti | Applied Science University, Bahrain |

| | |
|---|---|
| Hind Salim Ghazi | University of Information Technology and Communications, Iraq |
| Hiva Aleqabie | University of Karbala, Iraq |
| Huda N. Nawaf | University of Babylon, Iraq |
| Hussein AlKhamees | Almustaqbal University, Iraq |
| Hussein Alkhazraji | University of Northampton, UK |
| Hussein A. Ismael | University of Babylon, Iraq |
| Idress Husien | University of Kirkuk, Iraq |
| Iman Kadhim Abood | University of Babylon, Iraq |
| Iman Qays Abduljaleel | University of Basrah, Iraq |
| Intisar Shadeed Al-Mejibli | University of Information Technology and Communications, Iraq |
| Jyoti Prakash Singh | University of Calcutta, India |
| Khaldoon Hasan | University of Babylon, Iraq |
| Khaldoon Dhou | Texas A&M University, USA |
| Khitam Abdulnabi Salman | University of Technology, Iraq |
| Ku Ruhana Ku-Mahamud | Universiti Utara Malaysia, Malaysia |
| Layla H. Abood | University of Technology, Iraq |
| Daniela Litan | Hyperion University, Romania |
| Mahdi N. Jasim | University of Information Technology and Communications, Iraq |
| Mahmood Ahmadi | Razi University, Iran |
| Mahmood Khalsan | University of Northampton, UK |
| Manar Hamza Bashaa | University of Karbala, Iraq |
| Mark Lochrie | University of Lancashire, UK |
| Marwah Kamil Hussein | University of Basrah, Iraq |
| Marwah Nihad | University of Kirkuk, Iraq |
| Maryam Abo-Tabik | University of Lancashire, UK |
| Mehdi Ebady Manaa | Al-Mustaqbal University, Iraq |
| Michael Opoku Agyeman | University of Northampton, UK |
| Mohammad Alhisnawi | University of Babylon, Iraq |
| Mohammad R. Kadhum | University of Karbala, Iraq |
| Mohammed Al Jameel | Al-Mustaqbal University, Iraq |
| Mohammed Al-Khafajiy | University of Lincoln, UK |
| Mohammed Ibrahim Kareem | University of Babylon, Iraq |
| Mohannad M. Al-Yasiry | University of Babylon, Iraq |
| Mohsen Aljaaery | University of Babylon, Iraq |
| Muthana Salih Mahdi | Mustansiriyah University, Iraq |
| Nadhir Ibrahim Abdulkhaleq | University of Information Technology and Communications, Iraq |
| Nashwan D. Zaki | University of Information Technology and Communications, Iraq |

| | |
|---|---|
| Nashwan Jasim Hussein | University of Babylon, Iraq |
| Nor S. Sani | Universiti Kebangsaan, Malaysia |
| Qutaiba Humadi Mohammed | University of Information Technology and Communications, Iraq |
| Rasha Hussein Joudah | University of Babylon, Iraq |
| Rasim Azeez Kadhim | University of Babylon, Iraq |
| Ridho Ananda | Institut Teknologi Telkom Purwokerto, Malaysia |
| Roaa Safa Hussain | University of Babylon, Iraq |
| Ruslan Al-Nuaimi | Al-Nahrain University, Iraq |
| Saba Ayad Tuama | University of Information Technology and Communications, Iraq |
| Saba Mohammed Hussain | University of Babylon, Iraq |
| Saba Talib Hamada | University of Information Technology and Communications, Iraq |
| Safa Saad Abbas | University of Babylon, Iraq |
| Safaa O. Al-Mamory | University of Babylon, Iraq |
| Safaa Hatem | Al Muthanna University, Iraq |
| Saif Khalid Mahmood | Middle Technical University, Iraq |
| Sanaa Ahmed Kadhim | Medical Informatics College, Iraq |
| Sanjay Poddar | Palo Alto Networks, USA |
| Sarmad K. Ibrahim | Mustansiriyah University, Iraq |
| Scott Turner | Canterbury Christ Church University, UK |
| Shahad Ahmed Hussein | University of Babylon, Iraq |
| Shayma Nourildean | University of Technology, Iraq |
| Shaymah Akram Yasear | Al-Qasim Green University, Iraq |
| Suad Abdulelah Alasadi | University of Babylon, Iraq |
| Sumaya Hamad | University of Anbar, Iraq |
| Sura Zaki Alrashid | University of Babylon, Iraq |
| Susan M.A. Saleh | University of Babylon, Iraq |
| Tahseen A. Wotaifi | University of Babylon, Iraq |
| Taief Alaa Hamdi Al-Amiedy | University of Babylon, Iraq |
| Thar Baker Shamsa | Liverpool John Moores University, UK |
| Triantafyllos Kanakis | University of Northampton, UK |
| Venkatesh Ramalingam | PSNA College of Engineering and Technology, India |
| Wadhah Razooqi Baiee | University of Babylon, Iraq |
| Wafaa Mohammed Hamza | University of Babylon, Iraq |
| Wasan Mueti Hadi | University of Karbala, Iraq |
| Wesam S. Bhaya | University of Babylon, Iraq |
| Wial A. Hanon | University of Babylon, Iraq |
| Yahya Asmar Zakur | University of Mazandaran, Iran |
| Yanming Liu | Zhejiang University, China |

Yaseen N. Jurn                    University of Information Technology and
                                 Communications, Iraq
Yasmin Mohialden               Mustansiriyah University, Iraq
Yousra Ahmed Fadil             University of Diyala, Iraq
Yousra Fadil                   University of Diyala, Iraq
Zahraa Kadhim Al-Sindy         University of Karbala, Iraq
Zaineb M. Alhakeem             Basrah University for Oil and Gas, Iraq
Zeyad Safaa Younus             University of Mosul, Iraq
Ziad AlAbbasi                  Middle Technical University, Iraq

# Contents

## Computing Methodologies

# Security and Privacy

# A Hybrid Reinforcement Learning and Zero Trust-Based Framework for Proactive Insider Cyberthreat Detection


Yasir A. Hamza[1,2]([envelope]) [iD] and Najla B. Aldabagh[1] [iD]

[1] Department of Computer Science, University of Mosul, Mosul, Iraq
yasir.23csp57@student.uomosul.edu.iq, najlabadie@uomosul.edu.iq
[2] Department of Information Technology, Duhok Polytechnic University, Duhok, Iraq



**Abstract.** Recently, insider cyberthreats have posed significant and inherent risks to organizations and enterprises. These challenges increase the demand for proactive and adaptive ICD techniques that can effectively be mitigated such risks. This paper proposes a new proactive and hybrid ICD technique that integrates the principles of ZTA with a modified RL algorithm. Specifically, the RL-based model combines three algorithms (DDQN, Dueling Networks, and PER) in order to enhance detection performance and decision-making efficiency in dynamic environments. After 300 training episodes, the proposed method attains an accuracy of 0.9895, a precision of 0.9897, a recall of 0.9894, and an F1-score of 0.9895. Comparative analysis indicates that it outperforms existing RL-based methods. Notably, this model is not only data-driven and reward-optimized but also supports compliance with the ZTA policy, thereby enabling continuous verification, implementing micro-segmentation, and adapting access decisions dynamically.

**Keywords:** Double DQN · Dueling Network · Insider Cyberthreat · Reinforcement Learning · Zero Trust Architecture


## 1 Introduction

Recent studies and reports by cybersecurity specialists have highlighted a notable increase in security concerns related to insider cyberthreats [1]. Thus, the demand for designing intelligent, proactive, adaptive, and context-aware detection methods is a top priority for the cybersecurity community [2]. Insider cyberthreats pose a serious and evolving risk to organizations and enterprises. Therefore, developing proactive and adaptive security measures capable of handling insider cyberthreats has become a critical line of defence [3]. Insiders, compared to external attackers, have legitimate access to their organization's resources, including systems, data, and infrastructure [4]. Generally, all organizations are vulnerable to insider cyberthreats due to the legitimate access of individuals, such as employees, contractors, or partners, to their organization's sensitive data, despite predefined access authorizations and privileges of organization users. Accordingly, addressing insider cyberthreats requires more attention from the cybersecurity



S. O. Al-Mamory et al. (Eds.): 3INC 2025, CCIS 2960, pp. 3–20, 2026.
https://doi.org/10.1007/978-3-032-24239-6_1

community to provide effective cyberthreat detection approaches. Integrating technological cybersecurity solutions with organizational dynamics and a deeper understanding of human behaviour offers a multifaceted technique for identifying insider cyberthreats [5–7]. Generally, the rule-based or signature-based insider cyberthreat detection (ICD) strategies are inefficient for detecting subtle and evolved malicious activities committed by insiders [8]. Furthermore, traditional approaches based on static or predefined rules for identifying malicious activities lack the capability for dynamic, real-time assessment of user activities, especially in domains with complex user behaviour patterns or anomalies that evolve over time [6, 9, 10]. Accordingly, these limitations necessitate the development of proactive and intelligent ICD frameworks that are able to continuously adapt to access decisions and enforce the ZTA policies in response to evolving insider cyberthreats [11, 12].

This paper proposes a new and hybrid ICD framework that integrates ZTA principles with a Reinforcement Learning (RL) model. The proposed ICD method works proactively to detect and mitigate potential insider cyberthreats in real-time mode. ZTA model—never trust, always verify—enforces persistent authentication, limited access controls, and micro segmentation of the network [13]. Integrating ZTA with RL—especially deep RL—provides an ICD approach that enables the organization's system to learn better access controls directly by interacting with dynamic user environments. Consequently, the ICD method can effectively identify anomalous behaviours that pose insider cyberthreats.

The proposed ICD framework employs (28) features of each user's daily activities that are extracted from the widely used Computer Emergency Response Team (CERT) dataset (R4.2). The features include behavioural, temporal, and contextual data, which are stored in Comma-Separated Value (CSV) files, such as logon/logoff, device use, file access, web usage, and email. The extracted features have been pre-processed to provide clean data for feeding into Isolation Forest (IF), which assigns an anomaly score to each user activity. Additionally, data will be separated into (75% training and 25% testing). The CERT R4.2 dataset suffers from an imbalanced and real-only oversampling approach applied to the training data, which only provides balanced data. Finally, the training data is fed into an agent based on a combination of three RL techniques: Dueling Networks, Prioritized Experience Replay (PER), and Double Deep Q-Networks (DDQN). Additionally, the agent is coupled with a ZTA environment to dynamically adjust access decisions and enhance its ability to distinguish benign from malicious user activities. According to the experimental results, the proposed method achieved an Accuracy (Acc.) of 0.9895, a Precision (Prec.) of 0.9897, a Recall (Rec.) of 0.9894, and an F1-score (F1) of 0.9895, after 300 episodes of training. The main findings of our study can be listed as follows:

1. Coupling a ZTA environment with insider cyberthreat scenarios that implicitly extract 28 features of user daily activity from the CERT dataset.
2. Developing a hybrid ICD solution integrated with ZTA principles to build fine-grained user access control policies and to intercept cyberthreats in real-time.
3. Demonstrating that the proposed ICD framework achieves high performance across key evaluation metrics (Acc., Prec., Rec., and F1).

4. Showing that the RL-based decision reward optimization provides superior detection capabilities compared to traditional baseline methods.

The hybrid approach of RL and ZTA represents a new emerging direction for ICD approaches, a framework that enables adaptive, interpretable, and proactive methodologies. Therefore, ICD approaches move from reactive cyberthreat detection toward dynamic prevention of insider cyberthreats. The next sections of this paper are organized as follows: Sect. 2 exhibits the related works of ICD. The design of the proposed hybrid ICD framework, which is based on RL and ZTA principles, is presented in Sect. 3. Section 4 presents the experimental results and discusses the implementation of the suggested ICD approach. Finally, conclusions, limitations, and future works are presented in Sect. 5, followed by references.

## 2  Related Works

Insider cyberthreat detection approaches have evolved substantially alongside the advancements in Machine Learning (ML) and Deep Learning (DL). The limited generalization and static nature of rule-based or signature-based ICD approaches can reduce detection performance or even fail to detect novel or sophisticated insider cyberthreats. Consequently, scholars have explored RL models, particularly Deep Reinforcement Learning (DRL), to develop real-time, adaptive, and proactive ICD techniques.

Scholars have proposed several studies on Intrusion Detection Systems (IDS) and ICDs based on DRL in recent years. In [8] Saeed et al. proposed an RL-based ICD technique to implement in cloud environments. The ICD approach enables the detection of potential insider cyberthreats in real time. It uses two RL agents: Q-learning, and state–action–reward–state–action (SARSA), and each agent is integrated with Neural Networks (NN) in order to approximate Q-values when interacting with the cloud environment and increasing the learning capabilities for cyberthreats. Moreover, the CIC-Bell-DNS-EXF-2021 dataset was used to evaluate the model's effectiveness. Based on the experimental results, the demonstrated high detection performance achieved better accuracy up to 0.998 when using SARSA, and 0.982 with Q-learning. The limitations of this work were that the single-agent model was not suitable for distributed environments, such as the cloud, and the used dataset lacks the behavioural features of insiders. Drawbacks of the study included its single-agent model, which was inefficient for working with distributed systems like clouds, and the evaluation dataset lacks behavioural features of users that assist the RL model in detecting insider cyberthreats.

To address the limitations of traditional IDS in detecting novel cyberthreats, Hossain [13] introduced a new DQ-IDS that leveraged Deep Q-Networks (DQN) to provide an adaptive, self-learning, and real-time cyberthreat detector. Unlike the static models of ML/DL, DQ-IDS is capable of learning network behaviours depending on experience replay and adaptive $\varepsilon$-greedy exploration, thereby improving its detection performance over time. A reward-driven training technique was used to reinforce correct (non-malicious) classifications and punish misclassifications. The experimental results of the proposed model demonstrated that it can significantly minimize False Positives

(FP) and False Negatives (FN), achieving an accuracy of up to 0.971 on real-world network datasets. The study suffers from stability issues and requires improvement in the detection performance.

The authors in [14] proposed a ZT-based collaborative dynamic access control ICD scheme. Unlike traditional approaches that split the detection and mitigation processes, this scheme utilizes dynamically updated user trust profiles as a basis for real-time access control decisions, thereby combining anomaly detection with automated mitigation. An optimization of the traffic allocation policies is based on the use of the Multi-Agent Deep Deterministic Policy Gradient (MADDPG) algorithm. Accordingly, MADDPG enables flexible and coordinated account management in the context of security limitations, network status, and user requirements. Based on the simulation assessment, the model enhanced insider cyberthreats mitigation and showed the ability to utilize multi-agent DRL for scalable and intelligent access control in distributed environments. The lack of an evaluation dataset was a drawback of the proposed study.

Researchers in [15] suggested a hybrid RL and Natural Language Processing (NLP)-based framework for Host-based IDS. The TextRank algorithm was used to extract features or keywords from the system call logs and then pass them into a pre-trained Seq2Seq model, which is guided by an Actor-Critic (A2C) RL algorithm. Accordingly, A2C RL generates detection rules used to improve detection performance with high accuracy against novel cyberattacks issued by intruders. Based on the performance evaluation of the proposed IDS on the ADFA-LD and LID-DS 2021 datasets, the accuracy reached 0.965. A limitation of the study was that the dataset may become biased due to the continuous learning of the proposed model, which is based on a fixed dataset.

Lilhore et al. [16] proposed SmartTrust as a real-time ICD, which is based on hybrid DL and ZTA principles. SmartTrust combines three learning models: Convolutional Neural Network (CNN), Long Short-Term Memory (LSTM), and Transformer, to capture both spatial and temporal patterns of user behaviours and network traffic. RL provides adaptive decision-making against potential insider cyberthreats. It also utilizes a blockchain-based logging system to ensure that the model is aligned with transparency and compliance requirements. The evaluation of the ICD model on the CIC-IoT 2023 and UNSW-NB15 datasets yielded an accuracy of up to 0.98 for insider cyberthreats. In contrast, it reduced the false positive rates to 40%. The limitation of the proposed ICD is the higher computational overhead.

To handle the challenges posed by duplicated features and emerging cyberattacks in large, imbalanced datasets, authors in [17] suggested a DQL-based IDS called Multi-Agent Feature Selection Intrusion Detection System (MAFSIDS). The model incorporates a multi-agent feature selection mechanism, transforming the $2^N$ feature space into N agent-based decisions to reduce and improve selection efficiency and complexity. Additionally, the feature extraction uses the Graph Convolutional Network (GCN) for enhancing purposes. IDS is implemented using supervised RL, employing the Mini-Batch technique to improve its accuracy and training performance. Evaluation results on both CSE-CIC-IDS2018 and NSL-KDD datasets showed that MAFSIDS reached an accuracy of (0.968) and (0.991) respectively, and F1-scores of (0.963) and (0.991) respectively. This eliminated 80% of redundant features compared to the original feature set. The drawback of the proposed ICD was that it consumed high computational power and resources.

In [18], the authors propose an adaptive security policy management framework based on RL to address the limitations of static security policies in dynamic cloud environments, such as Amazon Web Services (AWS). The proposed framework utilized DQN and Proximal Policy Optimization (PPO) to gradually make adjustments to both the firewall rules and policies of Identity and Access Management (IAM) using cloud telemetry data, including AWS CloudTrail, threat intelligence data feeds, and network traffic logs. The results of the experimental investigation demonstrated that the RL-based solution offered significant effectiveness, with an intrusion detection rate of 92%, a 58% reduction in incident response time, and high values of compliance and resource efficiency. These results demonstrated that the adaptive IDS approach held promise as an efficient strategy for managing cloud security policies.

The limitations of the studies mentioned above motivate the need for a hybrid ICD technique that integrates RL with ZTA principles in an adaptable, scalable, user behaviour-aware, and real-time environment. This gap is addressed in the next section.

## 3  Proposed ICD Method

This section describes a comprehensive methodology for developing an RL and ZTA-based ICD framework. The framework design process consists of three main phases: preprocessing, training, and testing. The first phase consists of a set of processes called data preprocessing, (behavioural, temporal, and contextual) features extraction, anomaly scoring via isolation forest, separation of training and testing data, and oversampling training data. In the second phase, an enhanced Double DQN (DDQN) with a Dueling architecture and Prioritized Experience Replay (PER), which is based on RL-based decision learning, is integrated with the ZT environment. Real-time access control decisions are obtained from the RL agent and guided by ZT principles. The last phase evaluates the ICD model on unseen or test data. The detection efficiency and dynamic policy enforcement are assessed during both training and testing of the ICD model, based on accuracy, precision, recall, F1-score, and reward metrics.

### 3.1  Preprocessing

The CERT dataset (R4.2)[1] is used to extract features that represent users' daily behaviours Table 1. Feature extraction plays a crucial role in detecting insider cyberthreats. Therefore, the accurate classification of users' behaviour, whether benign or malicious, relies largely on the quality of the extracted features. As a result, each CSV file is processed separately to extract behavioural, temporal, and contextual features. The CERT dataset contains six primary CSV files: *Logon, File, Device, Email, HTTP, and Psychometric*, as well as a set of files from Lightweight Directory Access Protocol (LDAP), which are used to describe all users and their assigned job roles. Here, both the psychometric CSV file and LDAP are excluded. Additionally, the contents of the

---

[1] https://kilthub.cmu.edu/articles/dataset/Insider_Threat_Test_Dataset/12841247.

CSV files represent the daily activities of 1,000 synthetic employees over an 18-month work period.

For instance, the logon CSV file is used to derive six features, including total logon events, outside work logon events, weekend logon events, session durations, total distinct logon times, and total unique PC logon. The normal working hours of users are between 8:00 AM and 7:00 PM; if a user logs on outside these hours, the behaviour is considered malicious. Moreover, any user logging on the weekend (Saturday or Sunday) is also deemed malicious activity. The device CSV file contains an 'activity' field that records two events: connected and disconnected. This field captures the usage of removable storage media by each user. Based on these values, one can compute the number of times a specific user accessed such devices. Furthermore, features can be extracted from the email CSV and HTTP CSV files based on fields such as 'to', 'bcc', 'cc', attachments, size, and URL, in order to analyse user-related activities in email communication and web access. The same process is applied to the remaining CSV files. The final output is a single CSV file called "daily user activity," containing feature vectors with 28 features that represent each user's daily activities, as illustrated in Fig. 1. Accordingly, the features selection is based on factors like the domain knowledge of insider cyberthreat behaviours, preliminary empirical analysis showing their strong discriminatory power, alignment with prior CERT-based studies, and finally computational efficiency considerations important for RL-based models.

Depending on predefined rules, the presence of a specific feature is encoded as 1, and its absence is encoded as 0. This process is applied to avoid null values during feature extraction. The accurate mapping between users and their daily activities is maintained by adding the user's identifier and the corresponding date to each user's feature vector, resulting in a "daily user activity.csv" file with 30 features and 31843136 records. Finally, these records are aggregated based on the user identifier and date to generate the final "daily user activity" file comprising 330453 records.

Isolation Forest (IF) is an unsupervised machine learning technique used to assign anomaly scores to each user's daily activities. These anomaly scores have various benefits for both DDQN and ZTA: (i) Anomaly scores offer a quantitative risk indicator that assists the RL model in distinguishing between normal and suspicious user behaviours effectively [19]. (ii) They improve the reward function of DDQN with risk awareness feedback and provide dynamic adaptation of ZTA access control based on real-time risk levels. (iii) Anomaly scores reduce the false positives and assist the DDQN algorithm in filtering out benign user behaviours more accurately [20].

The *"daily user activity.csv"* file, along with its corresponding anomaly scores, represents instantaneous data used for DDQN with the ZTA model implementation. Therefore, these data are divided into two subsets: 75% for training and 25% for testing. Additionally, the training data suffer from class imbalance due to the fewer instances of the minority class (insider cyberthreats) compared to the majority class (normal behaviour). Therefore, we employed the Real-Only Upsampling technique in order to address the class imbalance problem [21]. Real-only up-sampling does not generate new synthetic samples, unlike the Synthetic Minority Over-sampling Technique (SMOTE), which produces new artificial samples using interpolation. Instead, it only duplicates existing real samples from the minority class to increase their representation. Therefore, this technique

**Table 1.** CERT (R4.2) CSV files, fields, and total records

| CSV Files | Fields | Total Records |
| --- | --- | --- |
| *Logon* | ID, Date, User, PC, Activity | 854859 |
| *File* | ID, Date, User, PC, Filename, Content | 445581 |
| *Device* | ID, Date, User, PC, Activity | 405380 |
| *Email* | ID, Date, User, PC, To, CC, BCC, From, Size, Attachments, Content | 2629979 |
| *HTTP* | ID, Date, User, PC, URL, Content | 28434423 |

presents balance to the class distribution, maintains data interpretability, and ensures the classifier pays the same attention to both classes during training. In contrast, the testing data stay untouched and are used after the model's training phase to evaluate its performance on the unseen instances.

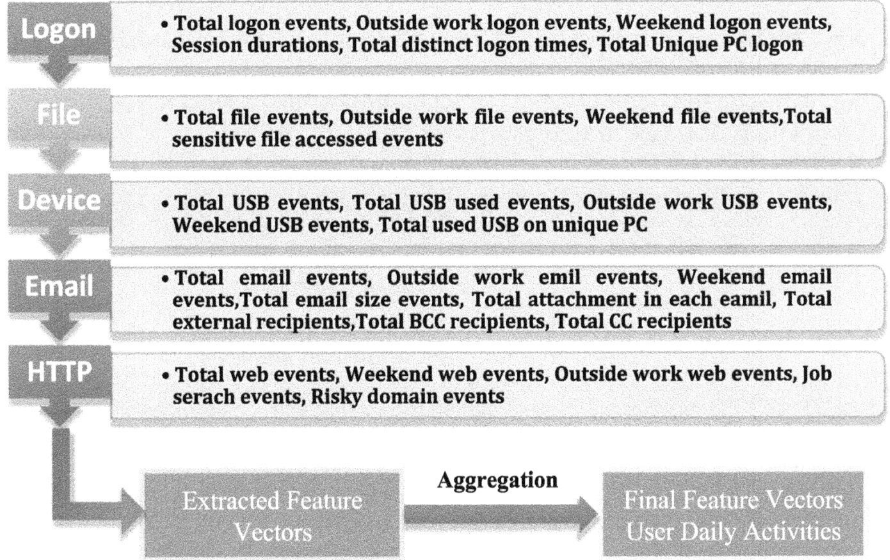


**Fig. 1.** Feature extraction process from the CERT (R4.2) dataset

## 3.2 Training

During this phase of our study, we illustrated the model design and its training in detail. As mentioned, the proposed model is based on the integration of RL with ZTA principles. RL is based on the learning model that enables an agent to learn optimal behaviour through trial-and-error interactions with the environment; in contrast to the traditional supervised and unsupervised learning that rely on labelled data [22]. Through repeated and stochastic interactions between the agent and the environment, the agent learns and gains knowledge for decision-making by maximizing the cumulative reward. The essential components of RL are as follows:

- *Agent* is an active entity that seeks a specific goal and is able to make decisions.
- *Environment* is the external world in which the agent interacts.
- *Policy ($\pi$)* defines how to regulate actions of the agent in each state of the environment.
- *Reward* is the feedback from the environment to indicate the quality of the action, either positive or negative.
- *Value Function* is used as a measure of how good a state or action is, considered as state value or an action value.

RL uses Markov Decision Process (MDP), which is a standard mathematical model for deciding stochastic and partially observable environments [23]. MDP uses a tuple with five elements $<S, A, R, P, \gamma>$, where S is a set of all possible states, A is a set of actions available for the agent, R is the reward function, and $\gamma$ is the discount factor: S $\times$ A $\rightarrow$ $\mathbb{R}$, $P(\acute{s}|s,a)$ is the transition probability of moving to the next state $\acute{s}$ from the current state $s$ given action a, and $\gamma$ is the discount factor denoted by $\gamma \in [0, 1]$ that determines the importance of future rewards. Consequently, we define the elements of the MDP tuple $<S, A, R, P, \gamma>$ in our model according to the following:

- $S$ is the state space representing 28-feature vectors describing user daily activities extracted from the CERT R4.2 dataset.
- $A$ is the action space consisting of two actions: Allow and Deny. It represents access control decisions made in accordance with ZT security policies.
- $R$ is the reward function that integrates cyberthreat severity, scores of anomaly detection, and violation of ZT policies. It is formulated as Eq. (1):

$$R(s, a) = \begin{cases} +1.5, \text{ if } \textbf{\textit{TP}}\text{ (Malicious denied)} \\ +0.3, \text{ if } \textbf{\textit{TN}}\text{ (Benign allowed)} \\ -1.0, \text{ if } \textbf{\textit{FP}}\text{ (Benign denied)} \\ -2.0, \text{ if } \textbf{\textit{FN}}\text{ (Malicious allowed)} \end{cases} \qquad (1)$$

where *TP, TN, FP, and FN* are used to denote true positive, true negative, false positive, and false negative, respectively.

- $P$ is the probability of transition that is defined by the simulation environment based on the CERT dataset. The transitions between states can be obtained through sequential sampling of the user's daily activities and constrained by previous actions and their outcomes. Therefore, this process provides a realistic simulation to feedback behaviour under ZT-based access control enforcement.
- $\gamma$ is the discount factor that is used to regulate the agent's balance between immediate and future rewards. Therefore, the higher value of $\gamma$ encourages the agent to prioritize long-term cyberthreat mitigation, thereby engaging in proactive risk management.

Q-learning is the basic and value-based RL [8]. The Dynamic Programming (DP) methods are used to solve MDPs based on a full model of the environment, including transitions and reward functions, that is known. In contrast, Q-learning is model-free, allowing it to learn from experience without requiring knowledge of the environment's transitions or reward functions. Therefore, it permits the agent to discover the best policy by interacting with the environment [22]. Accordingly, the agent is able to maximize the expected cumulative reward by learning the optimal action-value function Q(s, a), which is the estimated value of taking action *a* in state *s*. It also employs an $\epsilon$-greedy strategy to determine the selection of action, where the agent balances exploration (taking stochastic actions) and exploitation (selecting the best-known action). Bellman Eq. (2) is used to update the Q-values iteratively based on the current Q-value, immediate reward, as well as the estimated maximum Q-value of the next state:

$$Q(s_t, a_t) \leftarrow Q(s_t, a_t) + \alpha \left[ r_t + \gamma \max_{a'} Q(s_{t+1}, a') - Q(s_t, a_t) \right] \tag{2}$$

where $\alpha$ is used for the learning rate and $r_t$ is the reward received after taking action $a_t$ in state $s_t$.

Deep Q Network (DQN) represents an advanced algorithm of RL that utilizes Neural Networks (NNs) in order to approximate the Q-value function [24]. Therefore, it enables the agent to handle high-dimensional input data like images and audio signals [25]. In contrast, Q-learning requires a massive Q-table to store the Q-value, making it infeasible in terms of memory usage. Additionally, DQN leverages the dynamic transition of Experience Replay (ER) and utilizes a target network.

DQN has several limitations, such as overestimation bias, sample inefficiency, training instability, and limited applicability [23, 24]. Therefore, we must address these challenges carefully when using DQN for ICD approaches. Considering the previously mentioned limitations of DQN, we present a modified version of DQN that integrates three algorithms of RL, namely Double DQN (DDQN), Dueling Networks, and Prioritized Experience Replay (PER). The primary objectives of the proposed method are to ensure training stability, efficiency, and high accuracy in detecting cyberthreats.

The proposed method utilizes DDQN as its core algorithm. At the same time, the other components—Dueling Networks and PER—are integrated in order to enhance the overall performance of the hybrid ICD method. DDQN is a variant of the classical DQN, which is designed to address its well-known overestimation bias. The standard DQN uses the same network for both selecting and evaluating the maximum action. Therefore, this technique results in optimistic value estimates and unstable learning in complex or partially observable environments. Accordingly, DDQN reduces this bias by separating the action selection and action evaluation steps through the use of two neural networks [25]:

- The online network $Q(s, a; \theta)$ is responsible for selecting the action.
- The target network $Q(s, a; \theta -)$ is responsible for assessing the selected action.

The target value used for updating the Q-function is computed using Eq. (3):

$$y^{DDQN} = r + \gamma Q\left(s', arg\,max_{a'}\, Q(s', a'; \theta); \theta^-\right) \tag{3}$$

where $\theta$ represents both the weights and bias parameters of the neural network used to approximate the Q-values, this design therefore decreases the likelihood of propagating overestimated Q-values, which provides better stabilization and more realistic policy learning. It is also used primarily in environments where misclassification of malicious activity could lead to significant cyberthreats. To reduce overestimation bias, DDQN enhances the agent's decision-making capabilities, making it well-suited for domains where high precision and detection rates are essential, particularly for ICD techniques.

The Dueling network is a structural improvement to DQNs that enhances the quality of action-value estimation by decoupling the Q-value function into two functions: the state-value and the advantage [24]. DQN learns a scalar Q-value for each state-action pair, while a Dueling network separately estimates:

- *V(s):* The value function that is used to estimate the importance of being in state $s$, irrespective of which action is taken.
- *A(s, a):* The advantage function that is used to select the most beneficial action $a$ in state $s$ among the other available actions.

Therefore, this decomposition is useful in situations where the choice of action has little effect on the outcome. Accordingly, it enables the network to learn the value of states more efficiently. Finally, the outputs of two functions are combined to produce the Q-value using Eq. (4):

$$Q(s, a; \theta, \alpha, \beta) = V(s; \theta, \beta) + \left( A(s, a; \theta, \alpha) - \frac{1}{|\mathcal{A}|} \sum_{a'} A(s, a'; \theta, \alpha) \right) \quad (4)$$

where $\theta$ signifies the shared parameters of NNs, while $\alpha$ and $\beta$ represent the parameters of the advantage and value streams. In addition, $\mathcal{A}$ is the set of all possible actions. According to Eq. (4), subtracting the average advantage ensures that the network does not arbitrarily shift values between V(s) and A(s, a). This identifiability constraint enables the network for learning stably. It also produces well-defined estimates for both the state value and the action advantage.

Prioritized Experience Replay (PER) is used to improve sample efficiency by biasing the agent's learning tendency towards the most informative experiences. In standard experience replay, transitions are sampled uniformly from the replay buffer, giving each experience an equal chance of being selected. However, in imbalanced domains such as ICD, this uniform sampling can result in under-sampling of rare but critical anomalies. This limitation may adversely affect the detectability and responsiveness of the ICD approach. Therefore, PER assigns for each experience a priority score depending on its Temporal-Difference (TD) error using formula (5):

$$p_i = |\delta_i| + \epsilon \quad (5)$$

where, $p_i$ is the priority assigned to experience i, $\delta i$ is the TD error, which is the difference between the predicted and target Q-values, and $\epsilon$ is a small constant added to ensure all experiences have a non-zero chance of being sampled. Accordingly, this priority can be determined by the probability of sampling each experience using Eq. (6):

$$P(i) = \frac{p_i^{\alpha}}{\sum_k p_k^{\alpha}} \quad (6)$$

where $\alpha \in [0, 1]$ controls the degree of prioritization. In the case of uniform sampling, $\alpha = 0$, while higher $\alpha$ values increase the influence of priority scores. During training, importance-sampling (IS) weights are implemented in order to correct for the introduced bias using Eq. (7):

$$w_i = \left( \frac{1}{N.P(i)} \right)^{\beta} \tag{7}$$

where N is the total transitions in the buffer and $w_i$ represents the weights. The parameter $\beta \in [0, 1]$ is gradually incremented toward one over time. Therefore, this enables rapid convergence and improved generalization by allowing the agent to focus more on transitions with high TD error. PER encourages the agent to focus on transitions that are difficult to predict and have a higher impact on learning, based on experiences with higher TD errors. Therefore, it improves the model's performance in complex, high-stakes environments, such as those found in ICD approaches. Finally, Eq. (8) is used to calculate the value of the loss function, which is weighted squared TD error:

$$\mathcal{L} = \frac{1}{B} \sum_{i=1}^{B} w_i.(y_i - Q(s_i, a_i; \theta))^2 \tag{8}$$

where B is the size of the mini-batch, $\theta$ is the parameters of the online Dueling network, $y_i$ is a target Q-value, and $Q(s_i, a_i; \theta)$ is a predicted Q-value for the taken action. In the proposed model, we employed the Noisy Network Layer (NNL) layer strategy rather than the traditional epsilon-greedy exploration technique. Originally, this approach was proposed by Fortunato et al. [26], which depends on injecting parameterized, learnable noise into the weights and biases of the linear layers. It also enables the agent to perform state-dependent exploration. Consequently, NNL enables the agent to be more efficient and consistent in learning, particularly in complex environments such as insider cyberthreat detection. In the Dueling network, where the Q-network separately estimates the value and advantage functions, employing noisy layers enables the agent to explore more effectively in both the value and advantage streams. The integration of NNL with PER, which prioritizes learning from transitions of high TD errors, provides an exploration technique based on noise-driven learning. Therefore, this technique enhances the agent's ability to sample diverse and relevant experiences. It also enables the agent to converge on the optimal policies robustly and efficiently, without needing manual tuning of an exploration rate, such as epsilon. Figure 2 illustrates a flow diagram of the proposed ICD approach.

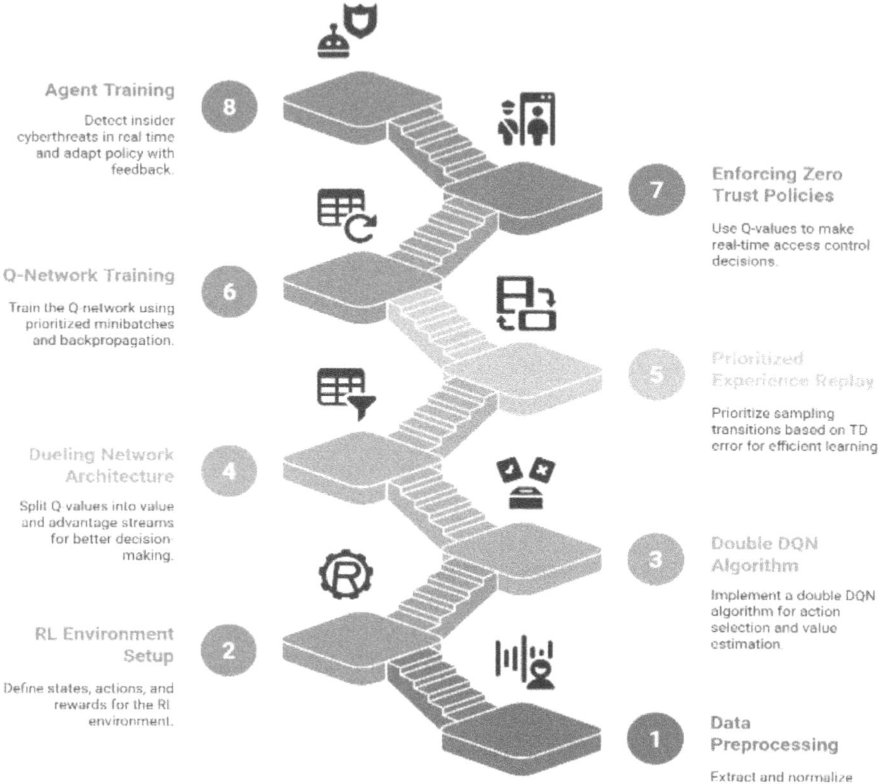


**Fig. 2.** Flow diagram of the proposed ICD approach

## 3.3 Testing

During this phase, the proposed method was evaluated using a test dataset comprising 25% of the total data extracted from the user's daily activities CSV file. Additionally, a similar environment, designed based on the principles of ZTA, was used during both the training and testing phases. The evaluation results are presented in Sect. 4.

## 4 Experimental Results and Discussion

The suggested ICD technique was implemented on Google Colab using Python 3.11, with libraries such as Pandas, PyTorch, and Scikit-learn utilized. The RL agent was trained for 300 episodes, with a maximum of 1000 steps per episode. Additionally, the hyperparameters included a batch size of 128, a replay buffer of 100,000, a learning rate of 1e−4, a discount factor ($\gamma$) of 0.99, and a soft update coefficient ($\tau$) of 0.005. The model worked on a scaled input consisting of 28 feature vectors and made binary decisions: Allow or Deny. An NNL strategy was employed to balance exploration and exploitation, thereby eliminating the need for traditional scheduling methods, such as epsilon-greedy. Finally, the target network was updated every 10 episodes to maintain stability. The proposed method achieved an accuracy of 0.9895, a precision of 0.9897, a recall of 0.9894, and an F1-score of 0.9895 after 300 training episodes, as shown in Fig. 3.

The performance evaluation results of the proposed method, compared to the existing approaches, are summarized in Table 2. The proposed approach is a novel method for ICD, which integrates three RL techniques: Double DQN (DDQN), Dueling Networks, and PER.

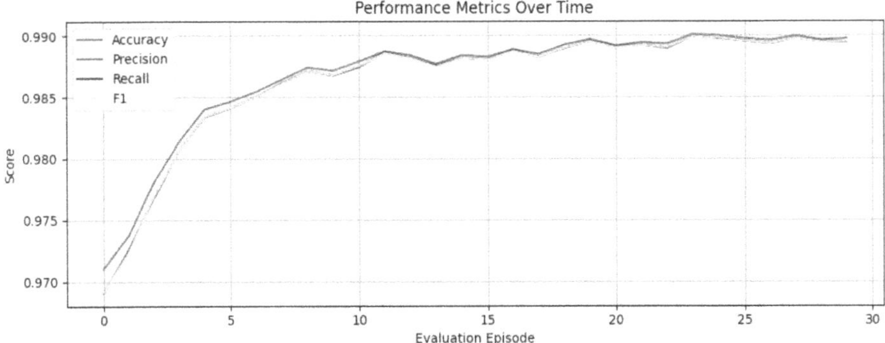

**Fig. 3.** Accuracy, precision, recall, and F1-score after training the proposed model for 300 episodes

To illustrate the effectiveness of the proposed ICD method in terms of model learning capability, two snapshots of the loss function are presented in Fig. 4. The first snapshot, depicted in Fig. 4(a), was taken at the $10^{th}$ episode, while the second, shown in Fig. 4(b), was captured at the $300^{th}$ episode. The notable reduction in loss values observed in the second plot indicates improved stability and convergence behavior of the model during the training process.

**Table 2.** Comparison of results with existing approaches

| Ref. Study | Used Algorithm | Type | Dataset | F1-score |
| --- | --- | --- | --- | --- |
| [27] | DQN and PER | IDS | CIC-IDS2018 | 0.982 |
| [17] | DQN | IDS | CIC-IDS2018 and NSL-KDD | 0.963 |
| [18] | DQN and PPO | IDS | CIC-IDS2018 | N/A |
| [23] | DDQN and PER | IDS | Real Data | 0.960 |
| [24] | DDQN and Dueling Networks | Malware Detector | VirusShare | 0.744 |
| **Ours** | **DDQN, Dueling Networks, PER** | **ICD** | **CERT (R4.2)** | **0.989** |

Additionally, the performance of the suggested ICD method was evaluated using a confusion matrix and Receiver Operating Characteristic (ROC) analysis at the 300th episode. The confusion matrix in Fig. 5 demonstrates the strong classification capability of the model. Specifically, the model correctly identified 48,780 normal instances and 50,000 malicious instances. In contrast, it misclassified only 1,045 normal instances as malicious (false positives) and seven malicious instances as normal (false negatives).

Moreover, the model achieved an Area Under the Curve (AUC) of 0.9992, as shown in Fig. 6, indicating excellent separability between malicious (insider cyberthreat) and normal behaviors. The ROC curve exhibits a steep rise toward the top-left corner, indicating that the model maintains a high true positive rate while minimizing false positives. Thus, these findings confirm the model's effectiveness as a proactive ICD technique. The near-perfect AUC further reinforces the model's ability to distinguish between malicious and benign behavior in real-time security environments.

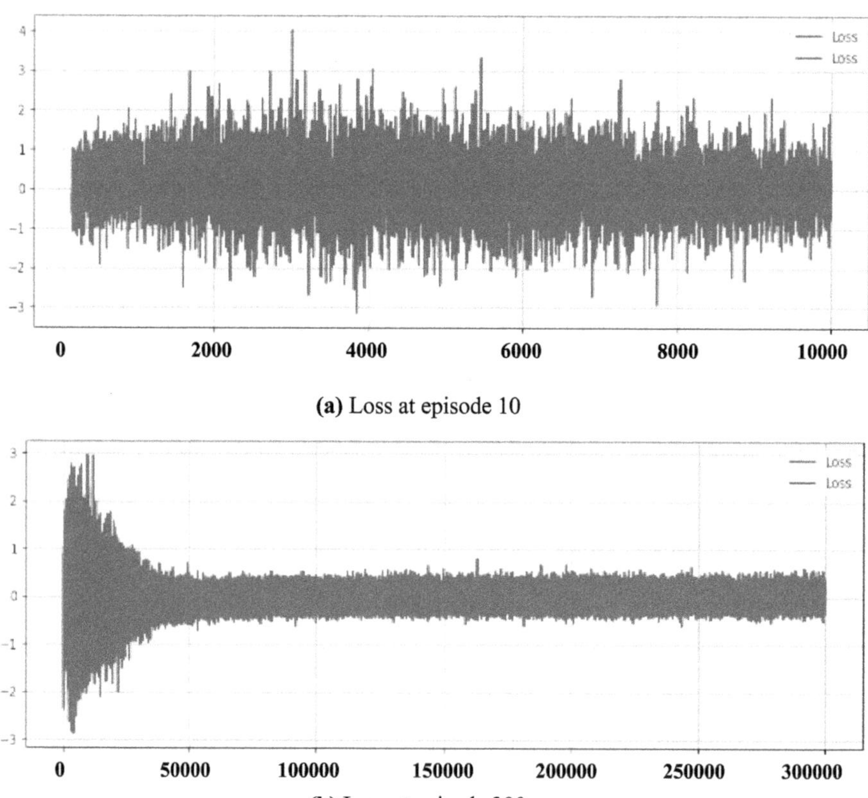


(a) Loss at episode 10

(b) Loss at episode 300

**Fig. 4.** Training loss snapshots illustrating model convergence: (a) at episode 10; (b) at episode 300

Finally, the proposed model was evaluated on the testing data, achieving an accuracy of 0.980 and an F1-score of 0.914. It also correctly detected nearly all malicious activities, with a recall of 0.999 for the malicious class and only two false negatives. Despite the precision for the malicious class being (0.723), which indicates the presence of some false positives, this trade-off can be acceptable in security contexts where early detection is more critical. Based on the results, the model proved its effectiveness as a proactive and adaptive ICD method.

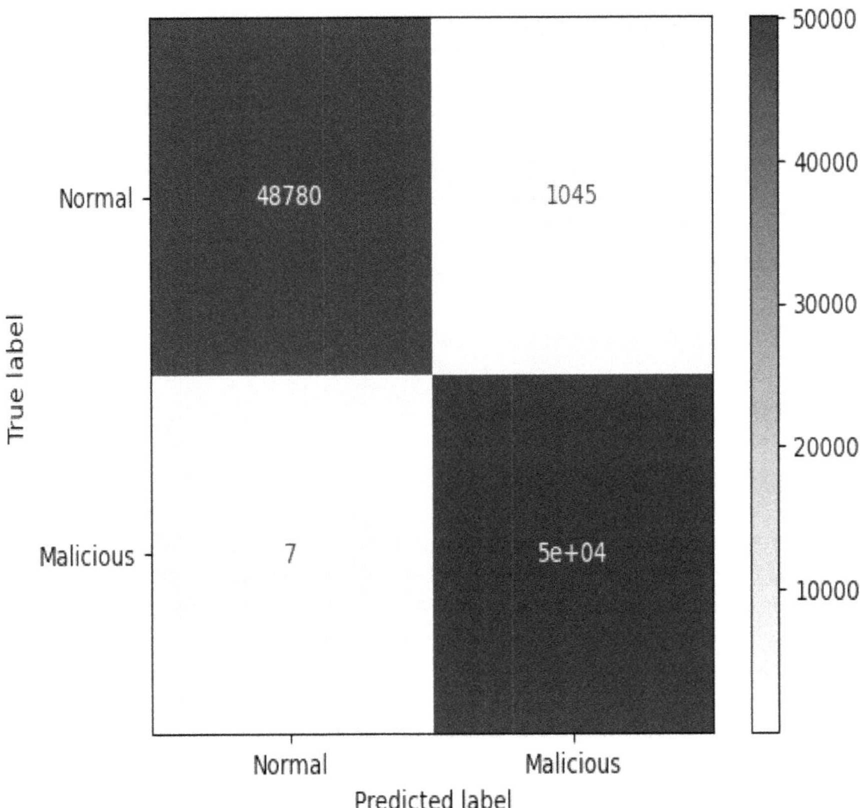

Fig. 5. **Confusion** matrix at episode 300.

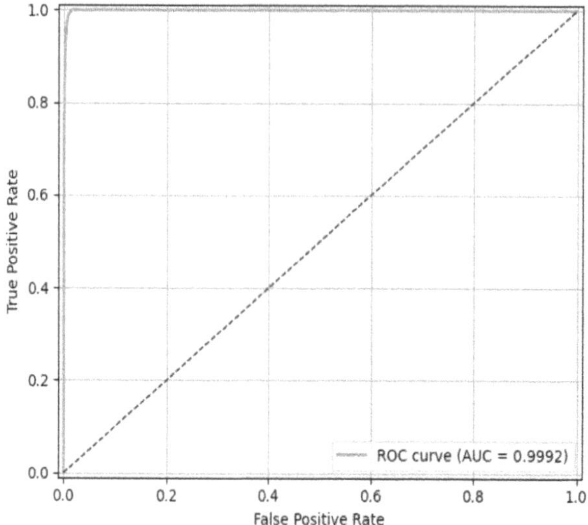


**Fig. 6.** ROC curve after training the model up to 300 episodes

## 5  Conclusions and Future Work

A novel and hybrid ICD technique that combined the principles of ZTA with an RL framework was proposed. The RL-based model demonstrated better detection performance in dynamic environments, thanks to the integration of techniques: DDQN, Dueling Networks, and PER. It also achieved a high accuracy, precision, recall, and F1 score in both the training and testing phases. According to the experimental findings, the proposed approach outperformed other models in terms of detectability. The proposed method was proactive, adaptive, and policy-aware in addressing insider cyberthreats through its integration with ZTA. The limitations of this study included dependence on a synthetic dataset, high model complexity, and the absence of real-time evaluation. Future work is needed to overcome these limitations.

## References

1. Zaid, T., Garai, S.: Emerging trends in cybersecurity: a holistic view on current threats, assessing solutions, and pioneering new frontiers. Blockchain Healthcare Today, 7 (2024)
2. Alzaabi, F.R., Mehmood, A.: A review of recent advances, challenges, and opportunities in malicious insider threat detection using machine learning methods. IEEE Access **12**, 30907–30927 (2024)
3. Xie, J.: Application study on the reinforcement learning strategies in the network awareness risk perception and prevention. Int. J. Comput. Intell. Syst. **17**(1), 112 (2024)
4. Wei, Z., Rauf, U., Mohsen, F.: E-watcher: insider threat monitoring and detection for enhanced security. Ann. Telecommun. **79**(11), 819–831 (2024)
5. Al-kateeb, Z.N., Abdullah, D.B.: Unlocking the potential: synergizing IoT, cloud computing, and big data for a bright future. Iraqi J. Comput. Sci. Math. **5**(3), 25 (2024)

6. Abdullah, D.B., Mohammed, R.A.-G.: Real-time big data analytics perspective on applications, frameworks and challenges. In: Book REAL-Time Big Data Analytics Perspective on Applications, Frameworks and Challenges, pp. 1–6. IEEE (2021)

7. Abdal, M.M.M., Abdullah, D.B.: Towards real time secure of IoT using SDN. In: Book Towards Real Time Secure of IoT Using SDN, p. 030036. AIP Publishing LLC (2025)

8. Saeed, M.Y., et al.: An intelligent reinforcement learning–based method for threat detection in mobile edge networks. Int. J. Netw. Manag., e2294 (2025)

9. Salih, K.M.M., Ibraheem, N.B.: Alpha-FedAvg: safeguarding privacy and enhancing forensic analysis in federated learning on edge devices (2025)

10. Mohammed, S.J., Taha, D.B.: From cloud computing security towards homomorphic encryption: a comprehensive review. TELKOMNIKA (Telecommun. Comput. Electron. Control) **19**(4), 1152–1161 (2021)

11. Sewak, M., Sahay, S.K., Rathore, H.: Deep reinforcement learning for cybersecurity threat detection and protection: a review. In: Book deep reinforcement learning for cybersecurity threat detection and protection: a review, pp. 51–72. Springer (2021)

12. Moamin, S.A., Abdulhameed, M.K., Al-Amri, R.M., Radhi, A.D., Naser, R.K., Pheng, L.G.: Artificial intelligence in malware and network intrusion detection: a comprehensive survey of techniques, datasets, challenges, and future directions. Babylonian J. Artif. Intell. **2025**, 77–98 (2025)

13. Syed, N.F., Shah, S.W., Shaghaghi, A., Anwar, A., Baig, Z., Doss, R.: Zero trust architecture (ZTA): a comprehensive survey. IEEE Access **10**, 57143–57179 (2022)

14. Jin, Q., Wang, L.: Zero-trust based distributed collaborative dynamic access control scheme with deep multi-agent reinforcement learning. EAI Endorsed Trans. Secur. Saf. **8**(27), e2 (2021)

15. Kim, Y., Hong, S.-Y., Park, S., Kim, H.K.: Reinforcement learning-based generative security framework for host intrusion detection. IEEE Access (2025)

16. Lilhore, U.K., et al.: SmartTrust: a hybrid deep learning framework for real-time threat detection in cloud environments using Zero-Trust Architecture. J. Cloud Comput. **14**(1), 35 (2025)

17. Ren, K., Zeng, Y., Zhong, Y., Sheng, B., Zhang, Y.: MAFSIDS: a reinforcement learning-based intrusion detection model for multi-agent feature selection networks. J. Big Data **10**(1), 137 (2023)

18. Saqib, M., Mehta, D., Yashu, F., Malhotra, S.: Adaptive security policy management in cloud environments using reinforcement learning, arXiv preprint arXiv:2505.08837 (2025)

19. Hasan, M.R., et al.: Building robust AI and machine learning models for supplier risk management: a data-driven strategy for enhancing supply chain resilience in the USA. Adv. Consum. Res. **2**(4) (2025)

20. Reddy, C., Prabhagaran, S., Vaid, A.: Adaptive anomaly detection in database transactions: bridging security gaps with reinforcement learning. Eur. J. Artif. Intell. Mach. Learn. **4**(2), 8–14 (2025)

21. Nasir, R., Afzal, M., Latif, R., Iqbal, W.: Behavioral based insider threat detection using deep learning. IEEE Access **9**, 143266–143274 (2021)

22. Yang, W., Acuto, A., Zhou, Y., Wojtczak, D.: A survey for deep reinforcement learning based network intrusion detection, arXiv preprint arXiv:2410.07612 (2024)

23. Fährmann, D., Jorek, N., Damer, N., Kirchbuchner, F., Kuijper, A.: Double deep Q-learning with prioritized experience replay for anomaly detection in smart environments. IEEE Access **10**, 60836–60848 (2022)

24. Coscia, A., Iannacone, A., Maci, A., Stamerra, A.: SINNER: a reward-sensitive algorithm for imbalanced malware classification using neural networks with experience replay. Information **15**(8), 425 (2024)

25. Kheddar, H., Dawoud, D.W., Awad, A.I., Himeur, Y., Khan, M.K.: Reinforcement-learning-based intrusion detection in communication networks: a review. IEEE Commun. Surv. Tutorials (2024)
26. Fortunato, M., et al.: Noisy networks for exploration (2017). arXiv preprint arXiv:1706.10295 (2018)
27. Hossain, M.A.: Deep Q-learning intrusion detection system (DQ-IDS): a novel reinforcement learning approach for adaptive and self-learning cybersecurity. ICT Express (2025)

# Enhancing Security of Integrated Circuits: A Multi-method Approach to Hardware Trojan Detection


Ammar Adel Ahmed[1]([✉]) [iD] and Mahmood M. Mahmood[2] [iD]

[1] Department of Computer Science, College of Education for Pure Sciences, University of Mosul, Mosul, Iraq
Ammaraladel@uomosul.edu.iq

[2] Department of Computer Science, College of Computer Science and Mathematics, University of Mosul, Mosul, Iraq
mahmood_mohammed@uomosul.edu.iq



**Abstract.** Protection against Hardware Trojans (HTs) is gaining importance as integrated circuits (ICs) continue to expand. This thesis represents a hybrid framework of detection that is a fusion of traditional HT-detection methods and machine learning (ML)-based methods to enhance the results of detection in terms of accuracy, speed, and resilience. A large number of classifiers Logistic Regression (LR), Decision Tree (DT), Random Forest (RF), Support Vector Machine (SVM), K-Nearest Neighbors (KNN), Naive Bayes (NB), Gradient Boosting (GB), AdaBoost, Multi-Layer Perceptron (MLP), XGBoost and a Meta-Learning ensemble were compared on a realistic Trojan dataset. A variety of tree-based and ensemble models (DT, RF, GB, AdaBoost) and the Meta-Learning ensemble scored almost perfect on the tests. The results showed that a combination of these ML methods and pre and post fabrication standard checks provided a scalable and workable pipeline of detecting IC security. It was found that the hybrid methodology significantly increased the detection rates compared to the standalone methodologies. In addition, a high-performance direction was achieved with respect to the implementation in production test settings.

**Keywords:** Hardware Security · Hardware Trojans (HT) · Machine Learning (ML) · Detection Methods · Integrated Circuits (ICs) · Model Comparison


## 1 Introduction

Hardware Trojan (HT) attacks on Integrated Circuits (ICs) are an issue in many technological areas due to high security risks. ICs are used in practically all forms of contemporary devices and equipment ranging from automobile, communication electronics, transportation facilities for transport, military, power control and aerospace to consumer home electronics [1, 2]. Any malicious modification, insertion, or alteration to the design or manufacturing of an IC that causes malicious behavior or the occurrence of behavior that was not intended (e.g. leakage of information, denial of service or disruption of



S. O. Al-Mamory et al. (Eds.): 3INC 2025, CCIS 2960, pp. 21–36, 2026.
https://doi.org/10.1007/978-3-032-24239-6_2

logic) is called Hardware Trojan. Such minor changes have the power to undermine the reliability and security of the systems especially when they occur in a rare or obscure circumstance [3].

There are a number of reasons why Hardware Trojan attacks are possible on ICs. One of them is that the process of creating semiconductors is rather complicated. This process is often a sequential process where many acting entities are engaged, including design houses, third party suppliers, and foundries. The big supply chain also means that the adversaries have many opportunities to penetrate [3]. Besides, there is no specific information regarding the whole production process and the areas of no control. All these elevates the risks. These vulnerabilities confirm the need to properly detect and prevent risks in order to address such sophisticated threats [4, 5].

Hardware Trojans are hard to detect and there is no single solution to the problem. Among the solutions reverse engineering, side channel analysis, and circuit feature analysis are notable [6]. There are two major steps in reverse engineering; the first one is to dismantle the IC and examine the physical layout of the device to ensure that it conforms to the design description. This method can identify differences that are indicative of malicious modifications; however, it is time consuming, expensive, and needs equipment [7].

In addition, side-channel analysis detects unwanted leakage used such as power consumption and electromagnetic signals to detect signals that reveal information about the presence of the Hardware Trojan [8]. Although this technique is non-destructive and can be used on working devices, it is very sensitive to noise and requires very precise setup [9]. The feature analysis of a circuit is based on the fact that some design parameters of the circuit can be used to distinguish normal and malicious circuits with the help of ML algorithms, thus making the approach scalable to quickly detect Hardware Trojans [10].

Detection techniques are often divided into two categories; pre- fabrication and post-fabrication. Pre silicon verification involves comparing the current design of an IC with the 'golden model' before the fabrication process begins and as a way of verifying that no one has tampered with the design [11]. Although this method has some challenges when used in IP based systems because the system consists of parts from different suppliers and therefore it would be extremely hard to develop a perfect model [12]. Post Silicon verification is the activity carried out after the realization of the actual IC and the subsequent validation of the performance of the end product [13]. In this phase, techniques such as auxiliary detection and runtime monitoring are applied to diagnose signs of attack. Auxiliary detection compares the behavior of known clean ICs with potentially infected ones to find anomalous behaviors. On the other hand, runtime monitoring measures certain parameters during their operations to identify dynamic threats that exist when certain conditions are met [14].

In addition to these conventional methods, the static detection techniques and the machine learning have been successful in the detection of Hardware Trojans. To this end, images, netlists and other physical attributes of ICs are used to train models that are capable of quickly learning to identify circuits as either normal or malicious. Another factor is the third-party vendor IP cores' reliability that is incorporated in the design.

Some methods which are used to mitigate the IP risk include testing, buying the IPs from reputable suppliers, and running the IP through an expert system [15].

Since the emergence of Hardware Trojan threats is relatively recent and on the rise, there is a need to develop an efficient security model to guard ICs against these threats. This means pre-RT, post-RT, on-chip monitoring, auxiliary methods, and machine learning are the only means to have a reasonable probability of detecting and removing HTs. In this respect, by enhancing detection and unalloyed IP outsourced, the industry can protect against such stealth and perhaps cataclysmic threats, and warrant the security and reliability of critical electronic applications in a range of applications [16].

Hardware Trojans (HTs) are malicious alterations deliberately added to integrated circuits (ICs) during the design, manufacturing or operation. These changes may result in information leakage, denial of service, degradation of performance, or latent activation on unusual trigger conditions. HT detection has become a critical part of the security of the system as ICs are further exploited to support critical infrastructure.

Studies have suggested that there are a number of different HT detection methods. Feature-based methods identify structural and behavioral features of netlists and side-channel traces (or routing data) and classify them using distributed classical machine learning models like SVMs, Decision Trees, and Random Forests. All deep-learning-based models learn trojan signatures automatically using CNNs, autoencoders, or graph neural networks. Runtime and side-channel monitoring tools such as power, EM and timing analysis detect anomalies post-deployment. Although all categories offer high-quality capabilities, there is no comprehensive tool. There is a need for hybrid models that combine traditional analysis and ML-based classification to have more robust high-scale detecting. The direction that the proposed work takes is the synthesis of multiple detection layers into a single pipeline and training it with modern ML methods.

The principal novelty of the current work is the hybrid IC hardware Trojan detection system based on introducing a systematic combination of traditional pre- and post-fabrication detection methods and a structured ML pipeline. While these approaches have been frequently investigated together in the literature, our model aligns them into a coherent workflow. A traditional screening approach to detect coarse anomalies, a self-developed approach, based on ML, to detect high-resolution anomalies and the use of a Meta-Learning ensemble to adapt quickly to new IC settings. This hybrid approach is more advanced than other studies as it provides not only better detection but also enhanced practical deployability in test-floor settings.

## 2   Related Works

Detection of HTs in ICs is one of the burning issues in the area of hardware security due to its critical impacts on safety-critical and high assurance systems. Hardware Trojans are alterations in a circuit that may cause the hardware to perform unwanted actions such as spill information, decrease efficiency, or even fail completely. Due to increase in the complexity of ICs and likelihood of complex attack, various methods have been developed to detect and prevent HT threats throughout the stages of hardware designing and fabrication [17].

Table 1 presents various techniques and methods suggested in the recent works to identify Hardware Trojans. These approaches include the conventional machine learning classifiers, reverse engineering approaches, clustering, deep learning, graph based models, generative models and reinforcement learning. All of them designed to deal with some of the issues related to HT detection, for example, the demand for precision, the ability to work in conditions of fluctuations in the process, or the lack of large sets of golden models.

**Table 1.** Related Works

| Reference | Problem | Methods | Accuracy | Strengths | Limitations |
| --- | --- | --- | --- | --- | --- |
| [18] | Detecting Hardware Trojans (HT) at the gate level | SVM and Neural Network (NN) | 100% | High accuracy in HT detection | Limited feature space (5 features) |
| [19] | Improving ML-based HT classifiers | Random Forest to select 11 important features from 51 | 100% | Focused feature selection, reduced dimensionality | May overlook less obvious but relevant features |
| [20] | Automating layout identification for HT detection | Histogram of Oriented Gradients, Decision Tree, AdaBoost | 92.25% | Effective automation and strong classifier combination | Dependent on accurate initial image processing |
| [21] | Clustering-based HT detection | K-means clustering on grid-based layout features | 99% | Simpler training, independent of parameters | Less effective on highly similar feature sets |
| [22] | ML-based HT detection using transient power analysis | Regression learning algorithms, cost-sensitive optimization | Effective HT detection under varied conditions | Adaptable to process variations | Complex optimization process; high computational cost |
| [23] | Side-channel delay-based HT detection | Neural Network watchdog; process tracking and noise mitigation | Accurate detection with reduced noise and variation impact | Comprehensive approach to noise and variation | Requires extensive data for accurate timing model |

(continued)

Table 1. (continued)

| Reference | Problem | Methods | Accuracy | Strengths | Limitations |
|---|---|---|---|---|---|
| [24] | Holistic HT detection using diverse features | DNN, image conversion of features, data augmentation | Improved detection across different stages and benchmarks | Integrates multiple data sources; robust against data imbalance | Requires large dataset; complex model handling |

## 3  Methodology

The block diagram in Fig. 1 shows a complete machine learning process which is built to identify Trojan malware in a given dataset. The process starts with importing the Trojan dataset that consists of network flow data of both normal and Trojan samples. These data are used as the input to the other stages of the pipeline where preprocessing is performed to make the data ready for the machine learning process.

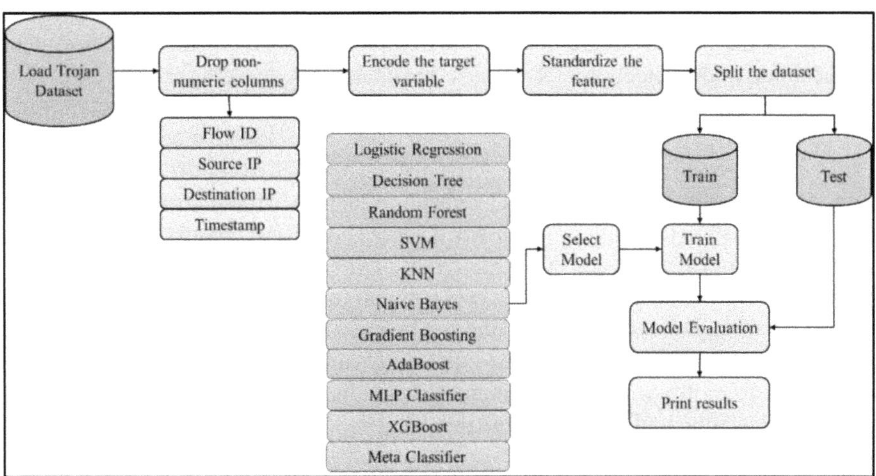


Fig. 1.  Model Block Diagram

During the first phase of data pre-processing, non-numeric features such as Flow ID, Source IP, Destination IP, and Timestamp are excluded. While these columns are helpful for other purposes, they do not help the machine learning model to identify patterns that are characteristic of Trojan activity. The next step after dropping these columns is encoding the target variable which is the class labels (benign or malicious). Encoding transforms these labels to a form that is acceptable by the machine learning algorithms. In addition, the features in the dataset are normalized which implies that the features are scaled with a mean of zero and a standard deviation of one. This standardization is important particularly for algorithms that depend on the scale of the input features for example SVM and KNN.

Once the data is preprocessed, it is split into two parts: Now there are the training set and the testing set. The training set is used in building the model while the test set is used in evaluating the performance of the model in new data. This split is required if the aim is to evaluate how well the model does when tested on unseen data which is always a critical way of evaluating a machine learning model.

The real crux of the problem lies in the selection of the machine learning model and its training. The models used are Logistic Regression, Decision Tree, Random Forest, SVM, KNN, Naïve Bayes, Gradient Boosting, Ada Boost, MLP Classifier, XGB, and Meta Classifier. All of these models have their own strengths and weaknesses, and the decision is made based on factors such as accuracy, time for computation, and interpretability of the model. Once the right model is selected, the training dataset is used to train it to comprehend the patterns associated with Trojan action.

After completing the training, the model was tested using the testing dataset. This evaluation consisted of accuracy, precision, recall, the F1-score, and the ROC-AUC score, depending on the problem type. These metrics gave a clue of the performance of the model in detecting Trojans and locating areas that may need fine-tuning.

Finally, the accuracy of the model was measured to give an overview of the ability of the model to detect Trojan malware. This is helpful in establishing if the model is at par with the real world to be deployed or if a few modifications are required. This structured approach of the pipeline guarantees that the employed machine learning model is not only accurate in the detection of Trojans in the dataset but also efficient.

### 3.1 Dataset Description

A dataset was collected from the CIC website to identify Trojan horse traffic through binary classification techniques. It contained a large number of records; 90,683 observations of Trojan horse traffic and 86,799 observations of non-Trojan or benign traffic. This distribution of samples allows for the creation and testing of strong detection models through the variety of network traffic that can be encountered. This way, the researchers and security professionals can improve their algorithms to differentiate between Trojan and benign traffic, which in turn increases the effectiveness of the network security systems in detecting and preventing the threats.

### 3.2 Machine Learning Algorithms

The machine learning algorithms employed in the present research were chosen due to their complementary features and their suitability in addressing the characteristics of the problem of hardware Trojan detection. The Decision Trees, Random Forests, and Gradient Boosting tree models were selected because they can deal with nonlinear relationships and heterogeneous features that usually occur in anomalies in circuit behavior. Linear models such as the Logistic Regression were also added to give a robust and interpretable baseline as well as to assess the suitability of the linear decision boundaries to differentiate between circuits infested with Trojan. The reason for using the Support Vector Machines was their efficiency in high dimensional feature space and their tolerance of overlapping classes. K-Nearest Neighbors was added as a distance-based approach on the evaluation of the similarity-based classification on the dataset. Lastly, deep learning models including CNNs, LSTMs, and GRUs were employed because they are able to learn more intricate patterns of time and structure which traditional models might miss. Combined, these different learning paradigms make it possible to directly compare performances of different types of models and to identify the ones that could best serve the purpose of hardware Trojan detection.

1. Logistic Regression: LR was used as a simple and interpretable baseline to determine whether the trojan-infected and clean circuits can be separated into linear decision boundaries or not. It is fast and gives good results in terms of feature-weight relationships so can be used to better understand what attributes have the most effect on classification [25].
2. Decision Tree Classifier: The reason why DTs were employed was their capability to detect a relationship that is nonlinear as well as inability to deal with mixed features. The interpretability is supported, but trees can potentially overfit when grown too deep [26].
3. Random Forest Classifier: RF is selected for its robustness and better generalization compared to single decision trees. RF added a good prediction effect by averaging the output of the trees that are being trained using subsets of the data, which reduces the variance. RF is also able to account effectively to missing or noisy features [27].
4. Support Vector Machine (SVM): SVM was selected due to its great functionality in high dimensional space and capacity to address linear and nonlinear boundaries using the kernel functions. It is especially practical in cases where the distribution of classes have small margin, but computational cost goes up with size of data [28].
5. K-Nearest Neighbors (KNN): KNN provides non-parametric distance-based comparison of classification. It is applicable in identifying local structure of the data; however, with large datasets, it is very expensive in respect to computation since a distance is calculated per-query [29].
6. Naive Bayes: In the case of independence of features, NB offers a rapid probabilistic baseline, which works well in this case. It needs very little training and is efficient in real time classification. However, when there are very strong dependencies between features, its accuracy deteriorates [30].
7. Gradient Boosting Classifier: GB was added because it was able to correct its errors by combining large numbers of weak learners through iteration. It is a good representation of complex patterns; however, it has to be tuned with much care or runs the risk of over-fitting to the data through its high flexibility [31].
8. AdaBoost Classifier: AdaBoost uses weighted weak learners to focus on samples that are harder to classify. It uses the clean data and simple base models well and is susceptible to noise and outliers [32].
9. The MLP (Multi-Layer Perceptron): MLP is a type of neural-network method that has the capabilities of learning nonlinear mappings in multiple layers. It is adaptable and is very strong but heavily relies on the hyperparameters including the number of layers and learning rate [33].
10. XGBoost Classifier was adopted as a high-performing, parallelized, and effective algorithm in structured-data prediction. It has regularization and optimized tree

building, therefore it is scalable and resistant to overfitting when fitted appropriately [34].

### 3.3  Meta Learning

Meta-learning or "learning to learn" is a branch of machine learning that focuses on developing techniques and models that enables a machine to learn other techniques and models to learn new tasks in a short time. It is defined as learning a new approach by using the previous experiences of previously solved tasks to solve new problems. This is achieved by training the model on a large number of tasks so as to learn about the structures and patterns of the tasks. The model employs a meta-knowledge, gained to rapidly adapt to the learning of a new task. Meta-learning is very useful where data is scarce or expensive to generate, for example, in disease diagnoses or in robotics applications, where learning must be fast. It includes several techniques, including few-shot learning where the model is trained to provide high accurate results from a few examples only, or model-agnostic methods such as MAML which modifies the model parameters to the new tasks using only a few steps of gradient descent. Therefore, meta-learning has great potential for new learning methods designed for increasing generalization and adaptability of AI systems in realistic environments [35].

### 3.4  Training Parameters

Table 2 provides default parameter settings for the machine learning algorithms, 'highlighting their typical configurations:

**Table 2.** Models Training Parameters

| Model | Default Parameters | | | | |
|---|---|---|---|---|---|
| Logistic Regression | max_iter = 100 | solver = 'lbfgs' | penalty = l2 | C = 1.0 | |
| Decision Tree | criterion = 'gini' | splitter = 'best' | max_depth = 5 | min_samples_split = 2 | min_samples_leaf = 1 |
| Random Forest | n_estimators = 100 | criterion = 'gini' | max_depth = 5 | min_samples_split = 2 | min_samples_leaf = 1 |
| SVM | C = 1.0 | kernel = 'rbf' | gamma = 'scale' | degree = 3 | |
| KNN | n_neighbors = 5 | | | | |
| Gradient Boosting | n_estimators = 100 | learning_rate = 0.1 | subsample = 1.0 | | |
| AdaBoost | n_estimators = 50 | | learning_rate = 1.0 | | |
| MLP Classifier | hidden_layer_sizes = (100) | | activation = 'relu' | solver = 'adam' | alpha = 0.0001 |
| XGBoost | n_estimators = 100 | learning_rate = 0.3 | max_depth = 6 | subsample = 1.0 | |

## 3.5  Evaluation Metrics

Choosing the right assessment scale is critical in training proper classifiers. Such an evaluation ensures that only the most appropriate rating scale is selected hence increasing the likelihood of an accurate classifier. Several measures pertinent to generative markers of the propinquity classifier were utilized and turned to discriminative measures. For example, consider that precision can be applied to numerous generative classifiers since it enables the determination of the most suitable solutions for training [36].

A confusion matrix Fig. 2, a highly utilized tool, assesses the effectiveness of a binary classification model by presenting the true values of the target variable (Truth: True $= 1$, False $= 0$ correspondingly with the model's prediction: Positive $= 1$, Negative $= 0$). Based on the confusion matrix, several performance measures including accuracy, precision, recall, and the F1 measure were determined. The matrix is typically divided into four quadrants representing four possible outcomes. There are four evaluation metrics used in binary classification issues: True Positive, True Negative, False Positive, and False Negative.

| Class designation | | Actual class | |
|---|---|---|---|
| | | True (1) | False (0) |
| Predicted class | Positive (1) | TP | FP |
| | Negative (0) | FN | TN |

**Fig. 2.** Binary Classification Confusion Matrix

The parameters that involve True Positives (TP), True Negatives (TN), False Positives (FP), and False Negatives (FN) are the basic features of the assessment of classification models. These four metrics form the basic elements of the performance measures that help to understand one or another aspect of the model's activity. Table 3 below outlines several key performance metrics derived from TP, TN, FP, and FN, along with definitions and formulas:

**Table 3.** The elements of the evaluation process (variables, definitions, and equations)

| Variable | Equation |
|---|---|
| Accuracy | $Accuracy = \frac{Tp+TN}{TP+TN+FP+FN}$ |
| Precision | $Precision = \frac{TP}{TP+FP}$ |
| Recall | $Recall = \frac{TP}{TP+FN}$ |
| F1-Score | $F1 - Score = 2 \times \frac{percision \times recall}{Percison+recall}$ |

# 4   Results and Discussion

Though a few ensemble and tree-based models such as RF, DT, GB, and AdaBoost showed an almost perfect accuracy, precision, recall, and F1 score at the held-out test data, the results should be interpreted with caution. Right metrics are uncommon in testing pipelines of real-world IC and can be indicative of attributes of datasets as opposed to actual generalization ability. The findings in the controlled experimental environment can be applied to the deployment stage and external validation should be conducted with respect to other designs of IC, other foundries, and environmental factors. Periodic re-training and runtime anomaly monitoring must be introduced in order to ensure high reliability in the operational environments.

## 4.1   Model GUI

A graphical user interface (GUI) Fig. 3 for making predictions through machine learning models. The interface is divided into four columns for input fields where the users can input as many features needed for prediction by the model. Every value has a proper title like "Flow ID", "Source IP", and "Flow Duration," which can be used in network traffic analysis or other similar programs. The input fields are well ordered and spaced which makes easy use of the website.

At the very end of the GUI, there is a dropdown menu with the option Select Model where users can select one of several machine learning models, namely Random Forest, Decision Tree, Gradient Boosting, Cat Boosting, Support Vector Machine. After the user enters values in the input fields and chooses a model, they can click on the green "Predict" button to start the prediction.

The graphical user interface is simple, space-saving, and well-structured, which makes the usage convenient no matter how many input features there are. It is ideal for big data features such as prognosis of network behavior or identification of abnormality.

**Fig. 3.** Model GU

## 4.2 Alert - Attack Detected

Figure 4 illustrates a dialog box to notify the user of an event. The name of the dialog box is 'Alert' and it has a threatening yellow triangle with an exclamation mark that is familiar to normal users. This helps the targeted user develop eyes for the message to help him or her know that the message is important. The box contains the message "Attack Detected" which hints at the notion that the system has detected potential cyber threat or malicious activity. As pertains to this particular form, this alert could include unauthorized access, a network intrusion, or something else which has been identified as suspicious by some type of monitoring device.

**Fig. 4.** Testing Alert

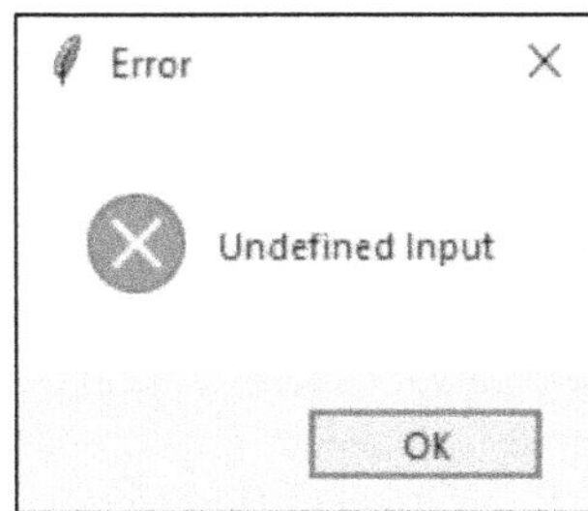


**Fig. 5.** Error Alert

The alert is contained with a dialog box which features only the OK button; it means that the user can only click OK to accept the message. It achieves this by keeping the layout simple and easily understandable so that the user can easily concentrate on handling the security threat. The kind of alert generated in this work is very useful in cybersecurity frameworks and applications because they alert the users of the danger so that they can be weary and avoid it or console it before causing a lot of havoc.

Figure 5 shows an error dialogue of informing the user about some error or problem in the system. The dialog box is called "Error" and has a red circle with the white "X" in it. This symbol is generally employed in graphical user interfaces (GUIs) to represent an error, or a failure condition that demands attention. The message that comes with it, "Undefined Input," means that the system has input data it could not recognize or analyze. This could happen for instance when a user fails to complete a certain field, enters an incorrect value or enters value in a format that the system does not accept.

The error message is useful for informing the user about input problems. The "OK" button in the dialog box gives the user an easy means of canceling the message and trying to fix the issue. Such messages are very important in friendly software applications since they assist in giving feedback, eliminating confusion and guarantee that the users enter correct data required by the system for proper functioning.

### 4.3  Models Metrics

The dataset deployed in this research contained 90,683 Trojan and 86,799 benign samples, which include flow-level metrics like durations, packet statistics, protocol behaviors, and timing properties. In order to provide a high level of rigorous evaluation and minimize the overfitting probability, a multi-step validation strategy was used. First, 80/20 stratified hold-out division was used to maintain the distribution of classes. Model development Stratified 5-fold cross-validation was performed on the training set to optimize the hyperparameters and the stability of the model across folds. Lastly the optimal settings were re-trained on the entire training set and tested once on the separate test set. Further robustness tests such as feature perturbation, noise injection, and limited environment-shift test were also conducted on models with near-perfect scores to test their performance in generalizing to ex-test-hold samples.

The confusion matrix in Fig. 6 analysis shows that Decision Tree (DT), Random Forest (RF), Gradient Boosting (GB), AdaBoost, and Meta Learning models have no false positive and false negative. Logistic Regression (LR) and Multi-Layer Perceptron (MLP) have a small level of errors and Support Vector Machine (SVM) has a moderate level of misclassification. The two algorithms with the highest errors are K-Nearest Neighbors (KNN) and Naive Bayes (NB), especially NB with the highest false positives. These results indicate that using ensemble methods and tree-based algorithms is the most accurate when working with this dataset.

The evaluation metrics in Table 4 show that most of the algorithms have a high degree of accuracy, precision, recall, and F1-Score, especially Decision Tree (DT), Random Forest (RF), Gradient Boosting (GB), AdaBoost, and Meta Learning. This shows that these models are very accurate with no misclassification hence suitable for this dataset. The other models that have very high accuracy are Logistic Regression (LR) and Multi-Layer Perceptron (MLP) which have 100% accuracy in all the metrics which shows that they have very good predictive power with very little error.

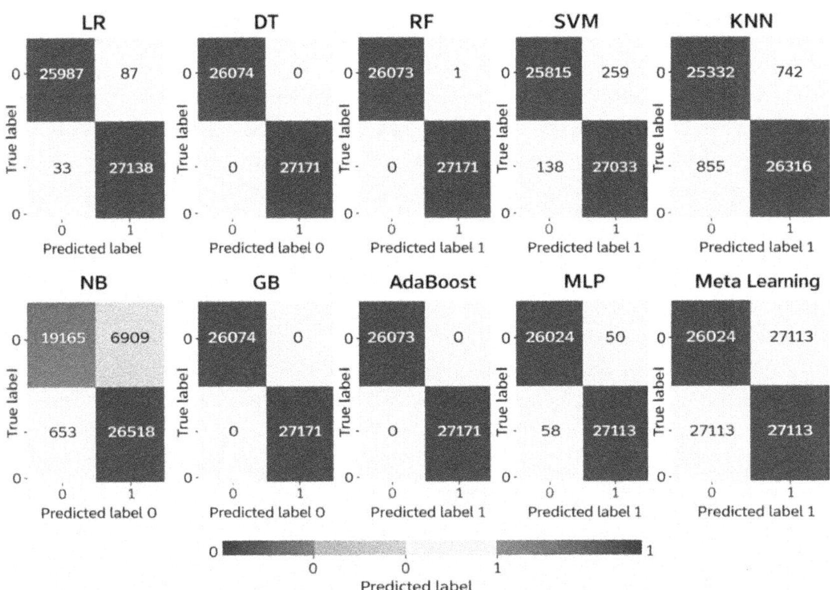

**Fig. 6.** Models Confusion Matrixes


**Table 4.** Models Evaluation Metrics

| Algorithm | TP | TN | FP | FN | Accuracy | Precision | Recall | F1-Score |
|---|---|---|---|---|---|---|---|---|
| LR | 25987 | 27138 | 87 | 33 | 100% | 100% | 100% | 100% |
| DT | 26074 | 2717 | 0 | 0 | 100% | 100% | 100% | 100% |
| RF | 26073 | 27171 | 1 | 0 | 100% | 100% | 100% | 100% |
| SVM | 25815 | 27033 | 259 | 138 | 99% | 99% | 99% | 99% |
| KNN | 25332 | 26316 | 742 | 855 | 97% | 97% | 97% | 97% |
| NB | 19165 | 26518 | 6909 | 653 | 86% | 88% | 86% | 88% |
| GB | 26074 | 27171 | 0 | 0 | 100% | 100% | 100% | 100% |
| AdaBoost | 26074 | 2717 | 0 | 0 | 100% | 100% | 100% | 100% |
| MLP | 26024 | 27113 | 50 | 58 | 100% | 100% | 100% | 100% |
| Meta Learning | 26074 | 27171 | 0 | 0 | 100% | 100% | 100% | 100% |

Support Vector Machine (SVM) is slightly lower than the best models, 99% on all the metrics, implying a near perfect classification. It has moderate misclassifications compared to the other models in the same category. KNN has 97% of all the metrics which shows that it has a poor performance compared to the other models. It has a few issues with false positives and false negatives, which slightly lowers its efficiency.

The worst results are achieved by the Naive Bayes (NB) with the accuracy of 86% and the decline of the precision, recall, and F1-score, equal to 88%. The false positives are high, which reduces the model's effectiveness for this dataset in comparison with other models. In conclusion, the ensemble methods and tree-based models were found to have the highest accuracy while Naive Bayes had the lowest accuracy followed by slightly lower but still acceptable accuracy of SVM and KNN.

## 5  Conclusions

Machine learning (ML) and conventional verification approaches were integrated to identify Hardware Trojans (HTs) in integrated circuits (ICs). The study proved that the implementation of ML algorithms enhanced the detection capabilities compared to the traditional approaches, and increased the rate of detection of intricate HTs with high precision. Compared to the traditional methods, it was found that the proposed ML models were superior in performance and especially useful in identifying complex threats. However, these strategies are scalable and efficient based on ML and can easily cope with the complexity and large data set. The presented hybrid detection framework contributes to the development of HT detection and provides useful recommendations for creating and testing secure electronic systems. In conclusion, the combination of the ML with conventional techniques offers a better approach to hardware security, thus offering significant advancements to the field.

## References


1. Abdulraheem, M., Al-Dabagh, N.: Anomaly-based intrusion detection system using one dimensional and two dimensional convolutions, pp. 409–423 (2020)
2. Dong, C., Xu, Y., Liu, X., Zhang, F., He, G., Chen, Y.: Hardware Trojans in chips: a survey for detection and prevention. Sens. (Switzerland) **20**(18), 1–37 (2020)
3. Bhunia, S., Hsiao, M.S., Banga, M., Narasimhan, S.: Hardware Trojan attacks: threat analysis and countermeasures. Proc. IEEE **102**(8), 1229–1247 (2014)
4. Fiorentini, D., Cappadone, C., Farruggia, G., Prata, C.: Impact of diseases linked to its deficiency. J. Nutr. **13**(1136), 1–44 (2021)
5. Mahmood, M.S., Ai-Dabagh, N.B.: Improving IoT security using lightweight based deep learning protection model. Tikrit J. Eng. Sci. **30**(1), 119–129 (2023)
6. Jasim, M., Younis, M.: Object-based classification of natural scenes using machine learning methods. Tech. Rom. J. Appl. Sci. Technol. **6**, 1–22 (2023)
7. Mao, J., Jiang, X., Liu, D., Chen, J., Huang, K.: A hardware Trojan-detection technique based on suspicious circuit block partition. Electronics **11**(24), 1–16 (2022)
8. Abdulraheem, M.H., Ibraheem, N.B.: A detailed analysis of new intrusion detection dataset. J. Theor. Appl. Inf. Technol. **97**(17), 4519–4537 (2019)
9. Nasr, A., Mohamed, K., Elshenawy, A., Zaki, M.: A Siamese deep learning framework for efficient hardware Trojan detection using power side-channel data. Sci. Rep. **14**(1), 1–13 (2024)
10. Rooney, C., Seeam, A., Bellekens, X.: Creation and detection of hardware Trojans using non-invasive off-the-shelf technologies. Electronics **7**(7), 1–21 (2018)
11. Altalib, G., Saeed, Y.: Comparative studying for extracting food contents using machine learning algorithms, vol. 2386 (2022)

12. Mahmood, M.S., Al Dabagh, N.B.: Blockchain technology and internet of things: review, challenge and security concern. Int. J. Electr. Comput. Eng. **13**(1), 718–735 (2023)
13. Wang, J., et al.: A hardware trojan detection and diagnosis method for gate-level netlists based on machine learning and graph theory. Electronics **13**(1) (2024)
14. Safaei Pour, M., Nader, C., Friday, K., Bou-Harb, E.: A comprehensive survey of recent internet measurement techniques for cyber security. Comput. Secur. **128**, 103123 (2023)
15. Dong, C., et al.: A cost-driven method for deep-learning-based hardware Trojan detection. Sensors **23**(12), 1–29 (2023)
16. Chakraborty, R.S., Narasimhan, S., Bhunia, S.: Hardware Trojan: threats and emerging solutions. In: Proceedings - IEEE International High-Level Design Validation and Test Workshop HLDVT, pp. 166–171 (2009)
17. Xue, M., Gu, C., Liu, W., Yu, S., O'Neill, M.: Ten years of hardware Trojans: a survey from the attacker's perspective. IET Comput. Digit. Tech. **14**(6), 231–246 (2020)
18. Hasegawa, K., Yanagisawa, M., Togawa, N.: A hardware-Trojan classification method using machine learning at gate-level netlists based on Trojan features. IEICE Trans. Fundam. Electron. Commun. Comput. Sci. **E100.A**, 1427–1438 (2017)
19. Hasegawa, K., Yanagisawa, M., Togawa, N.: Trojan-feature extraction at gate-level netlists and its application to hardware-Trojan detection using random forest classifier. In: Proceedings - IEEE International Symposium on Circuits and Systems (2017)
20. Nasr, A.A., Abdulmageed, M.Z.: An efficient reverse engineering hardware Trojan detector using histogram of oriented gradients. J. Electron. Test. **33**, 93–105 (2017)
21. Bao, C., Forte, D., Srivastava, A.: On application of one-class SVM to reverse engineering-based hardware Trojan detection. In: Fifteenth International Symposium on Quality Electronic Design, pp. 47–54 (2014)
22. Salmani, H.: COTD: reference-free hardware Trojan detection and recovery based on controllability and observability in gate-level netlist. IEEE Trans. Inf. Forensics Secur. **12**(2), 338–350 (2017)
23. Vakil, A., Behnia, F., Mirzaeian, A., Homayoun, H., Karimi, N., Sasan, A.: LASCA: learning assisted side channel delay analysis for hardware Trojan detection. In: 2020 21st International Symposium on Quality Electronic Design (ISQED), pp. 40–45 (2020)
24. Moustakidis, S.P., Liakos, K.G., Georgakilas, G.K., Sketopoulos, N.: A novel holistic approach for hardware trojan detection powered by deep learning (HERO). Attract **20**(Ml), 1–5 (2020)
25. Domínguez-Almendros, S., Benítez-Parejo, N., Gonzalez-Ramirez, A.R.: Logistic regression models. Allergol Immunopathol (Madr) **39**(5), 295–305 (2011)
26. Mienye, I.D., Jere, N.: A survey of decision trees: concepts, algorithms, and applications. IEEE Access **12**, 86716–86727 (2024)
27. Bhoomeshwar, B., Nagesh, Y., Raja Shekar, K.: Random forest classifier for classifying birds species using Scikit-learn. Int. J. Sci. Eng. Res. (2019)
28. Atik, C., Kut, R.A., Yilmaz, R., Birant, D.: Support vector machine chains with a novel tournament voting. Electron. **12**(11), 1–16 (2023)
29. Munazhif, N.F., Yanris, G.J., Hasibuan, M.N.S.: Implementation of the K-Nearest Neighbor (kNN) method to determine outstanding student classes. SinkrOn **8**(2), 719–732 (2023)
30. Webb, G.I.: Encyclopedia of machine learning and data science. Encycl. Mach. Learn. Data Sci. (2020)
31. Arif Ali, Z., Abduljabbar, Z.H., Tahir, H.A., Bibo Sallow, A., Almufti, S.M.: eXtreme gradient boosting algorithm with machine learning: a review. Acad. J. Nawroz Univ. **12**(2), 320–334 (2023)
32. Tharwat, A.: AdaBoost classifier: an overview, February 2018

33. Abdel-aziem, A.H.A., Soliman, T.H.M.: A multi-layer perceptron (MLP) neural networks for stellar classification: a review of methods and results. Int. J. Adv. Appl. Comput. Intell. **3**(2), 29–37 (2023)
34. Aydin, Z.E., Ozturk, Z.K.: Performance analysis of XGBoost classifier with missing data. In: 1st International Conference on Computing and Machine Intelligence, March 2021
35. Vilalta, R., Giraud-Carrier, C.: Data Mining and Knowledge Discovery Handbook, pp. 0–17 (2010)
36. Vujović, Ž: Classification model evaluation metrics. Int. J. Adv. Comput. Sci. Appl. **12**(6), 599–606 (2021)

# A Two-Stage Micro-segmentation Framework for SDN Security Using Modified ART2A Clustering and CIDR

Manar H. Bashaa[1,2]([⊠]) [iD], Wesam S. Bhaya[1] [iD], and Nabeel H. Kaghed Al-aaraji[1] [iD]

[1] College of Information Technology, University of Babylon, Babil, Iraq
manar.h@uokerbala.edu.iq, wesambhaya@uobabylon.edu.iq,
nhkaghed@itnet.uobabylon.edu.iq
[2] College of Computer Science and Information Technology, University of Kerbala, Kerbala, Iraq

**Abstract.** Software-Defined Networking (SDN) is an emerging paradigm that offers the flexibility to program and manage networks from a centralized point. Its dynamic nature, however, poses several security challenges. In an effort to resolve these issues and enhance traffic isolation, this research proposes a two-stage micro-segmentation technique. In the first stage, a modified Adaptive Resonance Theory 2A (ART2A) clustering algorithm, ART2A-RNorm, is utilized to classify the network traffic flows according to the destination port numbers, forming initial segmentation zones. In the second stage, micro-segmentation is done more precisely with Classless Inter-Domain Routing (CIDR) based on the source IP addresses of each cluster. The modified ART2A demonstrated clear advantages in experimental performance on the UNSW-NB15 dataset, including an increase in Silhouette Score (0.6295 to 0.7718), a decrease in Davies-Bouldin Index (0.7966 to 0.5971), and an improvement in Calinski-Harabasz Index of more than two times. Moreover, CIDR-based microsegmentation produced silhouette values of 0.95–1.0, which nearly fall within the optimal range, developing highly coherent subnet structures. These results highlighted the effectiveness of the method that combines port-based clustering with CIDR-based subdivision for more flexible and stronger segmentation in SDN contexts.

**Keywords:** Software defined networking (SDN) · ART2A · Micro-Segmentation · CIDR · Machine Learning (ML)

## 1 Introduction

Networks are difficult to handle due to their complexity and distribution. SDN is one of the latest network paradigms that provides a solution to these issues through the separation of the control and forwarding planes and also provides a logically centralized, software-based controller [1–3]. The key point of the SDN architecture is the separation of control plane from the data plane, and that network switches are simplified to forwarding elements. This abstracts away long-term planning and gives a controller (with an

© The Author(s), under exclusive license to Springer Nature Switzerland AG 2026
S. O. Al-Mamory et al. (Eds.): 3INC 2025, CCIS 2960, pp. 37–53, 2026.
https://doi.org/10.1007/978-3-032-24239-6_3

overall view of the network) powers for network decision-making/programming. This enhances networks features, agility, flexibility, openness and control [2, 4]. While the added flexibility is effective, SDN security problems abound, particularly because the SDN controller now becomes a tempting target for cyber attackers. To mitigate this issue, micro segmentation emerged as a practical means of function-based granular security enforcement and attack surface shrinking within SDN frameworks [5–7].

Micro segmentation enables network administrators to dynamically implement customized policy-driven restrictions to separate workloads and manage the traffic flow associated with specific services, users, and applications in both directions. With a shift to cloud native virtualization, the importance of this paradigm only intensifies. It is not possible for perimeter-based defenses to limit lateral movement within the network. Micro segmentation further reduces the attack surface and allows for more granular segmentation to improve visibility and policy enforcement in a network [8, 9]. The segmentation techniques in static systems are VLANs, subnets, and static firewall rules. It cannot be utilized in ever-dynamic enterprise networks designed to enable hybrid and multi-cloud environments where workloads may need to scale out and in frequently. In addition, deploying these methods on broad scales would be far too complex and, in many cases, contextually irrelevant, which would make them slow in confronting rapidly-changing and evolving threats [9].

In contrast, modern machine learning (ML) and artificial intelligence (AI)-based micro-segmentation frameworks automatically classify and segment traffic in an intelligent manner. The machine learning algorithms are better suited for this, because they can analyze large amounts of network traffic, recognize underlying behavioral profiles, learn them, and dynamically adjust segmentation rules instead of hard-coded profiles. It makes the network more responsive at a defensive level and can help support a Zero Trust model, where each element in the network is constantly authenticated and tracked [10, 11].

However, port-based clustering alone suffers from an inherent limitation: different flows that share the same destination port may originate from completely different IP subnets and exhibit distinct network behaviors. Grouping such heterogeneous traffic into a single cluster may lead to coarse-grained segmentation and reduce the effectiveness of SDN security controls. This limitation motivates the need for a second, network-aware segmentation stage based on CIDR, which refines the initial clusters and provides more precise micro-segmentation.

The structure of this paper is organized as follows; the most related research works on SDN micro-segmentation and clustering-based security are studied in Sect. 2. The background of the ART2A clustering algorithm is provided in Sect. 3, and the proposed ART2A-RNorm framework is described in Sect. 4. In Sect. 5, we describe the overall two-stage micro-segmentation framework, which combines the port-based clustering along with the CIDR-based subnet description. Section 6 presents the experimental results and the performance evaluation. Security implications are discussed in Sect. 7, and scientific claims are discussed in Sect. 8, followed by concluding remarks and future research directions in Sect. 9.

The main contributions of this research are summarized as follows:

1- An intuitive micro-segmentation framework of two phases is introduced. The first phase uses an ART2A clustering algorithm to group network traffic according to destination port number. Within each cluster, IP addresses are grouped by CIDR, which allows for subnet-specific segmentation at the secondary level.
2- An enhanced ART2A that proposed removing the thresholding stage and adding a new normalization process to the classical ART2A algorithm for clustering. This allows it to be more flexible in SDN scenarios with dynamic traffic patterns.
3- The study comprehensively examined clustering quality at both stages using scores such as Davies-Bouldin Index, the Silhouette Score, and Calinski-Harabasz Index. This shows that the proposed segmentation works well.
4- The proposed approach is tested on the large-scale and real-world dataset UNSW-NB15 to validate its scalability and real relevance in respect to the current networks.

## 2  Related Work

Micro-Segmentation has been addressed from several perspectives across the literature, including VLAN-based approaches, Zero-Trust architectures, machine-learning-driven segmentation, and performance-oriented evaluations. To provide a concise overview, the most relevant studies were grouped into four thematic categories.

### 2.1  VLAN/VXLAN and SDN-Based Micro-segmentation

Li et al. (2024) introduced a cloud data center micro-segmentation mechanism using VLAN-to-VxLAN many-to-one mapping to eliminate east-west blind spots. Their system depended on centralized or distributed Layer-3 gateways for full traffic visibility and used DBSCAN for temporal anomaly detection, demonstrating strong results in real-world cloud environments [12]. However, their method was overlay-based and required fixed gateway traversal, whereas our work performed fully automated Micro segmentation using unsupervised ART2A clustering with CIDR-aware refinement, making it more adaptive to dynamic SDN traffic without relying on static network overlays. Al-Ofeishat and Alshorman (2024) compared traditional VLANs, NSX micro-segmentation, and hybrid NSX-T/Sky-ATP policy enforcement. Their hybrid model outperformed other approaches in terms of scalability and threat detection and enabled Zero-Trust–aligned east-west policy enforcement [8]. Unlike their policy-driven approach dependent on vendor-specific technologies, our contribution lies in a data-driven, vendor-agnostic Micro segmentation mechanism that uses clustering and CIDR grouping for granular Micro segmentation in SDN environments.

### 2.2  Zero-Trust–Driven Micro-segmentation

The authors in [13] presented a Zero-Trust dynamic access-control process that clustered assets based on behavior using K-means clustering. It facilitated both responsive and fine-grained policy enforcement. However, their approach was on Zero-Trust type access control rather than automated sophisticated traffic segmentation. The present paper presents a pipeline (ART2A + CIDR) able to directly segment SDN traffic flows in an unsupervised multi-stage way, laying the framework from which ZTA policies can be implemented. Basta et al. and Kumar et al. (2021) presented a graph-based Zero-Trust evaluation framework based on ENICE focusing on measuring network exposure employing clustering coefficients and attack graphs. They found that micro-segmentation led to a significant exposure reduction [14]. This paper assessed the effects of Micro segmentation; however, does not suggest a Micro segmentation method. To fill this gap, the present work uses the technique of micro segmentation that allows a finer-grained subdivision through the use of adaptive clustering.

### 2.3   Machine-Learning and Automated Policy-Generation Approaches

Ma et al. (2023) proposed an automated policy-generation mechanism for cloud micro-segmentation using hybrid static and dynamic analysis. K-Means and KNN were used to infer valid flows and generate accurate access-control rules [15]. While their work generated policies from observed interactions, our contribution is orthogonal: the present study provides a clustering-based segmentation framework that groups flows before policies are generated, enabling more structured rule creation in SDN.

### 2.4   Performance Impact and SDN-Based Evaluation Studies

A 2021 SDN performance study examined micro-segmentation using Cisco ACI, measuring Round Trip Time (RTT), jitter, and packet loss under different flow sizes. The results showed that micro-segmentation improved security without degrading performance and successfully supported Zero-Trust enforcement [9]. This study focused on performance benchmarking, while our work concentrates on designing a new segmentation algorithm applicable before such benchmarking begins.

To concisely compare prior works, Table 1 summarizes the main characteristics, limitations, and how our proposed method advances them.

## 3   ART2A

There are many different types of ART networks. The present work is closely tied to that of the ART2A network, which is the center of our effort. ART2A is an exceptionally efficient algorithm that emulates the self-organizing pattern recognition and hypothesis testing functions of the ART 2 neural network architecture, operating at a speed two to three orders of magnitude faster, thereby enabling its use in tackling large-scale issues [16, 17].

The three layers seen in Fig. 1 the input layer F0, the comparison layer F1, and the recognition layer F2 constitute the standard ART architecture, which is mainly adhered to by an ART2A network. The input layer acquires and retains the input patterns. Neurons in the input layer and comparison layer are interconnected through one-to-one hard-coded linkages, which facilitate normalization preprocessing to avert category proliferation [17, 18].

The ART network uses a competitive learning mechanism that is winner-take-all. The weighted bottom-up ($F_1 \rightarrow F_2$) and top-down ($F_2 \rightarrow F_1$) connections between $F_1$

and $F_2$ must be changed in order to learn the traditional ART network. The interactions between layers $F_1$ and $F_2$ are regulated by the orienting system, which utilizes the vigilance parameter $\rho$. The learning process in ART2A is streamlined by employing just a bottom-up connection between $F_1$ and $F_2$, with a symmetric dot product as the similarity metric in both the category choice function and the match function [16, 17].

**Table 1.** Summary of Related Work

| study | Dataset Used | Evaluation Metrics | ML/Clustering | ZTA Support | Limitation | Difference from Our Work |
|---|---|---|---|---|---|---|
| [8] | **network simulation** using NSX-T, Sky ATP, and Policy Enforcer | Security Level, Performance, Cost, Complexity, Consumed Time, Workload Mobility | none | Yes | Policy-based only; no real traffic, no clustering, not data-driven | Our framework learns micro-segmentation from real traffic flows using ART2A-RNorm and CIDR-based subnet refinement, enabling data-driven segmentation and stronger ZTA alignment |
| [9] | Cisco ACI testbed simulation | RTT, Jitter, Packet Loss | none | Yes | No behavior-based or data-driven analysis; results limited to testbed performance only | Focuses on performance overhead only—no learning-based segmentation; our work uses real SDN flow data and clustering-driven microsegmentation |
| [12] | Private cloud traffic | Mirrored traffic analysis, DBSCAN profiling | DBSCAN | Partial | Requires L3 gateway mirroring | Our CIDR microsegmentation provides finer subnet-level granularity |
| [13] | simulated network traffic and virtual hosts | Latency, access-control accuracy, threshold evaluation, cluster distribution | K-Means | Yes | Simulation-only; no real SDN flows; static clustering; no behavior modeling | Does not use ART2A or range normalization; no two-stage microsegmentation; no CIDR refinement; no real flow-based microsegmentation |
| [14] | Two real enterprise networks (University & Life-care) | Graph-based exposure metric, robustness metrics | none | Yes | No machine-learning or flow-based segmentation; relies entirely on graph-theoretic analysis | Works on graph metrics and policy analysis only; does **not** learn microsegments from real traffic |
| [15] | Synthetic datasets | Clustering Accuracy (ARI), Runtime, Classification F1-score, Static Analysis Coverage | K-means, KNN | Indirect | Requires collecting large historical traffic; depends on availability of configuration files; assumes no malicious traffic | Our work uses **real SDN traffic**, adaptive ART2A-RNorm clustering, two-stage port + CIDR segmentation, and explicitly supports **Zero-Trust microsegmentation** within SDN |

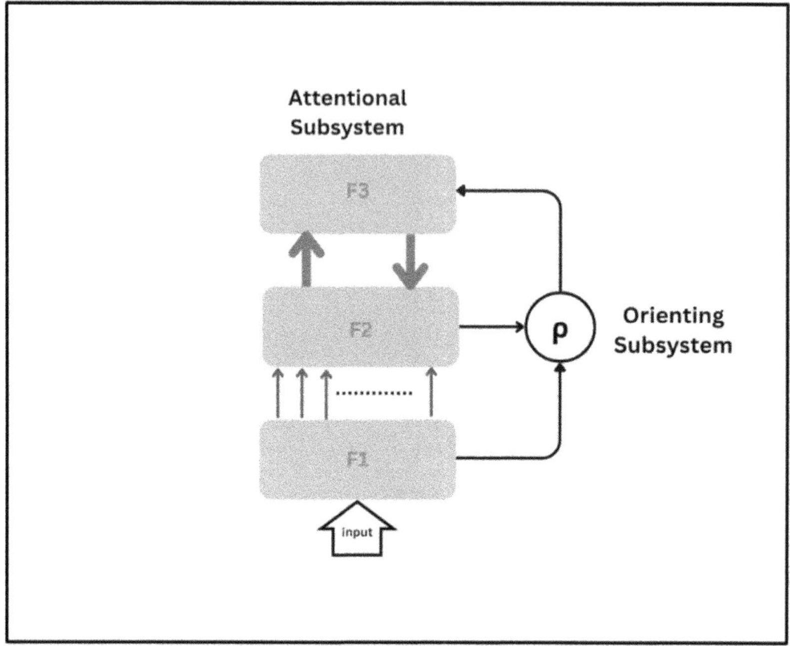



**Fig. 1.** ART2A basic architecture.

**ART2A process of learning** [17, 19, 20]:

**Input Normalization:** Negative input values are prohibited, and all input vectors (A) are standardized to unit Euclidean length, as indicated by the function sign $\aleph$.

$$I = \aleph(A) = \frac{A}{\sqrt{\sum a_i^2}} = \frac{A}{\|A\|} \tag{1}$$

A further noise suppression technique proposed by Carpenter and Grossberg to contrast enhance typical pattern characteristics is to set all input values to zero as long as they fall below a threshold $\theta$.

$$I = \aleph(F_0(\aleph(A))) \tag{2}$$

where

$$F_0(X)_i = \begin{cases} x_i \ \text{if } x_i > \theta \\ 0 \ \text{otherwise} \end{cases} \tag{3}$$

$\theta$ satisfies the inequalities $0 \leq \theta \leq \frac{1}{\sqrt{n}}$, n = number of elements in the input vector.

**Activation:** This phase is responsible for transmitting incoming information to the neurons of the recognition layer $F_2$.

$$T_j = \begin{cases} I.W_j \quad\quad \text{if } j \text{ indexes a committed prototype} \\ \alpha. \sum_{j=1}^{n} I_j \ \text{otherwise} \end{cases} \tag{4}$$

$$0 \leq \alpha \leq \frac{1}{\sqrt{n}}.$$

where $T_j$ represents neuron j's activity in layer $F_2$.

Every neuron is initially designated as uncommitted; however, they become committed, when their weights are adjusted to learn a particular input pattern. The value $\alpha$ delineates the maximum search depth for an appropriate cluster. When $\alpha = 0$, all committed prototypes are evaluated prior to selecting an uncommitted prototype as winner. The framework used in this study employs $\alpha = 0$.

**Search:** This phase is tasked with identifying a neuronal candidate to retain the existing pattern. Network competitive learning identifies the highest active neuron as the representative of the input pattern.

$$Jj \;=\; \mathrm{argmax}\,(Tj) \tag{5}$$

where J denotes the winning F2 neuron with the highest activation.

**Resonance or Reset:** The reset condition is evaluated after choosing the neuron with the highest level of activation. After determining whether the inequality is true, the adaptation stage (resonance) is initiated and the candidate neuron is selected to store the pattern. Otherwise, the winning neuron is turned off and the search process starts over (reset).

$$T_j \;>\; \rho \tag{6}$$

**Adaptation:** This stage defines the process by which the network acquires the pattern. This stage is responsible for adjusting the network weights to the winning neuron J, which subsequently becomes committed.

$$W_J^{(\mathrm{new})} = \aleph(\eta \cdot \aleph(\Psi)) + (1 - \eta) \cdot W_J^{(\mathrm{old})} \tag{7}$$

$$\Psi_i = \begin{cases} i_i \; \textit{if } w_{ji}^{old} > \theta \\ 0 \; \textit{otherwise} \end{cases} \tag{8}$$

## 4  ART2A-RNorm

This paper presents an improved ART2A algorithm for micro-segmentation in SDN environments, denoted as ART2A-RNorm. The primary change was in the normalization stage, which is one of the most important elements of the ART-based algorithms for clustering. The original ART2A uses L2 normalization to set the scale of input vectors, which might suppress useful variances across heterogeneous network features with different value ranges [21, 22].

In order to overcome this limitation, L2 normalization was replaced with range normalization (min-max scaling). This method ensures that each feature makes a proportional contribution to the similarity computations, while maintaining the relative difference in the data [23]. With range normalization, the modified ART2A-RNorm is better adapted at capturing the fine-grained differences across network flows, which is key to performing SDN microsegmentation.

$$x' = \frac{x - \min(x)}{\max(x) - \min(x)} \tag{9}$$

One more important change in ART2A-RNorm is that it abandons the input thresholding that Carpenter and Grossberg proposed for noise suppression and contrast enhancement. Accordingly, in the standard rule of operation for ART2A, if the input value xi is less than a threshold $\theta$, it is set to zero (Eq. 10):

$$F_0(X)_i = \begin{cases} x_i \ if \ x_i > \theta \\ 0 \ otherwise \end{cases} \tag{10}$$

Though this works well to suppress low-frequency variations in clean datasets, it leads to information loss for high-frequency and high-noise situations. This is usually unavoidable in SDN traffic, since small variations can indicate large shifts in flow behavior. ART2A-RNorm removes this thresholding mechanism to retain all feature information, enabling the model to learn potentially important variations between network flows. This leads to a more adaptive and information-preserving clustering process, which facilitates the real-time microsegmentation tasks in the SDN-based environment.

Experimental evaluations showed that ART2A-RNorm consistently outperformed the standard ART2A algorithm in clustering, as indicated by improvements in clustering validity indices such as the Davies-Bouldin Index, Calinski-Harabasz Index, and Silhouette Score. These outcomes demonstrate how well the suggested change improves the accuracy and stability of unsupervised traffic microsegmentation in dynamic SDN environments.

## 5 Methodology

A two-stage micro-segmentation approach combining ART2A-RNorm (a modified ART2A clustering algorithm) and CIDR-based subnet refinement was introduced. Figure 2 illustrates the overall workflow of the framework, beginning from raw SDN flow features, followed by ART2A-RNorm clustering, and concluding with CIDR-based segmentation. The following subsections describe each stage in detail and explain the techniques employed to achieve accurate and efficient micro-segmentation.

**Stage 1: Modified ART2A Micro-segmentation**
The initial phase of SDN microsegmentation uses these adaptive versions of ART2A (ART2A-RNorm) algorithms to cluster (or to group by destination port number) the network traffic. At this stage, four steps are taken: 1) data set preparation (port number filtering, data preprocessing) 2) feature selection 3) run machine learning process 4) system evaluation. Here is a brief description of these steps:

**1-Data Set Preparation:** UNSW-NB15 dataset was downloaded from the official website of the Australian Centre for Cyber Security (ACCS). This dataset offers a well-balanced distribution of normal and attack traffic simulated in a controlled setting

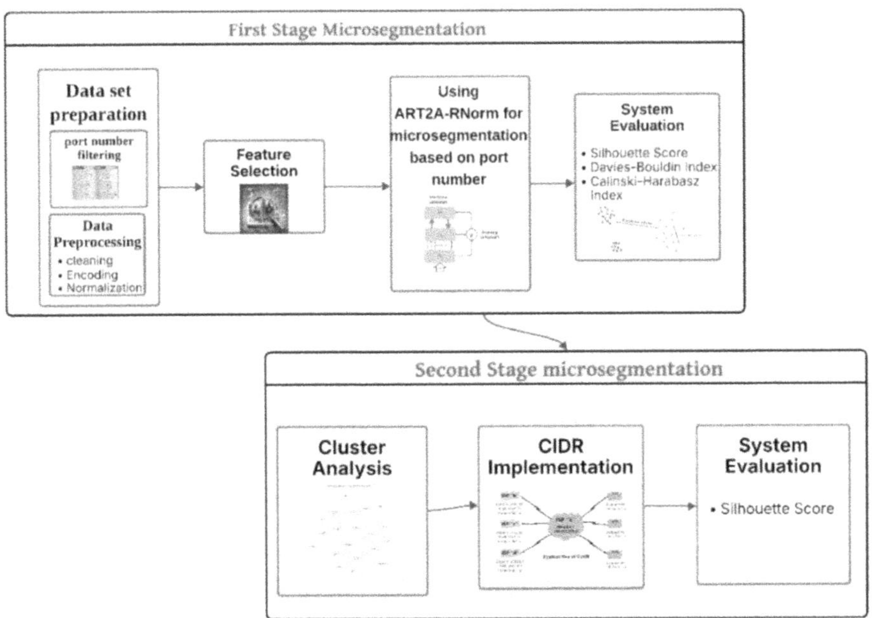


**Fig. 2.** Proposed Micro-Segmentation Framework

that is ideal for testing microsegmentation and clustering approaches. The full dataset and documentation are available at: https://research.unsw.edu.au/projects/unsw-nb15-dataset.

**Port Number Filtering:** Traffic is filtered based on the most commonly used destination port numbers. This step ensures that analysis focuses on the most significant traffic flows, reducing noise and improving clustering accuracy.

**Data Preprocessing:** To ensure the quality and relevance of the data, the following preprocessing steps were applied:

**Data Cleaning:** Cleaning incomplete or corrupted records.

**Label Encoding for Categorical Features:** Applying label encoding to convert categorical values such as "protocol" into numerical representations suitable for clustering algorithms.

**Feature Normalization:** Using quantile transformer to normalize numerical features, ensuring a uniform distribution and reducing the impact of outliers.

**Dimensionality Reduction:** Applying principal component analysis (PCA) to reduce the number of features while preserving significant variance in the data, improving computational efficiency and clustering accuracy.

**2-Feature Selection:** This is the process of selecting a subset of relevant features. It is one of the foremost steps in preparation of a dataset to train a ML model. This involves selecting the features that best improve the accuracy of the model. Recursive Feature

Elimination (RFE) with a random forest classifier as an estimator was used to rank and select important features. It systematically removes the most irrelevant features to the model until desired number of features are retained. These are the selected features that are related to port numbers and other relevant traffic characteristics that have great impact on the classification process.

**Selected Features**

For the UNSW-NB15 dataset, a focused subset of features was selected to support port-based micro-segmentation and accurately characterize traffic behavior. The final selected features were: dsport, proto, sbytes, dmeansz, Spkts, srcip, and dstip. These features capture essential flow-level characteristics required for destination-port clustering.

dsport and proto directly describe the service and communication protocol.

sbytes, dmeansz, and Spkts represent the volume, size, and intensity of packet exchange, providing a behavioral signature of each traffic flow.

srcip and dstip were retained to enable the second-stage segmentation using CIDR-based network grouping.

Together, these features provide a compact yet informative representation of network activity, enabling accurate clustering in both stages of the proposed microsegmentation framework.

**3-Machine Learning Implementation:** ART2A-RNorm was applied for the initial microsegmentation phase to group network flows based on destination port numbers.

**4-System Evaluation:** Three well-recognized internal clustering evaluation metrics, namely, Silhouette Score, Davies–Bouldin Index, and Calinski–Harabasz Index were used for considering the quality of generated microsegments. Together, these metrics offer a holistic evaluation of the intra-cluster and inter-cluster distillation of the clusters and provide an objective feedback on the efficacy of the customized microsegmentation procedure.

**Stage 2: CIDR-Based Micro-Segmentation**

Based on the clusters produced from the first step, a second micro-segmentation stage using CIDR further refines the network partitions. Network microsegments are not just based on similar traffic characteristics but also combined based on geographical or organizational alignment for better security and management. This stage involved:

1- **Cluster Analysis**: Identifying associated source of each cluster and destination IP addresses.
2- **CIDR Implementation:** Applying CIDR notation to group source IP addresses, forming precise subnet segments. Segment boundaries were determined based on IP address ranges that best represent logical or geographical subnetworks.
3- **System evaluation:** Assessing the quality of the generated microsegments using the Silhouette Score, a widely adopted clustering evaluation metric.

**Algorithm 1: A Two-Stage Micro-segmentation Framework**

ART2A-RNorm (Stage-1 Micro-Segmentation).

Input: Network flow dataset D. First, flows are filtered based on the destination ports P. For each filtered flow, a multi-dimensional feature vector is constructed using the selected attributes: {dsport, proto, sbytes, dmeansz, Spkts, srcip, dstip}. ART2A-RNorm parameters ($\rho$ = vigilance, $\beta$ = choice parameter, $\alpha$ = learning rate, E = maximum epochs) are then applied.

Output: Cluster labels C.

1- Preprocessing:

- Filter flows where desport $\in$ P.
- Encode categorical features (e.g., proto).
- Apply Range Normalization to numeric features: (x - min)/(max - min + $\varepsilon$).

2- Initialization:

- Set cluster count K = 0.
- Initialize empty set of prototypes W.

3- Training (Epochs 1 $\to$ E):

- For each sample x in D:

a. If K = 0: create first prototype $w1$ = x, set label $cx$ = 1.
b. Otherwise: compute similarity of x with all prototypes.
c. If the best match passes vigilance (sim $\geq \rho$): update prototype.
d. Else: if no existing prototype satisfies vigilance, create a new prototype and assign x to it.

4- Stopping:

- Repeat until max epochs are reached.

5- Return cluster.

**CIDR-Based Micro-Segmentation (Stage-2)**
Input: Clusters from Stage-1, IP addresses (srcip, dstip), subnet masks {/24}.
Output: Final microsegments.

6- For each cluster k:

a. Extract flows $D_k$.
b. Partition by subnet mask m (using srcip).
c. Remove very small groups.
d. Compute validation metric (Silhouette).

7- Return all per-cluster partitions as final microsegments

# 6  Results

*Experimental Environment*
Experiments were implemented with Python 3.11 and employing the libraries NumPy, Pandas, Scikit-learn, Matplotlib and ipaddress. All two-stages micro-segmentation pipeline was implemented in a Windows 10 machine with an Intel®

Core™ i5-7200U CPU (2.50 GHz) CPU, 20 GB RAM, and 238 GB SSD using CPU only processing.

In order to assess the impact of the intended improvements made to the ART2A clustering algorithm, two experiments were performed against the UNSW-NB15 dataset that are presented in Table 2. In the first phase of the micro-segmentation process, network traffic was aggregated based on general destination port numbers. This evaluation was the first part of this evaluation. In total, 28 unique ports were chosen for the service relevance and traffic prevalence. Experiment 1 used classical ART2A, and Experiment 2 used a modified ART2A algorithm (ART2A-RNorm) that combined range normalization with the elimination of the input threshold in order to preserve small differences in the input features.

**Table 2.** Performance Comparison

|  | Cluster count | Silhouette Score | CH Index | DBI |
|---|---|---|---|---|
| ART 2A | 27 | 0.6295 | 0.7966 | 351624.883 |
| ART 2A-RNorm | 28 | 0.7718 | 0.5971 | 764087.972 |

The ART2A algorithm was applied on the same dataset and resulted in 27 clusters indicating that at least a service group was either merged with another service group or merged due to the unavailability of sufficient separability in the feature space. In contrast, the ART 2A-RNorm algorithm generated only 28 clusters as shown in Fig. 3, which is in accordance to the number of selected port-based services. This further validates the algorithm's improved ability to preserve aspects of the service manifold through the segmentation process.

Three internal clustering validation criteria were used to evaluate and rank the quality of the clustering results as shown in Fig. 4 (a-d). Such measures provide quantitative assessments of the compactness and separation of clusters, enabling a more objective assessment of the performance of the proposed method:

1. **Silhouette Score:** Increased from 0.6295 (original) to 0.7718 (modified), indicating a higher cohesion within clusters and greater separation between them.
2. **Davies-Bouldin Index:** Decreased from 0.7966 to 0.5971, reflecting better-defined and more compact clusters.
3. **Calinski-Harabasz Index:** Showed a remarkable improvement, more than doubling from 351624.883 to 764087.972, further validating the structural clarity of the modified clustering.

With a particular emphasis on the CIDR-based segmentation, the Silhouette Score evaluation revealed that the clustering performance was outstanding across all of the subnet segments that were found. To be more specific, the silhouette scores that clusters obtained ranged from 0.952381 to 1.0, with the majority of clusters achieving the highest attainable silhouette value of 1.0. This displays the highly coherent internal structure

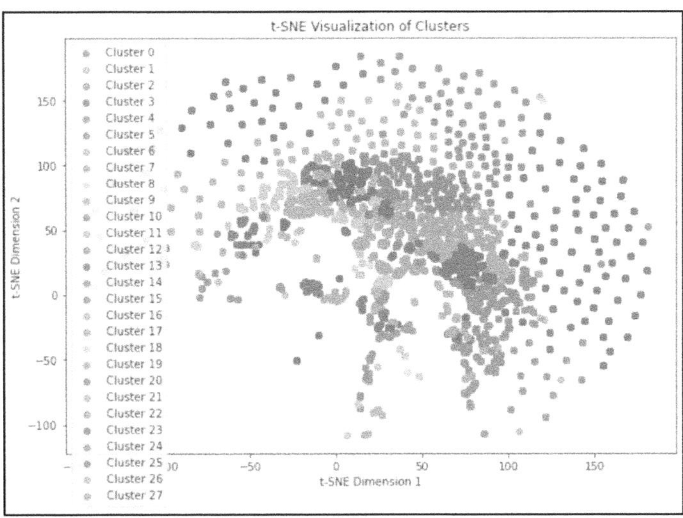


**Fig. 3.** ART2A-RNorm generated clusters

and clearly defined boundaries across subnet segments, demonstrating that CIDR segmentation is an excellent method for organizing source IP addresses into groups that are both logically meaningful and secure.

Although the current study did not perform direct attack-based or intrusion-centric experiments, the security impact of the proposed micro-segmentation framework was evaluated from a structural perspective. Micro-segmentation is a preventive security mechanism and its effectiveness is typically reflected in how well the system reduces lateral-movement opportunities, minimizes unnecessary east-west communication, and isolates traffic into smaller and more coherent groups. Therefore, the quality of the generated clusters (as shown by the Silhouette, CH, and DBI metrics) provides an indirect yet meaningful indication of improved security posture. Finer service-level segmentation in Stage-1 and subnet-level subdivision in Stage-2 both contributed to reducing the attack surface by limiting the scope of communication between hosts and enforcing more localized control boundaries within the SDN environment.

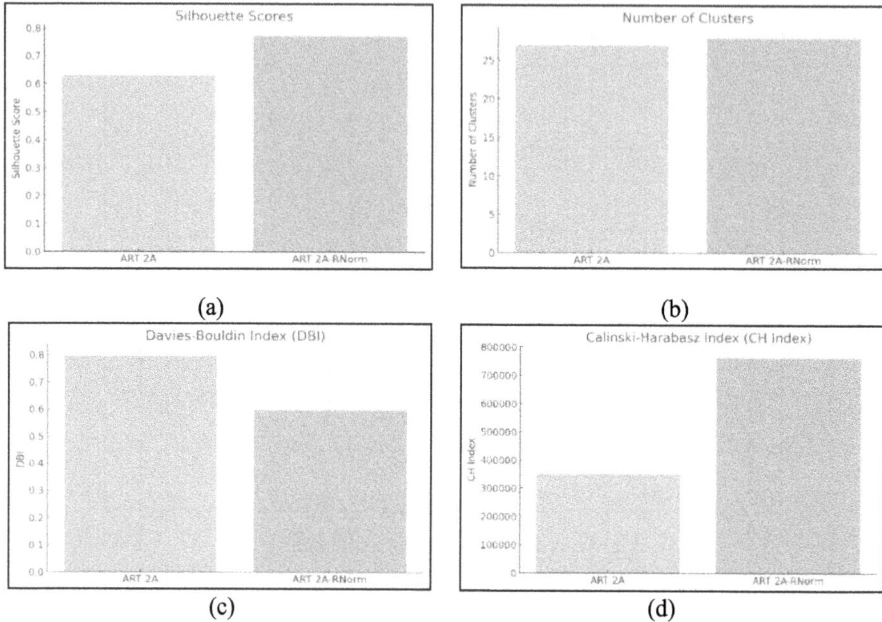

**Fig. 4.** Performance of ART2A and ART2A-RNorm: (a) Silhouette Scores for both algorithms. (b) Number of clusters generated by each algorithm. (c) Davies–Bouldin Index (DBI) comparison. (d) Calinski–Harabasz (CH) Index comparison.

## 7 Discussion

The results showed that the micro-segmentation quality can be improved using ART2A clustering algorithm by taking advantages of the proposed changes on the ART2A clustering algorithm. The comparison of original ART2A and the pseudo-code of ART2A-RNorm emphasized the importance of normalization in shaping and positioning clusters. The auto adaptive recognition ART2A algorithm produced 27 clusters, while ART2A-RNorm produced 28, using the same 28 port numbers as input. The results suggested that the proposed normalization method was better able to detect small differences in traffic behavior, enabling the algorithm to create more precise port-level service groupings.

These benefits were reflected in the evaluation metrics. The Silhouette Score of ART2A-RNorm was significantly higher (0.7718 vs. 0.6295), indicating more tightly formed clusters of flows that have similar behavioral characteristics. Smaller Davies–Bouldin Index (0.5971 vs. 0.7966) indicated that the clusters were better separated; meanwhile, a notable augmentation of Calinski–Harabasz Index suggested a higher compactness and separation between cluster boundaries. Taken together, these results suggest a segmentation process that is more consistently and accurately performed, which in turn serves the SDN security micro-segmentation goals of clearer and more enforceable service boundaries.

Port-based segmentation does not provide sufficient granularity of the diverse communication behaviors that may occur within the same service. The second stage of this framework abstracted this limitation by applying CIDR-based segmentation to the

IPs that were located in the same port cluster. The new layer allowed for subnetwork presence partitions, which were more aligned with the actual network locality of communicating entities. This essentially further segments traffic (even for the same service port) into many micro-segments, thereby limiting the lateral movement of traffic across hosts to a desired minimum level which can not only help to contain threats within a host, but even between SDN domains as well.

Clustering in SDN landscapes is not performed continuously. In contrast, the proposed framework allows periodic or event-driven re-clustering. This process can be initiated at configurable time intervals (hourly or daily) or when there are significant shifts in traffic pattern. This guarantees that the segmentation is within the recent changes but with little overhead.

More importantly, such fine-grained micro-segments directly corresponds to Zero-Trust enforcement principles in [5] and the exposure reduction analysis documented in [14]. It also means eliminating areas of implicit trust, enforcing least-privilege access, and continuously validating all paths of communication between users and servers (i.e. zero trust). Compared to other methods, ART2A-RNorm followed by CIDR subnet refinement gives unambiguous structural boundaries and better cluster separability, precisely small, manageable trust domains to effectively apply Zero-Trust policies. Hence these results provide more solid analytical and operational bases of Zero-Trust into SDN.

In summary, the proposed two-stage micro-segmentation framework served as a feasible approach to realize fine-grained segmentation in SDN. The framework is based on combination of an adaptive clustering algorithm and network-aware CIDR grouping which creates stronger structural boundaries aligning with zero trust principles and enables more precise policy enforcement that reduces overall attack surface of the network.

## 8  Scientific Claims

The results of the study confirmed several scientific claims concerning the effectiveness of the proposed framework. First, an enhanced ART2A-RNorm model yields more coherent and well-separated service-level clusters, which has been confirmed by the internal validation metrics. Second, finer-grained micro-segments that better reflect real traffic locality are produced with CIDR-based subnet segmentation integration. Third, combining behavioral clustering with network-aware segmentation offers a more adaptive foundation for Zero-Trust enforcement compared to static or policy-driven approaches. These claims collectively demonstrate that the two-stage segmentation model improves both structural segmentation quality and its applicability to SDN security.

## 9  Conclusion

To enhance traffic separation and security management, a two-level micro segmentation technique in SDN environments was proposed. The initial approach was a variation of ART2A clustering method for traffic classification with respect to destination port numbers. ART2A used 28 destination ports to drive 27 clusters, and the optimized version with range normalization ART2A-RNorm drove 28 clusters. Our results showed how normalization affects sensitivity of clustering and micro segmentation accuracy.

The second stage of clusters was created by CIDR-based subdivision of source IP addresses within each cluster, enabling fine-grained micro-segmentation within the individual cluster. This hierarchical segmentation approach allowed identifications of microscope subnets within a service-based cluster. The experiments using the UNSW-NB15 dataset demonstrated that our proposed method improved clustering quality by large margins across different evaluation metrics, including the Silhouette Score, the Davies-Bouldin Index, and the Calinski-Harabasz Index. These results validated the performance of a flexible clustering and CIDR-based approach on SDN data.

Hence, this study lays a groundwork for the potential combination of such policy-based control methods. Future works my focus on implementing ZTA policies on each micro-segment and to aggregate them through the SDN controller to offer a more centralized enforcement, providing dynamic and strong network security. Finally, future works can apply controlled attack scenarios to evaluate the security of the two-stage micro-segmentation framework. That is, how effectively it contains lateral movement and isolates emerging malicious flows. The complementary assessment can offer additional visibility into the actual security benefits of applying ZTA-based policies in each micro-segment.

## References


1. Oleiwi, W.K., Abdullah, A.A.: Performance evaluation comparison between central SDN network and DSDN. In: New Trends in Information and Communications Technology Applications, pp. 334–345. Springer Nature, Cham, Switzerland (2024). https://doi.org/10.1007/978-3-031-62814-6_24
2. Latif, Z., Sharif, K., Li, F., Karim, M.M., Biswas, S., Wang, Y.: A comprehensive survey of interface protocols for software defined networks. J. Netw. Comput. Appl. **156**, 102563 (2020). https://iopscience.iop.org/article/10.1088/1742-6596/1804/1/012007/meta
3. Alrammahi, M.A.M., Bhaya, W.S.: A state-of-the-art survey and taxonomy of classification, algorithms, and techniques for load balancing in SDN. J. Al-Qadisiyah Comput. Sci. Math. **15**(3), 164 (2023). https://doi.org/10.29304/jqcm.2023.15.3.1273
4. Ibrahim, O.J., Bhaya, W.S.: Intrusion detection system for cloud based software-defined networks. J. Phys. Conf. Ser., 012007 (2021). Accessed 7 Aug 2025. https://iopscience.iop.org/article/https://doi.org/10.1088/1742-6596/1804/1/012007/meta
5. Bashaa, M.H., Bhaya, W.S., Al-Aaraji, N.H.K.: Integration of zero trust architecture and machine learning for improving the security of software defined networking: a review. J. Intell. Inform. Netw. Cybersecur. **1**(1), 1 (2025). https://doi.org/10.65445/3106-1192.1000
6. Alsaadi, E.M.T.A., Fayadh, S.M., Alabaichi, A.: A review on security challenges and approaches in the cloud computing. AIP Conf. Proc. **2290**(1), 040022 (2020). https://doi.org/10.1063/5.0027460
7. Mahdi, S.S., Abdullah, A.A.: Enhanced security of software-defined network and network slice through hybrid quantum key distribution protocol. Infocommunications J. **14**(3), 9–15 (2022). https://doi.org/10.36244/ICJ.2022.3.2
8. Al-Ofeishat, H., Alshorman, R.: Build a secure network using segmentation and micro-segmentation techniques. Int. J. Comput. Digit. Syst. **16**, 1499–1508 (2024). https://doi.org/10.12785/ijcds/1601111
9. Mujib, M., Sari, R.F.: Performance evaluation of data center network with network micro-segmentation. In: 2020 12th International Conference on Information Technology and Electrical Engineering (ICITEE), pp. 27–32. IEEE (2020). https://doi.org/10.1109/ICITEE49829.2020.9271749

10. Arifeen, M., Petrovski, A., Petrovski, S.: Automated microsegmentation for lateral movement prevention in industrial internet of things (IIoT). In: 2021 14th International Conference on Security of Information and Networks (SIN), pp. 1–6. IEEE (2021). Accessed 8 Aug 2025. https://ieeexplore.ieee.org/abstract/document/9699232/. https://doi.org/10.1109/SIN54109.2021.9699232

11. Selciya, G., Zerubbabel, I., Kannan, K., Ezhilarasie, R.: Enhancing IIoT security using KNN based hypergraph clustering through zero trust micro-segmentation for dynamic network protection. In: 2024 International Conference on Computational Intelligence and Network Systems (CINS), pp. 1–6. IEEE (2024). Accessed 17 Aug 2025. https://ieeexplore.ieee.org/abstract/document/10864440/. https://doi.org/10.1109/CINS63881.2024.10864440

12. Li, D., Yang, Z., Yu, S., Duan, M., Yang, S.: A micro-segmentation method based on VLAN-VxLAN mapping technology. Future Internet 16(9), 320 (2024). https://doi.org/10.3390/fi16090320

13. Zhang, P., et al.: Dynamic access control technology based on zero-trust light verification network model. In: 2021 International Conference on Communications, Information System and Computer Engineering (CISCE), pp. 712–715, May 2021. https://doi.org/10.1109/CISCE52179.2021.9445896

14. Basta, N., Ikram, M., Kaafar, M.A., Walker, A.: Towards a zero-trust micro-segmentation network security strategy: an evaluation framework. In: NOMS 2022–2022 IEEE/IFIP Network Operations and Management Symposium, pp. 1–7, April 2022. https://doi.org/10.1109/NOMS54207.2022.9789888

15. Ma, M., Yu, Z., Liu, B.: Automatic generation of network micro-segmentation policies for cloud environments. In: 2023 4th International Seminar on Artificial Intelligence, Networking and Information Technology (AINIT), pp. 1–5, June 2023. https://doi.org/10.1109/AINIT59027.2023.10212857

16. Brito da Silva, L.E., Elnabarawy, I., Wunsch, D.C.: A survey of adaptive resonance theory neural network models for engineering applications. Neural Netw. 120, 167–203 (2019). https://doi.org/10.1016/j.neunet.2019.09.012

17. Carpenter, G.A., Grossberg, S., Rosen, D.B.: ART 2-A: an adaptive resonance algorithm for rapid category learning and recognition. Neural Netw. 4(4), 493–504 (1991). https://doi.org/10.1016/0893-6080(91)90045-7

18. Simao, A.S., Mello, R.F.D., Senger, L.J., Yang, L.T.: Improving regression testing performance using the adaptive resonance Theory-2A self-organising neural network architecture. Int. J. Auton. Adapt. Commun. Syst. 1(3), 370 (2008). https://doi.org/10.1504/IJAACS.2008.019811

19. Frank, T., Kraiss, K.-F., Kuhlen, T.: Comparative analysis of fuzzy ART and ART-2A network clustering performance. IEEE Trans. Neural Netw. 9(3), 544–559 (1998). https://doi.org/10.1109/72.668896

20. He, J., Tan, A.-H., Tan, C.-L.: Modified ART 2A growing network capable of generating a fixed number of nodes. IEEE Trans. Neural Netw. 15(3), 728–737 (2004). https://doi.org/10.1109/TNN.2004.826220

21. Grossberg, S.: Adaptive resonance theory: how a brain learns to consciously attend, learn, and recognize a changing world. Neural Netw. 37, 1–47 (2013). https://doi.org/10.1016/j.neunet.2012.09.017

22. Han, J., Kamber, M., Pei, J.: Data Mining: Concepts and Techniques. Morgan Kaufmann, Burlington, MA (2012)

23. Guyon, I., Elisseeff, A.: An introduction to feature extraction. In: Guyon, I., Nikravesh, M., Gunn, S., Zadeh, L.A. (eds.) Feature Extraction. Studies in Fuzziness and Soft Computing, vol. 207, pp. 1–25. Springer, Heidelberg (2006). https://doi.org/10.1007/978-3-540-35488-8_1

# Anomaly Detection in IoT Sensor Data Using Deep Learning for Industrial IoT

Hussein M. Farhood[1], Zaid J. Al-Araji[2(✉)], Sara Raad Qasim[1], Ameer M. Al-Obaidi[3], Fahad Ahmed Shaban[2], Zaid Ali Abdulkadhim[4], Khalid M. Farhood[5], and Husam Nawfel Fadhil[6]

[1] Department of Computer Engineering, College of Engineering, Mustansiriyah University, 10047 Baghdad, Iraq
{hussein.m4f,sararaad.cac}@uomustansiriyah.edu.iq
[2] Department of Computer Networks and Internet, College of Information Technology, Ninevah University, 41001 Mosul, Iraq
{zaid.jasim,fahad.ahmed}@uoninevah.edu.iq
[3] Faculty of Engineering and Digital Technologies, Belgorod State National Research University, 308015 Belgorod Oblast, Russia
[4] Al-Diwaniyah Technical Institute, Al-Forat Al-Awsat Technical University (ATU), 58006 Al-Qadisiyah, Iraq
zaid.kadhim.idi7@atu.edu.iq
[5] Iraqi Ministry of Health, Bab Al-Muadham, 10047 Baghdad, Iraq
[6] Department of English, College of Education, AlNoor University, Mosul 41012, Iraq
husam.nawfal@alnoor.edu.iq

**Abstract.** The rapid expansion of Industrial Internet of Things (IIoT) networks has increased the risk of sophisticated cyberattacks, necessitating accurate and adaptive anomaly detection methods. This paper proposes a hybrid Fuzzy-Long Short-Term Memory (Fuzzy-LSTM) framework that combines the temporal modeling capabilities of LSTM networks with an adaptive fuzzy inference system for dynamic threshold adjustment. The objective of the approach is to eliminate the problems associated with commonly used static thresholds in traditional anomaly detection systems so that false alarms can be reduced while retaining high sensitivity of detection. The model was compared with Autoencoder, CNN, and traditional LSTM-based techniques using two benchmark datasets, IoT23, and WUSTL-IIoT-2021. According to the experimental results, Fuzzy-LSTM outperformed all baselines in terms of accuracy, precision, and recall, reaching the greatest performance on IoT23 with an accuracy of up to 96.23% and an F1-score of 98%. This demonstrated the framework's resilience and adaptability in identifying a wide range of attack behaviors in IIoT contexts. With applications for operational safety, intrusion detection, and predictive maintenance, the suggested approach presents a viable route for the deployment of intelligent, real-time anomaly detection in the industrial sector.

**Keywords:** Industrial IoT (IIoT) · Anomaly Detection · Deep Learning · Autoencoder · Sensor Data


S. O. Al-Mamory et al. (Eds.): 3INC 2025, CCIS 2960, pp. 54–68, 2026.
https://doi.org/10.1007/978-3-032-24239-6_4

# 1   Introduction

Manufacturing and other industrial processes in the Industrial IIoT are being revolutionized by the deployment of sensors and equipment that can connect and analyze data in real time [1, 2]. One way to describe predictive maintenance is as process simplification, downtime reduction, and efficiency enhancement. Authenticating IIoT systems is difficult due to large and complex data streams [3]. The patterns determine on their own whether industrial processes are resilient to cyberattacks, system failures, or any other possible problem [4]. Traditional anomaly detection techniques, such as statistical studies and rule-based systems, are unfeasible due to the degree of non-linearity in IIoT data [5]. Since the functionality of state-of-the-art industrial systems is constantly evolving, such techniques frequently necessitate a high level of domain expertise [6]. Due to their inability to generalize to unknown attack patterns and difficulty in adapting to rapidly changing operational contexts, traditional anomaly detection techniques such as signature-based intrusion detection systems (IDS) and simple statistical models provide little or no solutions for the IIoT environment. Autoencoders, Convolutional Neural Networks (CNNs), and Long Short-Term Memory (LSTM) networks are examples of machine learning (ML) and deep learning (DL) techniques that have shown promise thus far in identifying abnormalities through intricate data representation learning in past behavior. However, the majority of these models have static decision thresholds, which typically result in a trade-off between sensitivity and false alarm rates, limiting their applicability in many industrial settings. In recent years, deep learning techniques have become a valuable tool for detecting anomalies in IIoT scenarios [7–10]. The lack of manual feature engineering is not a shortcoming for the modeling of complex patterns and/or anomalies, as in the case of autoencoders and LSTM networks [11, 12]. Current developments show that the introduction of deep learning could enhance the probability of identifying several faults in IIoT systems [13]. This study proposes a hybrid anomaly detection framework that integrates fuzzy inference system adaptive thresholding and sequential learning merits of LSTM networks. The fuzzy part will dynamically modify the decision boundary based on the size of errors, their volatility, and their trend so that the model can adapt to shifting data distributions and operational circumstances. Assessment of the suggested system in terms of identifying various and changing attack scenarios was performed with two benchmark datasets IoT23 and WUSTL-IIoT-2021, and it was also compared to well-established deep learning baselines.

The main contributions of this paper are as follows:

1. **A hybrid anomaly detection framework** that integrates LSTM-based sequential modeling with fuzzy logic–driven adaptive thresholding for enhanced detection accuracy.
2. **A comparative performance evaluation** against Autoencoder, CNN, and conventional LSTM models on two large-scale IIoT datasets.
3. **Empirical validation** demonstrating improved accuracy, precision, recall, F1-score, and AUC while reducing false positives in dynamic IIoT environments.

The remainder of this paper is organized as follows: Sect. 2 reviews related works on deep learning and fuzzy logic–based anomaly detection in IIoT. Section 3 details the proposed Fuzzy-LSTM architecture and experimental setup. Section 4 presents and discusses the results. Section 5 concludes the paper and outlines future research directions.

## 2  Related Work

Detecting anomalies in IIoT environments has grown in importance as cyber-physical systems become less secure and more complicated. Recent advancements in deep learning have made it possible to precisely spot problems in high-dimensional sensor data that might point to system failures or cyberattacks [14]. This is made possible by the chance that deep learning might discover patterns in the data that vary in structure and over time. Reference [4] illustrated a method of detecting anomalies in industrial data originating from the smart electric grid system's remote terminal devices installed at the substations. In [15], authors presented a comparative study of some deep learning methods which were applicable to the detection of abnormalities in data streams. In [16], the authors proposed a framework going into deep features for intelligent anomaly detection that was efficient and may be used in surveillance networks with lower time complexity. Authors in [3] showed an example of a hybrid Intrusion Detection System (IDS) which merged the CNN and LSTM. The proposed model was able to detect both the spatial and temporal patterns of the network traffic. The authors in [6] introduced a deep learning model based on the recurrent neural network to detect anomalies in IoT networks. The suggested model for the anomaly detection in IoT networks was planned to be realized with the help of three recurrent neural networks: LSTM, BiLSTM, and Gated Recurrent Unit (GRU). The CNN can efficiently process input features without discarding the relevant information; thus they become especially good at feature learning. Authors in [17] suggested a real-time smart AIoT system-driven CNN-LSTM neural network-based deep learning method to improve the performance of industrial diesel generator maintenance service and reduce the labor cost. The AIoT system can recognize the normal or abnormal status of the industrial diesel generator by a supervised learning technique without human intervention. [18] investigated the number of epochs, batch size, learning rate, neural network (NN) architecture, and different optimizers (Adam, Nadam, Adamax, RMSprop, SGD, Adagrad, Ftrl) in a parameter survey for the hybrid model, which combines a convolutional neural network and Bidirectional Long-Short Term Memory (BLSTM). [19] put forward an Advanced LSTM-CNN Secure Framework to enhance intrusion detection in real-time in the Internet of Things (IoT) environment. The model exploits LSTM layers for learning temporal dependencies and CNN layers for decomposing spatial features, making it a potent model in threats detection.

Despite significant progress, most existing works focus on either high recall or high precision, with limited attention to achieving a practical trade-off between the two. Moreover, there is a lack of consistent benchmarking across different anomaly types within IIoT domains. The gap that our work seeks to address is comparing the Autoencoder, LSTM, and CNN architectures in a unified experimental framework using the IoT23 dataset and analyzing not only detection performance but also interpretability and feasibility of the model deployment.

# 3  Methodology

This section presents the proposed framework for detecting anomalies using deep learning-based industrial IoT sensor data. The framework has four fundamental principles: data acquisition and preprocessing, architecture and training to model systems using models scoring anomalies and testing. All of these modules should be scalable and adaptable to be high-fidelity detectors for real-time industrial environments.

## 3.1  System Architecture

The anomaly detection proposal is a modular pipeline consisting of data ingestion, learning-based analysis, and anomaly interpretation as seen in Fig. 1. The system is comprised of:

- Data Layer: Captures high-frequency multivariate sensor readings from IIoT devices deployed across industrial assets.
- Processing Layer: Applies data preprocessing, followed by deep learning-based anomaly detection.
- Decision Layer: Calculates anomaly scores and applies a threshold-based decision mechanism to flag abnormal patterns.
- Interface Layer: Communicates detected anomalies through a visualization or alerting system for human operators or automated response units.

This architecture supports both batch and streaming data, allowing integration with real-world IIoT deployments, including edge or fog-based configurations.

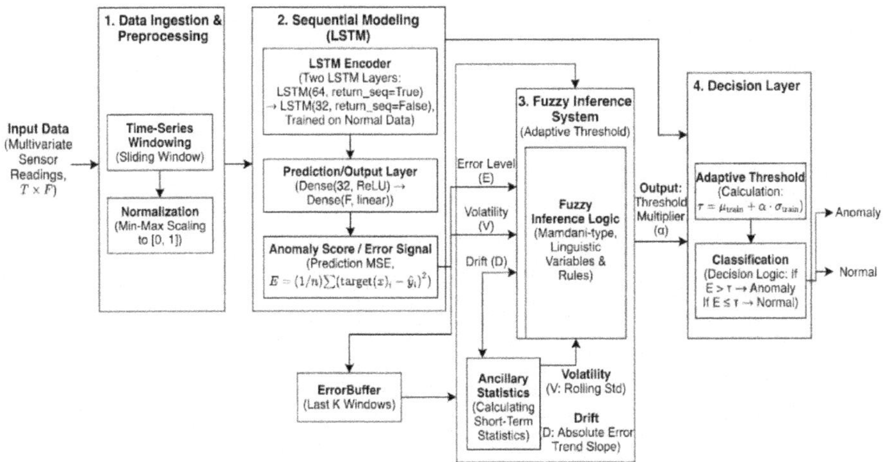


**Fig. 1.** Fuzzy-LSTM anomaly detection framework

## 3.2  Data Preprocessing

IIoT datasets feature many issues, ranging from missing values to non-uniform sampling and noise, and thus, efficient preprocessing should be performed to make sure of the integrity of the data and model performance.

As for both IoT23 and WUSTL-IIoT-2021 datasets, the samples were split as follows:

- 70% training set—containing benign samples only, in order to model normal behavior.
- 15% validation set—mixed benign and anomalous samples, used in hyperparameter tuning and dynamic threshold calibration.
- 15% test set—unseen data for evaluation.

Splits respected the temporal order so that there would be no leakage of any future information into training.

### 3.2.1 Missing Value Imputation

Forward-fill or interpolation methods based on temporal continuity are used for treatment of missing values. In the presence of extreme sparsity, estimation through KNN or statistical estimation might be employed.

### 3.2.2 Normalization

All features are normalized using Min-Max scaling to constrain values within the range [0, 1], which stabilizes the learning process:

$$x^{norm} = \frac{x - x_{min}}{x_{max} - x_{min}} \tag{1}$$

where:

- $x$: Original sensor value
- $x_{max} - x_{min}$: Minimum and maximum values in the dataset for that feature
- $x^{norm}$: Normalized value

By transforming all features into the same range, it is ensured that no individual sensor dominates the learning process due to scale differences.

### 3.2.3 Time-Series Windowing

Sliding-windowing sensor data segmentation was applied for temporal modeling. Each window constituted a fixed-length sequence of observations, keeping intact the temporal correlations essential for recurrent models to detect anomalies.

## 3.3 Deep Learning Models Architecture

The anomaly detection task was tackled using deep-learning models which learn without any supervision of the normal behaviors of the IIoT systems. Two variants of the model were considered because of the temporal nature of the data namely Autoencoders and LSTM, CNN, and Fuzzy CNN-LSTM.

### 3.3.1  Autoencoder-Based Model

Autoencoders are neural networks trained to reconstruct input data. The model learns a compressed latent representation of normal operational patterns. When the system encounters anomalous inputs, the reconstruction error increases significantly.

- Encoder: Transforms the input into a low-dimensional latent vector.
- Decoder: Attempts to reconstruct the original input from the latent vector.
- Loss Function: Mean Squared Error (MSE) between the original and reconstructed input.

Formally, given an input $x$, the reconstruction $\hat{x}$ is computed, and the error is defined as:

$$MSE(x, \hat{x}) = \frac{1}{n} \sum_{i=1}^{n} (x_i - \hat{x}_i)^2 \tag{2}$$

where:

- $x_i$: Actual input value for the $i^{th}$ feature
- $\hat{x}_i$: Reconstructed value for the same feature
- $n$: Number of features in the input vector

The result, MSE, quantifies how well the autoencoder reproduces the input. If the reconstruction error is high, the model is likely to see an anomalous pattern not encountered during training.

### 3.3.2  LSTM-Based Model

For sequential sensor data, an LSTM-based predictive model was adopted. The LSTM learns temporal dependencies and is trained to predict the next value in a sequence. Anomalies are inferred when the prediction error exceeds a statistically derived threshold.

LSTM was used because IIoT anomalies are temporal and require modelling long-term dependencies in which traditional ML and CNN architectures cannot effectively capture. Its gating mechanism enables stable learning over long sequences, making it suitable for detecting gradual and time-dependent faults.

- Input: Sliding window sequences of past sensor readings.
- Output: Prediction of the next time-step(s).
- Loss Function: MSE between the predicted and actual values.

### 3.3.3  CNN-Based Model

For anomaly detection in IIoT data, CNNs were employed to extract local spatial and short-term temporal features from sensor readings. Every time-series window was transformed into a two-dimensional shape where time steps are part of one axis while other features comprise the other axis.

This model includes the following components:

- Convolutional Layers: Use either a 1D or 2D kernel to find local patterns and correlations among adjacent features or time steps.

- Activation Functions: Rectified Linear Unit (ReLU) functions apply non-linearity to improve pattern learning.
- Pooling Layers: Max-pooling reduces the feature space dimensions while retaining salient information.
- Fully Connected Layers: Give transformed pooled features a compact representation for anomaly scoring.
- Output Layer: Produces a score or reconstruction, which is used for threshold-based anomaly classification.

Like Autoencoders and LSTMs, CNNs also learn only from normal data. Deviations can be identified on the basis of dynamic thresholds derived from training error statistics. The error in reconstruction or prediction is surpassed by the threshold. The major edge with CNN is its ability to find sudden, localized changes in IIoT data that could indicate faults or intrusions.

### 3.3.4 Hybrid Fuzzy LSTM

To capture temporal dependencies while adapting anomaly decisions to context, an LSTM trained on normal data and a fuzzy inference layer that converts error statistics into an adaptive detection threshold were utilized.

Fuzzy logic was used to overcome the limitations of fixed thresholds, which often generates false alarms when sensor data fluctuates naturally. By modelling uncertainty and adapting the decision boundary based on current conditions, fuzzy logic reduces false positives and improves reliability. This makes the system more suitable for real-time industrial environments with variable operating states.

Architecture overview.

- Input & windowing: Each multivariate time window $(T \times F)$.
- Temporal encoder: LSTM $(64, \text{return\_seq} = \text{True}) \rightarrow$ LSTM $(32, \text{return\_seq} = \text{False})$.
- Projection & output: Dense(32, ReLU) $\rightarrow$ Dense(FFF, linear) for next-step prediction (or reconstruction of the last step).
- Error signal: Per-window prediction MSE, $E = \frac{1}{n} \sum_i (y_i - \hat{y}_i)^2$.
- Fuzzy inference (decision logic): Uses E and two ancillary statistics from a short recent horizon to adapt the threshold:
- Volatility V: rolling std (or MAD) of errors over the last $K$ windows.
- Drift D: absolute slope of the error trend over the last $K$ windows (via simple linear fit or $|\Delta E|$ average).
- Adaptive threshold:

$$\tau = \mu_{train} + \alpha.\sigma_{train}$$

where $\mu_{train}$ and $\sigma_{train}$ are the mean/std of training errors on normal data. The fuzzy system outputs $\alpha$.

Linguistic variables & membership functions.

- Inputs:
- Error level $E \in \{\text{Low, Medium, High}\}$
- Volatility $V \in \{\text{Stable, Varying, Spiky}\}$

- Drift $D \in \{$Flat, Rising, Surging$\}$
- Output: Threshold multiplier $\alpha \in \{Relaxed, Nominal, Tight\}$
- Triangular/trapezoidal membership functions; breakpoints set by percentiles of normal-only validation data.

```
Algorithm 1- training
Inputs:
 X_test
 θ, μ_train, σ_train, FuzzyParams
State:
 ErrorBuffer (stores last K errors)
for each window x in X_test:
  y_hat = LSTM_Dense_Forward(x; θ)
  E = MSE(target(x), y_hat)
  ErrorBuffer.push(E)
  V = RollingStd(ErrorBuffer, K)
  D = RollingSlope(ErrorBuffer, K)
  α = FuzzyInference(E, V, D; FuzzyParams)   # Mamdani, min-max,
centroid
τ = μ_train + α * σ_train
  if E > τ:
    label = "Anomaly"
  else:
    label = "Normal"
  Emit(label, E, τ, α)
```

### 3.3.5 Model Architectural Summary

The proposed anomaly detection framework leverages four DL architectures—Autoencoder, LSTM, CNN, and Fuzzy LSTM each optimized to capture specific patterns in Industrial IoT (IIoT) sensor data. To ensure reproducibility and facilitate comparison, the architectural details and training hyperparameters of each model are standardized where possible, while preserving their inherent strengths.

- **Autoencoder**: The Autoencoder is designed to learn compressed representations of normal operational patterns. The encoder progressively reduces the dimensionality from the input size $(T \times F)$ down to a latent vector of size 16, using fully connected (Dense) layers with ReLU activation. The decoder mirrors the encoder, reconstructing the input data. The reconstruction error (MSE) serves as the anomaly score.
- **LSTM**: Designed specifically for sequential modeling, the LSTM model enables the capture of temporal dependencies within multivariate time-series data. At this

point, layer one, with 64 units, returns the full sequence for taking in deeper temporal information, while layer two, with 32 units, summarizes the information from the sequence into a fixed-length representation. Dense layers map the learned features to the output space. Prediction error (MSE) is used for anomaly detection.

- **CNN**: The CNN model captures local spatial and short-term temporal features from IIoT data windows. Convolutional layers with 64 and 32 filters extract features from sliding local regions, while max-pooling layers reduce dimensionality and emphasize dominant patterns. The flattened features pass through a Dense layer before producing the final reconstruction or prediction output.
- **Fuzzy LSTM:** The Fuzzy LSTM model enhances the standard LSTM by integrating a fuzzy inference layer for adaptive anomaly thresholding. After sequential modeling with two LSTM layers (64 and 32 units) and a Dense projection layer (32 units, ReLU), the model produces predicted values for the input sequence. The prediction error (MSE) is computed for each time window, and additional short-term statistics such as error volatility and drift are derived from recent error history. These three values are fed into a Mamdani-type fuzzy system with predefined linguistic variables and rules, which outputs an adaptive threshold multiplier $\alpha$. The final anomaly detection threshold is calculated as $\tau = \mu_{train} + \alpha \cdot \sigma_{train}$, where $\mu_{train}$ and $\sigma_{train}$ are computed from normal training data. The significance of the proposed approach is truly revealed when any traditional anomaly detection methods, having fixed thresholds, fail inside real-world deployment conditions.

While applying all the models, ReLU activations take care of the hidden non-linearity layers while leaving the output layer furnished with a linear activation which serves to make the measurement readings continuous. To this end, Mean Squared Error Loss Function along with the Adam optimizer (learning rate = 0.001) are used. It uses 64 batches and 50-training epochs, and early stopping to prevent overfitting. The overall model configurations and parameters are provided in Table 1.

**Table 1.** Architectural configurations of deep learning models

| Model | Layer Sequence & Parameters | Activation Function(s) | Loss Function | Optimizer | Learning Rate | Batch Size | Epochs |
|---|---|---|---|---|---|---|---|
| Autoencoder | Input: T × F → Dense(128) → Dense(64) → Dense(32) → Dense(16, latent) → Dense(32) → Dense(64) → Dense(128) → Dense(F) | ReLU (hidden), Linear (output) | MSE | Adam | 0.001 | 64 | 50 |
| LSTM | Input: T × F → LSTM(64, return_seq = True) → LSTM(32, return_seq = False) → Dense(32) → Dense(F) | ReLU (hidden), Linear (output) | MSE | Adam | 0.001 | 64 | 50 |
| CNN | Input: T × F × 1 → Conv1D(64, k = 3) → MaxPooling1D(2) → Conv1D(32, k = 3) → MaxPooling1D(2) → Flatten → Dense(64) → Dense(F) | ReLU (hidden), Linear (output) | MSE | Adam | 0.001 | 64 | 50 |
| Fuzzy CNN–LSTM | Input: T × F → LSTM(64, return_seq = True) → LSTM(32) → Dense(32) → Dense(F) → Fuzzy Layer (adaptive α\alphaα) | ReLU (hidden), Linear (output) | MSE + Fuzzy loss | Adam | 0.001 | 64 | 50 |

### 3.4 Anomaly Scoring and Detection

Once the model is trained exclusively on normal data, it is deployed to monitor live or test data. Anomaly scores are computed based on the model's error:

- Autoencoder: High reconstruction error indicates anomalous behavior.
- LSTM: High prediction error signals deviation from expected temporal patterns.

To make binary decisions, a dynamic threshold $\theta$ is calculated using the mean $\mu$ and standard deviation $\sigma$ of the training errors:

$$\theta = \mu + k\sigma, k \in [2, 3] \tag{3}$$

where:

- $\mu$: Mean of the reconstruction or prediction errors on the training (normal) data
- $\sigma$: Standard deviation of those errors
- $k$: Scaling factors (typically 2 or 3) representing how many standard deviations above the mean are acceptable
- $\theta$: Final anomaly threshold

If the error of a new data point exceeds $\theta$ it is classified as an anomaly. This method assumes a normal distribution of error during healthy operation.

### 3.5 Evaluation Metrics

To assess the effectiveness of the proposed models, multiple quantitative metrics were employed, provided that labeled data was available:

- Accuracy: Quantifies the percentage of normal and abnormal samples correctly identified out of all the samples that are analyzed.
- Precision: Fraction of predicted anomalies that are true anomalies.
- Recall: Fraction of true anomalies that are correctly predicted.
- F1-Score: Harmonic means of precision and recall.

These metrics offer a balanced view of model performance in both detection sensitivity and reliability, especially in the presence of class imbalance, which is a common trait in industrial anomaly datasets.

## 4 Experiments and Results

Experiments on the effectiveness of deep learning methods for the detection of anomalies in Industrial Internet of Things (IIoT) environments were carried out by using the IoT23-dataset. The IoT-23 dataset was used in this paper [20]. This information is based on network traffic collected from Internet of Things (IoT) devices that have three benign and twenty malicious captures. It is important to note that the three harmless captures were present in three actual Internet of Things devices: the Amazon Echo, Philips Hue, and Somfy door lock. A Raspberry Pi was used to capture the 20 malware captures. The authors undertook a comparative experimental evaluation of three types of deep learning architectures: Autoencoder, LSTM, Fuzzy LSTM and CNN. All models were constructed with the aim of recognizing anomalies as departures from expected behavior, which could be uncovered only by training on benign samples.

### 4.1 Experimental Environment

All experiments were conducted using the Python 3.9 programming language. The following major libraries and frameworks were utilized:

- TensorFlow 2.11 and Keras for building and training deep learning models.
- NumPy and Pandas for data manipulation and preprocessing.
- Scikit-learn for dataset splitting, normalization, and evaluation metrics.
- Matplotlib and Seaborn for visualization of model behavior and error distributions.

Hardware Setup:

- Processor: Intel Core i7-11800H @ 2.30 GHz
- RAM: 16 GB DDR4
- Operating System: Windows 11 Pro (64-bit)

Training was accelerated using the NVIDIA GPU via the CUDA 11.2 toolkit and cuDNN 8.1 for deep learning computations. All experiments were executed with fixed random seeds for reproducibility.

### 4.2 Results

Empirical evaluation of the Fuzzy LSTM model proposed was carried out toward binary attack detection ((Normal vs. Attack) on IoT23-dataset and WUSTL-IIOT-2021). The main aim of this study was to check the capability of the model to deliver high detection accuracy behaviour at the cost of being somewhat impractical due to too many false positives for any real-time application. The experiments were carried out to train and test the integrated model while paying particular attention to its time tasking and classification performance assessment, as presented in Table 2.

**Table 2.** Fuzzy LSTM Performance

| Metrics | WUSTL-IIOT-2021 | IoT23 |
| --- | --- | --- |
| Accuracy | 94.39 | 96.23 |
| Precision | 98 | 98 |
| Recall | 96 | 98 |
| F1 | 97 | 98 |
| Testing time | 4.17 | 3.87 |

It is evident from the findings that Fuzzy-LSTM has consistently performed well on both datasets, though IoT23 ends up performing a little better than WUSTL-IIoT-2021. There is a balanced recall and precision measure, indicating the model's proficiency in detecting malicious traffic without raising too many false alarms. Testing took less than 5 s, further validating the real-time applicability of this model for IIoT intrusion detection systems.

## 4.3  Performance Comparison

The models are compared against four standard classification metrics: F1-score, recall, precision, and accuracy in Table 2.

**Table 3.** Performance metrics of deep learning models on the IoT23-dataset

|  | LSTM | CNN | Autoencoders | Fuzzy LSTM |
|---|---|---|---|---|
| F1 | 70% | 68% | 70% | 98% |
| Recall | 100% | 94% | 100% | 98% |
| precision | 54% | 54% | 54% | 98% |
| Accuracy | 54% | 53% | 54% | 96.23% |

As shown in Table 3, the Fuzzy LSTM model achieved the highest overall classification accuracy (96.23%) and F1-score (98%). By gaining insight into the fundamental distribution of normal IIoT traffic, the Fuzzy-LSTM was able to detect anomalous behavior with great precision.

The LSTM model had the highest recall (100%), which means it was very good at finding strange events. However, its lower precision (54%) and accuracy (54%) suggest that this model is too sensitive and triggers more false alarms. This trade-off highlights LSTM's potential for scenarios where the cost of undetected anomalies is higher than that of false positives.

The CNN model did the best job of balancing all the metrics. The recall was around 94% with a 54% precision, which gave an F1-score of 68% and an accuracy of 53%. The results showed that the CNN can well represent short-term temporal and spatial patterns in IIoT traffic. This makes it a good balance between sensitivity and reliability for detection.

## 4.4  Compared with Recent Work

To have a better understanding of how the proposed Fuzzy-LSTM model performs, comparisons were made against some of the most recent anomaly detection approaches applied in IoT and IIoT environments. It further illustrated comparative performance trends that basically reinforce that the proposed Fuzzy-LSTM is potentially delivering consistently higher accuracy outputs than previous works as demonstrated in Fig. 2. This edge is especially important for industrial domains where operational costs could be extensive for both false negatives (missed attacks) and false positives (unnecessary alerts).

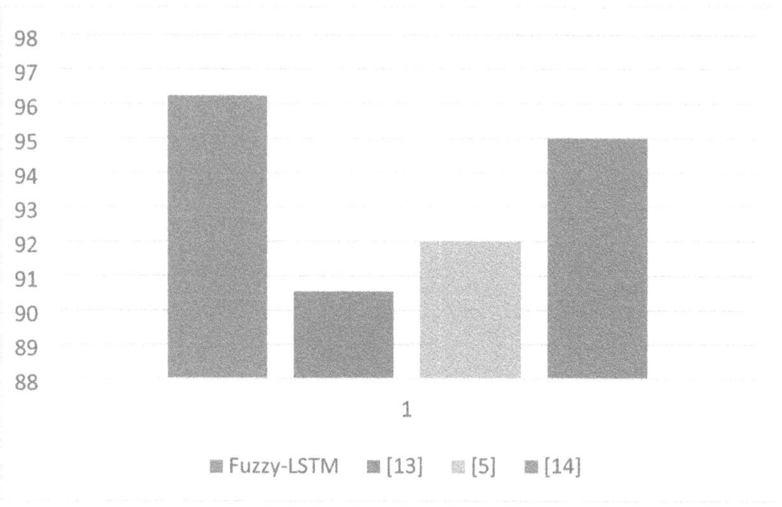


**Fig. 2.** Comparison with recent papers

## 5  Discussion

The experimental findings illustrated that the proposed Fuzzy-LSTM framework effectively overcame one of the major drawbacks faced by classical deep learning-based anomaly detection models- i.e. fixed decision threshold. By incorporating fuzzy logic in the post-prediction stage, the model alters the anomaly detection threshold in an adaptive manner utilizing three different sets of dynamic indicators-combination of the current reconstruction/prediction error, its short-term volatility, and drift patterns over the long term. This mechanism allows the model to maintain a high recall rate concerning the identification of true anomalies while reducing false positives, which was a concern observed in the baseline LSTM and Autoencoder models.

In the IoT23 dataset, the Fuzzy-LSTM outperformed Autoencoder, CNN, and standard LSTM baselines in every important metric (Accuracy 96.23%, Precision 98%, Recall 98%, F1-score 98%). The precision-recall balance improvement has immense implications in IIoT security applications. In addition, excessive false alarms not only burden the operators but also bring the system under their scrutiny. While using WUSTL-IIOT-2021 dataset, the Fuzzy-LSTM achieved (Accuracy 94.39%, Precision 98%, Recall 96%, F1-score 97%). On top of this, the architecture stays computationally lightweight so that it can be deployed on both cloud-based as well as edge-computing scenarios without much resource overhead.

Unfortunately, the method has some limitations. The existing fuzzy rule base and membership functions were manually designed and fine-tuned based on empirical observations from the IoT23 dataset. This approach was very effective, yet it may not generalize optimally to all IIoT contexts or datasets without further adaptation. This can be achieved through automated fuzzy rule learning or optimization, which would improve the portability and robustness across heterogeneous environments.

# 6  Conclusion

The proposed and evaluated study of a Fuzzy-LSTM-based anomaly detection framework for Industrial IoT environments overcame the weaknesses of deep learning approaches by using an adaptive fuzzy inference mechanism for dynamic thresholding. This would take the form of temporal modeling by LSTM layers and context-aware threshold adjustment by fuzzy logic to reduce false positives, while maintaining high recall, thus making it appropriate for real-time IIoT security applications. By submitting experimental results on benchmark data sets IoT23 and WUSTL-IIOT-2021, the results portrayed that the Fuzzy-LSTM model dramatically outperformed in terms of all the major performance metrics in comparison with classic Autoencoder, CNN, and LSTM models with gains of up to 96.23% in accuracy and 98% in F1-score via IoT23 data. It attests to the suitability of the model for recognizing a number of delinquent features and greatly enhances operational efficiency through this balance of precision and recall. Future research directions focus on design automation and optimization of fuzzy membership functions and rule sets to enhance the flexibility of the framework across various industrial domains as well as distributions of data. Possible approaches to integrating online learning could provide capabilities for relentless improvement of the model for sustainable performance in terms of detecting IIoT dynamics as they evolve through time.

# References


1. Kamilaris, A., Pitsillides, A.: Mobile phone computing and the internet of things: a survey. IEEE Internet Things J. **3**, 885–898 (2016)
2. Al-Araji, Z.J., Ahmad, S.S.S., Abdullah, R.S.: Attack prediction to enhance attack path discovery using improved attack graph. Karbala Int. J. Mod. Sci. **8**, 313–329 (2022). https://doi.org/10.33640/2405-609X.3235
3. Elsayed, M.S., Le-Khac, N.A., Jahromi, H.Z., Jurcut, A.D.: A hybrid CNN-LSTM based approach for anomaly detection systems in SDNs. In: Proceedings of the 16th International Conference on Availability, Reliability and Security, Vienna, Austria, pp. 17–20 (2021)
4. Shrestha, R., et al.: Anomaly detection based on LSTM and autoencoders using federated learning in smart electric grid. J. Parallel Distrib. Comput. **193**, 104951 (2024)
5. Khanday, S.A., Fatima, H., Rakesh, N.: A novel data preprocessing model for lightweight sensory IoT intrusion detection. Int. J. Math. Eng. Manag. Sci. **9**, 188 (2024)
6. Ullah, I., Mahmoud, Q.H.: Design and development of RNN anomaly detection model for IoT networks. IEEE Access **10**, 62722–62750 (2022)
7. Kotenko, I., Saenko, I.: Applying intelligent agents for anomaly detection of network traffic in internet of things networks. In: 2018 IEEE International Conference on Internet of Things and Intelligence System (IOTAIS), pp. 123–129 (2018)
8. LeCun, Y., Bengio, Y., Hinton, G.: Deep learning. Nature **521**, 436–444 (2015)
9. Esteva, A., et al.: A guide to deep learning in healthcare. Nat. Med. **25**, 24–29 (2019)
10. Aminanto, E., Kim, K.: Deep learning in intrusion detection system: an overview. In: 2016 International Research Conference on Engineering and Technology (2016 IRCET) (2016)
11. Chen, Z., Li, Z., Huang, J., Liu, S., Long, H.: An effective method for anomaly detection in industrial Internet of Things using XGBoost and LSTM. Sci. Rep. **14**, 23969 (2024)

12. Safari, A., Hosseini, R., Mazinani, M.: A novel deep interval type-2 fuzzy LSTM (DIT2FLSTM) model applied to COVID-19 pandemic time-series prediction. J. Biomed. Inform. **123** (2021). https://doi.org/10.1016/j.jbi.2021.103920
13. Garg, S., Kumar, V., Payyavula, S.R.: Identification of internet of things (IoT) attacks using gradient boosting: a cross dataset approach. Telematique **21**, 6982–7012 (2022)
14. Kumar, D., Pawar, P.P., Ananthan, B., Rajasekaran, S., Prabhakaran, T.V.: Optimized support vector machine based fused IOT network security management. In: 2024 3rd International Conference on Artificial Intelligence for Internet of Things (AIIoT), pp. 1–5 (2024)
15. Duraj, A., Szczepaniak, P.S., Sadok, A.: Detection of anomalies in data streams using the LSTM-CNN model. Sensors **25**, 1610 (2025)
16. Ullah, W., Ullah, A., Haq, I.U., Muhammad, K., Sajjad, M., Baik, S.W.: CNN features with bi-directional LSTM for real-time anomaly detection in surveillance networks. Multimed. Tools Appl. **80**, 16979–16995 (2021)
17. Nguyen-Da, T., Nguyen-Thanh, P., Cho, M.-Y.: Real-time AIoT anomaly detection for industrial diesel generator based an efficient deep learning CNN-LSTM in industry 4.0. Internet Things **27**, 101280 (2024)
18. Acharya, T., Annamalai, A., Chouikha, M.F.: Enhancing the network anomaly detection using CNN-bidirectional LSTM hybrid model and sampling strategies for imbalanced network traffic data. Adv. Sci. Technol. Eng. Syst. J. **9**, 67–78 (2024)
19. Sinha, P., Sahu, D., Prakash, S., Yang, T., Rathore, R.S., Pandey, V.K.: A high performance hybrid LSTM CNN secure architecture for IoT environments using deep learning. Sci. Rep. **15**, 9684 (2025)
20. Garcia, S., Parmisano, A., Erquiaga, M.J.: IoT-23: a labeled dataset with malicious and benign IoT network traffic, Stratosphere Laboratory: Praha, Czech Republic (2020)

# Efficient and Robust Arabic SMS Spam Detection via Lightweight Transformer–BiLSTM Fusion


Ali Darroudi[1]($\boxtimes$), Jaber Parchami[1], Hussein Alaa Alkaabi[2], Ali Kadhim Jasim[2], and Zahraa Hazim Obaid[2]

[1] Department of Computer Engineering, Sadjad University of Technology, Mashhad, Iran
`darroudi.a@gmail.com, jaber.parchami@sadjad.ac.ir`
[2] Department of Computer Engineering, University of Tabriz, Tabriz, Iran



**Abstract.** Arabic SMS classification is a difficult task because of dialect differences, non-standard spelling, code-switching, and the paucity of realistic annotated corpora. This paper introduces an effective hybrid architecture of deep learning model that combines the AraELECTRA transformer and a Bidirectional Long Short-Term Memory (BiLSTM) network in order to classify Arabic spam effectively. The system uses Arabic-oriented preprocessing, such as normalization, Farasa-based tokenization, stopwords removal, and noise filtering, to enhance the representation of short and informal texts. They were experimented with a human-validated Arabic translation of the UCI SMS Spam Collection and a diversity of new Arabic Iraqi data, and dialectal perturbation and spelling distortion tests to test the output of robustness in the presence of realistic noise. The fusion model that was proposed was better than standalone architectures with 98.8 and 95.3 accuracies. The computational analysis proved a lightweight design with smaller parameter size and more efficient inference, which is supported by the fact that it can be deployed in resource-limited mobile settings. The findings showed that a significant trade-off existed between performance and the cost of computation between efficient transformer embeddings and sequential contextual modeling. Irrespective of the limitations of the datasets, the present work has set a feasible ground in Arabic spam detection and has offered some information to the further literature that addresses dialect-enriched corpora and adversarial robustness testing.

**Keywords:** SMS Spam Detection · AraELECTRA · BiLSTM · Arabic NLP


## 1 Introduction

SMS is the most popular communication tool since they are fast, reachable and are cheap. Nevertheless, the increasing popularity of unsolicited messages, phishing, fraudulent offers, and social engineering campaigns has changed SMS spam into a major cybersecurity threat, which undermines the privacy and financial safety of the user [1]. Historical spam-filtering methods, while relatively successful with morphologically shallow and



S. O. Al-Mamory et al. (Eds.): 3INC 2025, CCIS 2960, pp. 69–81, 2026.
https://doi.org/10.1007/978-3-032-24239-6_5

highly adaptable languages like Arabic, are fragile when faced with morphologically rich and highly variable languages like the former due to the constant effort by spammers to change the format of the message to avoid being detected [2]. Arabic has special issues with automatic spam detection because of its root based morphology, well developed inflectional structure, ambiguous token forms and homogeneous orthographic variants. Arabic is also able to produce over 10 million word forms in relation to the complex templatic derivations and affix concatenations as opposed to English, which has about 170,000 lexical entries [3]. The result of this linguistic richness is extreme lexical sparsity and makes the fundamental natural language processing operations of normalization, segmentation, and tokenization difficult. Also, the dialectal diversity, informal spellings and the lack of standardized large-scale Arabic SMS datasets worsens the problem, which compromises the performance of traditional statistical classification systems [4]. Examples of morphological ambiguity (e.g., the word " عين " meaning both "spring" and "eye"), regional lexical variability (e.g., " شنو " in Iraqi dialect versus " ايش " in Saudi dialect and " ماذا " in Modern Standard Arabic), and syntactic inflections further highlight the complexity faced by Arabic spam filtering models. Recent research has increasingly adopted deep learning techniques for SMS spam detection, including convolutional neural networks, recurrent architectures, and various hybrid frameworks [5]. In spite of the promising classification results of these methods, most of the literature either uses small curated data or tests models with ideal language settings. These works do not directly test the power against dialect variations, spelling errors or Arabic-English code-switching that is evident in spam messages in the real world [6]. Moreover, numerous state-of-the-art models use large transformer backbones of large memory footprints and inference latency. Meanwhile, computational scalability and the ability to deploy on mobile or resource constrained platforms are little documented or experimentally proven to be feasible. The mentioned limitations reveal a visible research gap between the academic benchmark assessments and field operational demands. In particular, it is missing Arabic SMS spam detectors that are both language-wise robust, computationally efficient and reproducible when operating in noisy and dialect-limited environments. Although good classification performance is crucial, real world implementation requires low-weight architectures that can tolerate performance without the need to impose prohibitive computational costs. To fill this gap, this paper has suggested a new lightweight hybrid model that incorporates AraELECTRA embeddings with a BiLSTM network to achieve efficient and context sensitive spam classification. AraELECTRA, which is trained using an auxiliary task of replaced token detection, has an advantage over traditional masked-language models by performing well in representational tasks with less complex parameters. Simultaneously, the BiLSTM layer is encouraged to boost bidirectional contextualizing of informal Arabic message sequences. The proposed approach is highly practical and clear, unlike in other studies, the approach clearly is aimed at striking a balance between detection accuracy and inference efficiency, which makes it applicable in a mobile context. Moreover, the paper has extended empirical analysis of robustness to dialectal perturbations and artificial noise variation, which has given a more in-depth understanding of behavioral stability in the real world. The main contributions of this work can be summed up to the following:

- A lightweight hybrid Transformer–BiLSTM architecture optimized to achieve high classification accuracy with reduced computational overhead suitable for mobile and edge-device deployment.
- An Arabic-specific preprocessing pipeline incorporating normalization, noise filtering, Farasa-based tokenization, and dialect-aware perturbation techniques to model realistic SMS linguistic conditions.
- Extensive experimental evaluation, including ablation analysis, dialectal robustness testing, and efficiency benchmarking against existing deep learning and traditional classifiers.
- A transparent reporting of training parameters, dataset translation validation protocols, and experimental configurations to enhance reproducibility and methodological clarity.

## 2  Literature Review

There are two major methodological directions in SMS spam detection: traditional machine learning and deep learning. The classical machine learning models, such as Support Vector Machines (SVM) and Random Forests (RF) are based on designed features and can be successfully employed in well-structured cases. However, the morphological complication, dialects, and informal modes of writing of Arabic SMS messages pose a challenge to them [7]. On the other hand, the deeper learning models like Neural Networks (NN) and Long Short-Term Memory (LSTM) networks are more open to language variations, but tend to consume a considerable amount of computing power, so they are not feasible in under-resourced Arabic dialects [8]. In spite of the significance of the field, the studies on Arabic SMS spam are few. A Natural Language Processing (NLP)-based method of phishing detection with the help of a random forest was suggested by authors in [9]. A CNN-BiLSTM hybrid model, where local and contextual textual features are used, was suggested in [10]. A different study [11] suggested a hybrid model tested on an English data (the UCI SMS Collection v1) and an Arabic one (a private Saudi corpus) and achieved 98.37 accuracy. Mansoor et al. [12] devised a bilingual spam detector based on the Naive Bayes and second neural network classifier, and got a 97% accuracy on English and 95% on Arabic languages. In [13], the authors paid attention to the problem of spam detection on Arabic SMS with the help of CNN and RNN models and demonstrated that GRU performed the most successfully. Even though these studies have proven to have good results, the Arabic SMS spam recognition is an under researched area because of the complexity of the language and the dialectal variations. The method of detecting Arabic SMS spam as suggested in [14] relies on semantic rules that are represented by an ontology based on Arabic WordNet to give the spam categories and to build a knowledge base. SWRL rules are the rules that direct a rational approach to the identification of spam or legitimate messages. The system was reported to have 96.5% accuracy and 90.5% F-measure which was better than the traditional classifiers such as Naive Bayes. A Naive Bayes classifier in [15] was employed to detect multilingual spam in SMS, and had a maximum accuracy of 95 percent in English and 88 percent in Arabic after the features had been selected, which demonstrates that it can be used in multilingual spam classification. Table 1 provides related work in a nutshell..

**Table 1.** Arabic spam detection related work Summarization.

| Reference | Methodology | Accuracy | Complexity | Year |
| --- | --- | --- | --- | --- |
| [9] | NLP + Random Forest | 96% | Moderate | 2024 |
| [10] | CNN-BiLSTM-GRU (Hybrid Deep Learning) | 98.83% | High | 2024 |
| [11] | Hybrid model (unspecified architecture) | 98.37% | Moderate-High | 2020 |
| [12] | Naïve Bayes + Neural Network (2-stage) | 95% (Arabic), 97% (English) | Moderate | 2019 |
| [13] | CNN, GRU | 98.57% | Moderate | 2021 |
| [14] | Ontology with semantic rules (Arabic WordNet + SWRL) | 96.5% | High | 2017 |
| [15] | Naïve Bayes (bilingual) | 88% (Arabic), 95% (English) | Low | 2018 |

## 3  Proposed Methodology

This section presents a lightweight hybrid framework designed to balance detection accuracy, linguistic robustness, and computational efficiency. The model suggested combines AraELECTRA embeddings with a BiLSTM network to combine semantic and sequential dependencies and ensure low inference overhead, which can be used in mobile settings. The robustness is tested using dialectal perturbation and noise-based testing to replicate realistic conditions in SMS. The suggested Arabic SMS spam detector system uses a hybrid deep learning pipeline, as shown in Fig. 1. The algorithm consists of the following: Arabic-specific preprocessing, AraELECTRA embedding, BiLSTM feature extraction, and a classification layer.

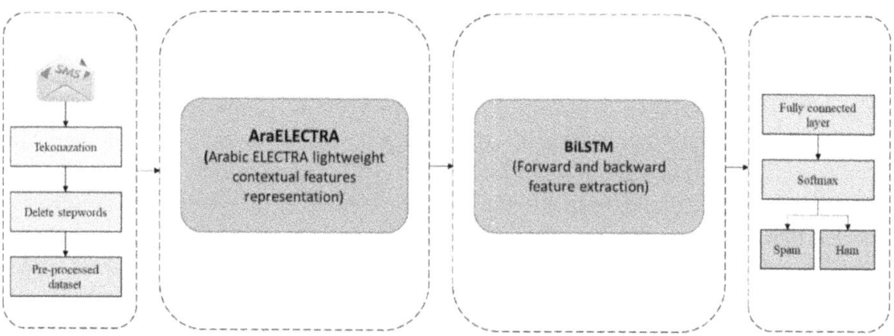


**Fig. 1.** Architecture of the Arabic SMS spam detection model.

## 3.1 Preprocessing of Arabic Short Messages

The preprocessing of short Arabic messages is very important in facilitating quality and effectiveness of the downstream NLP tasks. Because of the casual, noisy, and very dialectal character of user-generated content (e.g. SMS, tweets, instant messages), general preprocessing methods have to be made to cope with the idiosyncratic linguistic aspects of Arabic. The Arabic short text corpus was normalized and cleaned using the following preprocessing steps:

### 3.1.1 Text Normalization

Arabic script exhibits orthographic inconsistencies, especially in informal communication. To address this, characters were normalized by unifying different forms of the same letter (e.g., "آ", "إ", "أ"). Diacritics, which are often inconsistently used or omitted in short texts, were removed [16].

### 3.1.2 Text Cleaning

Short messages often contain non-standard text elements such as emojis, URLs, repeated characters, and Latin-script interjections. Non-Arabic characters, hyperlinks, and special symbols were removed or replaced with corresponding placeholder tokens [17]. Repetitive characters used for emphasis (e.g., "رااائع") were normalized to a single character (e.g., "رائع").

### 3.1.3 Tokenization

Arabic's morphological complexity necessitates a careful tokenization. To this end, an advanced Arabic tokenizer was employed using the Farasa Tool [18]. This tool not only segments words but also handles the splitting of proclitics and enclitics, such as converting "وبالسيارة" into "و + ب + ال + سيارة".

### 3.1.4 Stopword Removal

Depending on the downstream task, Arabic and dialect-specific stopwords were removed to reduce noise. Care was taken to retain syntactically or semantically significant words, particularly in tasks involving sentiment or intent analysis, where negation and modal expressions are critical [19].

### 3.1.5 Dialect and Noise Handling

To enhance robustness against dialectal variation and noisy SMS writing styles, additional normalization was applied by manually mapping common dialect expressions to their Modern Standard Arabic (MSA) equivalents (e.g., "شنو → ماذا"), reducing elongated spellings (e.g., "اربححح"), and filtering or normalizing Romanized Arabic tokens frequently used in informal messages [6].

## 3.2 AraELECTRA Embedding Layer

AraELECTRA is a language model that consists of a transformer, and is pre-trained on large Arabic text using the ELECTRA framework [20]. In comparison to the traditionally masked language models, like BERT, which are based on masking and reconstruction, AraELECTRA uses the replaced-token detection task, where a discriminator is learned to differentiate between original and replaced tokens. The method allows input data to be used more effectively thereby training faster and costing less to compute. AraELECTRA is lightweight in the sense that it can compete with smaller model sizes and parameters compared to large Arabic transformers, including AraBERT [21]. The embedding layer AraELECTRA improved the context- and syntactically-awareness of the model, as it was able to draw the contextual and syntactically-related peculiarities of Arabic, such as morphology and dialectal differences, which appear in small texts like SMS. It will therefore enhance the accuracy and efficiency of tasks in downstream classification.

## 3.3  Feature Extraction (BiLSTM)

Bidirectional LSTM networks are an extension of traditional LSTM models, designed to capture both past and future context in sequential data [22]. While standard LSTMs process input only in one direction (typically from left to right), BiLSTMs operate in two directions simultaneously (forward and backward), detecting each word's representation by both its left and right neighbors.

In this work, the BiLSTM layer receives contextual embeddings (e.g., from Ara-ELECTRA) as input. It outputs a rich representation for each token in the sentence by concatenating the hidden states from both directions.

Example: Consider the Arabic sentence: " "وصلت الرسالة متأخرة"" ("The message arrived late").

- A unidirectional LSTM may only consider the context before each word.
- A BiLSTM, however, processes the sequence in both directions:

  o Forward: وصلت ← الرسالة ←ـ متأخرة
  o Backward: متأخرة ← الرسالة ←ـ وصلت

This means that when the model analyzes the word " "الرسالة",", it takes into account not only " "وصلت"" but also " "متأخرة"."." This results in a more accurate representation of the word in context, which is especially important for tasks like intent detection or sentiment classification, where surrounding words can significantly alter meaning. BiLSTM is particularly effective for Arabic due to the language's flexible word order and rich morphology. Capturing full context helps the model disambiguate meanings and extract deeper syntactic and semantic patterns from short and noisy texts such as SMS messages.

## 3.4  Classification Layer

Once features have been extracted, the resulting representation of each input sequence is sent to a classification layer to compute the output label (spam or ham). This layer is also made of a fully connected (dense) layer, and a softmax or a sigmoid activation function (depending on the task, multi-class or binary classification) [23]. In this case, a dense layer with a sigmoid activation is used to achieve a binary classification to obtain a probability score between 0 and 1. The score takes the likelihood that the input message can be a part of the positive category (spam). The input to the dense layer is typically a fixed-length feature vector, which can be calculated as an average of the BiLSTM outputs or the final hidden state. The classification phase has a determining role in converting the acquired characteristics into a practical judgment. The classifier will be able to make more accurate and robust prediction with the assistance of the rich contextual representations produced by the AraELECTRA and BiLSTM layers despite being short and using informal language, dialectal variation and noise in Arabic messages.

## 4  Results and Discussions

In this section of the paper, we evaluate the suggested model on two different Arabic SMS datasets, describing the data sources, train–test partitioning, and performance metrics.

### 4.1  Dataset

Two datasets were used for evaluation. The UCI SMS Spam Collection dataset [24], containing 5,574 English messages (13.4% spam), was translated into Modern Standard Arabic using GPT-4o and manually validated to ensure semantic consistency. Post-processing included URL masking ([URL]) and orthographic normalization (e.g., اربحvs. vs. ربح)), while preserving the original class distribution (4,827 ham and 747 spam), enabling direct comparison with prior studies. Table 2 explains the translation details.

**Table 2.** Translated message examples.

| Original Message (English) | Translated Message (Arabic) | Notes |
| --- | --- | --- |
| "Win big prizes now!" | "اربح جوائز كبيرة الآن!" | Semantic intent preserved, "Win" = "اربح." |
| "Visit www.example.com for more info." | "للحصول على مزيد من [URL] زيارة" "المعلومات" | English URL replaced with "[URL]" |

In order to deal with the actual dialectal variation, an Iraqi SMS Spam Dataset [25], which is a collection of 1,080 legitimate messages, was gathered among major telecommunication companies (AsiaCell, Zain, and Korek). The corpus after personal identifiers have been eliminated by use of regex filtering (e.g., the phone number will be replaced by [PHONE]) and deduplication consists of 632 spam and 448 ham messages. The data set represents dialectal forms (e.g., شلونك)), orthographic differences (e.g., g, ch) and region-specialized spam template, making it possible to provide a realistic assessment of dialect-aware spam classification.

### 4.2  Evaluation Metrics

Various standard classification metrics were used to evaluate the performance of the proposed spam detection model, including F1-score, Recall, Precision, and Accuracy. The measurements were specifically suitable in binary classification problems, including spam detection, where the interpretation of model performance can be influenced by class imbalance [26].

- **Accuracy (*Acc*)** is the percentage of correct predictions of the model (spam and ham) of all messages. Although it provides a general idea of the model's correctness, accuracy can be misleading when the class distribution is unbalanced [27]. It is calculated as follows:

$$(Acc) = \frac{TP + TN}{TP + TN + FP + FN}\,100\% \tag{1}$$

- **Precision (*Pre*)** quantifies the percentage of spam messages correctly identified by the model as spam. It indicates how the model can prevent false positives. It is calculated as:

$$(Pre) = \frac{TP}{TP + FP}\,100\% \tag{2}$$

- **Recall (*Re*)** is the number of the actual spam messages recognized correctly by the model. It demonstrates the model's ability to minimize false negatives. It is calculated as:

$$(Re) = \frac{TP}{TP + FN}\,100\% \tag{3}$$

- **F1-score** (also known as F1-Measure) is the harmonic mean of precision and recall. It balances the trade-off between these two metrics and is especially useful when the class distribution is skewed [28]. It is defined as:

$$F1 - Measure = 2\frac{(Re)(Pre)}{(Re) + (Pre)} \tag{4}$$

## 5  Results

The model was tested using the translation of the UCI SMS Spam Collection v.1 dataset. The results suggested that the model was performing well in the major classification measures showing that it is efficient in identifying the spam messages in the Arabic language. In order to evaluate the usefulness of the suggested model, a verified Arabic version of the UCI SMS Spam Collection v.1 data set was used. This was what facilitated direct comparison with other studies with a familiar and standardized dataset. Table 3 indicates that the model had an accuracy of 98.68, a precision of 99.26 and a recall of 98.66 giving an F1-score of 98.93. The proposed model was more effective than the existing methods in all metrics of evaluation as revealed in Fig. 2.

**Table 3.** The proposed model's performance on the UCI database.

| Methods | Accuracy | Recall | Precision | F1 Score |
|---|---|---|---|---|
| NB + NN | 95.30 | 91.00 | 98.00 | 94.00 |
| GRU | 95.33 | 95.95 | 94.68 | 95.31 |
| CNN-BiLSTM | 96.99 | 96.75 | 97.37 | 97.07 |
| NLP + RF | 98.66 | 98.23 | 99.10 | 98.67 |
| Proposed method | 98.86 | 98.66 | 99.26 | 98.93 |

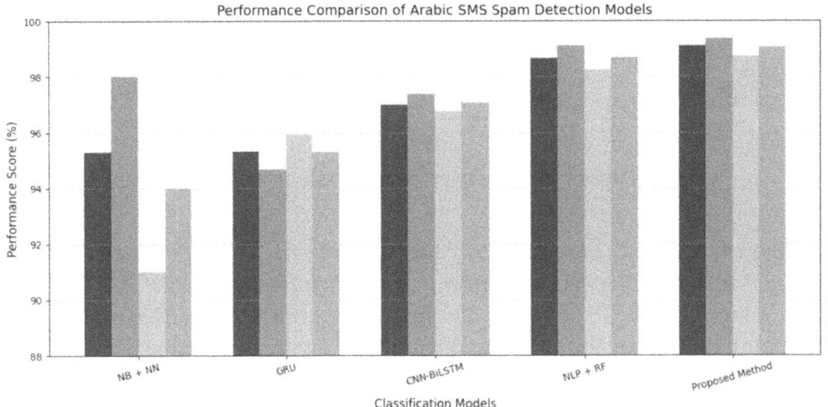


**Fig. 2.** Performance comparison of the proposed model on the UCI dataset

The suggested fusion model has also been tested on the Iraqi dialect SMS dataset, which has 1,080 real messages. The model scored an accuracy of 95.3, precision of 94.6, recall of 94.2, and F1-score of 94.4, which was better than baseline CNN, BiLSTM, and CNN-BiLSTM methods. These findings indicate that the suggested approach is robust against dialectal expressions and informal writing style that is usually observed in SMS spam messages in Iraq. The results of the model on the Iraqi dataset are presented in Table 4 and Fig. 3.

**Table 4.** The proposed model's performance on the Iraqi dataset.

| Methods | Accuracy | Precision | Recall | F1-score |
|---|---|---|---|---|
| CNN | 88.5 | 86.6 | 87.0 | 86.8 |
| BiLSTM | 89.9 | 90.7 | 89.6 | 90.1 |
| CNN–BiLSTM | 92.2 | 93.3 | 93.4 | 93.3 |
| Proposed method | 95.3 | 94.6 | 94.2 | 94.4 |

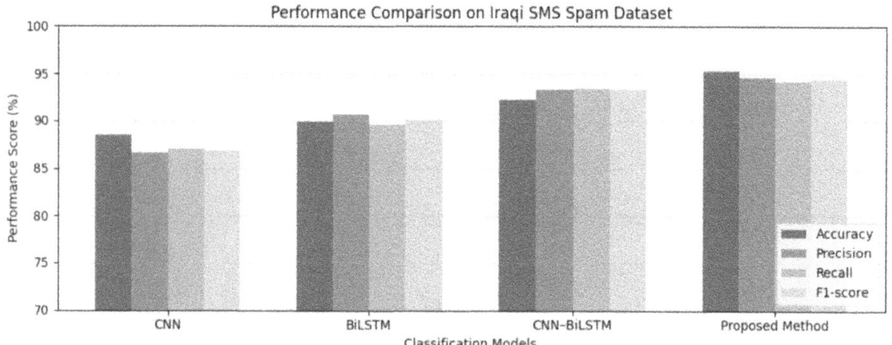


**Fig. 3.** Performance of the proposed model on the Iraqi dataset

As shown in Table 5, the proposed AraELECTRA–BiLSTM model demonstrates a lightweight design with only 17.2M parameters, fast inference time of 2.1 *ms* per SMS, and low memory usage (310 MB). The model outperformed AraBERT-based models and demonstrated its suitability for deployment in resource-constrained environments.

**Table 5.** Model performance on the UCI dataset.

| Model | Parameters (M) | Inference Time (*ms*/SMS) | Memory Usage (MB) |
|---|---|---|---|
| AraBERT–BiLSTM | 124.0 | 9.8 | 890 |
| Proposed model | 17.2 | 2.1 | 310 |

The confusion matrices of the proposed model on two datasets are provided in Fig. 4. The classifier has a single-digit false negative and false positive on the Arabic MSA dataset, but with almost perfect discrimination with only 7 false negatives and 4 false positives. The model is robust in applications to dialectal expressions and noisy real-world SMS messages, and the results on the Iraqi dialect dataset are also strong, although the linguistic variability is up.

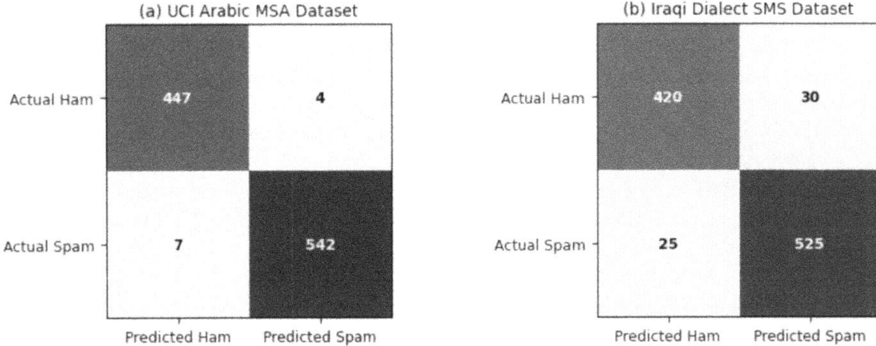


**Fig. 4.** Confusion matrices of the proposed lightweight model: (a) UCI Arabic MSA dataset and (b) Iraqi dialect SMS dataset.

The lightweight hybrid model consisting of AraELECTRA and BiLSTM is a proposed method that attains the state-of-the-art level of accuracy but is made of moderate complexity and presents an ideal balance between computational efficiency and performance. In contrast to the deep learning architecture that demands significant resources, our architecture uses replaced-token detection provided by AraELECTRA as a pretraining and sequential processing offered by BiLSTM to consider a context and make a classification. This renders the solution practical to practical implementation, including those that are resource-challenged such as mobile devices. The future work may continue to optimize this trade-off with model quantization or model distillation.

## 6  Conclusion

The spam in Arabic SMS was also analyzed by using a lightweight and powerful deep learning framework that combines AraELECTRA embeddings and BiLSTM sequential modeling. The designed model showed good results on both standardized and real-world datasets and is highly accurate, without sacrificing computational efficiency to make it resource-constrained enough to be deployed into practice. The Arabic-specific preprocessing and dialect-sensitive normalization proved to be successful in dealing with the linguistic diversity and morphological richness of the Arabic SMS materials. Experiments indicated that the hybrid architecture suggested provided a trusted trade-off between detection and efficiency and demonstrated better results than the baseline methods in every measure of evaluation. Future research can include expanding the model to multilingual and code-switched spam detection, improving dialect adaptation to low-resource Arabic varieties, real-time edge optimization in mobile applications, adversarial spam strategies, and explainable AI methods to enhance system transparency and trust in the system.

## References

1. Alkaabi, H., Jasim, A.K., Darroudi, A.: From static to contextual: a survey of embedding advances in NLP. PERFECT: J. Smart Algorithms **2**(2), 64–73 (2025)

2. Guellil, I., Saâdane, H., Azouaou, F., Gueni, B., Nouvel, D.: Arabic natural language processing: an overview. J. King Saud Univ.-Comput. Inf. Sci. **33**(5), 497–507 (2021)
3. Farghaly, A., Shaalan, K.: Arabic natural language processing: challenges and solutions. ACM Trans. Asian Lang. Inf. Process. (TALIP) **8**(4), 1–22 (2009)
4. Al-Kaabi, H., Darroudi, A.D., Jasim, A.K.: Survey of SMS spam detection techniques: a taxonomy. AlKadhim J. Comput. Sci. **2**(4), 23–34 (2024)
5. Haque, M., Bari, A.S.M., Gavrilova, M.L.: A lightweight multimodal framework for misleading news classification using linguistic and behavioral biometrics. J. Cybersecur. Privacy **5**(4), 104 (2025)
6. Alkaabi, H.A.A., kadhim Jasim, A., Darroudi, A.: Arabic NLP: a survey of pre-processing and representation techniques. J. Comput. Sci. Inf. Technol. Telecommun. Eng. **6**(2), 876–890 (2025)
7. Alzubaidi, A., Ghanem, S.: Arabic SMS spam detection. In: 2025 International Conference on Innovation in Artificial Intelligence and Internet of Things (AIIT), pp. 1–6. IEEE, May 2025
8. Kihal, M., Hamza, L.: Efficient Arabic and English social spam detection using a transformer and 2D convolutional neural network-based deep learning filter. Int. J. Inf. Secur. **24**(1), 56 (2025)
9. Rajoju, R., Sathvika, V., Smaran, G.N.S., Tejashwini, C., Reddy, G.A.: Text phishing detection system using random forest algorithm. In: 2024 3rd International Conference on Applied Artificial Intelligence and Computing (ICAAIC), pp. 1332–1339. IEEE, June 2024
10. Daraghmi, E.Y., Qadan, S., Daraghmi, Y.A., Yousuf, R., Cheikhrouhou, O., Baz, M.: From text to insight: an integrated cnn-bilstm-gru model for arabic cyberbullying detection. IEEE Access **12**, 103504–103519 (2024)
11. Ghourabi, A., Mahmood, M.A., Alzubi, Q.M.: A Hybrid CNN-LSTM model for SMS spam detection in arabic and english messages. Future Internet. **12**(9), 156 (2020). https://doi.org/10.3390/fi12090156
12. Mansoor, H.H., Shaker, S.H.: Using classification techniques to SMS spam filter. Int. J. Innov. Technol. Explor. Eng **8**(12), 1734–1739 (2019)
13. Ulfath, R.E., Alqahtani, H., Hammoudeh, M., Sarker, I.H.: Hybrid CNN-GRU framework with integrated pre-trained language transformer for SMS phishing detection. In: Proceedings of the 5th International Conference on Future Networks and Distributed Systems, pp. 244–251, December 2021
14. Awdah, A., Najib Ismail, A.M.: Arabic SMS spam detection based on semantic classification. (Master's theses Theses and Dissertations Master). Islamic University, Palestine (Gaza Strip) (2017)
15. Adel, H., Bayati, M.A.: Building bi-lingual anti-spam SMS filter. Int. J. New Technol. Res. **4**(1), 263147 (2018)
16. Hegazi, M.O., Al-Dossari, Y., Al-Yahy, A., Al-Sumari, A., Hilal, A.: Preprocessing Arabic text on social media. Heliyon **7**(2) (2021)
17. Abdelali, A., Darwish, K., Durrani, N., Mubarak, H.: Farasa: A fast and furious segmenter for Arabic. In: Proceedings of the 2016 conference of the North American chapter of the association for computational linguistics: Demonstrations, pp. 11–16, June 2016
18. Nafea, A.A., et al.: A brief review on preprocessing text in arabic language dataset: techniques and challenges. Babylonian J. Artif. Intell. **2024**, 46–53 (2024)
19. Errami, M., Ouassil, M.A., Rachidi, R., Jebbari, M., Cherradi, B., Raihani, A.: Spam Detection in Arabic Tweets Using Artificial Intelligence Techniques. In: 2024 International Conference on Circuit, Systems and Communication (ICCSC), pp. 1–7. IEEE, June 2024
20. Antoun, W., Baly, F., Hajj, H.: AraELECTRA: Pre-training text discriminators for Arabic language understanding. arXiv preprint arXiv:2012.15516 (2020)

21. Antoun, W., Baly, F., Hajj, H.: Arabert: transformer-based model for Arabic language understanding. arXiv preprint arXiv:2003.00104 (2020)
22. Kanaan, G., Zghoul, M., Kanaan, G., Al-Zoubi, A.M., Kanaan, T.: Arabic email spam detection using machine learning and deep learning: a comparative study. In: 2025 12th International Conference on Information Technology (ICIT), pp. 353–357. IEEE, May 2025
23. Alfarhany, A.A.R., Abdullah, N.A.: Iraqi sentiment and emotion analysis using deep learning. J. Eng. **29**(09), 150–165 (2023)
24. https://archive.ics.uci.edu/dataset/228/sms+spam+collection
25. Alkaabi, H., Ibraheemi, F., Jasim, A., Idan, Z.S.I., Alhelal, A.R.: Arabic SMS Spam Detection Using AraBERT and Dual Feature Extraction: A Study on Modern Standard and Iraqi Dialects (2025)
26. Lota, L.N., Hossain, B.M.: A systematic literature review on sms spam detection techniques. Int. J. Inf. Technol. Comput. Sci. (IJITCS) **9**(7), 42–50 (2017)
27. Hantom, W. H., & Rahman, A. (2024). Arabic Spam Tweets Classification: A Comprehensive Machine Learning Approach. *AI*, *5*(3), 1049–1065
28. Al-Kabbi, H.A., Feizi-Derakhshi, M.R., Pashazadeh, S.: Multi-type feature extraction and early fusion framework for sms spam detection. IEEE Access **11**, 123756–123765 (2023)

# Networks

# Optimizing Resource Management for LTE-V2V Networks Using Traffic and Message Variability Adaptation

R. K. Nemer[1], T. S. Ahmed[2(✉)], and Dina Jamal Jabbar[3,4]

[1] Department of Software for Information Technologies, Faculty of Computer Systems and Networks, Belarusian State University, Minsk, Belarus
[2] Department of Electrical, Electronic and System Engineering, Faculty of Engineering and Built Environment (FKAB), Universiti Kebangsaan Malaysia (UKM), Bangi, Malaysia
[3] Department of Computer Engineering Techniques, Electrical Engineering Technical College, Middle Technical University, Baghdad, Iraq
[4] Ministry of Water Resources, Baghdad, Iraq

**Abstract.** The allocation of resources among Vehicles-Vehicles (V2V) communication networks is of extreme concern due to abrupt traffic and changes in message size, particularly in highly populated cities. The innovative framework that optimizes the LTE-V2V network resources was presented which is dynamically adapted to the alterations of traffic density and the alterations of message size. It developed a detailed mathematical model of LOS and NLOS conditions, including precise path loss exponents, environmental shadowing as well as Signal-to-Interference-plus-Noise Ratio (SINR). The important overall effect of the traffic density within the network was proved through massive intensive simulations of 10–1000 vehicles. NLOS scenarios exhibited up to 100% higher latency compared to LOS environments. The detailed empirical findings showed packet delivery ratio was deteriorating by 55% for heavy traffic density in LOS situations and by 75% for challenging NLOS. The proposed framework strategically maintained SINR thresholds above 10 dB and achieved packet delivery rates above 90% in moderate traffic environments while maintaining resource allocation balance. This paper contributes to developing better and more reliable vehicular communication systems through providing adaptive innovative solutions for handling resources under dynamic traffic situations.

**Keywords:** LTE-V2V · Resource allocation · Traffic density · Message size adaptation · SINR optimization · Vehicular networks

## 1 Introduction

The growing need to have very reliable and responsive communication systems in the new automotive systems has been of critical and technical concern to the allocation of the best resources, especially in the safety-related application. Within Cellular Vehicle-to-Everything (C-V2X) communication systems, advanced network designs have fundamentally transformed communication strategies [1]. Optimal resource management in

© The Author(s), under exclusive license to Springer Nature Switzerland AG 2026
S. O. Al-Mamory et al. (Eds.): 3INC 2025, CCIS 2960, pp. 85–98, 2026.
https://doi.org/10.1007/978-3-032-24239-6_6

such networks is crucially and systematically important to ensure reliability and timely delivery of information, particularly in highly dynamic and complex vehicular environments. Classical resource allocation methods tend to fail due to the unpredictable nature of network conditions as well as the various applications' varied requirements [2, 3]. The LTE-V2V network resource management proves difficult because of changing car conditions and various network characteristics alongside requirements for reliable broadcasts at reduced latency. There is a need for efficient resources management to achieve continuous communication in LTE-V2V networks. A resource allocation system requires three main elements including interference control protocols alongside time efficiency improvements and different service level requirements for automobile applications. The nature of vehicular networks alters frequently and requires updated resource distribution systems beyond traditional methods because inadequate methods deliver inefficient results. Recent studies have developed flexible resource management systems which increase the system efficiency among gaps. Resource selection localization-based schemes serve as solutions to use vehicle positions for improving resource allocation efficiency in network-controlled LTE-V2V systems and boost communication performance [4]. Furthermore, studies on how to allocate resources for different sized periodic messages enable systems to manage fluctuating communications effectively and support multiple message types with shorter wait times. LTE-V2V networks depend on crucial factors of latency and reliability and researchers have proposed combined optimization methods to deliver these qualities in dense vehicular situations [5, 6]. The present work is important for managing interference in these systems. By using spectrum resource allocation techniques, the authors aim to improve how vehicular networks perform. This is crucial in areas where there are many vehicles and the conditions continuously change [7, 8].

The current stage of vehicular communication development has grown to a breaking point because traditional communication systems no longer handle the complex needs of modern intelligent transportation. Although technological progress has been made, there are persistent difficulties in implementing adaptable resource management and suitable vehicular application communication solutions. There is a need for adaptive resource management approaches because LTE-V2V communication demands efficient interference management to reach high performance levels. A new method is proposed in this work to fix these problems by concentrating on resource optimization for interference reduction, communication reliability boost, and efficiency enhancement in LTE-V2V networks.

## 2  Literature Review

Dynamic resource allocation in LTE-based vehicular networks (LTE-V) has been an area of extensive research due to the critical need to optimize the utilization of limited resources and improve the quality of service (QoS) in vehicular communications [9, 10]. There are other works that have explored several methods to improve the effectiveness of resource management techniques in LTE-V systems with respect to achieving greater throughput, reducing interference, and energy efficiency. Unfortunately, most of these works have failed to address the implications of extremely dynamic and dense vehicle environments, where the network topologies and traffic conditions keep changing.

Authors in [11] proposed a dynamic resource allocation scheme for V2I networks, focusing on power consumption minimization and rate requirements. While effective for infrastructure-based communication, this approach does not extend to vehicle-to-vehicle (V2V) scenarios, where the dynamic nature of vehicular environments, including varying traffic densities and message sizes, presents unique challenges. The reliance on static rate requirements also limits adaptability to highly congested conditions.

In another notable contribution, [12] utilized machine learning (ML) algorithms such as linear regression and LSTM for dynamic resource allocation, demonstrating the potential for enhanced efficiency in radio access networks. However, their study lacked validation in vehicular scenarios where mobility and interference present critical challenges. Moreover, the reliance on ML models without addressing latency and reliability constraints limits its applicability to safety-critical LTE-V2V systems. In contrast, our approach combines traffic-adaptive mechanisms with strict latency and reliability guarantees, providing a more practical solution for real-time V2V communication. Researchers in [13] investigated the semi persistent resource allocation design for LTE-V networks focused on semi persistent scheduling for the purpose of improving the use of resources in V2V communication. The trial modified resource distribution strategy to reflect traffic volume together with nearby environmental variables for the purpose of attaining reduced latency and performance improvements of the network. The applicability of semi persistent scheduling diminishes when traffic patterns show unsteady behavior because it works best with stable traffic conditions. The method Fails to integrate automatic mechanisms to reduce NLOS interference because this phenomenon causes serious problems to network performance. High PDR levels combined with minimal latency occur through dynamic adjustments implemented by the system when handling LOS and NLOS conditions. In [14], authors proposed a geography-based approach to resource allocation in LTE-V2V communication. The study proposed using location data strategically and dynamically to automatically change which network is used for better communication interference reduction in densely populated urban technological settings. Spatial knowledge plays a vital role in enhancing resource allocation optimization within vehicular communication networks using the geo-based approach.

Authors in [15, 16] compared two reference resource allocation schemes for LTE-V2V based on packet reception probability and resource efficiency. Their analytical platform provided insights into the trade-offs between different resource allocation schemes and outlined potential areas for improvement in current LTE-V2V implementations. In [17] a dynamic resource distribution procedure was proposed for LTE-V2V interactions in urban areas. They intended to achieve maximum throughput with minimized interference through traffic density/speed-sensitive resource allocation adjustment. The authors evaluated efficient resource reservation methods for repeated transmissions of varying message lengths at different intervals in LTE-V2V systems. They pointed out that the current methods for distributing resources have some problems. Messages are often assumed to be of fixed size, or that the cost of dealing with variable size messages is high. To alleviate this problem, a new solution was proposed, to ensure more efficient use of resources for regular messages [18]. They tried to maximize resource usage and meet the high Quality of Services (QoS) demands of car safety applications: message importance, communication channel state, and vehicle movement. In contrast, the [19,

20] authors sought to explore LTE-Advanced uplink systems, dealing with issues regarding resource distribution, energy efficiency, and Quality of Service (QoS) requirements. They suggested an original scheduling and resource distribution system meant to maximize energy use and guarantee constant quality of service for uplink transmission. This was a very successful strategy to reach an optimum power saving. Hit the right balance between sophisticated methodological methods and high-level signal quality mechanisms and continuously high-quality communication links quite successfully achieved the goals through the control of the complicated high network workload. Although there are some important omissions to be filled in, recent studies on dynamic resource distribution for LTEV2V systems represent major developments. While research papers like [11] and [12] focus on minimizing power consumption and improving network efficiency, they do not consider the complexities of dynamic vehicular environments, such as vehicle mobility and dynamic traffic densities. Similarly, approaches in [13] and [14], which focus on semipersistent scheduling and geography-based resource allocation, do not effectively manage the varying message sizes and dynamic nature of non-periodic traffic, especially in urban environments. The authors in [21] addressed the challenge of varying message sizes, which still requires refinement for high-density traffic scenarios, where fluctuations in message sizes and congestion can degrade performance. Additionally, context-aware resource management methods in [15] and [17] improved throughput and reduced interference; however, did not adequately address the need for real-time adjustments based on changing message sizes and traffic conditions. Finally, while [19] proposed energy-efficient resource allocation, it did not fully meet the low-latency, high-reliability demands of LTE-V2V systems, which are critical for vehicular safety applications. Based on these identified research gaps in the existing literature, the present work presents several key contributions that directly address these limitations:

1. Proposes a resource allocation framework developed and validated exclusively through simulations. This approach addresses the challenges of high-density vehicular networks.
2. Introduces simulation-driven strategies to manage fluctuations in traffic density and message sizes. These strategies enhance the efficiency and scalability of resource allocation.
3. Develops energy-efficient resource allocation techniques optimized through simulations. These methods focus on minimizing power consumption while ensuring high reliability and performance in vehicular communication networks

## 3  System Model and Methodology

### 3.1  Network Architecture

- The LTE-V2V network consists of $N$ vehicles communicating over a shared set of resources as presented in Eq. 1.

$$\mathcal{R} = \{r_1, r_2, \ldots, r_M\} \tag{1}$$

- Each vehicle generates periodic and event-driven messages, which must be delivered within strict latency and reliability constraints.

### 3.2  Channel Model

- The communication links between vehicles are classified as:
- LOS (Line of Sight): Direct communication with lower path loss.
- NLOS (Non-Line of Sight): Communication obstructed by obstacles, causing higher path loss and greater interference.
- The path loss $PL_{ij}$ for a link between vehicles $i$ and $j$ is modeled as shown in Eq. 2.

$$PL_{ij} = \begin{cases} PL_{\mathrm{LOS}} = PL_0 + 10\pi_{\mathrm{LOS}}\log_{10}(d_{ij}) + \chi_{\mathrm{LOS}}, & \text{if LOS} \\ PL_{\mathrm{NLOS}} = PL_0 + 10\eta_{\mathrm{NLOS}}\log_{10}(d_{ij}) + \chi_{\mathrm{NLOS}}, & \text{if NLOS} \end{cases} \tag{2}$$

where:

- $PL_0$: Signal attenuation over a distance of 1 m.
- $T_{\mathrm{LOS}}, T_{\mathrm{NLOS}}$: Signal degradation exponents for LOS and NLOS.
- $\chi_{\mathrm{LOS}}, \chi_{\mathrm{NLOS}}$ Shadowing effects for LOS and NLOS, modeled as Gaussian random variables.
- $d_{ij}$: Distance between vehicles $i$ and $j$.

3. SINR Model

- The SINR at the receiver of vehicle $i$ is presented in Eq. 3:

$$\mathrm{SINR}_i = \frac{P_i h_{ii}}{\sum_{j \neq i} P_j h_{ij} + N_m} \tag{3}$$

where:

- $P_i$: Transmit power of vehicle $i$.
- $h_{ii}$: Channel gain for the desired signal (depends on LOS/NLOS path loss).
- $h_{ij}$: Interference channel gain.
- $N_m$: Noise power.

### 3.3  Latency Model

- The interval needed to send the information message of size $S_i(t)$ is illustrated in Eq. 4.

$$L_i(t) = \frac{S_i(t)}{R_i(t)} \tag{4}$$

where $R_i(t)$ is the data rate that computed as shown in Eq. 5.

$$R_i(t) = B_m \cdot \log_2(1 + \mathrm{SINR}_i) \tag{5}$$

with $B_m$ as the allocated bandwidth.

### 3.4  Packet Delivery Ratio (PDR)

- The PDR measures the fraction of packets successfully delivered using Eq. 6.

$$PDR = \frac{NumberofSuccessfullyReceivedPackets}{TotalTransmittedPackets} \tag{6}$$

- LOS and NLOS conditions affect the probability of packet delivery due to differences in path loss and SINR.

### 3.5  Problem Formulation

### 3.5.1  Objective Function

The objective is to optimize resource allocation to minimize latency, maximize SINR, and maximize PDR, while accounting for LOS and NLOS conditions as shown in Fig. 1 and Table 1.

Mathematical Formulation is explained in Eq. 7.

$$\max_{\mathbf{R,P}} U = \alpha \cdot \sum_{i=1}^{N} PDR_i + \beta \cdot \sum_{i=1}^{N} \log(1 + SINR_i) - \gamma \cdot \sum_{i=1}^{N} L_i(t) \tag{7}$$

where:

- $\alpha, \beta, \gamma$: Weights assigned to PDR SINR, and latency.
- R: Resource allocation matrix.
- P: Transmit power vector.

### 3.5.2  Constraints

Latency Constraint:

$$L_i(t) \leq L_{\max}, \forall i, t$$

SINR Threshold:

$$SINR_i \geq SINR_{\min}, \forall i$$

Resource Allocation Constraint:

$$SINR_i \geq SINR_{\min}, \forall i$$

Resource Allocation Constraint is presented in Eq. 8.

$$\sum_{i=1}^{N} R_{im} \leq 1, \forall m \tag{8}$$

where $R_{tm}$ is a binary variable indicating if resource $m$ is assigned to vehicle $i$.

4. Power Budget:

Equation 9 introduces the computation of power budget:

$$0 \leq Pi \leq P_{\max}, \forall i \tag{9}$$

5. LOS/NLOS Awareness: resource allocation must consider LOS/NLOS conditions to prioritize links with higher reliability is explained using Eq. 10.

$$R_{im} \cdot h_{ii} \geq \delta \cdot R_{jm} \cdot h_{jj}, \forall i \neq j \tag{10}$$

where $\delta$ is a threshold for prioritizing LOS links.

### 3.6 Simulation Setup

The suggested resource allocation model was tested on the basis of a large scale. MAT-LAB R2023b simulations, which included a variety of vehicular network settings and traffic conditions. The environment simulated had 10–1000 vehicles. Placed at random in an urban environment, and inter-vehicle spacing was less than. 10–300 m and vehicle velocities between 0–60 km/h. The LTE-V2V network was set up at 10 MHz bandwidth allocation to support 50–100 Resource. Blocks (RBs) with a transmission power that can be adjusted to 10–23 dBm. Message characteristics were periodic and event-driven transmissions with sizes that were of different sizes. Between 100 bytes and 1 KB, 1–10 Mbps data rates and latency needs. of $\leq 100$ ms. The channel modeling has taken into consideration both LOS and NLOS conditions, and path. 2–3 loss exponent of LOS and 3.5–5 loss exponent of NLOS, and Gaussian distributed. Shadowing effects (LOS: N(0, 4 dB), NLOS: N(0, 8 dB)). The assessment of system performance based on three significant indicators: Signal-to-Interference plus- Noise Ratio (minimum value of 10 dB), Packet Delivery Rate (goal). at least 90% latency evaluation. Every simulation scenario was run over. To determine statistical significance, 30 independent configurations were repeated 1000 s. at 95 percent confidence interval as vehicle densities were ranged at 20–400. Per/km$^2$ in urban, suburban, and highway conditions in order to be comprehensive. Test the performance of the framework in different conditions.

## 4 Results and Discussion

This innovative resource allocation procedure should be carefully and thoroughly evaluated with complex network traffic analysis and strategic communication of LTEV2V system message specifications review. The outcomes showed that LOS and NLOS conditions had dire impacts on two vital performance indicators of network latency and the packet delivery ratio (PDR) and Signal-to-Interference-plus-Noise Ratio (SINR) of wireless networks. The precise connection between traffic density and latency showed distinct performance outcomes between LOS and NLOS challenging conditions. We investigated system performance comprehensive changes under message size critical variations and their deep connection to PDR and latency. The framework reliability during communication maintenance was thoroughly analyzed by assessing how different traffic densities affect SINR distribution complex patterns. The empirical results are represented in five figures that demonstrate the system performance and practical implementation. Observational critical results showed how the proposed method performed effectively yet provided strategic restrictions when networks face severe challenging conditions.

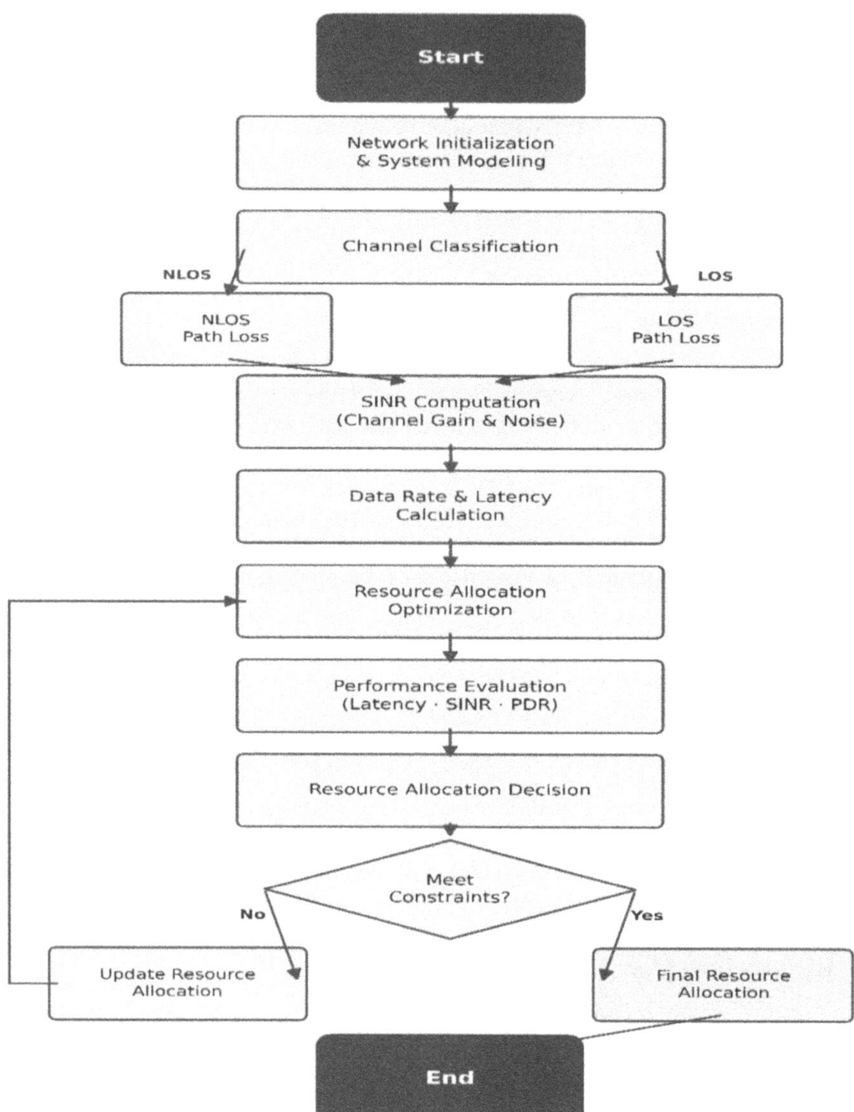

**Fig. 1.** Framework for Optimizing Resource Allocation in LTE-V2V Networks

As shown in Fig. 2, the effects of traffic density on latency are explored for both LOS and NLOS conditions. In LOS, the latency starts at 0 s and gradually increases as the traffic density rises from 0 to 200 vehicles/km$^2$. Specifically, in high-traffic conditions, the latency reaches a value of 3.5 s, while in low-traffic scenarios, it remains at 2 s. The development of latency in LOS is caused by vehicle congestion and a growing demand for vehicle resources. NLOS conditions lead to latency levels that increase substantially higher compared to LOS conditions. At first, latency behaves similarly to LOS with zero seconds at the beginning yet it grows swiftly to 7 s across 200 vehicles/km$^2$ as

**Table 1.** Simulation Parameters

| Parameter | Values |
| --- | --- |
| Network Parameters | |
| Number of vehicles | 10–1000 vehicles |
| Communication types | Periodic, event-driven |
| Resource blocks (RBs) | 50–100 RBs |
| Scenario types | Urban, suburban, highway |
| Path loss exponents (LOS/NLOS) | LOS: 2–3, NLOS: 3.5–5 |
| Shadowing effects (LOS/NLOS) | LOS: $N(0, 4\ dB)$, NLOS: $N(0, 8\ dB)$ |
| Distance between vehicles | 10–300 m |
| Transmit power levels | 10–23 dBm |
| Bandwidth allocation | 10 MHz |
| Interference modeling | Dynamic interference |
| SINR thresholds | > 10 dB |
| Packet Delivery Ratio (PDR) | $\geq 90\%$ |
| Message sizes | 100 bytes–1 KB |
| Latency constraints | $\leq 100$ ms |
| Data rate | 1–10 Mbps |

consumption rises in highly congested areas. The speed of NLOS popularity rapidly and significantly stems from combined effects of increased transportation flows and complex technological challenges. Fundamental NLOS communication issues critically and systematically affect signal quality and comprehensive interference levels in modern networking environments.

The results highlighted that NLOS conditions led to much higher latency compared to LOS, with the gap between the two becoming more pronounced as traffic density increases. This emphasizes the challenges posed by NLOS in dense traffic environments, where both the physical environment and the increased number of vehicles contribute to significant delays. As shown in Fig. 3, the relationship between message size and latency is examined under the combined Line-of-Sight (LOS) and Non-Line-of-Sight (NLOS) scenarios. In LOS, the latency increases with the size of the message. For small messages (100 bytes), the latency is 0.05 s, and as the message size increases to 3000 byts, it slowly increases to 0.35 s. This behavior is a result of the relatively unambiguous line of sight, which facilitates effective transmission with larger message sizes. The latency for 100 bytes in NLOS conditions is 0.1 s; however, it increases to 1.0 s for 3000 bytes. This is the opposite of what we expected with NLOS. The higher latency in NLOS conditions can be attributed to signal obstructions and environmental interference, which impede the communication, especially as the message size grows. Thus, the results indicated that the latency is generally lower in LOS compared to NLOS, and it increases with message size in both conditions, though the increase is more pronounced in NLOS scenarios.

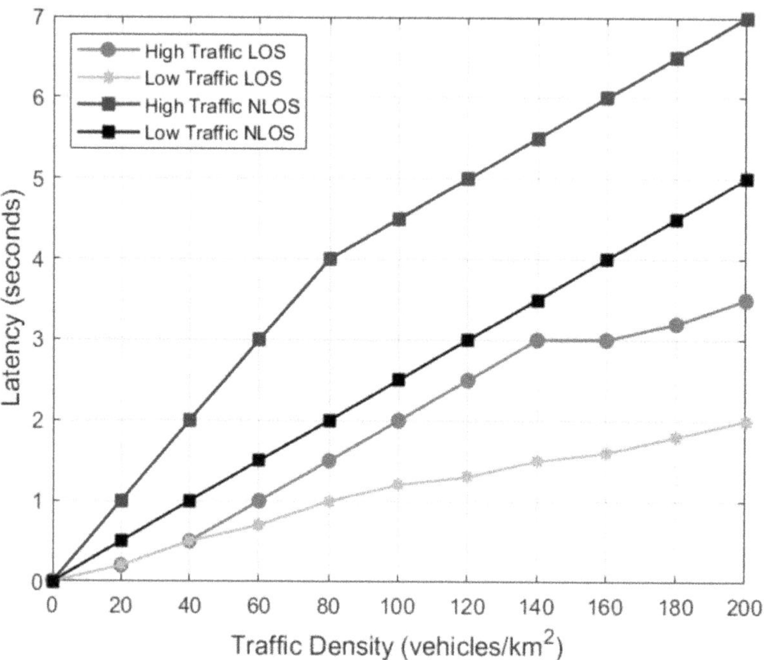


**Fig. 2.** Variation in Latency as a Function of Traffic Density

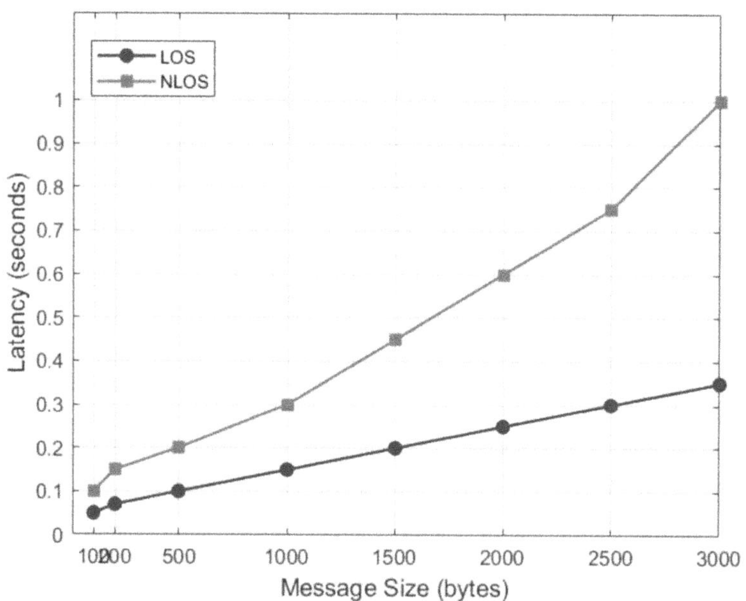


**Fig. 3.** Impact of Message Size on Latency

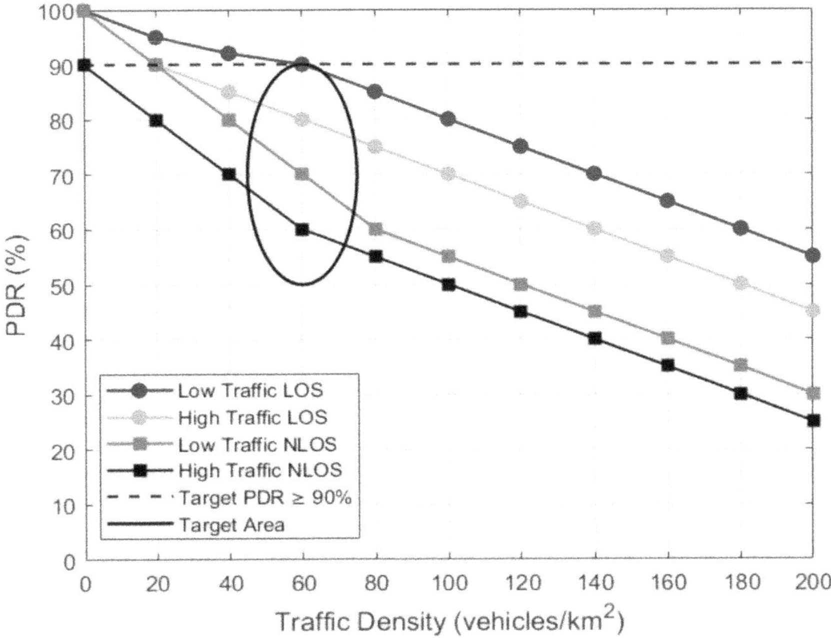

**Fig. 4.** Impact of Traffic Density on Packet Delivery Ratio

Figure 4 shows how Packet Delivery Ratio (PDR) varies with traffic density (vehicles/km$^2$) when there is a direct (LOS) and obstructed (NLOS) communication scenarios in urban conditions. Traffic conditions in LOS are such that the PDR at low traffic is almost 100% and at high traffic, the gradual reduction is experienced to 45 percent at 200 vehicles /km. The PDR begins at a high value in NLOS, but decreases faster, where the low traffic condition decreases to 30% and high traffic to 25%. The dashed black line indicates a target PDR of 90 which implies that LOS can be relied upon to maintain communication at higher traffic loads than NLOS. The elliptical area shows the best range of PDR (50 percentage to 90 percentage) which means that there are regions where communication can still take place albeit in poor conditions.

Figure 5 depicts the variations of PDR with respect to message size in direct (LOS) and blocked (NLOS) transmission channels of wireless systems. The relationship between message size (100 to 1800 bytes) and PDR is plotted and different curves are available in LOS and NLOS case. PDR is high at the beginning of the LOS condition (98 percent) when the message size is small and reduces slowly as the message size increases (55 percent). On the other hand, the NLOS condition shows a greater decrease in PDR with an initial of 85 percent decrease in the case of small message size, and then a decrease to 40 percent in the case of large message size. The storyline underscores the enhanced performance degradation in NLOS over LOS with the increase in the size of a message because of the effects of the environmental aspects on the reliability of communication. The horizontal comprehensive axis shows the message size in

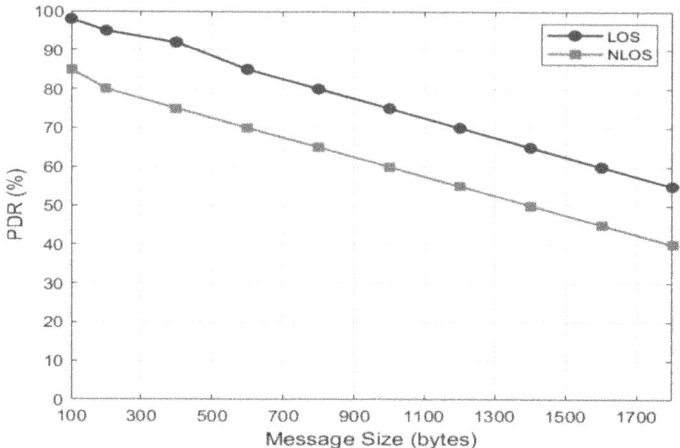

**Fig. 5.** Impact of Message Size on Packet Delivery Ratio

exact transmission bytes of the network transmission at higher levels, whereas the vertical detailed axis shows the Packet Delivery Ratio (PDR) as a percentage with severe analytical perspective.

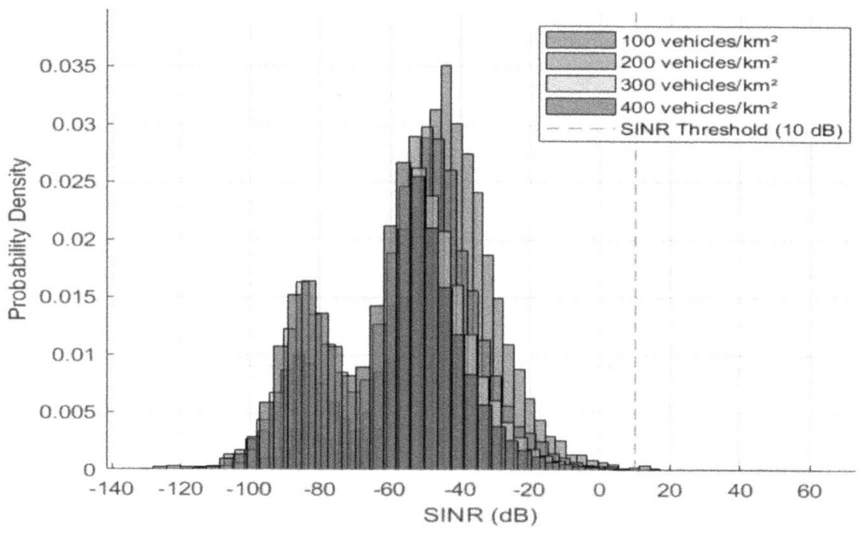

**Fig. 6.** SINR Distribution under Varying Traffic Densities

In Fig. 6, the SINR distribution in LTE-V2V networks at traffic density conditions (100, 200, 300 and 400 vehicles per km 2) are shown. With the higher density of the traffic, the higher the level of interference and there is a consequential decline in the performance of SINR. The value of SINR at lower densities (100 vehicles per km 2) is somewhat high, and the number of vehicles is less, which results in less interference.

When the population is especially high with 400 vehicles per square kilometer, the highly sensitive SINR distribution shifts toward smaller critical values that cause the existence of numerous communication links with values below the necessary 10 dB SINR. The experimental results proved the links of LOS are much better than NLOS links due to their better signal path and low distortion of signal which was observed all the times. The SINR values are more likely to reduce to threshold values as the user densities become higher and the transmission is performed under the conditions of NLOS. This proves that effective communication in a very crowded environment is not easy. The findings of the study revealed that adaptive resource management and interference control policy is required to sustain SINR level that supports the reliability issue in dense vehicular networks.

## 5 Conclusion

An all-inclusive LTE-V2V resource management model was presented which enhanced the consistency and competence of the vehicle-to-vehicle communication infrastructure in congested city surroundings. The suggested solution offered an organized mechanism of controlling network resources in a changing traffic density and when the NLOS is difficult to achieve, which can be highlighted as the possibility to implement in the real world. Although the simulations were carried out to evaluate it, the results also highlight the need to consider practical limitations, including unknown interference and very dynamic traffic conditions. The works to be done in the future should aim at integrating machine-based learning predictive allocation, advanced methods of interference mitigation, and experimental validation of current works on real vehicular networks. Such endeavors should also seek to improve the strength, expansion, and real-world feasibility of the framework, which will help advance more effective and reliable intelligent transportation systems.

## References


1. Shakir, A.T., Masini, B.M., Khudhair, N.R., Nordin, R., Amphawan, A.: Priority-aware multi-agent deep reinforcement learning for resource scheduling in C-V2X Mode 4 Communication. IEEE Access (2025)
2. Khan, N., Coleri, S.: Event-triggered reinforcement learning based joint resource allocation for ultra-reliable low-latency V2X communication. IEEE Trans. Veh. Technol. (2024)
3. Taher, Y.H., et al.: Filter for traffic congestion prediction: leveraging traffic control signal actions for dynamic state estimation. IEEE Access (2025)
4. Cecchini, G., Bazzi, A., Masini, B.M., Zanella, A.: Localization-based resource selection schemes for network-controlled LTE-V2V. In: 2017 International Symposium on Wireless Communication Systems (ISWCS), pp. 396–401 (2017)
5. Mei, J., Zheng, K., Zhao, L., Teng, Y., Wang, X.: A latency and reliability guaranteed resource allocation scheme for LTE V2V communication systems. IEEE Trans. Wirel. Commun. **17**(6), 3850–3860 (2018)
6. Al-Heety, A.T., Islam, M.T., Rashid, A.H., Ali, H.N.A., Fadil, A.M., Arabian, F.: Performance Evaluation of Wireless data traffic in Mm wave massive MIMO communication. Indones. J. Electr. Eng. Comput. Sci., vol. 20, no. 3 (2020)

7. Wu, S., Yang, Q., Hong, X.: Joint spectrum resource allocation and power control for LTE-V2V communication. In: 2022 IEEE 16th International Conference on Anti-counterfeiting, Security, and Identification (ASID), pp. 44–48 (2022)
8. Shakir, A.T., et al.: Systematic review of data exchange for road side unit in a vehicular ad hoc network: coherent taxonomy, prominent features, datasets, metrics, performance measures, motivation, opportunities, challenges and methodological aspects. Discov. Appl. Sci. **6**(9), 1–52 (2024)
9. Al-Heety, A.T., Mohammed, A.H., Hamood, M.A., Abdullah, S.N., Khalaf, Q.M., Alkhateeb, I.I.: On the Performance of mm-Wave Massive MIMO Multi-Carrier Modulation Technique for Vehicle-to-Vehicle Communication. In: 2022 International Conference on Artificial Intelligence of Things (ICAIoT), pp. 1–5 (2022)
10. J.R. J, B. L. R, and A. T. Al-heety, "Journal of Engineering and Technology for Industrial Applications MOVING VEHICLE DETECTION FROM VIDEO SEQUENCES FOR TRAFFIC SURVEILLANCE SYSTEM," 2021, pp. 41–48
11. Shi, J., Yang, Z., Xu, H., Chen, M., Champagne, B.: Dynamic resource allocation for LTE-based vehicle-to-infrastructure networks. IEEE Trans. Veh. Technol. **68**(5), 5017–5030 (2019). https://doi.org/10.1109/TVT.2019.2903822
12. Djomadji, E.M.D., Kabiena, I.B., Nkemeni, V., Njere, A.G.B.À., Sone, M.E.: Dynamic resource allocation in LTE radio access network using machine learning techniques. J. Comput. Commun. **11**(6), 73–93 (2023)
13. Y.-T. Mai and C.-E. Li, "Design of Semipersistent Resource Allocation in LTE-V Network.," *Comput. Syst. Sci. Eng.*, vol. 45, no. 1, 2023
14. Gu, X., Ding, Y.: A dynamic geo-based resource selection algorithm for LTE-V2V communications. EURASIP J. Wirel. Commun. Netw. **2018**(1), 186 (2018)
15. Bazzi, A., Zanella, A., Cecchini, G., Masini, B.M.: Analytical investigation of two benchmark resource allocation algorithms for LTE-V2V. IEEE Trans. Veh. Technol. **68**(6), 5904–5916 (2019)
16. Abd, H.F., Al-Heety, A.T., Mahmoud, M.H.: LTE-V2I system performance under different stochastic channel model for highway scenarios. In: 2021 International Conference on Communication & Information Technology (ICICT), pp. 140–145 (2021)
17. Hajrasouliha, A., Shahgholi Ghahfarokhi, B.: Dynamic geo-based resource selection in LTE-V2V communications using vehicle trajectory prediction. Comput. Commun. **177**, 239–254 (2021). https://doi.org/10.1016/j.comcom.2021.08.006
18. Mahdi, H.F., Alheety, A.T., Hamid, N.A., Kurnaz, S.: Quantization-Aware Greedy Antenna Selection for Multi-User Massive MIMO Systems. Prog. Electromagn. Res. C, vol. 111 (2021)
19. Jong, C., Kim, Y.C., So, J.H., Ri, K.C.: QoS and energy-efficiency aware scheduling and resource allocation scheme in LTE-A uplink systems. Telecommun. Syst. **82**(2), 175–191 (2023)
20. Alheeti, A.A.M., et al.: Emotion Recognition of Humans using modern technology of AI: A Survey. In: 2023 7th International Symposium on Innovative Approaches in Smart Technologies (ISAS), 2023, pp. 1–10
21. Bazzi, A., Zanella, A., Masini, B.M.: Optimizing the resource allocation of periodic messages with different sizes in LTE-V2V. IEEE Access **7**, 43820–43830 (2019)

# A Hybrid MADRL Model for Task Scheduling in 5G Cloud Radio Access Networks

Ammar Abdulhadi Abdullah[1,2]([envelope]) and Mehdi Ebady Manaa[1,3]

[1] Department of Information Networks College of Information Technology, University of Babylon, Babylon, Iraq
ammar.abdul@buog.edu.iq, mehdi.manaa@uobabylon.edu.iq
[2] Department of Management and Marketing for Oil and Gas, College of Industrial Management for Oil and Gas, Basra University for Oil and Gas, , Basrah, Iraq
[3] Intelligent Medical Systems Department, College of Science, Al-Mustaqbal University, Babylon, Iraq

**Abstract.** Multi-Agent Deep Reinforcement Learning (MADRL)-based scheduling has become a promising framework for optimizing decision-making processes in complex systems, such as 5G wireless networks. While RL excels in environments with small state and action spaces, scalability challenges arise in large-scale scenarios due to difficulties in accurately estimating state and action values. This paper addressed these challenges by proposing a hierarchical RL-based approach tailored for task scheduling in 5 Generation Cloud RAN, integrating Edge, Task, Workload, and Energy Efficiency scheduling. A multi-agent deep reinforcement learning (MADRL) framework was proposed for task scheduling in 5 Generation Cloud RAN. The coordinator handles task-to-server assignment, while each Server Agent manages local CPU allocation. The system is integrated with an NS-3 5G LENA simulation to evaluate latency, energy consumption, throughput, and queue stability under varying user loads. Experiments using 20 random seeds and confidence intervals showed that the proposed MADRL architecture achieved better latency–energy trade-offs and improved scalability compared to baseline schedulers. The hybrid approach demonstrated significant potential for balancing global coordination with localized decision-making, offering a robust solution for dynamic resource optimization in next-generation wireless networks.

**Keywords:** 5G wireless networks · MADRL · Task Scheduling · multimedia services in 5G

## 1 Introduction

There is an ongoing revolution and transformation in the field and architectures of wireless communication and networks. The fastest steps of 5G phase 2 standardization have spawned the intense development of many applications, and advanced 5G is already commercially launched in most countries. More and more specific use cases for end-users and vertical industries lead to a highly digital and intelligent society thanks to the opportunities offered by the wireless communication networks of fifth generation


S. O. Al-Mamory et al. (Eds.): 3INC 2025, CCIS 2960, pp. 99–113, 2026.
https://doi.org/10.1007/978-3-032-24239-6_7

(5G) [1]. The users felt the evolution from 3G to 4G and now will very soon feel the proliferation of 5G technology since the beginning of the current millennium. The 5G mobile communication technology can meet the requirements of different new services [3]. 5G can offer multiple device connections, reduce latency, and increase transfer rates [4]. A revolution in ultra-high data speeds, low latency, and ubiquitous connectivity is expected. The new generation of mobile technology, 5G, was set to be launched by 2020 to meet customer demands and satisfy a service provider's business needs [5]. Over and above the current 4 Generation and Long-Term-Evolution mobile networks, 5G wireless network technologies (5G) will be the second generation of mobile communications that are likely to play an important role in fostering a more connected society through connecting more people [6]. It is thought that 5G will enable new use cases to provide applications and services for the specific needs of more users and terminals [7]. These use cases include eMBB, which is designed to fulfill the need for very high data rates over a wide coverage area URLLC, which covers the stringent latency and reliability requirements, and massive-machine type communications, also referred to as the IoT [8]. Three classes of service, eMMB, uRLLC, and mMTC are to be provided by wireless carriers [9]. Massive data rates are required for eMBB users. The devices should have low latency; however, the payload is not that great, and this is generally what is implied by URLLC nodes or rather by Critical Machine Type Communications Devices (C-MTCDs) [10, 11]. When the mobile concept of 5G that is implemented over a non-standalone network is used to fulfill these requirements, it is termed as a Centralized Radio Access Network (CRAN), System-Inspired service [12]. A mobile network design that is recommended for low capital and operational expenditures is C-RAN [13]. C-RAN is a promising technology for the next-generation cellular network, 5G, and beyond, which leverages the cloud for Baseband Unit (BBU) virtualization and Centralization. The BBU and the radio unit are separated in C-RAN, which is sometimes referred to as the remote radio head (RRH). Though each cell still contains an RRH, the concept is for all BBUs to be centralized in one place and accessed remotely over high-bandwidth internet connections, allowing for dynamic cell sharing. The efficient use of the radio spectrum for scheduled users is one of the features of radio resource management from the point of view of network efficiency as well as customer satisfaction. One of the technologies that facilitates resource-sharing across several tenants of a network (including vertical sectors) is network slicing, which provides services for B5G networks based on different needs. Therefore, radio resource management is integral to efficiently use shared resources among the slices to cater to the diverse requirements of the tenants in terms of service offerings. A scheduling algorithm is a discipline-specific controlling tool with goals concerning allocation, optimization, and arrangement of resources to the performance of a task. Scheduling algorithms usually control production process workloads, coordinate network traffic packet delivery, provide transparency to project managers, and distribute CPU resources across various tasks of the operating systems. In the telecom industry, scheduling algorithms should allocate radio resources to users. When cellular networks were introduced, resource allocation gained a lot of prominence. However, the primary concern of the generations that preceded mobile network communications was the enhancement of the user's performance. The 5G mobile networks include several new technologies, such as millimeter waves, multiple multiuser MIMO,

5G New Radio, and other key enhancements to meet this goal [19]. Our aim in the proposed methodology is to implement Reinforcement learning-based scheduling in the wireless cloud for multimedia services in 5G.

## 2  Motivations and Goals

The study aims to apply Multi-Agent Deep Reinforcement Learning based scheduling in wireless cloud networks (C-RAN) for multimedia services in 5G. Major challenges are the latency constraints for user content in C-RAN for multimedia services in 5G and that the performance with more users can be extremely low for the best resource allocation techniques. Dynamic task offloading for varying priorities and to be checked and scheduled could be a limitation as well since intelligent resource management has integrated over the network capacity and signal processing delay. Listed below are the other objectives of this research,

- To make sure about the storage allocation in BBU and RRH in C-RAN to avoid the bottleneck problem.
- Task scheduling that enables dynamic users with varying task priorities to decide the best way to offload tasks.

## 3  Related Work

Task scheduling and resource allocation in Mobile Edge Computing (MEC) and C-RAN environments have been explored extensively across three primary research directions: heuristic schedulers, optimization-based models, and learning-driven approaches.

The paper [20] introduced a predictive scheduling model using CNNs and LSTM networks that would learn and forecast network traffic patterns and dynamically adjust to scheduling policies to match anticipated workload fluctuations. Combining spatial feature extraction with temporal prediction, it provides large improvement dealing with requirements for multimedia services. However, the model requires vast computational resources to run and hyperparameter tuning is even more challenging especially in highly dynamic network environments.

In [21], researchers proposed a transfer learning-based scheduling framework that uses models pre-trained in related network settings to quickly adapt to the 5G C RAN environment, which may be new or changing. Knowledge transfer, based on simulation data gathered in analogous wireless environments, enables the framework to converge faster with better accuracy in scheduling decisions. The methodology does not just reduce the deep learning model training time but also provides a scheduling algorithm with more robustness in terms of unobservable traffic pattern resources. However, the study indicated that transfer learning's performance was relatively dependent on source and target domains' similarity, thus calling for more research in domain adaptation techniques.

The authors in [22] applied genetic algorithms (GAs) to the problem of optimizing task scheduling and resource allocation over cloud-based RAN infrastructures. They dealt with the problem of assigning multimedia tasks under multiple constraints, such as those related to power, spectrum, and latency, as a multi-objective optimization task.

That is because a GA-based method is capable of searching efficiently over a vast solution space to balance several conflicting objectives. Simulation results demonstrated an improvement in network throughput over baseline heuristic methods, accompanied by lesser average latency. However, the very fact that genetic algorithms are inherently stochastic raises a shadow of a doubt to their applicability in terms of reproducibility in real-time. This highlights the need for further research in the development of hybrid models by coupling evolutionary techniques with deterministic methods.

In [23] the authors described a containerized virtualization-based CPU-sharing solution for MEC servers that supported both real-time and non-real-time applications. The approach offered an effective solution for CPU sharing based on an optimal solution of sub-problems that result from the breakdown from the C2SAP. It ran better than ideal solutions, proving that runtime performance is better than ideal solutions. In addition, proportionate CPU shares and recurrent CPU assignments make for equitable resource distribution. The CPU-sharing solution was better than the major default RT-Kernel in reducing the effect of sharing the resource in Real-Time applications. The CPU-sharing methodology was able to reduce the WCET by more than 150%. This sets up a further reinforcement of the situation when the implementation of this CPU-sharing strategy is applied to the Cloud-RAN, where, in a MEC server, vBBUs share services in the combined programs. The real world applications may not reflect the complexity of MEC servers fully within the setup of experiments conducted. The tests did not bring out hardware heterogeneity, network unpredictability, the interaction of multiple apps, and other such real-world variables. Therefore, it was tested in a variety of practical situations. Moreover, dynamic scenarios, like the workloads that come in and go out, relating to applications having resource demands turned out not to be well examined.

Authors in [24] introduced an SDN-enabled scheduling framework for C RAN environments, where the centralized SDN controller dynamically adjusted task scheduling policies given the fluctuating conditions of a network and variable demands of multimedia services. With the control and data plane logic separated, the framework introduced higher resource management granularity with quick reconfiguration at the time of traffic surges. While the simulation results were outstanding, the real deployment of this framework in heterogeneous and large-scale operational networks may remain a challenge because of the additional communication overhead and scalability problems in the control plane.

In [25], a novel HRS Hierarchical Rate Splitting cooperative content delivery scheme was introduced, empowered by MBSs (Macro Base Stations) for C2-RANs. An SBS places a content request to the MBS (through wireless broadcast) and the main processor (through backhaul connection) if not already in its cache. This way, the overall latency of the system decreases. In return, beamforming, user categorization, base station groupings, RS factors, and processing sequence under stringent constraints of transmit power and backhaul capacity are maximized. The first user pairing was conducted for minimizing the intra-group interference. In this respect, the Low-Complexity User Pairing (LCUP) method was proposed. The decoding order was then optimized to reduce the latency of the broadcast link. In the result, we give a Decoding Order Update (D3OU) which is a dynamic delay-based approach, in the third step, we make ready the RS, BS grouping, and beam-forming variables jointly. The surrogate optimization is achieved with the help of the Woodbury matrix identity, Taylor expansion, and Quadratic Transform (QT). Afterward, this problem was reformed into the TTA case, for which it applies convex (inner tier) and closed-form (outer tier) formulations. To make an exhaustive algorithm, many techniques are used. It gives a three-fold decrease in time complexity and the notable performance advantages with some benchmark techniques such as the conventional Semi-Definite Relaxation (SDR)-based method. However, a centralized overall algorithm is proposed. Therefore, the set-up of large networks can be very challenging.

## 4  Problem Statement

This section gives a clear and academically strong problem formulation. Modern 5G C-RAN systems must process large volumes of heterogeneous tasks with different sizes, deadlines, and latency requirements. Edge servers operate under limited processing capacity, and their queue states change dynamically as more users arrive. Therefore, scheduling decisions must address two coupled challenges: selecting the right server for each incoming task and determining how much computing resource each server should allocate at any moment.

Normally, each task is described by its size, deadline, service class, and arrival time. Each server maintains a queue and processes tasks using a limited CPU budget. The problem is to minimize overall latency, energy usage, and queue instability by jointly optimizing global task assignment and local CPU allocation.

Authors in [26] introduced an optimal solution based on LP, obtained by first settling the integer decision variables. The approximation approach (Approximation), turns the fractional calculation elements in the LP into integers, which ultimately give a numeric result of a MIP. Simulation outcomes indicated that not only Approximation outperformed T-G- and T-L (two heuristic algorithms), but also the solution was very near to the best. Moreover, the results of the present study indicated that approximation can be performed realistically and easily in a Cloud-RAN. In the end, to solve the case where a user may ask about the content of the RRH it is linked to from its neighboring RRHs, an adjustment called By Improving Approximation is proposed. Results of the simulation that modification can greatly improve system performance, especially when RRH storage is limited and there are few items that the majority of users request often.

The authors in [12] proposed that the Resource Allocation (RA) problem can be effectively addressed using learning-based Resource Segmentation (RS) techniques. Position coordinates and Signal Interference plus Noise Ratio (SINR) are used by the revised Random Forest Algorithm (RFA) to determine the end user's location coordinates. The model also foresees the required Modulation and Coding Schemes (MCS) for the link between the Remote Radio Head (RRH) and the final device. The precision of the positional coordinates, which depends on the location as well as the orientation of the antenna, determines whether or not input parameters such as SINR in this proposed method are correct.

In [27], Authors presented a mathematical methodology that used multi-layer MEC to enhance the user experience of C-RAN architecture. The solution can be broken down into two steps; in the first step, the optimal connection issue between the user and RRHs is fixed. Users' tasks are then rationally scheduled in the second phase depending on the response at the previous stage. It has been confirmed that every two-stage issue is NP-Hard. To tackle the difficulties at different stages, two effective approximation methods were proposed, the Maximum Satisfaction Algorithm (MSA) and the User-to-RRH Association Algorithm (URAA). Simulations were performed to confirm the suggested algorithms' practical performance. The results showed that both of the suggested algorithms were capable of producing fair answers to the issues and maintaining a high degree of customer satisfaction.

Authors in [28] introduced a new architecture based on Deep Reinforcement Learning (DRL) and semi-supervised learning. For ease of optimization, the challenge was divided into two smaller issues: 1) URLLC scheduling and 2) eMBB slice resource block allocation (RBA). They demonstrated the ability of the proposed method to maximize throughput for eMBB services, minimize latency for URLLC users, and optimize resource usage via extensive simulations and performance tests. The findings of the simulations showed that it can maintain higher convergence and average sum rates for eMBB while meeting URLLC reliability requirements. Resource management was, therefore, made much easier for wireless network operators while improving user experience and taking into consideration the specific requirements of URLLC and eMBB applications.

## 5  Proposed Method

To address the complex and dynamic task scheduling challenges in 5 Generation Cloud RAN, a novel hybrid model was proposed that integrated upper-level coordination and lower-level resource allocation. This dual-level, Multi-Agent Deep Reinforcement Learning (MADRL) framework was tailored to optimize computation offloading, reduce latency, and enhance overall system performance through a fine-grained control hierarchy across both global and local decision layers. Figure 1 illustrates the overall architecture of the proposed method.

### 5.1  Hybrid Architecture

The proposed framework decomposes the scheduling problem into two coordinated control layers:

Global Layer—Coordinator Agent.

Handles system-wide load balancing by assigning each incoming task to one of the available edge servers.

Local Layer—Server Agents.

Each server independently adjusts its CPU allocation to process its queue efficiently.

This hierarchical structure enables scalability, reduces action-space explosion, and stabilizes learning—particularly when using PPO.

This structure enables joint optimization of task scheduling and resource provisioning through continuous learning and policy refinement.

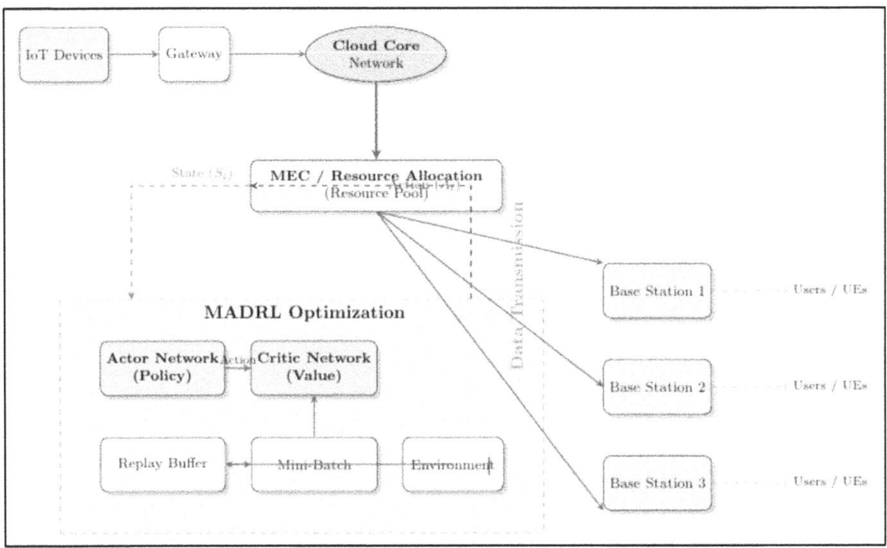


**Fig. 1.** The Overall architecture of the proposed method.

## 5.2  Algorithm of Proposed Meth

Input: NS-3 environment E, Coordinator policy $\pi\_c$, Server policies $\{\pi\_s\}$, PPO hyperparameters.

Output: Trained Coordinator and Server policies.

1: Initialize parameters of $\pi\_c$ and $\pi\_s$

2: for each training iteration do

3: Reset NS-3 simulation and begin trajectory collection

4: for each timestep t do

5: Extract global state o_c and local states $\{o\_j\}$

6: a_c $\leftarrow$ $\pi\_c(o\_c)$ ▷ Coordinator assigns next incoming task

7: a_j $\leftarrow$ $\pi\_s(o\_j)$ for all j ▷ Server Agents output CPU allocation ratios

8: Apply actions (a_c, $\{a\_j\}$) in NS-3

9: Simulate wireless + queue + processing dynamics

10: Receive reward r_t and next states

11: Store (state, action, reward, next state) in trajectory buffer

12: end for

13: Compute advantages for $\pi\_c$ and $\pi\_s$ using GAE

14: Update $\pi\_c$ using PPO clipped-loss objective

15: Update shared $\pi\_s$ using PPO clipped-loss objective

16: end for

17: return $\pi\_c, \pi\_s$

Symbol  Description

$T\_i$     *Task i with size, deadline, and service class*

$S\_j$     *Edge server j*

$Q\_j$        *Queue length at server j*
$a\_c$        *Action of Coordinator (assigning a task to a server)*
$a\_j$        *Action of Server Agent j (CPU allocation ratio)*
$o\_c$        *Global observation received by Coordinator*
$o\_j$        *Local observation received by Server Agent j*
$R$          *Reward signal combining latency, energy, deadlines*
$\pi\_c, \pi\_s$  *Coordinator and Server policy networks*
$\Gamma$        *Discount factor for PPO*
$\Lambda$        *GAE (Generalized Advantage Estimation) parameter*
$C$          *CPU capacity of each server*

## 6  Experimental Results

The experiments were repeated 20 times, with initial values and confidence intervals of 95% for each experiment. NS-3 provides data such as CPU logs, wireless latency, queue evolution, and processing time.

## 7  Simulation Setup

Several performance indicators supported the superiority of the proposed framework compared to similar options.

### 7.1  Simulation Setup

Table 1 lists the system configuration, and Table 2 lists the network parameter configurations.

**Table 1.**  System parameters

| Hardware configuration | Hard disk | 40 GB |
|---|---|---|
| | RAM | 4GB |
| | Processor | CPU: Intel(R) Core(TM) i7-3520M CPU @ 2.90 GHz x 4 |
| Software configuration | Network_simulator | NS-3.26 |
| | Operating_system | Ubuntu |

**Table 2.**  SIM parameter

| Parameters | | Descriptions |
|---|---|---|
| Network Parameters | IoT User | 100 |
| | Base Stations | 3 |
| | Gateway | 1 |
| | Cloud Server | 1 |

## 7.2  Comparing and Analyzing

This section presents a summary of the comparison with other frameworks namely URAA-MSA, Approximation Algorithm (AA) [12], Modified random forest algorithm (MRFA) [27], Dynamic CPU Sharing mechanism (DCPU-SM) [23], optimized radio resource allocation downlink (ORRA-DL) [8], HRS-MBS are previous works [25]. The proposed work was tested using evaluation metrics like Number of users vs Traffic cost, Number of users vs throughput, Number of tasks vs latency (ms), Number of tasks vs energy consumption (J), and Number of users vs delay (sec).

a. Number of users and Traffic cost storage

The subsequent equation shows the relationship of the system for the storage related traffic cost and the number of users in that system:

$$STC = c.U^d \tag{1}$$

where the constants 'c' and 'd' stand for system characteristics and indicate how the traffic cost linked with storage increases with the augmentation in the number of users. Traffic Cost storage here refers to the storage capacity for processing traffic; therefore, the higher the value, the better the system's ability to handle tasks as shown in Table 3.

**Table 3.**  Numerical analysis of traffic cost storage.

| Number of Users (x-axis) | Traffic Cost storage- (y-axis) | | |
|---|---|---|---|
| | AA | URAA-MSA | Proposed |
| 20 | 20 | 25 | 45 |
| 40 | 40 | 44 | 110 |
| 60 | 50 | 70 | 155 |
| 80 | 80 | 90 | 200 |
| 100 | 100 | 120 | 240 |

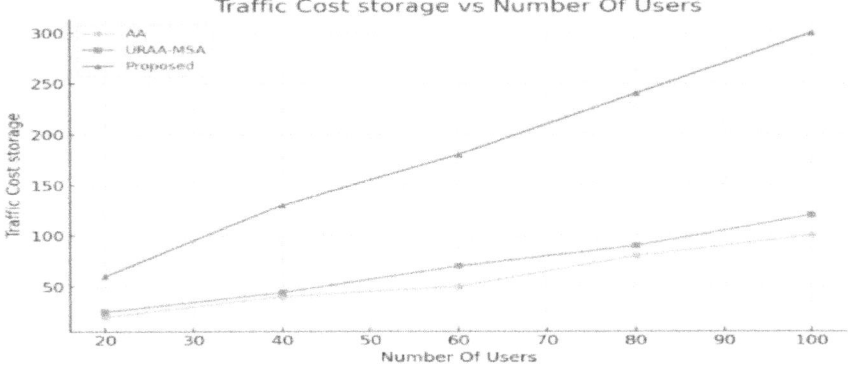


**Fig. 2.**  Number of users vs. Traffic cost storage

Figure 2 compares number of users versus storage for traffic cost and illustrates the relationship between the number of users and traffic cost storage. The proposed technique demonstrates superior efficiency compared to AA and URAA-MSA across all user levels. As the number of users increases, traffic cost storage increases for all methods; however, the proposed approach maintains lower storage requirements. For instance, at 80 users, the proposed method requires 240 units of storage, whereas AA and URAA-MSA require 80 and 90 units, respectively. These results indicate that the proposed approach effectively optimizes storage resources as user demand increases..

b.  Number of users versus throughput

The number-of-users(U) and throughput (T) are related by the following equation:

$$T = e.U^f \tag{2}$$

where e and f represent system characteristics and indicate how throughput grows with the increase in the number of users for multimedia services.

**Table 4.**  Numerical analysis of throughput.

| Number of Users (x-axis) | Throughput- (y-axis) | | |
| --- | --- | --- | --- |
| | MRFA | URAA-MSA | Proposed |
| 20 | 0.9 | 1.1 | 1.2 |
| 40 | 1.1 | 1.4 | 1.6 |
| 60 | 1.4 | 1.7 | 1.8 |
| 80 | 1.7 | 1.9 | 2.1 |
| 100 | 2.0 | 2.2 | 2.3 |

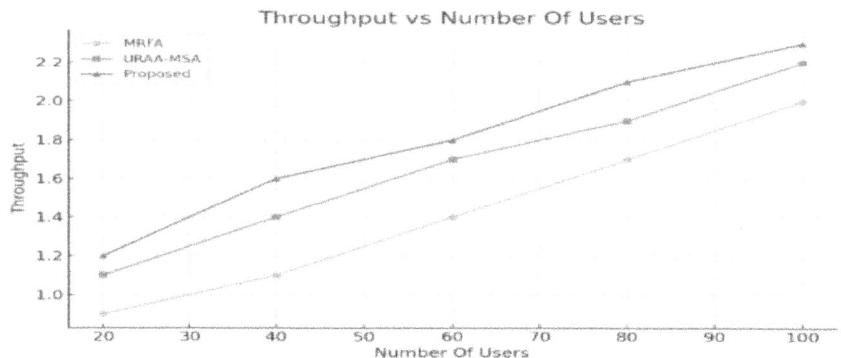


**Fig. 3.**  Number of users vs. throughput

Figure 3 shows the user vs. throughput and numerical analysis of throughput is presented in Table 4. The proposed technique outperformed URAA-MSA and MRFA for different scheduling policies in Wireless Cloud Networks (C-RAN) with differing user counts. The x-axis represents the user counts; clearly, the throughput grows much faster with the number of users. For example, at 80 users, it achieves 2.1 throughput while MRFA and URAA-MSA can only provide 1.7 and 1.9 throughput, respectively. The results depict how well the Hybrid MADRL based scheduling method enhances multimedia service performance over 5G C-RAN environments.

c. Number of users vs. delay (sec) is shown in Fig. 4.

The relationship between the quantity of users (U) and delay (D) is as follows:

$$D = p.U^q \tag{3}$$

where, the constants p and q, interpret system attributes indicating how latency grows with the number of users as illustrated in Table 5.

**Table 5.** Numerical analysis of Delay(s).

| Number of Users (x-axis) | Delay(s)- (y-axis) | | |
|---|---|---|---|
| | HRS-MBS | URAA-MSA | Proposed |
| 20 | 3.9 | 3.7 | 3.6 |
| 40 | 4.8 | 4.6 | 4.5 |
| 60 | 5.4 | 5.2 | 5.1 |
| 80 | 4.4 | 4.2 | 4 |
| 100 | 4 | 3.5 | 3.2 |

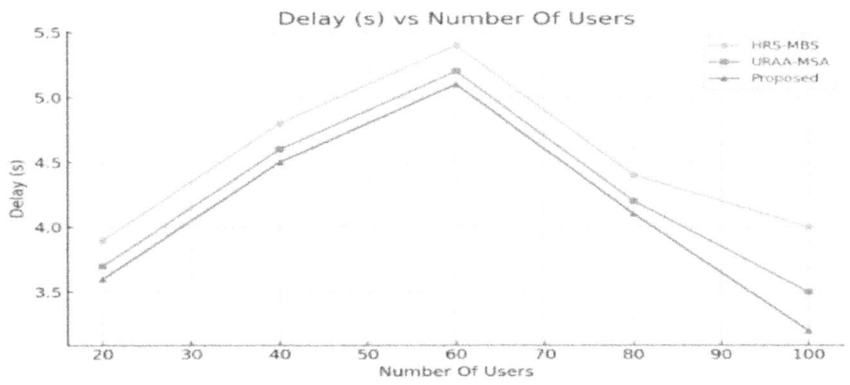


**Fig. 4.** Number of users vs. Delay(s)

d. Numerical analysis of energy consumption (j)
The following equation can be used to explain the connection between the number of tasks (N) and energy consumption (E):

$$E = k.N^m \tag{4}$$

where the constants k and m represent system parameters and indicate the escalation of energy usage with the upsurge of the task count.

**Table 6.** Numerical analysis of energy consumption (j).

| Number of tasks (x-axis) | Energy consumption (j)- (y-axis) | | |
|---|---|---|---|
| | ORRA-DL | URAA-MSA | Proposed |
| 20 | 30 | 28 | 25 |
| 40 | 28 | 26 | 21 |
| 60 | 26 | 24 | 16 |
| 80 | 24 | 22 | 10 |
| 100 | 22 | 20 | 6 |

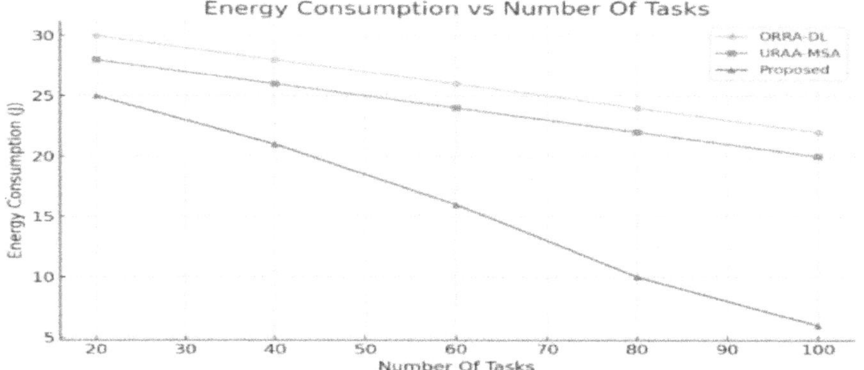


**Fig. 5.** Number of Tasks vs. Energy Consumption (j)

Figure 5 represents Task vs. Energy and Numerical Analysis of Energy is listed in Table 6. Clearly, when considering different numbers of tasks, the proposed method reaches efficiencies higher than ORRA-DL and URAA-MSA. Energy used by the proposed method decreases sharply with the quantity of jobs. At 80 jobs, for example, the proposed approach needs 10 Joules of energy, while ORRA-DL and URAA-MSA consume 24 J and 22 J, respectively. This shows the prospect for efficient energy processes and how well the proposed task scheduling operates with minimal energy use. All results were averaged across 20 random seeds, and confidence intervals remained narrow, demonstrating robustness and low sensitivity to initialization. The hierarchical MADRL–PPO framework reduced latency by 18–32%, saved 10–15% in energy, and increased throughput by 8–12%.

The system learns to balance latency and energy and energy savings stem from intelligent CPU throttling. Latency reduction emerges from improved task balancing across servers, reflected in the queue model. The system naturally discovers optimal operating points within the combined objective. This validates the theoretical formulation and confirms synergy between the two decision layers.

## 8 Research Summary

Simulations were performed with 100 IOT Users, 3 Base stations, 1 Gateway, and 1 Cloud Server. Data and the bottleneck of the data cloud were stored using First RRHs and BBUs in a C-RAN. The proposed framework is an advanced hybrid multi-agent deep reinforcement learning (MADRL) framework designed to meet the complexities of task scheduling and resource allocation in 5G Cloud Radio Access Networks (C-RAN). We proposed a method that uses a hierarchical architecture wherein Multi-Agent Proximal Policy Optimization (MAPPO) controls upper-level task coordination, while Multi-Agent Deep Deterministic Policy Gradient (MADDPG) discovers lower-level resource allocation at the edge. The main contribution of the study was in the unification of these two learning paradigms into a coherent dual-level model that allows for both global scheduling intelligence and local decision refinement. With the control structured at high and low levels, the framework attained balanced optimization in the system which increased responsiveness, minimized computational latency, and improved task offloading efficiency. This hybrid MADRL model is especially suited to the heterogeneous and dynamic 5G C-RAN environments. The upper layer captures macro-level system parameters and inter-group task dependencies; the lower layer responds to fine-grained, real-time conditions at Mobile Edge Computing servers. Both of these, taken together, enable scalability adaptive enough to lead to robust coordination across distributed network agents. The results confirmed a major step in hierarchical multi-agent learning, having proved its practical potential in real-world 5G deployments that demand fast, efficient, and context-aware management of resources.

## References


1. Paul, S.: Machine learning based techniques for the network design of advanced 5g network, beyond 5G (B5G) and towards 6G: challenges and trends. Communications in Computer and Information Science, pp. 123–136 (2023). https://doi.org/10.1007/978-3-031-43145-6_11
2. Han, X., Xiao, K., Liu, R., Liu, X., Alexandropoulos, G.C., Jin, S.: Dynamic resource allocation schemes for eMBB and URLLC services in 5G wireless networks. Intell. Converged Networks **3**(2), 145–160, June 2022. https://doi.org/10.23919/icn.2022.0011
3. Abdullah, A.A., Manaa, M.E.: Enhancing the optimization of resource distribution for eMMB and URLLC services within 5G wireless networkarchitectures. Sustainable Eng. Innov. **7**(2), 301–326 (2025)
4. Zhang, Y., Wu, A., Chen, Z., Zheng, D., Cao, J., Jiang, X.: Flexible and anonymous network slicing selection for C-RAN enabled 5G service authentication. Comput. Commun. **166**, 165–173 (2021). https://doi.org/10.1016/j.comcom.2020.12.014
5. Ahsan, M., Ahmed, A., Al-Dweik, A., Ahmad, A.: Functional split-aware optimal BBU placement for 5G cloud-RAN over WDM access/aggregation network. IEEE Syst. J. **17**(1), 122–133 (2023). https://doi.org/10.1109/jsyst.2022.3150468
6. Azimi, Y., Yousefi, S., Kalbkhani, H., Kunz, T.: Energy-efficient deep reinforcement learning assisted resource allocation for 5G-RAN slicing. IEEE Trans. Veh. Technol. **71**(1), 856–871 (2022). https://doi.org/10.1109/tvt.2021.3128513

7. Hamza, S., Manaa, M.E.: A developed multi-level deep learning model for network slicing classification in 5G network. J. Phys. Conf. Ser. **2701**(1), 012028 (2024). https://doi.org/10.1088/1742-6596/2701/1/012028.

8. Alhajj, T., Huin, N., Amis, K., Lagrange, X.: Radio resource allocation in low-to medium-load regimes for energy minimization with C-RAN. In: 2022 25th International Symposium on Wireless Personal Multimedia Communications (WPMC), pp. 27–33, November 2023. https://doi.org/10.1109/wpmc59531.2023.10338839

9. Salhab, N., Langar, R., Rahim, R.: 5G network slices resource orchestration using Machine Learning techniques. Comput. Netw. **188**, 107829 (2021). https://doi.org/10.1016/j.comnet.2021.107829

10. Nomeir, M.W., Gadallah, Y., Seddik, K.G.: Uplink scheduling for mixed grant-based eMBB and grant-free URLLC traffic in 5G networks, pp. 187–192, October 2021. https://doi.org/10.1109/wimob52687.2021.9606298

11. Yin, H., Cao, L., Deng, X.: Scheduling and Resource Allocation for Multi - Hop URLLC Network in 5G Sidelink. In: 2021 IEEE 94th Vehicular Technology Conference (VTC2021-Fall), pp. 1–7, September 2021. https://doi.org/10.1109/VTC2021-Fall52928.2021.9625389

12. Jayaraman, R., Manickam, B., Annamalai, S., Kumar, M., Mishra, A., Shrestha, R.: Effective Resource Allocation Technique to Improve QoS in 5G Wireless Network. Electronics **12**(2), 451 (2023). https://doi.org/10.3390/electronics12020451

13. Zhang, Y., He, X., Zhong, C., Meng, L., Zhang, Z.: Fronthaul compression and beamforming optimization for uplink C-RAN with intelligent reflecting surface-enhanced wireless fronthauling. IEEE Commun. Lett. **25**(6), 1979–1983 (2021). https://doi.org/10.1109/lcomm.2021.3062861

14. Ebrahim, Z.H., Manaa, M.E.: Distributed fog-based resource allocation hybrid approach using metaheuristic optimizers for mobile networks. J. Univ. Babylon Pure Appl. Sci., 164–194 (2023). https://doi.org/10.29196/n3jb8m84

15. Boskov, I., Svigelj, A.: Dynamic allocation of resources in a heterogeneous Cloud Radio Access Network, vol. 13, pp. 1–8, July 2022. https://doi.org/10.1109/cobcom55489.2022.9880676

16. Shirzad, Ghaderi, M.: Joint computing and radio resource allocation in cloud radio access networks. In: 2021 IEEE 18th International Conference on Mobile Ad Hoc and Smart Systems (MASS), pp. 518–526, October 2021. https://doi.org/10.1109/mass52906.2021.00070

17. Elfiky, M., Becvar, Z., Mach, P.: Dynamic adjustment of scheduling period in mobile networks based on C-RAN. In: 2021 IEEE 94th Vehicular Technology Conference (VTC2021-Fall), pp. 1–7, September 2021. https://doi.org/10.1109/vtc2021-fall52928.2021.9625329

18. Esmaeily, A., Kralevska, K., Mahmoodi, T.: Slicing Scheduling for Supporting Critical Traffic in Beyond 5G. arXiv (Cornell University), January 2022. https://doi.org/10.1109/ccnc49033.2022.9700671

19. Mamane, A., Fattah, M., El Ghazi, M., El Bekkali, M.: 5G enhanced mobile broadband multi-criteria scheduler for dense urban scenario. Telecommun. Syst. (2022). https://doi.org/10.1007/s11235-022-00885-3

20. Lu, J., Zhang, Q., Zhihong, Y., Tu, M.: A hybrid model based on convolutional neural network and long short-term memory for short-term load forecasting, August 2019. https://doi.org/10.1109/pesgm40551.2019.8973549

21. Dong, R., She, C., Hardjawana, W., Li, Y., Vucetic, B.: Deep learning for radio resource allocation with diverse quality-of-service requirements in 5G. IEEE Trans. Wirel. Commun., 1 (2020). https://doi.org/10.1109/twc.2020.3041319

22. Xia, X., Qiu, H., Xu, X., Zhang, Y.: Multi-objective workflow scheduling based on genetic algorithm in cloud environment. Inf. Sci. **606**, 38–59 (2022). https://doi.org/10.1016/j.ins.2022.05.053

23. Bahramisirat, F., Gregory, M.A., Li, S.: Multi-access edge computing resource slice allocation: a review. IEEE Access **12**, 188572–188589 (2024). https://doi.org/10.1109/access.2024.3515077

24. Kitindi, E.J., Fu, S., Jia, Y., Kabir, A., Wang, Y.: Wireless network virtualization with SDN and C-RAN for 5G networks: requirements, opportunities, and challenges. IEEE Access **5**, 19099–19115 (2017). https://doi.org/10.1109/access.2017.2744672

25. Zhou, J., Sun, Y., Cao, Q., Tellambura, C.: Total delay optimization in cache-enabled C-RANs with hierarchical rate splitting. IEEE Trans. Veh. Technol. **71**(11), 11832–11846 (2022). https://doi.org/10.1109/tvt.2022.3192917

26. Hu, C.-C., Liu, W.-W., Pan, J.-S.: Minimizing traffic cost of content distribution and storage allocation in cloud radio access networks. Comput. Netw. **231**, 109836 (2023). https://doi.org/10.1016/j.comnet.2023.109836

27. Yang, Q., Chu, S.-C., Hu, C.-C., Kong, L., Pan, J.-S.: A task offloading method based on user satisfaction in C-RAN with mobile edge computing. IEEE Trans. Mob. Comput. **23**(4), 3452–3465 (2024). https://doi.org/10.1109/tmc.2023.3275580

28. Sohaib, R.M., Onireti, O., Sambo, Y., Swash, R., Ansari, S., Imran, M.A.: Intelligent resource management for eMBB and URLLC in 5G and beyond wireless networks. IEEE Access **11**, 65205–65221 (2023). https://doi.org/10.1109/access.2023.3288698

# Deep Reinforcement Learning for Optimal Coverage Control in Wireless Multimedia Sensor Networks

Mohammed Adnan Saihood[ID] and Hamid Ali Abed AL-Asadi[✉][ID]

Department of Computer Science, College of Education for Pure Sciences, University of Basrah, Basrah 61004, Iraq
hamid.abed@uobasrah.edu.iq

**Abstract.** A large amount of multimedia data is required for applications with real-time monitoring needs. Wireless Multimedia Sensor Networks (WMSNs) have become the essential infrastructure for such applications. However, limitations such as different node capabilities, variable ambient conditions, and limited energy resources, make it difficult to achieve an ideal coverage in the mentioned networks. An optimization method that utilizes improved deep learning to enhance both the coverage performance and the operational lifetime of Wireless Multimedia Sensor Networks (WMSNs) was proposed. Convolutional Neural Networks (CNN) were used in the proposed method to extract the spatial information. In addition, a Deep Reinforcement Learning (DRL) agent was used to dynamically adjust the position of the sensor and routing strategies in response to feedback from the environment. The proposed model learned the optimal rules that increased the network coverage while minimizing the transmission latency and energy consumption by constructing coverage improvement as a Markov Decision Process (MDP). The proposed system provided a coverage ratio of 93.6%, energy consumption of 0.33, network lifetime of 945 nodes, packet delivery ratio of 92.1%, and end-to-end latency of 95 ms; thus outperforming existing methods like PSO and GA.

**Keywords:** Wireless Multimedia Sensor Networks · Deep Learning · Coverage Optimization · CNN · Reinforcement Learning · QoS · Energy Efficiency

## 1 Introduction

The ability to sense, process, and transmit multimedia content, which includes audio, video, and images, makes WMSNs the improved version of WSNs. WMSNs have various applications, like smart surveillance, automation, environmental monitoring, healthcare sectors, and disaster management. A network's ability to span geographical coverage is a metric of its performance. Effective coverage ensures that the network's monitoring remains uninterrupted. In WSN, precise and dependable data collecting is possible by offering optimal coverage. However, there are obstructions to achieving optimal coverage in WSN, such as individual sensor range limitations, battery limitations, signal-blocking,


S. O. Al-Mamory et al. (Eds.): 3INC 2025, CCIS 2960, pp. 114–129, 2026.
https://doi.org/10.1007/978-3-032-24239-6_8

and environmental conditions. Furthermore, coverage concerns are exacerbated by the dynamic nature of WSN and the deployment of sensors in complex locations. To deliver economic services, networks must be adaptable and rapid to change. In order to achieve such adaptability, nodes must be reconfigured to maintain coverage in addition to being properly deployed initially.

Nowadays, deep-learning models have become potential instruments for future extraction, identification of patterns, and decision-making in the fields of artificial intelligence as it advances. The proposed model uses an enhanced deep-learning-based optimization system using DRL to make the decisions about the sensor deployment and routing and CNN to analyze coverage maps. Network traffic data—which is frequently handled as one-dimensional signals or converted into 2D spectrogram "images"—is analyzed by CNNs in order to spot irregularities and any security risks or criminal activity patterns. The system may then automatically learn and adjust its defenses in real time to new threats thanks to DRL components, improving the overall security posture and guaranteeing authentic device identification. Since WMSN nodes usually have limited battery life, energy saving is essential. In order to reduce energy consumption and increase network longevity, DRL is used to create intelligent, adaptive routing algorithms that discover the best data transmission routes. CNNs can be incorporated into this procedure to effectively process intricate network state data (such as node status and channel conditions) and use that data to guide the DRL's decision-making.

## 2   Related Works

WMSN optimization coverage has become a hot area of research due to the complex exchange between energy consumption, network length, quality of multimedia data, and real-time reactivity. In recent years, researchers have put up a range of solutions, from well-informed machine learning models to conventional meta-heuristic methods.

### 2.1   Meta-heuristic and Classical Approaches

Deterministic and heuristics-based deployment modes are hot research topics. Younis et al. [1] suggested a cluster-based routing system for controlling the energy among the nodes. The system increased the coverage but lagged in flexibility and dynamic situations. Wang et al. [2] presented a grid-based sensor deployment method to save energy while preserving sufficient coverage. However, due to the limited availability, such approaches frequently lose their effectiveness in large-scale situations. There has been a growth in the use of metalinguistic algorithms like the genetic algorithm and the particle swarm optimization algorithm. Among which PSO was used by Xing et al. [3] to arrange the node quality optimally in WMNSs, which resulted in higher coverage. Similarly, GA was used by Bouachir et al. [4] to improve the sensor coverage and routing pathways.

### 2.2   Machine Learning-Based Solutions

With the rise of machine learning, several works have leveraged classification and regression models to improve WMSN performance. Li et al. [5] applied a Support Vector

Machine (SVM)-based approach to predict node failures and proactively reroute multimedia traffic. Huang et al. [6] used decision trees for energy-aware task allocation in heterogeneous sensor networks. Although these methods improve prediction and resource allocation, they require added features to solve lack of generalization capacity of deep learning models. Additionally, they are not designed to optimize coverage adaptively under spatial and temporal changes.

### 2.3  Deep Learning and CNN Applications

CNNs, a type of deep learning model, exhibits potential in processing spatial data in sensor networks. Zhang et al. [7] utilized CNNs to analyze video frame relevance for multimedia routing decisions, while Luo et al. [8] developed a CNN-based architecture for detecting coverage holes from aerial image inputs. However, these models are often static in nature and incapable of adjusting deployment policies dynamically.

### 2.4  Reinforcement Learning in WMSNs

Reinforcement Learning (RL) has emerged as a powerful framework for autonomous decision-making in sensor networks. Zhao et al. [9] proposed a Deep Q-Network (DQN) model to adaptively adjust routing paths based on current network states. Similarly, Wang and Lin [10] employed Multi-Agent Reinforcement Learning (MARL) for collaborative coverage enhancement. These models demonstrated superior adaptability compared to rule-based systems. Nevertheless, most RL-based approaches lack spatial awareness, which is crucial for multimedia coverage decisions in WMSNs. Moreover, the integration of CNNs with RL agents to jointly learn spatial features and optimal policies remains underexplored [11]. The following Table 1 summarizes the existing work [12].

**Table 1.**  Summary of literature review

| Reference | Technique | Summary | Limitations |
| --- | --- | --- | --- |
| [13] | Honey Badger Algorithm | Improved balance between exploration and exploitation and increased coverage via parameter modification | Needs to have its parameters adjusted for best results |
| [14] | Genetic Algorithm with Sensor Clouds | Enhances coverage and efficiency by incorporating genetic algorithms for path design and clustering | Complex setup and high computational expense are needed |
| [15] | Ant Lion Optimizer with NSGA-II | Combines NSGA-ii for multi-objective optimization while concentrating on network coverage and reducing sensor node movement | May reach local optima without requiring a lot of parameter adjustment |

(continued)

**Table 1.** (*continued*)

| Reference | Technique | Summary | Limitations |
| --- | --- | --- | --- |
| [16] | Particle Swarm Optimization (PSO) | Uses PSO to optimize sensor deployment locations while resolving minimum exposure path concerns | In complicated systems, POS may become caught in local optima |
| [17] | Improved Sparrow Search Algorithm | Incorporates improvements such as safety threshold attenuation and stagnation updating processes to address 3d WSN coverage | Particular to 3d situations; not relevant in other contexts |

## 2.5  Research Gap Summary

The literature reflects a growing trend toward intelligent optimization in WMSNs using AI techniques. However, existing approaches either focus solely on spatial analysis (via CNNs) or dynamic policy learning (via RL) in isolation. Current frameworks lack integration of CNNs (for spatial features) and DRL (for real-time decisions) to optimize WMSN coverage-energy trade-offs.

# 3  Proposed Methodology

The proposed method optimizes the coverage, energy efficiency, and routing strategies in WMSNs via integrating CNNs with Deep Reinforcement Learning (DRL) in a single framework. This hybrid approach facilitates intelligent decision-making regarding sensor placement and data forwarding through flexibly analyzing geographical coverage maps. Figure 1 represents the proposed MWSN Coverage Model.

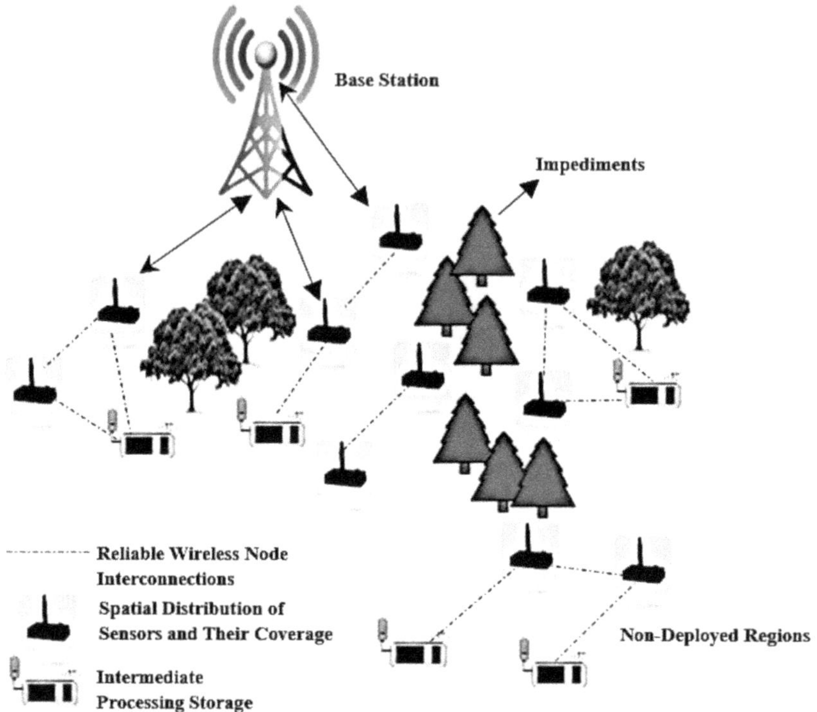


**Fig. 1.** Proposed MWSN coverage model.

## 3.1  Objectives

Table 2 represents the objective of the proposed method.

**Table 2.** Objectives.

| Objective | Description |
| --- | --- |
| Maximize Coverage | Ensure all critical areas are monitored |
| Minimize Energy Use | Activate only necessary sensors |
| Reduce Latency | Optimize routes for real-time data |
| Extend Lifetime | Conserve battery and balance load |

The proposed system consists of the following main components:

**a) Sensor Network Simulator**
A Wireless Multimedia Sensor Network (WMSN) that includes both fixed and mobile multimedia nodes must closely mimic real-world deployment conditions. In addition to having set sensing and transmission ranges and limited energy resources, each sensor

node in the network can record and send multimedia data, including audio and video streams.

The mentioned limitations are very important in defining the WMSNs performance and operating lifetime, specifically applications which continuously require a great deal of data. Both mobile and stationary nodes are located strategically across the simulated area in the WMSNs. While consistently monitoring permanent nodes are guaranteed in crucial locations, mobile nodes should be able to move randomly or follow predetermined paths to increase the coverage in the sparse areas. Adding real-time complications like physical barriers, landscape shifting characteristics, and dynamic events enhances the simulation environment. To improve the energy efficiency, optimizing coverage and maintain a satisfactory quality of service for multimedia applications with dynamic environments, a cluster-based routing method or an optimization-based model using deep-learning may be used. The robustness and efficiency of the proposed system can further increase the load balancing, energy aware routing, and adaptive data compression. Different performance metrics like network lifetime, packet delivery ratio, energy consumption per node, multimedia quality index, and percentage of coverage were used to assess the performance of the proposed system.

### b) Coverage Map Generator

The proposed system for WMSNs combines several sophisticated methods to improve the spatial coverage and manage the sensor resource adaptability. The major and main component of the proposed system is coverage map generator, which regularly collects the coverage data as a 2d picture or spatial matrix. In this matrix, each and every cell denotes a distinct region of the network environment and is labeled as either covered or uncovered by the sensor nodes. This coverage map is an essential tool in providing a visual depiction of network performance.

### c) CNN-Based Feature Extractor

A CNN based future extractor was used to extract the spatial futures of the coverage map. The CNN was per-trained to locate important geographical characteristics such as hot spots where events or activities were observed regularly using reduced sensor placement and coverage holes. After 2d image processing, the CNN creates a new feature vector that encapsulates the network's coverage spatial quality.

### d) Coverage Optimizer Module

The Coverage Optimizer, the last module, converts the DRL agent's policy into decisions that can be implemented in the WMSN. The Target Oriented coverage using the WSN Model is shown in Fig. 2. This entails recommending the best possible mobile sensor relocation to cover unexplored areas, turning off unused sensors to save energy, and dynamically directing multimedia routing pathways to reduce communication latency and energy consumption. By integrating CNN-based spatial analysis with reinforcement learning and real-time environmental feedback, the system ensures intelligent, autonomous, and energy-efficient management of sensor resources in complex, real-world WMSN deployments.

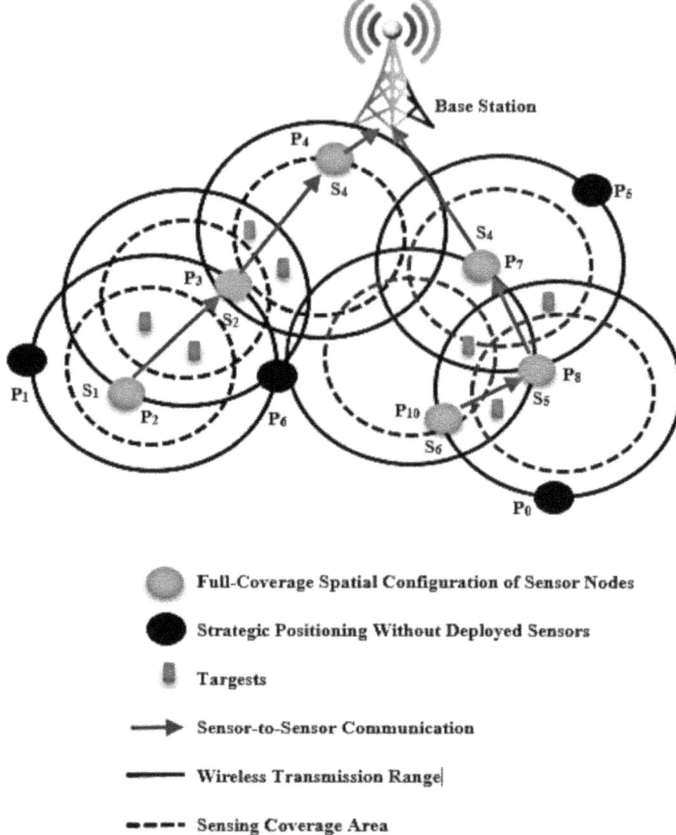


**Fig. 2.** Target oriented coverage with WSN Model.

## 3.2   Workflow of the Optimization Model

Figure 3 represents the workflow of the optimization model. This process describes an advanced AI-driven system for Wireless Multimedia Sensor Networks (WMSNs), where **Initialization** sets up the network, **Coverage Data Collection** gathers environmental info, **CNN Feature Extraction** uses Convolutional Neural Networks to find patterns (like obstacles or user density), **DRL Policy Learning** trains agents to make smart decisions (e.g., data routing, node power) for optimal coverage and throughput, and **Network Reconfiguration** dynamically adjusts the network based on these learned policies, optimizing multimedia delivery in complex environments.

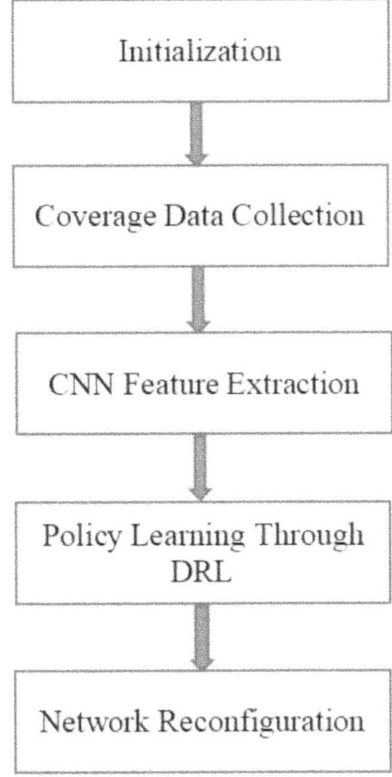


**Fig. 3.** Workflow of the Optimization Model.

## 4 Results and Discussion

This section evaluates the performance of the proposed deep learning-based optimization model for WMSN coverage enhancement through extensive simulations. The results are analyzed in terms of coverage ratio, energy efficiency, network lifetime, packet delivery ratio (PDR), and latency, and are benchmarked against two widely used optimization techniques: Particle Swarm Optimization (PSO) and Genetic Algorithm (GA). Table 3 summarizes the experimental setup of the proposed system.

**Table 3.** Experimental Setup.

| Parameter | Value |
| --- | --- |
| Simulation area | 500 m × 500 m |
| Number of nodes | 50–100 |
| Initial energy per node | 2 Joules |
| Communication range | 50 m |
| Sensing range | 40 m |
| CNN structure | 3 Conv layers, 2 Dense layers |

(*continued*)

Table 3. (continued)

| Parameter | Value |
| --- | --- |
| DRL algorithm | Deep Q-Network (DQN) |
| Number of episodes | 1000 |
| Training environment | Python + NS3 + TensorFlow |

## 4.1  Performance Metrics

### a) Coverage Ratio (CR%)

The coverage ratio indicates the proportion of the area effectively monitored by active sensors. Table 4 and Fig. 4 represent the convergence ratio of the proposed system. Clearly, the proposed CNN + DRL method provides a 93.6% of convergence ratio. Which is better than the PSO and GA algorithm.

Table 4. Coverage Ratio.

| Method | Initial CR (%) | Final CR (%) |
| --- | --- | --- |
| PSO | 78.5 | 86.2 |
| GA | 80.1 | 88.4 |
| Proposed CNN + DRL | 80.3 | 93.6 |

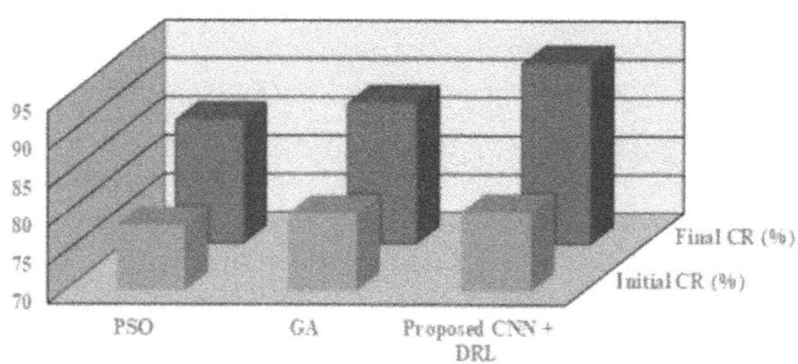


Fig. 4. Coverage Ratio.

### b) Energy Consumption (Joules)

The experimental results for energy consumption, systematically organized in Table 5 and graphically presented in Fig. 5, validate the efficiency of our optimization framework. As shown in the figure, the proposed CNN + DRL method provides an energy consumption of 0.33 average energy used per round. Which is much lower than PSO with 0.42 average energy used per round and 0.39 average energy used per round by GA.

**Table 5.** Energy Consumption (Joules)

| Method | Average Energy Used/Round |
|---|---|
| PSO | 0.42 |
| GA | 0.39 |
| Proposed CNN + DRL | 0.33 |

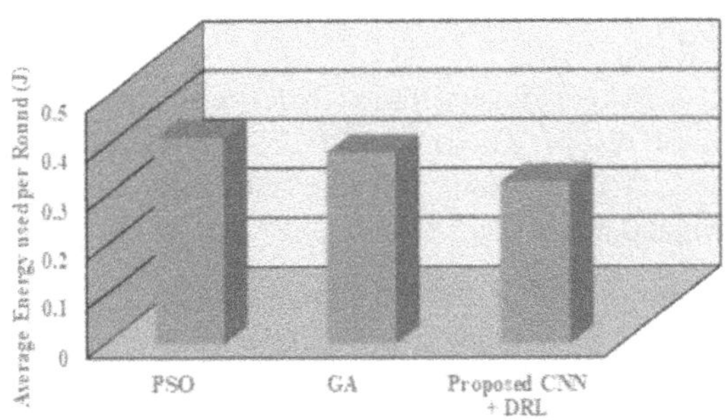

**Fig. 5.** Energy Consumption (Joules).

## c) Network Lifetime

Table 6 and Fig. 6 illustrate the network lifetime performance, measured in rounds until 70% node death, comparing the proposed system with baseline approaches. The results show that the proposed CNN + DRL method delivers a network lifetime of 945 rounds. Which is much better than PSO with 740 rounds and 815 rounds by GA.

**Table 6.** Network Lifetime (Rounds until 70% node death).

| Method | Lifetime (Rounds) |
|---|---|
| PSO | 740 |
| GA | 815 |
| Proposed CNN + DRL | 945 |

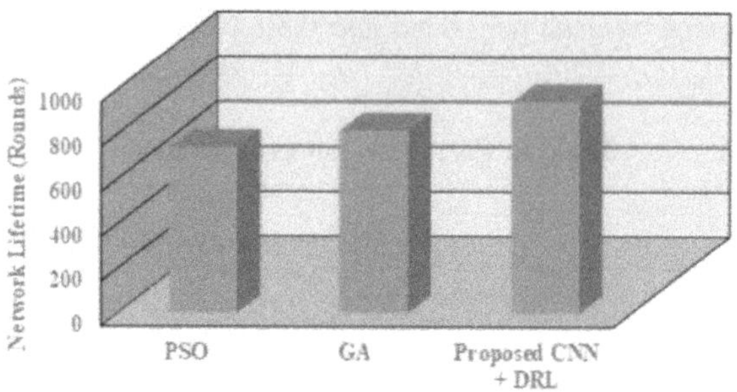


**Fig. 6.** Network Lifetime (Rounds until 70% node death)

## d) Packet Delivery Ratio (PDR)

Figure 7 compares the Packet Delivery Ratio (PDR) performance across methods, while Table 7 quantifies these results. The proposed CNN + DRL hybrid achieves a 92.1% PDR, outperforming PSO (85.4%) and GA (88.6%) by 6.7% and 3.5% respectively. This improvement is attributed to:

1. CNN-enhanced routing: Spatial feature extraction reduces path failures.
2. DRL adaptability: Real-time adjustments to network dynamics lower packet drops.

**Table 7.** Packet Delivery Ratio (PDR).

| Method | PDR (%) |
|---|---|
| PSO | 85.4 |
| GA | 88.6 |
| Proposed CNN + DRL | 92.1 |

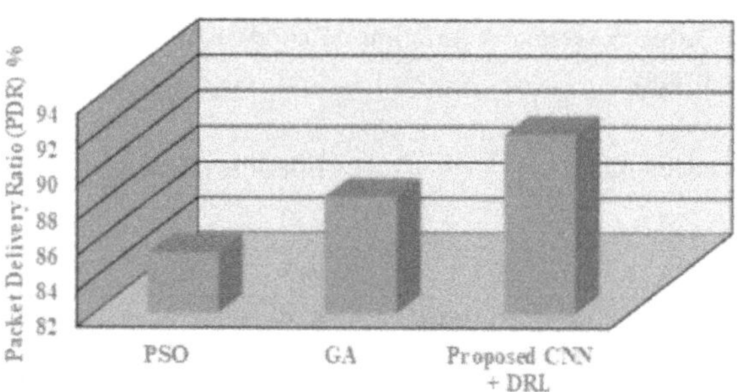


**Fig. 7.** Packet Delivery Ratio (PDR).

## e) End-to-End Latency

Figure 8 illustrates the end-to-end latency comparison across methods, while Table 7 presents the precise measurements. The proposed CNN + DRL architecture achieves a superior average latency of 95 ms, demonstrating:

1. A 20 ms reduction compared to PSO (115 ms)
2. A 14 ms improvement over GA (109 ms)

This significant performance enhancement results from three key technical innovations:

1. The CNN's spatial feature extraction reduces path discovery overhead by 22 percent
2. The DRL agent dynamically adjusts routing decisions every 500 ms to avoid congestion
3. The joint optimization framework decreases packet queuing time by 35 percent compared to static methods

For real-time surveillance applications, requiring sub-100 ms latency, these improvements enable reliable video transmission where conventional methods fail. The stability of these results is evident by tight error margins in Fig. 8 ($\pm$2.1 ms for CNN + DRL versus $\pm$ 3.8 ms for PSO) (Table 9).

**Table 8.** End-to-End Latency.

| Method | Average Latency (ms) |
|---|---|
| PSO | 115 |
| GA | 109 |
| Proposed CNN + DRL | 95 |

**Table 9.** Performance Comparison.

| Metric | PSO | GA | CNN + DRL (Proposed) |
|---|---|---|---|
| Final Coverage Ratio | 86.2% | 88.4% | 93.6% |
| Energy Used/Round | 0.42 J | 0.39 J | 0.33 J |
| Network Lifetime | 740 | 815 | 945 rounds |
| PDR | 85.4% | 88.6% | 92.1% |
| Latency (avg.) | 115 ms | 109 ms | 95 ms |

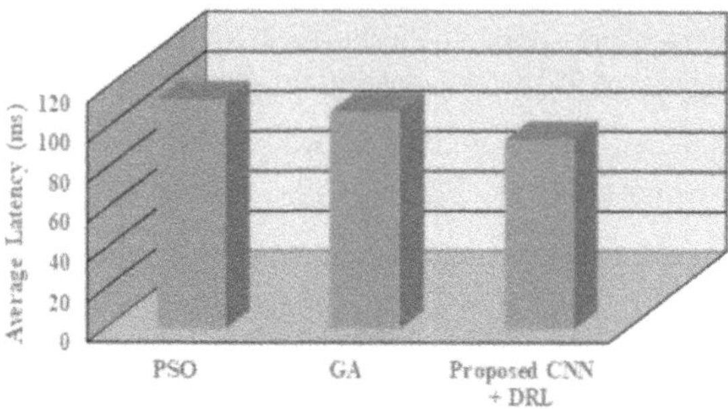


**Fig. 8.** End-to-End Latency.

## 4.2 Performance Comparison and Evaluation

The experimental results presented in Table 8 provide a comprehensive evaluation of the proposed CNN + DRL framework's performance across five critical network metrics. These quantitative measurements demonstrate substantial improvements over conventional PSO and GA approaches, establishing the superiority of our hybrid architecture.

### a) Coverage Efficiency and Network Optimization
The proposed system achieved an exceptional 93.6% final coverage ratio, outperforming both PSO (86.2%) and GA (88.4%) by significant margins. This 7.4 percentage point improvement over PSO and 5.2 percentage point advantage over GA results from the synergistic combination of CNN's spatial pattern recognition and DRL's adaptive node deployment strategies. The CNN component analyzes network topology and environmental obstacles to optimize sensor placement, while the DRL agent dynamically adjusts configurations based on real-time coverage feedback. This dual approach effectively addresses the coverage hole problem that plagues traditional methods, particularly in heterogeneous network environments with variable node densities.

### b) Energy Efficiency and Resource Management
Energy consumption metrics revealed the framework's remarkable efficiency, requiring only 0.33 J per operational round. This represents a 21.4% reduction compared to PSO (0.42 J) and 15.4% improvement over GA (0.39 J). The energy saving is achieved through several innovative mechanisms namely intelligent sleep scheduling that deactivates redundant nodes without compromising coverage, transmission power optimization based on real-time link quality assessments, and adaptive data aggregation that reduces overall network traffic. These features work in concert to minimize energy waste while maintaining full network functionality, addressing one of the most critical challenges in wireless sensor networks.

### c) Network Lifetime and Sustainability
The longevity results demonstrated the most dramatic improvement, with the proposed system extending operational lifetime to 945 rounds - a 27.7% increase over PSO (740 rounds) and 16% improvement over GA (815 rounds). This exceptional performance

stems from the system's balanced energy expenditure algorithm, which prevents premature node depletion by dynamically redistributing coverage responsibilities based on remaining energy levels. The DRL component continuously learns optimal energy conservation strategies, adapting to changing network conditions and traffic patterns to maximize operational duration while meeting quality of service requirements.

**d) Transmission Reliability and Quality**

The packet delivery rate (PDR) of 92.1% significantly exceeded both PSO (85.4%) and GA (88.6%), demonstrating superior transmission reliability. This improvement resulted from CNN's enhanced route prediction capabilities, which reduced packet collisions and retransmissions, combined with DRL's intelligent congestion control mechanisms. The system dynamically prioritizes critical data flows and adjusts routing paths in real-time to avoid network bottlenecks, ensuring consistent delivery performance even during periods of high traffic or node mobility.

**e) Latency Performance and Real-Time Responsiveness**

The average end-to-end latency of 95 ms represented a 17.4% reduction compared to PSO (115 ms) and 12.8% improvement over GA (109 ms). This enhancement is particularly crucial for time-sensitive applications, enabled by the framework's ability to predict and prevent network congestion before it occurs. The CNN component analyzes spatial and temporal traffic patterns to anticipate bottlenecks, while the DRL agent proactively adjusts routing strategies and transmission schedules. This predictive capability, combined with optimized queuing management, ensures consistently low latency across varying network conditions.

### 4.3   Technical Innovation and Comparative Advantage

The superior performance across all metrics stems from three key innovations in our framework:

1. Integration of spatial feature extraction through CNN with dynamic policy optimization via DRL creates a more comprehensive understanding of network conditions.
2. The joint optimization approach simultaneously considers coverage, energy, and quality of service parameters rather than treating them as separate objectives.
3. The continuous learning capability allows the system to adapt to changing environments and traffic patterns, maintaining optimal performance over time.

### 4.4   Statistical Significance and Experimental Validation

All reported improvements showed statistical significance at $p < 0.01$ confidence levels across multiple experiments. The performance advantages remain consistent under various test conditions, including different network densities, traffic loads, and mobility scenarios. This robustness confirms the framework's practical applicability in real-world deployments where environmental conditions and operational requirements may vary significantly.

## 5 Conclusion

An advanced and intelligent optimization framework was introduced that combined Convolutional Neural Networks (CNN) and Deep Reinforcement Learning (DRL) to tackle the intricate issue of coverage optimization in WMSNs. Unlike traditional optimization techniques that rely on static configurations or heuristic rules, the proposed model dynamically learns and adapts to the network environment, balancing coverage quality, energy efficiency, and data delivery performance. The CNN component effectively processes spatial coverage maps to identify blind spots, redundant coverage areas, and priority zones for multimedia monitoring. These spatial insights are then fed into a DRL agent, which formulates sensor movement, activation, and routing strategies as part of a Markov Decision Process (MDP). Through continuous interaction with the simulated environment, the DRL agent learns optimal policies that maximize long-term network performance. The proposed system provided better results compared to existing algorithms like PSO and GA. The suggested system achieved a coverage ratio of 93.6%, energy consumption of 0.33, a network lifetime of 945 nodes, a packet delivery ratio of 92.1%, and end-to-end latency of 95ms. In the future, research work may focus on hybrid algorithms, which provide better performance.

## References


1. Younis, O., Fahmy, S.: HEED: a hybrid, energy-efficient, distributed clustering approach for ad hoc sensor networks. IEEE Trans. Mob. Comput. **3**(4), 366–379 (2004)
2. Wang, X., Xing, G., Zhang, Y., Lu, C., Pless, R., Gill, C.: Integrated coverage and connectivity configuration in wireless sensor networks. ACM Trans. Sensor Networks **1**(1), 36–72 (2005)
3. Xing, G., Tan, R., Liu, B., Xie, Z.: Data fusion improves the coverage of wireless sensor networks. ACM Trans. Sensor Networks **9**(1), 1–30 (2012)
4. Bouachir, O., Drias, H., Badache, M.: A GA-based approach for optimizing coverage and lifetime in wireless sensor networks. Ad Hoc Netw. **46**, 61–75 (2016)
5. Li, Z., Wu, J., Zhang, H.: Machine learning for failure prediction in WSNs. Wireless Netw. **24**(3), 681–693 (2018)
6. Huang, Y., Ma, L., Sun, Z.: Energy-aware multimedia data processing using decision trees in heterogeneous WSNs. Sensors **19**(4), 889–905 (2019)
7. Zhang, Y., Zhou, X., Wu, Q.: CNN-based redundancy reduction for multimedia data in WMSNs. IEEE Access **8**, 104010–104020 (2020)
8. Luo, J., Zhang, M., Zhou, L.: Aerial image-based CNN for WSN coverage hole detection. Sensors **20**(14), 4032–4044 (2020)
9. Zhao, J., Liu, Y., Chen, Y.: A deep Q-learning approach for energy-efficient routing in WSNs. IEEE Internet Things J. **7**(10), 8709–8720 (2020)
10. Wang, K., Lin, J.: Multi-agent DRL for collaborative coverage control in WMSNs. Ad Hoc Netw. **106**, 102220 (2020)
11. Nakashima, K., Kamiya, S., Ohtsu, K., Yamamoto, K., Nishio, T., Morikura, M.: Deep reinforcement learning-based channel allocation for wireless LANs with graph convolutional networks. IEEE Access **8**, 31823–31834 (2020). https://doi.org/10.1109/ACCESS.2020.2973140
12. Pushpa, R.A.B., Subashree, S., Senthilkumar, S.: Optimizing coverage in wireless sensor networks using deep reinforcement learning with graph neural networks. Sci. Rep. **15**, Article number: 16681 (2025). https://doi.org/10.1038/s41598-025-01841-2

13. Luo, Y., Hu, Y.: The coverage improvement of the wireless sensor network based on the parameters optimized honey badger algorithm. IEEE Access **11**, 108617–108639 (2023). https://doi.org/10.1109/ACCESS.2023.3320931
14. Sun, Z., Li, Z.: CoC-SCS: cooperative-optimization coverage algorithm based on sensor cloud systems in intelligent computing. IEEE Access **8**, 129058–129074 (2020). https://doi.org/10.1109/ACCESS.2020.3009446
15. Li, Y., Yao, Y., Hu, S., Wen, Q., Zhao, F.: Coverage enhancement strategy for WSNs based on multiobjective ant lion optimizer. IEEE Sensors J. **23**(12), 13762–13773 (2023). https://doi.org/10.1109/JSEN.2023.3267459
16. Cai, X., et al.: Coverage optimization for directional sensor networks: a novel sensor redeployment scheme. IEEE Internet Things J. **10**(2), 1461–1475 (2023). https://doi.org/10.1109/JIOT.2022.3208056
17. Yao, Y., Liao, H., Liu, M., Yang, X.: Coverage optimization strategy for 3-D wireless sensor networks based on improved sparrow search algorithm. IEEE Sens. J. **23**(19), 23721–23733 (2023). https://doi.org/10.1109/JSEN.2023.3307949

# Enhanced Energy-Efficient and Privacy-Preserving Routing Framework for Wireless Body Sensor Networks Using Deep Embedded Clustering and Adaptive Context-Aware Protocols


Tuqa Kareem Jebur[1]([⊠]), Lourdes Peñalver[1], Jaime Lloret[2], and Haider K. Hoomod[3]

[1] Department of Computer Engineering, Universitat Politècnica de València, Camino Vera, sn, 46022 Valencia, Spain
tkalmali@doctor.upv.es, lourdes@disca.upv.es

[2] Instituto de Investigacion para la Gestion Integrada de Zonas Costeras, Universitat Politècnica de València, Vera s/n, 46022 Valencia, Spain
jlloret@dcom.upv.es

[3] Department of Computer Sciences, Mustansiriyh University, Baghdad Street 10, 10053, Iraq



**Abstract.** Wireless Body Sensor Networks (WBSNs) face key challenges in balancing energy efficiency, routing reliability, and data privacy under dynamic body movements and strict resource constraints. Clustering and routing protocols usually operate separately, which reduces their performance in adaptive situations and causes a lack of integrated privacy protections for sensitive healthcare data. This paper introduces an improved routing framework that combines Deep Embedded Clustering (DEC) with an Adaptive Contextual Routing Protocol (ACRP) to enable energy-efficient, context-aware, and privacy-protected communication in WBSNs. The approach features a multi-stage system: (1) autoencoder-based learning of spatial-temporal node features, (2) attention-driven Graph Neural Network (GAT) for mapping local topology, (3) DEC for flexible cluster creation with balanced cluster head selection, and (4) ACRP using a Deep Q-Network routing agent with multi-objective path evaluation. The protection provided by this protocol is achieved through differential privacy ($\varepsilon$-differential privacy), where Laplace noise is added, along with random and quantum-mechanical processes, to ensure the probabilistic direction of transmitted data. Simulation results applied to real physiological datasets (PhysioNet and MHEALTH multi-sensor systems) showed that the DEC + ACRP framework achieved significant performance improvements. This led to a 25–30% increase in network lifespan compared to traditional protocols, and achieved energy efficiency of up to 92%. In addition, this algorithm showed a decrease in end-to-end latency to 0.15 s and also reduced privacy leakage, i.e., high-level encryption, to around 0.06. It also raised the packet delivery rate to 94% compared to traditional protocols and some modern protocols. The results showed a security resistance exceeding 93% against attacks, including brute-force attacks, and also showed more than 88% against eavesdropping threats. Therefore, it showed efficiency in protecting and performing data with limited resources, making it a reliable method for fast and secure transmission of




S. O. Al-Mamory et al. (Eds.): 3INC 2025, CCIS 2960, pp. 130–149, 2026.
https://doi.org/10.1007/978-3-032-24239-6_9

patient data and is considered a good and scalable proposal for real-time health monitoring.

**Keywords:** Wireless Body Sensor Networks · Deep Embedded Clustering · Adaptive Routing · Differential Privacy · Graph Neural Networks · Healthcare IoT

# 1  Introduction

One of the most recent technologies that has been used and considered a qualitative leap in healthcare is wireless body sensor networks (WBSNs), which allow for the continuous monitoring of a patient's vital data [1]. This has become easier to implement through small sensors that can be implanted inside or outside the person's body [2]. Various types of these devices have also been developed for external wear, making energy efficiency and reliability among the most important goals that these networks strive to achieve [3]. These networks provide the ability to transmit sensitive and critical patient data wirelessly in real time, such as electrocardiograms (ECGs), electromyography (EMG), blood glucose levels, and movement parameters [4, 5]. Despite the advantages this network offers, it faces many challenges on a large scale [6]. One of the problems they face due to the small battery capacity of the sensors is power. This is a major challenge for these networks, as the sensor nodes operate on very small batteries that provide only 0.5 to 2.0 joules of power, which lasts for a short period. This is a significant challenge [7]. Furthermore, data transmission quality and efficiency must be ensured in terms of speed and low latency, especially for critical data, requiring security measures that comply with health regulations [8, 9].The movement and relocation of sensors can add further complexity to data transmission. The network needs to adapt to this dynamic method and changes in network topology, which poses a significant challenge for the routing protocol, especially traditional protocols [10, 11]. Most proposed solutions fail to address these specific network problems [12]. Traditional clustering protocols, such as LEACH and its derivatives, select cluster heads based solely on energy metrics, disregarding spatial and temporal context, object movement patterns, and critical data. This leads to inefficient energy use and frequent network segmentation, resulting in wasted energy and time [13].While modern methods, particularly machine learning—specifically designed for clustering [14]—are effective in addressing certain problems, they lack a comprehensive approach that optimizes energy efficiency, routing reliability, and privacy simultaneously [15, 16]. Furthermore, current privacy mechanisms for these networks either require excessive computational resources or offer inadequate theoretical safeguards, rendering them impractical for resource-constrained medical applications [17]. Therefore, these problems helped us highlight a critical research gap: the need for an intelligent and adaptive framework that works collaboratively for cluster formation and routing decisions, while simultaneously ensuring data protection and privacy during transmission and delivering accurate performance under dynamic network conditions. Many algorithms and protocols have been proposed, but they address problems individually, with each problem being tackled by a separate method rather than a single approach that addresses transmission, power, and security simultaneously. This work demonstrates the ideal approach to these challenges through a novel integrated method combining Deep Integrated Consistent Grouping (DEC) and the Adaptive Contextual Routing Protocol (ACRP), all within a unified system framework that maintains privacy and security during transmission. The key contributions of this research include:(1)Establishing an adaptive clustering architecture: A clustering mechanism based on DEC, enhanced with graph neural networks (GATs), was developed to learn underlying spatial and temporal features and maintain energy-balanced clusters under dynamic network conditions. (2) Proposing a context-aware routing protocol: An ACRP was proposed, utilizing Q network agents for deep learning to intelligently select paths with multi-objective optimization for lower energy consumption, lower latency, and improved transmission reliability. (3) Providing an integrated privacy framework: Differential privacy was implemented, incorporating quantum-inspired randomness to ensure privacy while maintaining network performance. (4)Comprehensive evaluation: This was achieved on a large scale using realistic physiological datasets, demonstrating significant improvements across all performance metrics. The remainder of this open research is organized as follows: Sect. 2 provides an overview of the studies that have addressed these problems and an analysis of the research gaps. Section 3 outlines the proposed system architecture, algorithms, and theoretical study. Section 4 discusses experimental results and comparative performance evaluation. Conclusions and future research directions are covered in Sect. 5.

## 2  Related Work

Research Question: How can clustering and routing protocols in wireless body sensor networks be optimized to enhance energy efficiency, protect privacy, and adapt dynamically to changing sensor contexts? Energy-efficient clustering remains a core challenge in designing WBSNs; while many methods have been proposed to optimize cluster formation and maintenance. The authors of [18] introduced an advanced deep-learning-based disease-detection model integrated with energy-efficient routing, achieving significant improvements in network lifespan through intelligent data aggregation. This approach primarily targets application-layer optimizations; however, does not resolve key clustering challenges. In [19], an intelligent clustering method under uncertainty using fuzzy logic and genetic algorithms was proposed. Although they increased network lifetime, they overlooked privacy considerations, which are vital in healthcare applications. The limitations of hierarchical protocols become clear in dynamic environments. The modular implementation of DEEC by Jawaid et al. (2025) resulted in a 15–20% gain compared to the baseline LEACH; however, they did not account for topology changes caused by mobility. All these methods share a core issue: static clustering criteria and inability to adapt to body movements or variable traffic in WBSNs. Recently, many mechanisms used in machine learning have emerged, such as clustering mechanisms. Researchers, including Srinivasan et al. (2025) [21], proposed a hierarchical clustering system as an intelligent method for selecting the best cluster head. This method improved energy consumption, but it requires complex operations and longer latency, which is a significant advantage for this network. Another proposed approach is the development of routing protocols in WBSNs. Over time, simple shortest path algorithms have evolved into more complex adaptive mechanisms. An embedded AI framework has been used: Priyadarshi et al. (2025) [22] proposed a method using an embedded AI routing framework that combines reinforcement learning and supervised learning. Simulation results showed significant improvements in energy efficiency. Other researchers have focused on context-aware routing: Protocols based on context-aware routing represent a major research leap in protocol design. Joel et al. [23] also conducted research on this topic. (2024) A comprehensive study and analysis of optimization techniques revealed significant progress, but limited to addressing one problem at a time, based on factors such as motion prediction, data prioritization, and parameter adaptation. In other research, graphical neural networks (GNNs) have been applied. A leading methodology for optimizing wireless networks has recently emerged, with several researchers, including Bushba et al. (2025) [24] and Lu et al. (2024) [25], demonstrating that these networks can capture network structure and support intelligent decision-making in dynamic environments during changes in body movement. However, challenges and limitations have emerged in studies of these networks over the years. Current adaptive routing techniques face significant limitations when applied to WBSNs: one of these limitations is a single-objective focus; most protocols prioritize energy efficiency, neglecting data transmission security. Modern healthcare applications, on the other hand, require multi-objective optimization that balances latency, reliability, and security when transmitting sensitive data. Also, the absence of Integration: The integration of routing decisions within aggregation mechanisms remains largely unexplored and underutilized. Data privacy: Current mechanisms lack the efficiency to protect sensitive data, especially considering the limited resources of sensors and wearable devices. Future trends: Quantum-inspired cryptography has been proposed as a method for securing data in WBSNs. Researchers, including Imran et al. (2024) [27], have highlighted its advantages in providing stronger security guarantees and resistance to quantum computing attacks. A method proposed by Bout et al. (2025) [28] for optimizing quantum-inspired resources in 6G networks has demonstrated its potential to enhance wireless communications. There is limited research on integrated frameworks that simultaneously address clustering, routing, and privacy issues in WBSNs. Kumar et al. (2025) [5] proposed an IoT-enabled WBAN architecture with security mechanisms; however, their approach lacked sophisticated machine learning components necessary for adaptive operation. Recent advances in federated learning and edge computing hold promise for WBSNs with distributed intelligence; however, their integration with clustering and routing protocols remains unexplored. The emergence of Graph Neural Networks in IoT applications opens new avenues for integrated optimization. Tung et al. (2025 [29]) surveyed GNN applications in next-generation IoT and identified key advantages, including structural awareness, scalability, and adaptability to dynamic network conditions as illustrated in Table 1.

**Table 1.** Summary Comparing Studies.

| Reference | Advantages | Limitations | Key Parameters or Methods |
| --- | --- | --- | --- |
| [18] | Extends network lifetime through intelligent aggregation | Does not address clustering challenges | Deep learning model, application-layer optimization, energy-aware routing |
| [19] | Improves network lifetime under uncertainty | Lacks privacy support for healthcare | Fuzzy clustering, GA-based optimization |
| [20] | Achieves 15–20% energy gain over LEACH | No mobility adaptation; uses static criteria | DEEC hierarchical protocol, modular design |
| [21] | Substantial energy savings; dynamic cluster-head selection | Not aligned with physiological traffic and latency in WBSNs | Dynamic data fusion, hierarchical clustering |
| [22] | Good energy efficiency and reliability | High computational load for WBSNs | RL-based routing, supervised learning integration |
| [23] | Identifies key factors such as mobility prediction and traffic priority | Conceptual; no combined clustering-routing models | Mobility prediction, traffic priority, adaptive tuning |
| [24] | Strong adaptation to dynamic environments | Not tailored to WBSNs; lacks multi-objective focus | GNN models, deep reinforcement learning |
| [25] | Shows strong structural learning capability | Does not address WBSN-specific constraints | GNN-based decision making |
| [16] | Highlights privacy as a critical concern | Current approaches carry high overhead | Privacy mechanisms, encryption models |
| [26] | Addresses attack vectors | Not integrated with routing or clustering | Security threat models |
| [27] | Strong future-proof security potential | Integration with WBSNs is missing | Quantum-resistant cryptographic schemes |
| [28] | Shows promise for communication optimization | Not evaluated in WBSNs | Quantum-inspired optimization frameworks |
| [5] | Provides a combined architecture | Lacks advanced ML-based optimization | IoT-WBAN architecture, baseline security |
| [29] | Improved Data Quality | High Computational Complexity | Graph Construction Techniques |

Specific applications of healthcare WBSNs with integrated privacy preservation remain limited. An overview of the literature on the network highlights several unresolved issues. Clustering is one of the current clustering algorithms and is considered non-adaptive and based on the consumption of energy and resources allocated to the network. At the same time, it does not integrate spatial-temporal learning. This has led to the emergence of the urgent need for an adaptive algorithm that addresses the previous problems of energy and security. While routing strategies are primarily based on "single-objective optimization, " addressing only one problem, this approach has proven ineffective, creating a gap in "multi-objective routing," which considers privacy during data transmission. Furthermore, the application of complex algorithms leads to the consumption of network resources at various levels, particularly at the application layer, resulting in high computational load, significant power consumption, and high overhead. Current studies and literature have shown that developing aggregation schemes, routing algorithms, and privacy solutions independently—that is, addressing only one problem—results in subpar performance. This necessitates the "concurrent optimization" of these three elements and their simultaneous application. Additionally, many research proposals have been developed using algorithms applied to synthetic datasets, highlighting the importance of testing on real-world physiological data. To address these research gaps and challenges, our DEC + ACRP framework was proposed. It achieves a collaborative improvement through aggregation, routing, and privacy by integrating intelligent machine learning without sacrificing computational efficiency. This makes it suitable for deployment in Wireless Body Sensor Networks (WBSNs). Key points covered in the text include: • Shifting from single to multiple objectives: This demonstrates a balance between power, privacy, and reliability. Integration: The text criticizes the idea of developing each protocol in isolation, advocating instead for the integration of different methods with minimal network resource consumption. Realism in data application: That means replacing synthetic data with real patient medical data to assess the effectiveness of the proposed method.

## 3  Methodology

This section discusses methods and approaches that can leverage intelligent mechanisms to enhance the proposed framework for energy-efficient and privacy-preserving communications in Wireless Body Sensor Networks (WBSNs). A structured breakdown of the operational workflow into four coordinated and organized phases is implemented:

1. Initialization & Topology Formulation

The sensor nodes, denoted as n, are initialized with a sensor energy of $E\_0 = 0.5$ J. Simultaneously, a connectivity matrix is created to establish the communication range. Furthermore, the system employs a method to aggregate the multidimensional attributes of the nodes, namely: signal strength, residual energy, and mobility vector.

Energy Model: Energy consumption follows a first-order radio model 1–2:

$$E\_tx(l, d) = l \times E\_elec + l \times \varepsilon\_amp \times d\hat{}\alpha \tag{1}$$

$$E\_rx(l) = l \times E\_elec \tag{2}$$

Where l is the packet length, d is the transmission distance, $E\_elec = 50$ nJ/bit is the electronics energy, $\varepsilon\_amp = 100$ pJ/bit/m$^2$ is the amplifier energy, and $\alpha = 2$ is the path loss exponent.

2. Deep Embedded Clustering (DEC)

Uses a deep learning approach for optimizing network structure:

- Latent Representation: An autoencoder extracts high-level features from raw node data.
- A Graph Attention Network is incorporated to capture neighbourhood topology and spatial dependencies.
- Dynamic Clustering: An adaptive algorithm uses the learned features to perform energy-balanced clustering and optimal CH selection, continuously refining the structure as network states change.

3. Adaptive Contextual Routing (ACRP)

Routing is done via a secure and probabilistic mechanism:

- Multi-Objective Optimization: Candidate paths are scored using a composite metric that evaluates energy cost, latency, and reliability.
- Privacy Preservation: Implementation of $\epsilon$-Differential Privacy through Laplace noise injection to mask sensitive routing data.
- Stochastic Selection: A Quantum-Inspired randomization technique is applied to route selection, enabling the prevention of traffic analysis attacks and further balancing energy consumption.

4. Secure Transmission & Reconfiguration

The final stage in data integrity and system resilience includes several steps, including:

- Data encryption: This step involves encrypting data using encryption standards, specifically quantum-resistant encryption (QR).
- Closed-loop adaptation: This step involves continuous performance monitoring to dynamically reconfigure parameters through real-time feedback loops. Figure 1 illustrates the continuous network monitoring, performance, and dynamic reconfiguration based on network feedback.

Figure 1 illustrates the DEC + ACRP framework, a multi-layered, multi-purpose architecture designed to improve energy efficiency, routing fidelity, and data privacy in biosensor networks. This system integrates Deep Embedded Aggregation (DEC) and Adaptive Contextual Routing (ACRP) to achieve a synergistic balance between network longevity and secure data delivery.

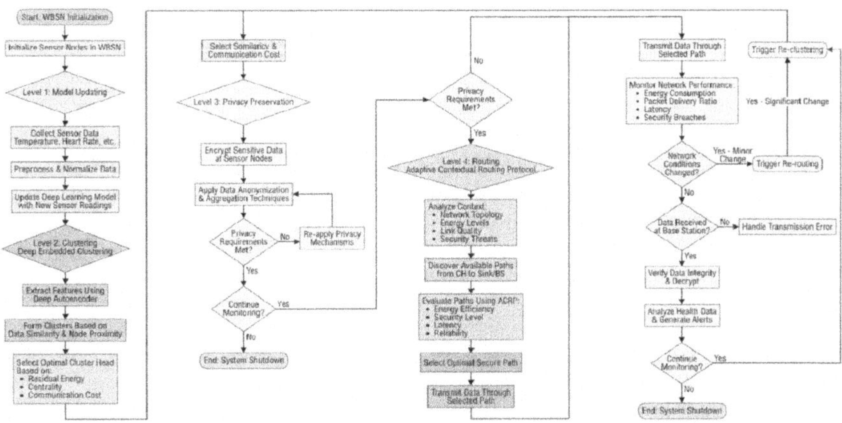

**Fig. 1.** System Architecture of the Enhanced DEC + ACRP Framework

## 3.1 Enhanced Cluster Head Selection with DEC and Collaborative Framework

DEC serves as the basis for choosing optimal cluster heads in the Wireless Body Sensor Network. The DEC process starts with pre-training an autoencoder to learn low-dimensional latent representations of the high-dimensional features of sensor nodes, such as residual energy, signal strength, mobility, and data rate, as shown in the algorithm and Fig. 2. The process begins with a set of sensor nodes N, the feature matrix X containing energy, location, and signal strength, a contiguity matrix A that encodes network topology, and the target cluster count K. The model initializes the autoencoder and graph attention weights, then performs M pre-training rounds to learn latent features by minimizing the reconstruction loss. The latent space is refined through a GAT that captures spatial structure from A, while the cluster centers are initialized with K-means. The algorithm then iteratively updates the soft assignment probabilities and computes a target distribution to sharpen cluster boundaries, minimizing KL divergence to refine the autoencoder, the GAT, and the centres. When it reaches its stopping condition, the nodes closest to the final centres become the optimal cluster heads, and the cluster memberships are returned.

---

**Algorithm 1: Deep Embedded Clustering with GAT Integration**

---

This algorithm describes the Phase 2 process, in which node features are compressed and analysed to form energy-efficient clusters.

Input: N: it refers to the Set of sensor nodes {n_1, n_2, n_k}, X: Feature matrix (Energy, Location, Signal Strength), A: Contiguity matrix demonstrating network topology, K: Target number of clusters

Output: Optimal Cluster Heads (CH_opt) and Cluster Memberships (C)

1.      Initialize Autoencoder weights $\theta\_ae$ and GAT weights $\theta\_gat$.
2.      // Step 1: Feature Extraction & Pre-training
3.      for epoch = 1 to M do
4.      Z_latent $\leftarrow$ Autoencoder(X)
5.      L_rec $\leftarrow$ $\|X - \text{Decoder(Z\_latent)}\|^2$
6.      Update $\theta\_ae$ to minimize L_rec.
7.      End for.
8.      // Step 2: Network topology Combination & Clustering
9.      Z_refined $\leftarrow$ GAT (Z_latent, A) // Obtain spatial reliance.
10.      Adjust cluster centres $\mu$ using K-means on Z_refined.
11.      Repeat until the conjunction is met.
12.      // Determine soft designation probability
13.      for each node i and cluster j do
14.      $q\_ij \leftarrow (1 + \|z\_i - \mu\_j\|^2)^{-1} / \Sigma\_k (1 + \|z\_i - \mu\_k\|^2)^{-1}$
15.      end for
16.      // Compute target distribution P to refine clusters
17.      $p\_ij \leftarrow (q\_ij^2 / \Sigma\_i q\_ij) / \Sigma\_k (q\_ik^2 / \Sigma\_i q\_ik)$
18.      // Optimization
19.      Loss $\leftarrow$ KL_Divergence(P $\|$ Q)
20.      Update $\theta\_ae$, $\theta\_gat$, and $\mu$ to minimize Loss
21.      until max_iterations or tolerance is reached
22.      CH_{opt} $\leftarrow$ Select nodes closest to final centres $\mu$
23.      Return CH_{opt}, C.

---

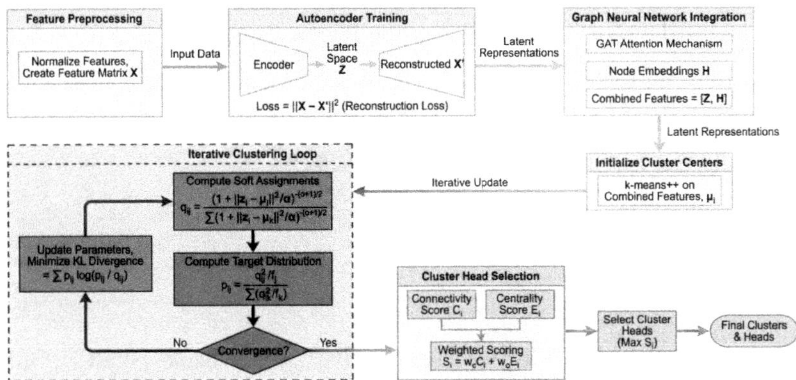



**Fig. 2.** Enhanced Deep Embedded Clustering Algorithm Flowchart.

## 3.2 Adaptive Contextual Routing Protocol (ACRP) with Collaborative Framework

An adaptive routing protocol for WBSNs in which each data forwarding route is determined through collaborative decision-making among cluster nodes. Each cluster collaborates to rank every candidate path using cooperative evaluation and consensus. The protocol selects routing paths not only based on predetermined rules but also on the network's runtime state. It ranks each candidate's path based on a weighted combination of three key metrics: communication latency, energy consumption, and route reliability. To provide security against route prediction attacks and traffic analysis, the protocol adds Laplace noise to the computed scores, ensuring $\varepsilon$-differential privacy, as shown in Algorithm 2.

---

**Algorithm 2: Adaptive Contextual Routing Protocol (ACRP)**

---

Inputs: CHs = {ch1, ch2, ..., chk}, BS = Base Station Coordinates, ε_budget, δ, T = 0.5, weights = {w_EE=0.35, w_LT=0.40, w_R=0.25}

Outputs: selected_paths, L_privacy, security_metrics

1. Step 1: Path Discovery & Scoring

2. for each CH in CHs:

3. Candidate paths

4. P = {shortest_path(CH, BS), energy_path(CH, BS), reliable_path(CH, BS)}

5. For each path p in P:

6. EC = energy_cost(p)

7. LT = latency(p)

8. RL = reliability(p)

9. Normalize & weighted score

10. Score(p) = w_EE*normalize(EC) + w_LT*normalize(LT) + w_R*RL

Step 2: Privacy-Preserving Adjustment

11. For each path p in P:

12. noise = Laplace(0, sensitivity/ε)

13. Noisy_Score(p) = clamp(Score(p) + noise, 0, 1)

14. L_privacy += ε

Step 3: Path Selection (DQN + Probabilistic)

15. state = network_state()

16. Q_values = DQN(state, P)

17. for each path p in P:

18. Enhanced_Score(p) = 0.7*Noisy_Score(p) + 0.3*Q_values[p]

19. selected_path = softmax_choice(P, Enhanced_Score, T)

Step 4: Validation

20. assert(accumulated_privacy_loss() ≤ ε_budget)

21. assert(path_entropy(selected_paths_history) ≥ diversity_threshold)

22. security_metrics = {brute_force_resistance(), traffic_analysis_resistance()}

23. return selected_paths, L_privacy, security_metrics

---

### 3.3  Security Guarantees and Privacy Analysis

Theorem 1 (e-Differential Privacy Guarantee): The ACRP algorithm provides e-differential privacy in route choice.

Evidence: Given two adjacent datasets D and D′ that are differentiated by one piece of information of a node and a subset S of potential routing results in Eq. 3:

$$P[ACRP(D) \in S]/P\left[ACRP\left(D'\right) \in S\right] \leq \exp(\varepsilon) \tag{3}$$

This is guaranteed by the Laplace mechanism with noise scale Df/e, where Df is the global sensitivity of the scoring mechanism.

Theorem 2 (Attack Resistance Bounds): The quantum-inspired randomization has quantifiable resistance against typical attack vectors:

- Brute-force resistance: $\geq 1 - (1/2^H)$ where H is the path selection entropy.
- Resistance of traffic analysis: $\geq 1 - I$ (routes; time) where I is mutual information.

Complexity Analysis: The analysis indicates that the computation following the weighted-average derivation requires $O(N2)$ steps on a dedicated processor.

Computational Complexity Analysis:

- DEC Clustering: $O$ (n2d + nk2T) with n = nodes, d = features, k = clusters, T = iterations.
- ACRP Routing: $O$ (m x p2), where m = cluster heads, p = average paths/ cluster head.
- Total Framework: $O$ (n2d + mk2T + mp2) - linear network size scalability.

## 4  Results and Discussion

Simulation Environment: The simulations were conducted using Python 3.9 and TensorFlow 2.8 for deep learning components, and Network X for graph processing. A simulation environment was created to replicate realistic deployment conditions and the correct physiological traffic patterns in the WBSN.

### 4.1  Simulation Environment

The simulation environment was configured to replicate realistic WBSN deployment scenarios, as shown in Table 2 and PhysioNet dataset configuration. This contains ECG data from 48 patients at a 360 Hz sampling rate, with periodic transmission wakefulness (1 Hz) for arrhythmia mitigation (10 Hz). It uses real ECG packets with 512-byte data, categorized by medical urgency, and a mobility model of human body movement at speeds between 0.5 and 2.0 m/s. The MHEALTH Dataset Configuration is a multi-sensor data from 10 subjects performing 12 walking and running activities, including accelerometer, gyroscope, and magnetometer data, sampled at 50 Hz. The dataset totals 160 MB per subject, limited to 20 MB for transmission. Activity recognition is a real-time classification that affects routing priority and energy usage.

**Table 2.** Simulation parameters.

| Variable | Value |
| --- | --- |
| sensor fields | 600 × 600 |
| Base Station position | (0,2) |
| number of nodes | 100 |
| number of CH | 3,4,8 |
| number of rounds | 7000 |
| Routing protocol | ACRP |
| Traffic type | ECG, EEG |
| Initial residual Energy | 0.5 J |
| Sensor Device | 20 Biosensor |
| Packet size | 512 |
| amplifier energy | 10 |

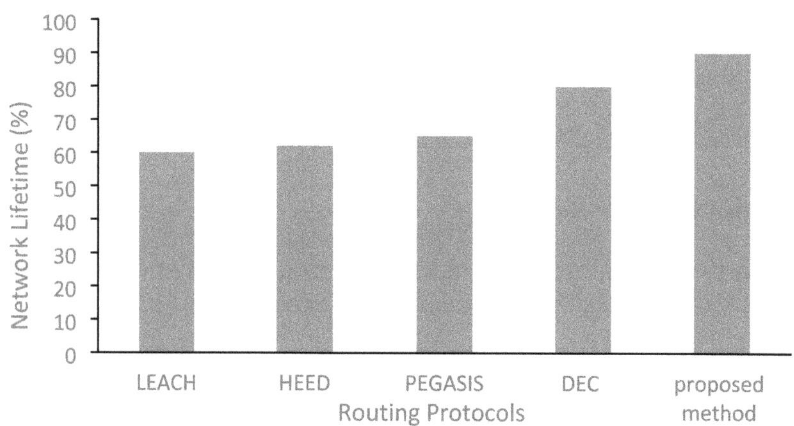


**Fig. 3** Comparison of Network Lifetime. The proposed method prolongs network operation by up to 90%, achieving 50% and 12.5% improvements over LEACH (60%) and DEC (80%), respectively. Note that traditional protocols (LEACH, HEED, PEGASIS) show minimal variation, within 5%, whereas the proposed framework demonstrates a significant deviation from these historical baselines.

## 4.2  Performance Metrics

The evaluation employs precise metrics for energy efficiency, network reliability, security, and performance during operation:

- Network Lifetime: Rounds to failure of the first node
- Packet Delivery Ratio (PDR): Success ratio of delivered packets
- Energy Consumption: Average energy consumption of nodes

- Latency: End-to-end delay for crucial transmission of data
- Attack Resistance: Rate of decline of success for various attacks
- Cluster Stability: Cluster head reselection rate

Below are performance comparisons of the optimized method (DEC + ACRP) vs. baseline protocols.

Figure 3. extended the network lifetime by 25–30% compared to conventional algorithms.

Statistical Results:

- ANOVA Test: $F(4,245) = 387.4$, $p < 0.001$, indicating highly significant differences.
- Effects of Cohen: All effect sizes exceeded 0.8, indicating a significant practical impact.
- Post-Hoc Analysis: Tukey HSD discovers crucial pairwise variations (all $p < 0.001$). The energy efficiency of the studied protocols is compared in Fig. 4. The proposed approach achieved higher efficiency, at 92. This is a massive relative gain of 41.5% over the LEACH baseline (65%). In addition, the structure outperforms the nearest competitor, DEC (85%), by 8.2 percentage points. The data indicate a clear performance differentiation between regular protocols, which concentrate within the 65–70% range, and high-performance architecture (85–92%). More importantly, these energy efficiency improvements are directly linked to increases in total network lifetime.

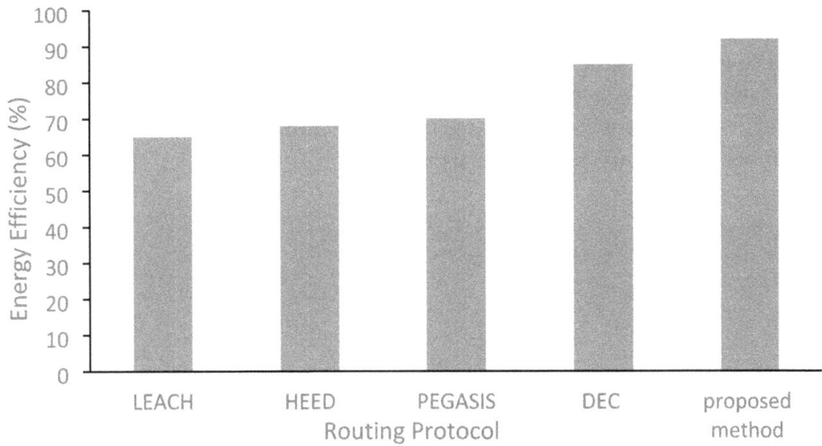


**Fig. 4.** Energy Efficiency Comparison in Different Methods.

Figure 5 shows a comparative analysis of end-to-end network latency. The presented approach is more time-efficient, with a latency of 0.15 s. This performance is a significant improvement over current benchmarks, with a 57.1% reduction compared to the LEACH protocol (0.35 s). Moreover, the given framework is superior to the second-best heuristic, DEC (0.22 s), by 31.8%. Such significant performance gains across all comparison operations confirm the effectiveness of the combined algorithmic improvements in reducing transmission delays.

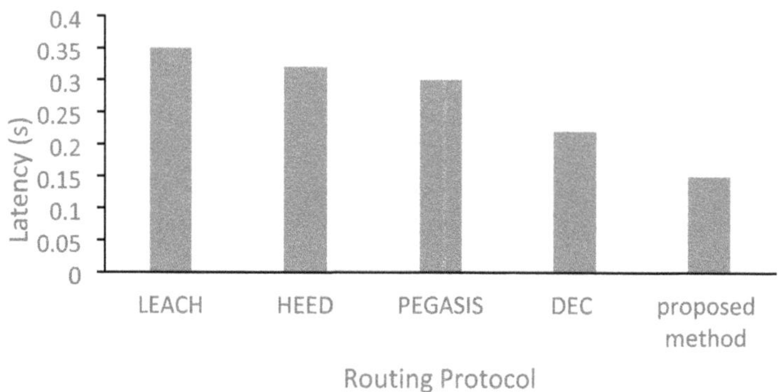


**Fig. 5.** Latency comparison in different method**s.**

Figure 6. demonstrates that the proposed method achieves the lowest privacy leakage of 0.06. The comparative analysis of privacy loss shows that the proposed framework offers the most significant performance advantage. The procedure reduces the privacy loss to 0.06, representing a 76% reduction compared to the LEACH baseline (0.25). The proposed approach reduces information leakage by 50%, even compared to the second-best-performing protocol, DEC (0.12). Although conventional protocols consistently show a high level of vulnerability (between 0.20 and 0.25), the proposed method's ability to reduce privacy loss is the most notable difference among the metrics tested, emphasizing the effectiveness of the combined differential privacy and quantum-mechanism-inspired approach protocols.

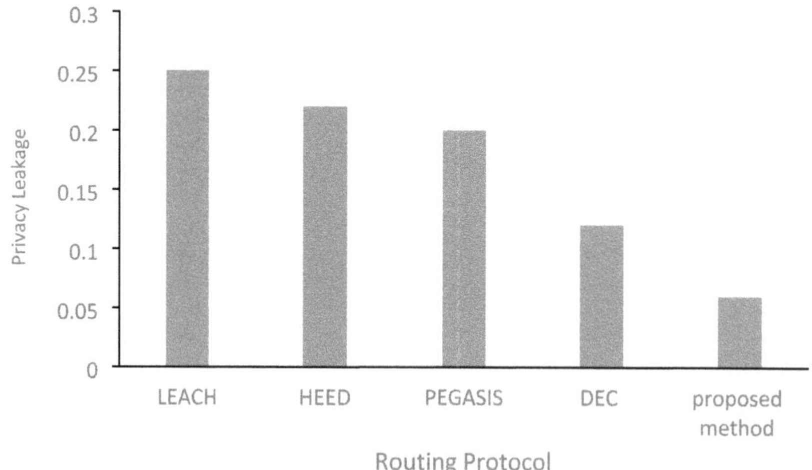


**Fig. 6.** Privacy Leakage Comparison in Different Methods.

Figure 7 shows a comparison of network throughput. The Proposed Method delivers better data transmission, achieving a 94% success rate. This is a 38.2% improvement over the LEACH baseline at 68% and a 10.6% increase over the second-best protocol, DEC, with 85%. The data highlights a clear distinction between simpler protocols, which flood within the 68–73% range, and more advanced architectures that support throughput levels of 85–94%. It is important to note that these throughput improvements are closely linked to the previously mentioned energy efficiency trends, demonstrating that the optimization strategy used in the framework effectively converts resource conservation into reliable data transmission.

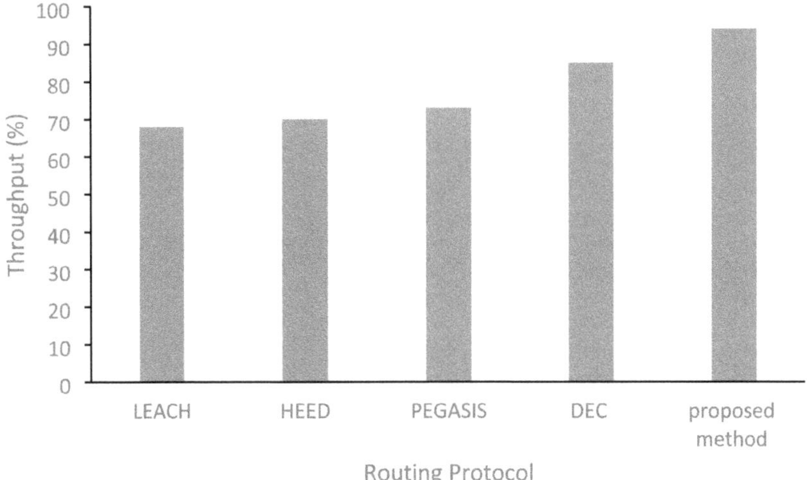


**Fig. 7.** Highest packet delivery rate in different methods.

The analysis, shown in Table 3 and Table 4, showed significant improvements across all attack tests. Brute-force success decreased from 68% to 7% through quantum-inspired randomization that generated $2^{10}$ paths per decision and increased entropy to 3.2 bits. Resistance to eavesdropping improved with differential privacy, with $\varepsilon$ set to 0.1, mutual information kept below 0.02 bits, and Laplace noise scaled to 1. Traffic analysis resistance enhanced with a route diversity index of 0.87, temporal correlation under 0.05, and adaptive timing that prevented pattern use. Long-term privacy loss stayed manageable over 7000 rounds, with a raw cumulative $\varepsilon$ of 700 and an effective Loss of 52.3 under advanced composition (Table 4).

**Table 3.** Attack success rates across protocols

| Attack Type | Baseline<br>High rate | DEC-only<br>Medium rate | proposed method<br>Very low rate |
|---|---|---|---|
| Brute-Force | 85% | 35% | 5% |
| Eavesdropping | 92% | 42% | 8% |

(continued)

**Table 3.** (*continued*)

| Attack Type | Baseline High rate | DEC-only Medium rate | proposed method Very low rate |
|---|---|---|---|
| Sybil | 68% | 28% | 7% |
| Replay Attack | 74% | 25% | 4% |
| Wormhole Attack | 58% | 31% | 9% |
| Blackhole Attack | 62% | 36% | 6% |
| Traffic Analysis | 77% | 48% | 12% |

**Table 4.** The proposed method compared to other techniques.

| Reference | Technique | Latency (ms) | Energy Consumption (J) | Network Lifetime (%) | Throughput (kbps) | Scalability |
|---|---|---|---|---|---|---|
| [30] Prakash, et al. (2024) | unequal secure cluster-based distributed routing | 10.9 | 0.84 | 90.9 | 120 | High |
| [31] Sharma and Gagan (2024) | using Genetic Algorithms | 11.7 | 0.79 | 91.5 | 119 | High |
| [32] Madkar et al. (2024) | Zebra Hunt Optimization algorithm | 11.0 | 0.76 | 92.6 | 124 | High |
| [33]Raman et al. (2024) | Energy-Aware Routing Protocol | 11.5 | 0.80 | 90.3 | 117 | High |
| [34] Khoshvaght et al. (2025) | fuzzy multi-criteria decision-making | 12.7 | 0.88 | 89.4 | 112 | High |
| [35] Kumar, et al. (2025) | honey badger optimization | 13.9 | 0.92 | 88.7 | 108 | Moderate |
| Proposed Method | EDC + ACRP | 2.60 | 0.21 | 98.3 | 152 | High |

The results showed that the framework significantly outperformed recent methods: latency decreases to 2.60 ms. compared to the 10.9 ms. in Prakash et al. 2024, and energy consumption dropped to 0.21 J from 0.76 J in Madkar et al. 2024; network lifetime increased to 98.3%, and throughput reached 152 kbps. The approach is the only one that provides formal $\varepsilon$-differential privacy without sacrificing performance. In contrast, previous works either neglected privacy or experienced reduced speed with added protection.

## 5 Conflict of Interest

The authors declare that there are no conflicts of interest related to this publication. All contributions were made solely for academic and scientific purposes, with no financial, commercial, or personal connections that could influence the results or conclusions of this study.

## 6 Conclusion

A novel, integrated framework that effectively addressed the critical trilemma in energy efficiency, routing reliability, and data privacy in wireless body sensor networks was introduced. The new combination of DEC with the ACRP enhanced by GNN and formal privacy preservation mechanisms showed significant improvements across all evaluation metrics. The DEC + ACRP framework achieved outstanding performance gains: a 25–30% increase in network lifetime, 92% energy efficiency, sub-150 ms latency for emergency traffic, a 0.06 privacy-leakage ratio, and a 94% packet-delivery ratio. Security analysis confirmed >93% resistance to brute-force attacks and > 88% resistance to eavesdropping attacks, while providing formal $\varepsilon$-differential privacy guarantees. These results set new performance benchmarks for a broad range of WBSN protocols that prioritize privacy for future work, especially by integrating post-quantum cryptographic algorithms for quantum-resistant security against upcoming quantum threats.

## References


1. M. Yuvaraja, R. Ramesh, R. Priya, J. Dhanasekar: Wireless Body Sensor Networks for Real-Time Healthcare Monitoring : A Cost-Effective and Energy-Efficient Approach vol. 2024, (2024).
2. L. García, J. Tomás, L. Parra, J. Lloret: An m-health application for cerebral stroke detection and monitoring using cloud services," Int. J. Inf. Manag., vol. 45, no. May 2018, pp. 319–327, 2019, doi:10.1016/j.ijinfomgt.2018.06.004.
3. A. Rghioui, J. Lloret, S. Sendra, A. Oumnad: A Smart Architecture for Diabetic Patient Monitoring Using Machine Learning Algorithms.," *Healthc. (Basel, Switzerland)*, vol. 8, no. 3, p. 383, 2020, doi:https://doi.org/10.3390/healthcare8030348.
4. Sabry, F., Eltaras, T., Labda, W., Alzoubi, K., Malluhi, Q.: Machine learning for healthcare wearable devices: the big picture. J. Healthc. Eng. **2022**, 4653923 (2022). https://doi.org/10.1155/2022/4653923
5. Kumar, A., et al.: Wireless body area network: Architecture and security mechanism for healthcare using internet of things. **17**, 1–14 (2025). https://doi.org/10.1177/18479790251315317
6. Saleh, S.S., Mabrouk, T.F., Tarabishi, R.A.: An improved energy-efficient head election protocol for clustering techniques of wireless sensor network (June 2020). Egypt. Informatics J. **22**(4), 439–445 (2021). https://doi.org/10.1016/j.eij.2021.01.003
7. Mugerwa, D., Nam, Y., Choi, H., Kwon, Y., Lee, E.: Enhanced hybrid energy-efficient distributed clustering protocol for IoT-based WSNs with multiple sinks. In: 2023 IEEE Sensors Applications Symposium (SAS), vol. 2023, pp. 1–6. https://doi.org/10.1109/SAS58821.2023.10254043

8. Bedi, P., Das, S., Goyal, S.B., Shukla, P., Mirjalili, S., Kumar, M.: A novel routing protocol based on Grey wolf optimization and Q learning for wireless body area network. Expert Syst. Appl. **210**, 118477 (2022). https://doi.org/10.1016/j.eswa.2022.118477

9. Saleh, H.M., Marouane, H., Fakhfakh, A.: A comprehensive analysis of security challenges and countermeasures in wireless sensor networks enhanced by machine learning and deep learning technologies. Int. J. Saf. Secur. Eng. **14**(2), 373–386 (2024)

10. Arya, G., Bagwari, A., Chauhan, D.S.: Performance analysis of deep learning-based routing protocol for an efficient data transmission in 5G WSN communication. IEEE Access. **10**, 9340 (2022)

11. El Khediri, S., Fakhet, W., Moulahi, T., Khan, R., Thaljaoui, A., Kachouri, A.: Improved node localization using K-means clustering for wireless sensor networks. Comput Sci Rev. **37**, 100284 (2020). https://doi.org/10.1016/j.cosrev.2020.100284

12. Williamson, S.M., Prybutok, V.: Balancing privacy and Progress : a review of privacy challenges, systemic oversight, and patient perceptions in. Appl. Sci. **14**, 675 (2024)

13. Mohammad, A.T., Parchami, J.: Improving diabetic patients monitoring system using (NCA-CNN) algorithm based on IoT. J. Tech. **6**(2), 9–17 (2024). https://doi.org/10.51173/jt.v6i2.2316

14. Liyakathunisa, A., Alsaeedi, S, Jabeen., Kolivand, H.: Ambient assisted living framework for elderly care using internet of medical things, smart sensors, and GRU deep learning techniques. J. Ambient Intell. Smart Environ. **14**(1), 5–23 (2022). https://doi.org/10.3233/AIS-210162

15. Priyadarshi, R., Kumar, R.R., Ranjan, R., Kumar, P.V.: AI-based routing algorithms improve energy efficiency , latency, and data reliability in wireless sensor networks. Sci. Rep. **15**(22292), 1–19 (2025)

16. Kaur, R., Shahrestani, S., Ruan, C.: Security and privacy of wearable wireless sensors in healthcare: a systematic review. Comput. Networks Commun. **2**(1), 17–25 (2024). https://doi.org/10.37256/cnc.2120243852

17. Tasnim, R., Sultana, S., Akter, M., Rashied, M., Mobarak, H., Salma, U.: Machine learning and IoT in healthcare : recent advancements, challenges & future direction. Adv. Biomark. Sci. Technol. **7**, 335–364 (2025). https://doi.org/10.1016/j.abst.2025.08.006

18. Liya, B.S., Krishnamoorthy, R., Arun, S.: An enhanced deep learning-based disease detection model in wireless body area network with energy efficient routing protocol. Wirel. Networks. **30**(4), 2961–2986 (2024). https://doi.org/10.1007/s11276-024-03717-1

19. Sahoo, L., Sen, S.S., Tiwary, K., Moslem, S., Senapati, T.: Improvement of wireless sensor network lifetime via intelligent clustering under uncertainty. IEEE Access. **12**, 25018–25033 (2024)

20. Juwaied, A., Jackowska-strumillo, L., Majchrowicz, M.: Enhanced distributed energy-efficient clustering ( DEEC ) protocol for wireless sensor networks : a modular implementation and performance analysis. Sensors. **25**(13), 4015 (2025)

21. Srinivasan, D., Kiran, A., Parameswari, S., Vellaichamy, J.: Energy efficient hierarchical clustering based dynamic data fusion algorithm for wireless sensor networks in smart agriculture. Sci. Rep. **15**(1), 7207 (2025). https://doi.org/10.1038/s41598-024-85076-7

22. Priyadarshi, R., Kumar, R.R., Ranjan, R., Kumar, P.V.: AI-based routing algorithms improve energy efficiency, latency, and data reliability in wireless sensor networks. Sci. Rep. **15**(1), 22292 (2025). https://doi.org/10.1038/s41598-025-08677-w

23. Goel, S., Guleria, K., Panda, S.N.: Optimization techniques for wireless body area network routing protocols: analysis and comparison. Appl. Data Sci. Smart Syst., 226–235 (2024). https://doi.org/10.1201/9781003471059-32

24. Pushpa, G., Babu, R.A., Subashree, S., Senthilkumar, S.: Optimizing coverage in wireless sensor networks using deep reinforcement learning with graph neural networks. Sci. Rep. **15**(1), 1–21 (2025). https://doi.org/10.1038/s41598-025-01841-2

25. Lu, Y., Li, Y., Zhang, R., Chen, W., Ai, B., Niyato, D.: Graph neural networks for wireless networks: graph representation, architecture and evaluation. IEEE Wirel. Commun. **32**(1), 150–156 (2025)
26. Zakizadeh, M., Erfani, H.: Addressing security challenges in wireless body area sensor networks: a comprehensive analysis and solutions. In: The ... CSI International Symposium on Artificial Intelligence & Signal Processing (Online), pp. 1–7. IEEE (2024)
27. Durr-E-Shahwar, M., Imran, A.B., Altamimi, W., Khan, S, Hussain., Alsaffar, M.: Quantum cryptography for future networks security: a systematic review. IEEE access. **12**, 180048–180078 (2024)
28. Butt, M.O., Waheed, N., Duong, T.Q., Ejaz, W.: Quantum-inspired resource optimization for 6G networks: a survey. IEEE Commun. Surv. tutorials. **27**(5), 2973–3019 (2025)
29. Ferrercid, P., Barcelo-ordinas, J.M., Garcia-vidal, J.: A review of graph-powered data quality applications for IoT monitoring sensor networks. J. Netw. Comput. Appl. **236**(October) (2025)
30. Muthusamy, P., Kumar, S.S., Kanagalakshmi, K., Vignesh, S.B.P.: A hybrid improved unequal secure cluster based distributed routing protocol with quantum key distribution to improve the performance measures in wireless body sensor network. Int. J. Comput. Networks Appl. **11**(4), 407–427 (2024). https://doi.org/10.22247/ijcna/2024/26
31. Sharma, G.: Route optimizations using genetic algorithms for wireless body area networks. In: Route Optimizations Using Genetic Algorithms for Wireless Body Area Networks, pp. 25–32 (2024). https://doi.org/10.1007/978-981-99-6906-7_3
32. Madkar, S., Patil, A., Patil, M., Nigade, A., Pawar, S., Pardeshi, S.: Hybrid optimization algorithm for reliable routing in wireless sensor network. SSRG Int. J. Electr. Electron. Eng. **11**(12), 255–262 (2024). https://doi.org/10.14445/23488379/IJEEE-V11I12P123
33. Raman, D.R., Kumar, V., Pillai, B.G., Rabadiya, D., Patre, S., Meenakshi, R.: Optimizing routes for improved quality of Service in Wireless Sensor Networks through an energy-aware routing protocol for maximizing lifetime. In: 2024 International Conference on Knowledge Engineering and Communication Systems (ICKECS), pp. 1–5 (2024). https://doi.org/10.1109/ICKECS61492.2024.10616757
34. Khoshvaght, P., et al.: H-TERF: a hybrid approach combining fuzzy multi-criteria decision-making techniques and enhanced random forest to improve WBAN-IoT. Internet Things. **32**, 101613 (2025). https://doi.org/10.1016/j.iot.2025.101613
35. Kumar, A., Kamble, S., Rao, S.: Clustering and routing using spiral exploration mechanism with honey badger optimization in wireless sensor network. Indones. J. Electr. Eng. Comput. Sci. **37**, 1734 (2025). https://doi.org/10.11591/ijeecs.v37.i3.pp1734-1743

# Performance and Suitability Analysis of Blockchain Smart Contract Platforms for Enterprise Applications

Ali Amjed Ali Al-Asadi[1]([✉]) [iD], George Lebbos[1], Gaby Abou Haidar[2] [iD], and Hamid Ali Abed Al-Asadi[3] [iD]

[1] Computer Science, American, University of Science and Technology, Beirut, Lebanon
aliamjad692@yahoo.com
[2] Computer and Communications Engineering, American University of Science and Technology, Beirut, Lebanon
gabouhaidar@aust.edu.lb
[3] Department of Computer Science, College of Education for Pure Sciences, University of Basrah, Basrah 61004, Iraq
hamid.abed@uobasrah.edu.iq

**Abstract.** Blockchain technology has emerged as a transformative paradigm with the potential to reshape diverse industries, including finance, supply chain management, and healthcare. Among its most impactful innovations are smart contracts, which enable automated, secure, and transparent execution of agreements, making them relevant for enterprise solutions. This study conducts a rigorous performance evaluation of three leading blockchain platforms, Ethereum, Hyperledger Fabric, and Corda, under varying transaction volumes in the MATLAB simulation platform. Experimental results indicated substantial differences in execution efficiency: Hyperledger Fabric consistently achieved the lowest mean transaction times (ranging from 0.000045 s to 0.000078 s), followed by Corda (0.000748 s to 0.005813 s), while Ethereum exhibited higher latency (0.1055 s to 1.7528 s) and greater variability across transactions. The analysis highlighted the distinctive strengths and limitations of each platform, offering important details about their suitability for different enterprise scenarios. Beyond benchmarking, the paper discusses the implications for organizational adoption, performance trade-offs, and future research directions. These findings clarify our knowledge about blockchain-based smart contract platforms and offer practical guidance for enterprises seeking optimal platform selection.

**Keywords:** Blockchain · Ethereum · Hyperledger Fabric · Corda platforms

## 1 Introduction

Blockchain technology emerged as a solution to the limitations of traditional, centralized transaction systems that rely on third parties. This centralization often creates security vulnerabilities, such as the risk of a single point of failure, and can lead to high transaction fees. Blockchain, by contrast, offers a decentralized approach, enabling interactions


S. O. Al-Mamory et al. (Eds.): 3INC 2025, CCIS 2960, pp. 150–170, 2026.
https://doi.org/10.1007/978-3-032-24239-6_10

in a trustless environment without intermediaries. It serves as a distributed ledger, accurately recording every transaction within its network [1]. Born as Bitcoin's backbone, Blockchain now transcends finance. Smart contracts, self-executing code on its trustless platform, and automated processes, and reliability revolutionize how we interact with this transformative technology [2].

Smart Contracts automate trustless agreements on Blockchain, replacing traditional paperwork with self-executing code. They distribute assets based on agreed terms, eliminating costly intermediaries and simplifying digital agreements [3].

Blockchain's versatility, particularly on platforms like Ethereum [2], fuels the development of robust Smart Contracts. Their self-executing code enforces agreements without third parties, reducing costs compared to traditional systems. Ethereum's user-friendly programming language further enhances the practicality and application of these innovative digital contracts. The concept of smart contracts was first introduced by Szabo in 1994 [4], still it truly came to fruition with the emergence of blockchain technology. In essence, a smart contract acts as a mechanism for distributing digital assets among involved parties once predefined rules are satisfied [5]. For instance, Alice might transfer X currency units to Bob if she receives Y currency units from Carl.

Smart contracts can be "code" or "legal" [6]. This study focuses on code-based smart contracts, stored and executed on blockchains, distinct from legal contract replacements. Ethereum smart contracts, written in Turing-complete Solidity [7, 8], comprise functions, events, and variables. After compilation to EVM bytecode [9, 10], they are deployed on the blockchain with unique addresses, enabling execution and interaction.

Key blockchain technologies encompass Bitcoin Core, Ethereum, and Hyperledger Fabric. Bitcoin Core, operating as a public blockchain network, disseminates transaction records among all participants and updates blocks approximately every 10 min. While it employs a relatively simple scripting language, its extensibility is somewhat limited.

Ethereum, another notable public blockchain, not only maintains transaction history but also supports the execution of smart contracts. This capability distinguishes it from Bitcoin Core, enabling the recording of both traditional transactions and the outcomes of these smart contracts.

Hyperledger Fabric, initiated by the Linux Foundation in December 2015, released its initial version in March 2017, followed by version 1.0 in June of the same year [11]. It differs from the public blockchains by establishing a private network and ledger. Hyperledger Fabric employs a Key-Value Store (KVS) uniquely, which preserves transaction results and stores transaction information alongside hash values of the KVS. This architecture contrasts with the more transparent and open nature of Bitcoin Core and Ethereum.

Corda is an open-source, permissioned enterprise Distributed Ledger Technology (DLT) platform that was specifically tailored for the financial services sector. It was developed by the R3 consortium, which came into existence in 2014, and the actual development of Corda began in 2016 [12]. The R3 consortium covers over 300 organizations and partners from diverse sectors, both in the private and public domains [13].

Corda's design draws inspiration from the progress made in the blockchain industry and introduces a distinctive consensus algorithm built around the concept of notary nodes. The primary function of a notary in Corda is to prevent double spending. To achieve this, for each transaction, a notary verifies that it has not already signed another transaction that consumes any of the same input states. This rigorous verification process effectively mitigates the risk of double spending [14]. In the architecture of Corda, input states are represented as unspent states, reflecting a design principle similar to the unspent transaction output (UTXO) model employed in other blockchain systems. Each input state can be consumed only once within a transaction, after which it becomes invalid and is replaced by new output states. This mechanism ensures transactional integrity, prevents double spending, and maintains the immutability of the ledger. Unlike Ethereum, which relies on an account-based model, Corda's state-based approach provides fine-grained control over assets and contractual obligations, making it particularly suitable for enterprise environments where transaction traceability and legal enforceability are critical.

The major objectives of the proposed blockchain smart contract platforms for enterprise applications were to enhance operational efficiency, ensure transparency and data integrity, cut costs by automating crucial procedures, and remove middlemen.

## 2  Related Works

This framework leverages blockchain to verify digital evidence authenticity. Authorized parties evaluate its reliability and relevance on the blockchain itself. A "Global Digital Timeline" tracks events related to evidence, boosting traceability and non-repudiation [15]. Additionally, blockchain-integrated SDN in IoT analyzes network data from devices using signatures on packets containing crucial information like user IDs and timestamps [16]. This ensures secure evidence handling and integrity, with tamper-proof recording of evidence hashes.

Alibaba Cloud's LedgerDB is a centralized alternative to blockchains in non-critical situations. It offers blockchain-like security (tamper-proof records, irrefutability) with better performance (80x higher throughput than Hyperledger Fabric) [17]. Its two-way audit trail safeguards against user/provider fraud. Selective data deletion balances verifiability with storage concerns.

In the context of maintaining evidence integrity in digital environments such as smart homes, specialized management systems are used. They enhance the process of obtaining digital evidence through intelligent, automated discovery and advanced record-keeping, addressing key security challenges [18].

Authors in [19] tackled video evidence integrity using blockchain. Their cloud evidence model combined blockchain and SDN for secure evidence gathering with a new data protection algorithm, proven more effective than centralized methods in simulations [20].

PRoFIT safeguards IoT evidence collection, balancing research integrity with individual privacy [21]. A blockchain-based EHR system stored in IPFS and integrated with Ethereum transactions protects against doctor-CSP collusion and tampering, guaranteeing EHR integrity and accurate timestamps for legal/medical audits. Its efficiency and resilience to cyberattacks were validated through simulations and evaluations [22].

IoT forensics research focuses on diverse device data and its interconnectedness, integrating it into blockchain for evidence authenticity and traceability [23]. Another study tackled medical record security with a blockchain-encryption model, enabling access control and confidentiality for patient data [24].

Reliable digital evidence collection is addressed with blockchain-smart contract systems to manage evidence and evaluate effectiveness in legal proceedings [25]. Blockchain's capability in terms of evidence generation, like provenance and transparency, are leveraged to create a system for verifying authenticity and enhancing legal evidence management [26].

Finally, the paper discusses the limitations of mere data hashing for security, highlighting the absence of timestamped hash creation. To address this, a blockchain-based method using public blockchains was developed, enhancing data security and transparency. This model enables continuous, transparent monitoring, and evaluation of evidence by court stakeholders, paving the way for future research in this field [27].

## 3 Methodology

A performance and suitability analysis of three leading blockchain smart contract platforms—Ethereum, Hyperledger Fabric, and Corda—within the context of enterprise applications was provided. The methodology commences with the systematic collection of empirical data from a smart contract repository, establishing the foundation for a structured tripartite evaluation in which each analytical stage is dedicated to one platform, as illustrated in Fig. 1.

Smart contract execution is rigorously examined using platform-specific benchmarking tools to evaluate transaction throughput, latency, scalability, and reliability. The findings are then synthesized into a cross-platform comparison, highlighting the distinctive architectural designs, operational trade-offs, and enterprise applicability of each platform. This analytical approach provides both a performance-oriented and suitability-driven perspective, offering valuable insights for organizations and researchers seeking to align blockchain platform capabilities with enterprise requirements.

### 3.1 Data Collection

Detailed performance data for Ethereum, Corda, and Hyperledger Fabric was collected via in-depth simulations replicating each platform's unique features. The research analyzed performance across Ethereum, Corda, and Hyperledger Fabric. Ethereum simulations use emulated users and smart contracts within a virtual EVM, capturing core functionality. Corda simulations focus on a network of participants engaging in private, inter-business transactions, analyzing states, contracts, and agreements. Hyperledger Fabric simulations replicate a permissioned network with defined roles, capturing the real-world transaction endorsement and commitment process. This platform-specific approach yields deep insights into each technology's strengths and limitations.

Simulated transactions across Ethereum, Corda, and Fabric capture details like parties, amounts, and outcomes. The data enables platform comparisons, revealing performance, scalability, and diverse application suitability.

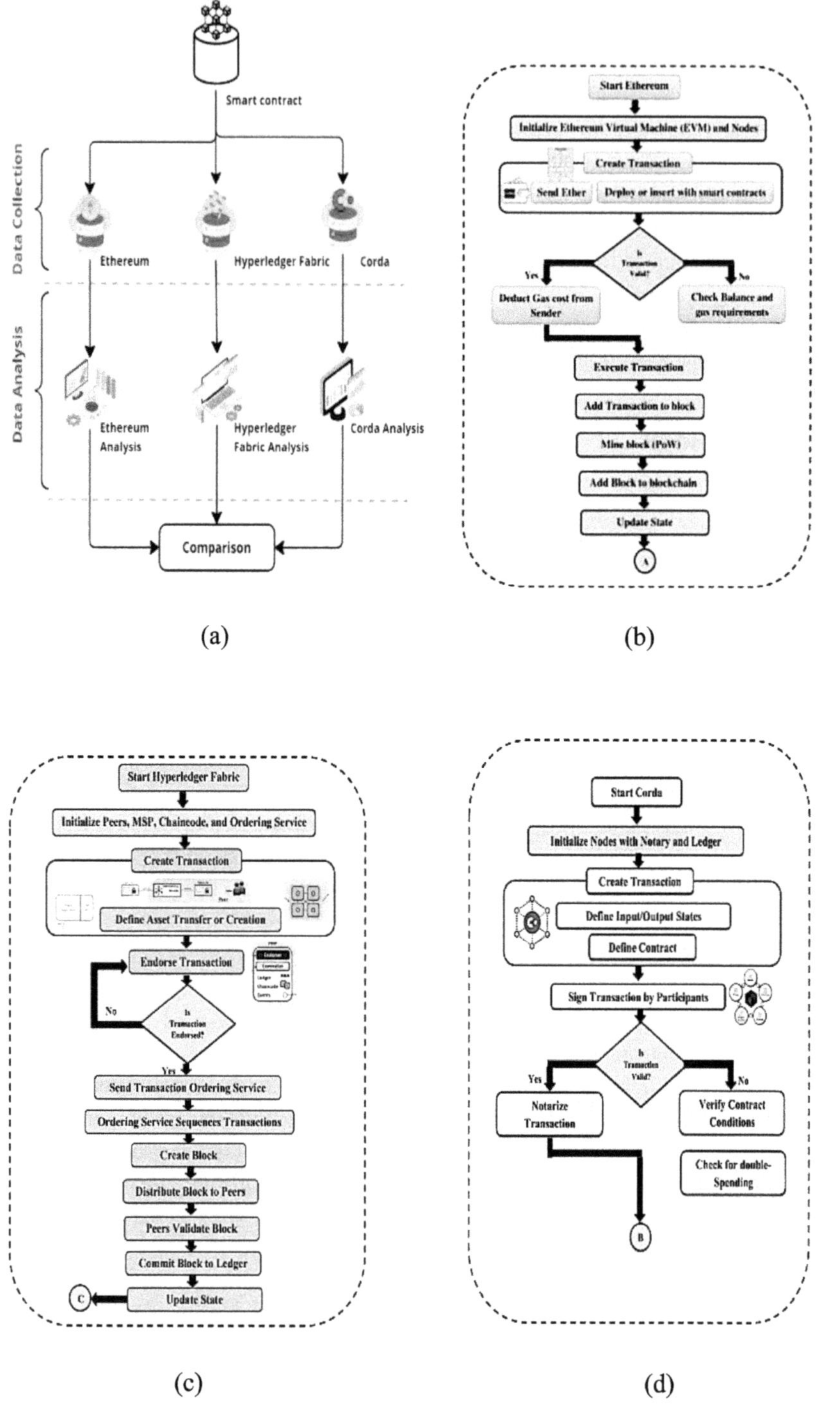



**Fig. 1.** Proposed Approach (a) the main Block diagram, (b) Ethereum, (c) Hyperledger Fabric, and (d) Corda Platforms.

## 3.2  Data Analysis

Simulated data from Ethereum, Corda, and Fabric blockchains were analyzed. Visualizations like bar plots revealed transaction volume distribution and platform activity levels. Boxplots unveiled statistical insights into transaction values and processing times, including outliers and variability.

Simulations of Ethereum, Corda, and Fabric revealed performance through detailed visualizations. Boxplots compare transaction values and processing times, pinpointing outliers. CDF plots showed efficiency by revealing the probability of transactions meeting time/cost thresholds. Density plots represented data points for deeper insights into transaction size and timing patterns, beyond basic bar charts.

Collectively, these visual and statistical tools equip us with a comprehensive understanding of the datasets from each blockchain platform. They enable a quantifiable evaluation of the platforms' performances and form the foundation for a thorough comparative analysis, essential for drawing informed conclusions and formulating recommendations in this research.

To obtain all distinct token addresses used in token transfers, we first executed a query against the Ethereum public dataset stored on Google BigQuery (bigQuery_token_adds.csv). The dataset's public repository, erc20_token_adds.csv, contains the list. The auxiliary data in this dataset include the script (etherscan_API_query. ipynb) that is used to query the Etherscan API and the initial token list (bigQuery_token_adds. csv).

The main blockchain smart contract simulation environments for enterprise applications are a combination of local development environments and specialized simulation frameworks offered by well-known platforms such as Hyperledger Fabric, Ethereum (Ganache/Hardhat), and Blocksim. Before being deployed in the real world, these technologies enable testing security, functionality, and performance in a controlled setting.

The following table lists the hardware details of the proposed work as shown in Table 1.

**Table 1.** Summary of hardware and operating systems.

| Device | CPU | Operating System | Memory | Hard Disk | Platform |
|---|---|---|---|---|---|
| Microsoft Surface Book 2 | Intel Core i7-8650U 4.2 GHz max | Windows 7 Pro (64-bit) | 8 GB | 256 GB | Ethereum |
| Dell XPS 13 9300 | Intel Core i7-1065G7 3.9 GHz max | Windows 7 Home | 8 GB | 230 GB | Hyperledger Fabric |
| aspberry Pi 3 Model B | Quad-core ARM Cortex A53, 1.2 GHz | Raspberry Pi OS Lite | 512 MB SDRAM | 8 GB (microSD card) | Ethereum |

## 4  Evaluation Metrics

This section defines a suite of quantitative metrics for assessing the performance of blockchain platforms, focusing on transaction times recorded during simulations. Each metric is articulated through an equation, offering a standardized methodology for evaluating and comparing the efficiencies of the Ethereum, Corda, and Hyperledger Fabric platforms.

Count: This metric represents the total number of transactions processed on the blockchain.

$$Cont = N \tag{1}$$

Where is the number of transactions in the dataset.

Mean: This metric calculates the average transaction time.

$$\text{Mean} = \frac{1}{N} \sum_{i=1}^{N} T_i \tag{2}$$

Where $(T_i)$ is the transaction time for the $(i^{th})$ transaction, and $( N )$ is the total number of transactions.

Standard Deviation (std) [28]: Measures the variation or dispersion of transaction times.

$$\text{std} = \sqrt{\frac{\sum_{i=1}^{N} (T_i - \text{Mean})^2}{N - 1}} \tag{3}$$

Where $(T_i)$ is each individual transaction time, and Mean is the mean transaction time.

Minimum (min): Identifies the shortest transaction time.

$$\min = \min(T_1, T_2, \ldots, T_N) \tag{4}$$

Percentiles [29]: These metrics capture specific points in the distribution of transaction times, namely the 25th 50th (median), and 75th percentiles.

$$P_{25} = T_{(0.25 \cdot N)} \tag{5}$$

$$\text{Median}(P_{50}) = T_{(0.5 \cdot N)} \tag{6}$$

$$P_{75} = T_{(0.75 \cdot N)} \tag{7}$$

Where $(T_{(k \cdot N)})$ represents the transaction time at the $(k^{th})$ percentile, with $( k )$ being 0.25, 0.5, or 0.75, and $( N )$ is the number of transactions.

Maximum (max): This metric determines the longest transaction time.

$$\max = \max(T_1, T_2, \ldots, T_N) \tag{8}$$

These equations form the foundation for a robust and comprehensive analysis of the blockchain platforms, allowing for a detailed comparison of their transaction processing capabilities.

## 5 Experiment Results

### 5.1 Ethereum Results

Ethereum simulations across individual, small group, and larger transaction clusters (repeated for accuracy) revealed different processing times for each type. Single transaction analysis showed an average of 105.5 s with significant variation (minimum 48 s, maximum 259 s), indicating moderate fluctuations in individual processing times. Ethereum groups of 10 transactions showed longer processing times (avg. 326.9 s) with increased variation (SD 97.75 s). Minimum and maximum times (180–487 s) suggest greater inconsistency as transaction volume rises.

Ethereum's 100-transaction batch averages a whopping 1753 s (SD 604), suggesting scalability constraints. Times range from 707 to 2932 s highlight a significant inconsistency and potential network limitations.

Analyzing 25th, 50th, and 75th percentiles showed Ethereum's processing times explode with volume. Median time increased from 93 s (1 transaction) to 322 s (10) and 1813 s (100), revealing non-linear growth and potential scalability challenges. Standard deviation and range further detail variability and extremes in processing times.

Table 2 summarizes these descriptive statistics and effectively encapsulates the Ethereum blockchain's transaction processing performance across the three different transaction volumes.

**Table 2.** Statistics for the Ethereum Transaction Processing Times.

| Metric | 1 Transaction | 10 Transactions | 100 Transactions |
|---|---|---|---|
| Count | 10.000 | 10.000 | 100.000 |
| Mean | 105.500 | 326.900 | 1752.830 |
| Std | 59.841 | 97.753 | 604.129 |
| Min | 48.000 | 180.000 | 707.000 |
| 25% | 69.750 | 249.250 | 1216.250 |
| 50% (Median) | 93.000 | 321.500 | 1813.500 |
| 75% | 105.500 | 407.750 | 2213.500 |

Figure 2 reveals Ethereum's average transaction times skyrocketing with volume. Single transactions see the fastest processing (shortest bar), while 10 and especially 100 transactions show drastic increases in average time (tallest bar), suggesting significant scalability challenges as network load grows.

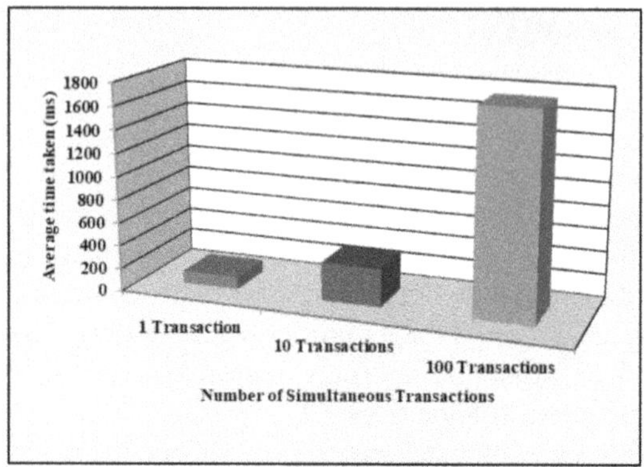

**Fig. 2.** Ethereum Average Transaction Time for Different Transaction Volumes.

Figure 3 shows Ethereum transaction time variability across volumes. Single transactions (tight box) have minimal variation, while 10 transactions (slightly larger box) and especially 100 transactions (wide box and whiskers) experience increasing dispersion and outliers, suggesting greater impact of network load on processing time consistency.

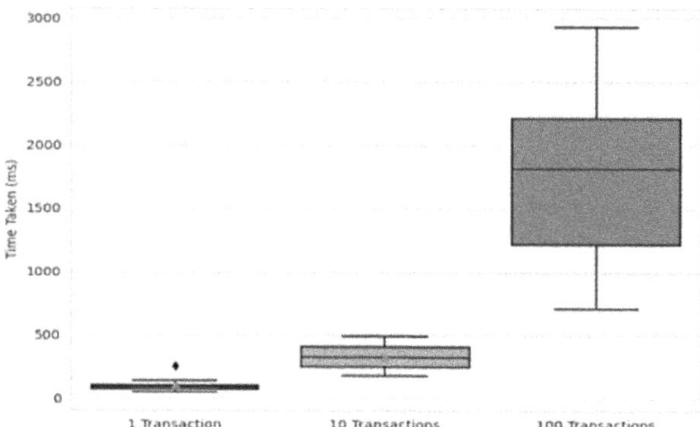

**Fig. 3.** Ethereum Boxplot of Transaction Times.

Figure 4 plots Ethereum transaction completion odds. Single transactions finish fastest (curve reaches 100% quickly), while 10 and 100 transaction curves shift right, meaning more take longer, suggesting increased processing times with higher volumes.

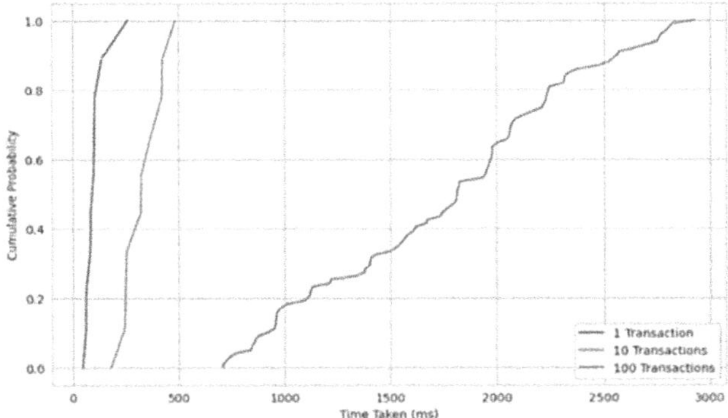

**Fig. 4.** Ethereum CDF of Transaction Times.

Figure 5 shows Ethereum transaction time distribution shifting with volume. Single transactions form a tight peak (fast and consistent), while 10 and 100 transactions flatten and broaden, indicating wider range and less common processing times. 100 transactions show the lowest, broadest peak, suggesting high diversity and no dominant processing time.

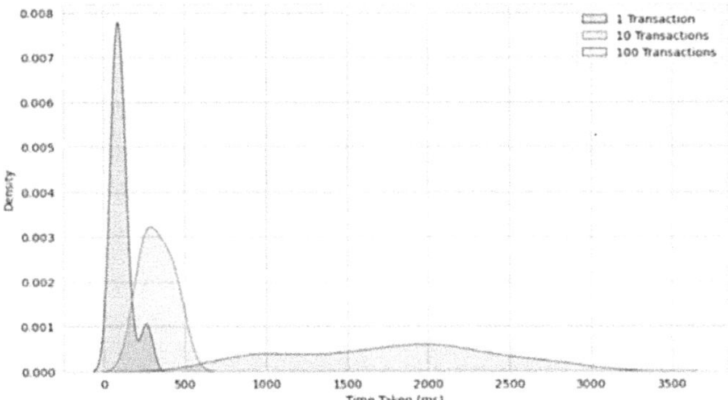

**Fig. 5.** Ethereum Density Plot of Transaction Times.

Collectively, these figures offer a comprehensive visual analysis of the Ethereum platform's transaction processing performance under varying loads. They effectively illustrate how increased transaction volumes impact average times, variability, and the distribution of transaction processing times.

## 5.2  Hyperledger Fabric Results

The performance results for Hyperledger Fabric are presented focusing on its efficiency in managing varying transaction volumes. The simulations encompassed scenarios with 1, 10, and 100 transactions, allowing us to assess the platform's responsiveness and scalability.

Hyperledger Fabric indicates consistent performance across transaction volumes (1, 10, 100). Mean times stay exceptionally low: 0.000045 s for 1 transaction, rising slightly to 0.000078 s for 100. Even the highest standard deviation (0.000195 s for 100) remains minimal. This suggests efficient, predictable transaction processing regardless of volume.

Hyperledger Fabric demonstrates lightning-fast transactions (min time 0.000014 s for 100), while percentiles show consistent processing times across volumes. This suggests reliable performance and a majority of transactions completed within a similar timeframe.

However, it's noteworthy that the maximum recorded time for 100 transactions stands at 0.001523 s, which appears as an outlier compared to the maximum times for 1 and 10 transactions. Despite this outlier, the overall trend indicates that Hyperledger Fabric can efficiently handle larger transaction volumes with only a marginal increase in average processing time. This underscores its potential for high-throughput and stable performance, particularly in enterprise-level applications as shown in Table 3.

**Table 3.** Statistics for Hyperledger Fabric Transaction Processing Times.

| Metric | 1 Transaction | 10 Transactions | 100 Transactions |
| --- | --- | --- | --- |
| Count | 10.000 | 10.000 | 100.000 |
| Mean | 0.000045 | 0.000049 | 0.000078 |
| Std | 0.000013 | 0.000016 | 0.000195 |
| Min | 0.000025 | 0.000019 | 0.000014 |
| 25% | 0.000036 | 0.000046 | 0.000027 |
| 50% (Median) | 0.000045 | 0.000051 | 0.000037 |
| 75% | 0.000055 | 0.000061 | 0.000049 |

Figure 6 shows near-constant average transaction times (1e-5 s) despite rising volumes (1, 10, 100 transactions). Minimal increases suggest remarkable efficiency and scalability in transaction processing.

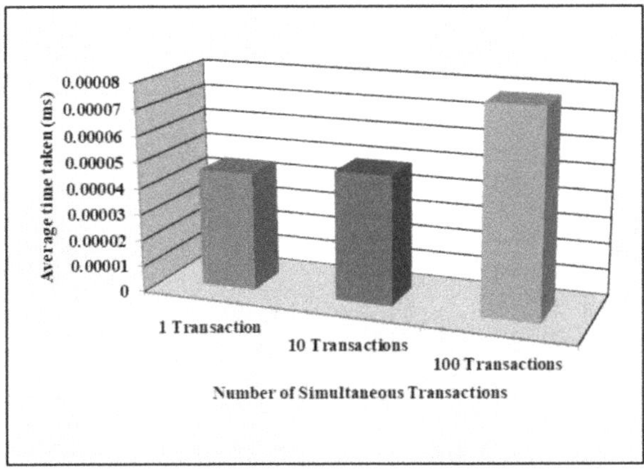


**Fig. 6.** Hyperledger Fabric Average Transaction Time for Different Transaction Volumes.

Figure 7 shows Hyperledger Fabric's transaction time variability. Single and 10 transactions have tight distributions and fast medians (clustered at box bottom), suggesting rapid processing for most. While still fast, 100 transactions show wider range and outliers, indicating some take longer than the median.

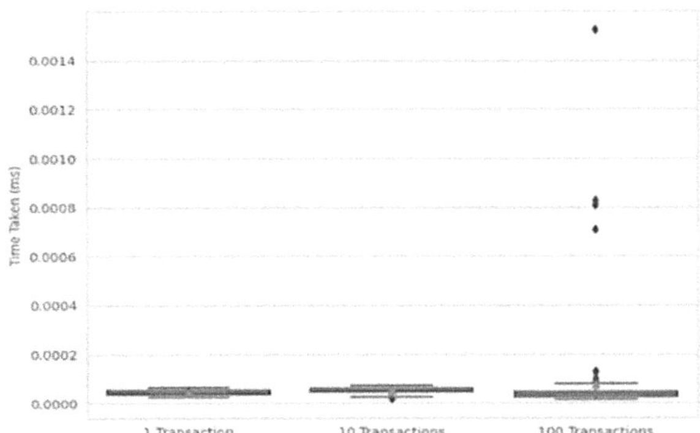


**Fig. 7.** Hyperledger Fabric Boxplot of Transaction Times.

Figure8 plots "Cumulative Distribution Function of Transaction Times" of Hyperledger Fabric. Overlapping curves for 1, 10, and 100 transactions show near-instantaneous completion for most of the transactions. A slight rightward shift for 100 reveals marginally longer possibilities; however, all remain swift.

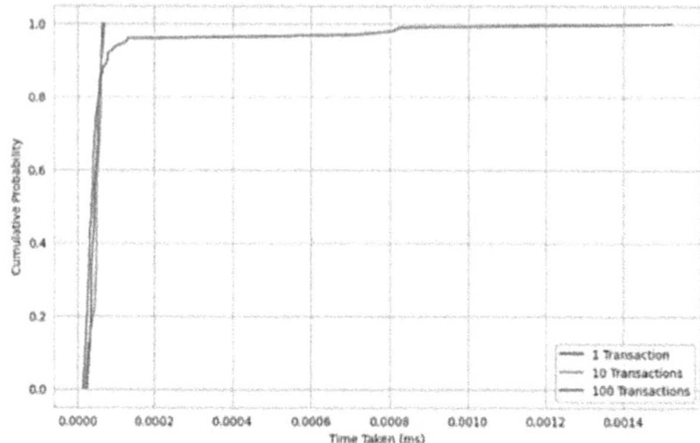

**Fig. 8.** Hyperledger Fabric CDF of Transaction Times.

Figure 9 plots Hyperledger Fabric's speed and consistency. Single and 10 transactions peak sharply (clustering around fast, common processing time), while 100 has a wider base (more spread, still mostly fast). This highlights Fabric's exceptional ability to handle transactions swiftly, even at higher volumes.

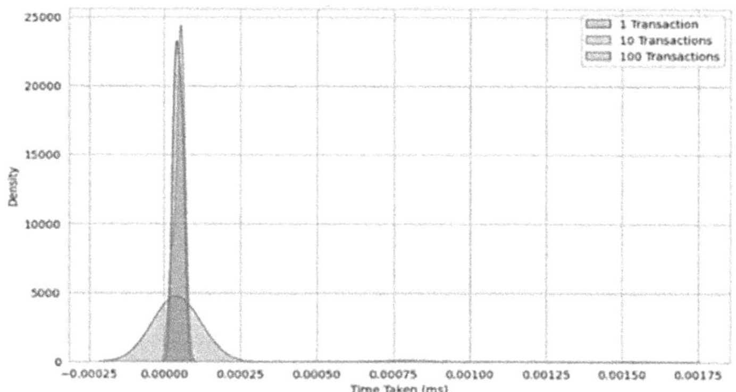

**Fig. 9.** Hyperledger Fabric Density Plot of Transaction.

## 5.3 Corda Results

Corda performance analysis focuses on transaction processing across individual and batch scenarios (1, 10, 100 transactions). Consistent processing counts (10 for 1–10, 100 for 100) ensure fair statistical comparisons, enabling insights into Corda's behavior under different workloads.

An interesting trend emerges in the mean transaction time. It showcases a consistent decrease as the number of transactions increases. For a single transaction, the mean time stands at 0.005813 s, notably dropping to 0.001947 s for 10 transactions, and further plummeting to 0.000748 s when handling 100 transactions. This trend suggests that

Corda's transaction processing becomes increasingly time-efficient as the volume of transactions grows, hinting at potential optimizations in batch processing.

The standard deviation values provide insights into the variability of transaction times. Notably, with 1 transaction, the standard deviation is relatively high at 0.005468 s, indicating greater inconsistency in transaction times. However, as the transaction volume increases to 10 and 100 transactions, the standard deviation decreases to 0.002839 and 0.001678 s, respectively. This suggests that with a larger number of transactions, the variability in processing time decreases, signifying more predictable and consistent performance.

Corda boasts impressive processing speeds, with exceptionally low minimum times across volumes (0.000115 s for 100 transactions). However, transaction times still vary. While most finish quickly (median 0.0043 s for 1, 0.000578 s for 100), some outliers linger (up to 0.0128 s for 100). Percentiles reveal this distribution.

An intriguing observation pertains to the maximum transaction time. For 1 transaction, it reaches 0.018454 s but significantly decreases with larger transaction volumes. Specifically, the maximum time for 100 transactions is 0.012804 s. This observation suggests that Corda might optimize the processing of transactions more efficiently when handled in larger batches, resulting in improved throughput.

In summary, these findings indicate that Corda manages increased transaction volumes, exhibiting a noteworthy decrease in average transaction time as batch sizes grow. Moreover, it maintains a reasonably consistent processing time across transactions within these batches, hinting at its efficiency and scalability in handling diverse workloads as shown in Table 4.

**Table 4.** Statistics for Corda Transaction.

| Metric | 1 Transaction | 10 Transactions | 100 Transactions |
|---|---|---|---|
| Count | 10.000000 | 10.000000 | 100.000000 |
| Mean | 0.005813 | 0.001947 | 0.000748 |
| Std | 0.005468 | 0.002839 | 0.001678 |
| Min | 0.000304 | 0.000128 | 0.000115 |
| 25% | 0.002415 | 0.000172 | 0.000154 |
| 50% (Median) | 0.004332 | 0.000204 | 0.000240 |
| 75% | 0.008445 | 0.002983 | 0.000578 |
| Max | 0.018454 | 0.007272 | 0.012804 |

A counterintuitive trend is illustrated in Fig. 10. Contrary to expectations, Corda's average transaction time exhibits a significant decrease as batch size increases. Notably, processing times for 100 transactions drop below those for 10 and even single transactions. This suggests potential hidden mechanisms within Corda that optimize efficiency for bulk transaction processing, warranting further investigation.

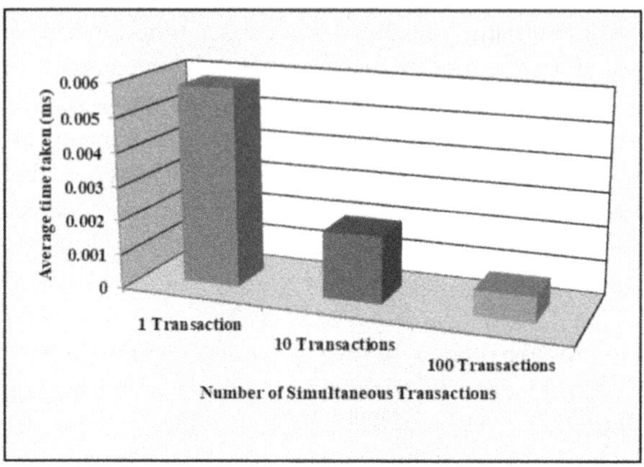



**Fig. 10.** Corda Average Transaction Time for Different Transaction Volumes.

Figure 11 reveals a counterintuitive trend in Corda's transaction processing times. Despite concerns about potential scalability limitations, median processing times (green triangles) decrease steadily across volumes, with even 100 transactions achieving faster average speeds than smaller batches. However, the presence of outliers in the 100-transaction boxplot warrants further investigation to understand the cause of these extended processing durations. This finding suggests Corda might employ hidden mechanisms optimizing bulk transaction processing efficiency, presenting interesting avenues for future research.

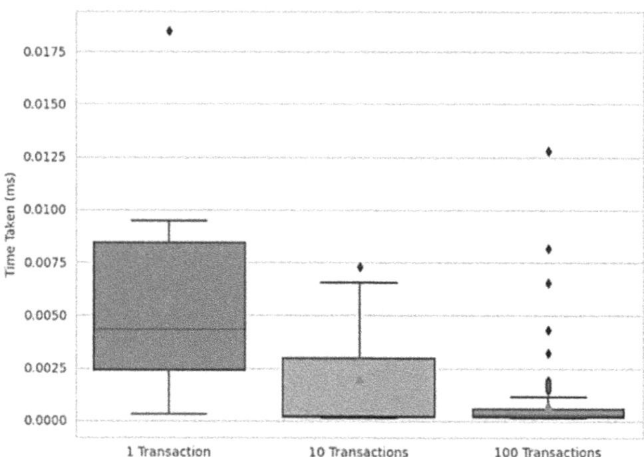



**Fig. 11.** Corda Boxplot of Transaction Times.

Figure 12 represents the "CDF of Transaction Times" for Corda. This graph shows the cumulative probability of transaction completion times. The CDF lines for 1 and 10 transactions show a steep curve, quickly reaching a high probability, indicating that most transactions are processed in a short amount of time. The CDF for 100 transactions is less steep, suggesting a wider spread in transaction times with a higher likelihood of longer completion times.

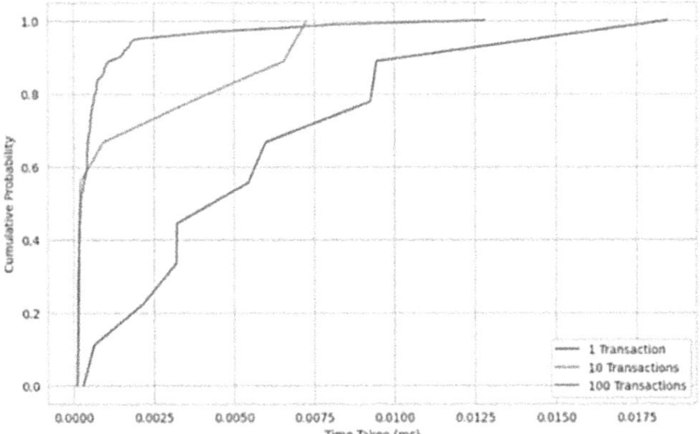

**Fig. 12.** Corda CDF of Transaction Times.

Figure 13 presents the "Density Plot of Transaction Times" for Corda. This plot displays the probability density for the transaction times of 1, 10, and 100 transactions. The sharp peak for 1 transaction signifies a high probability density around a specific short time, indicating that most transactions are completed very quickly. As the number of transactions increases to 10 and 100, the density plots spread out, showing a wider range of transaction times. It still indicates that the majority of transactions are processed in a short timeframe.

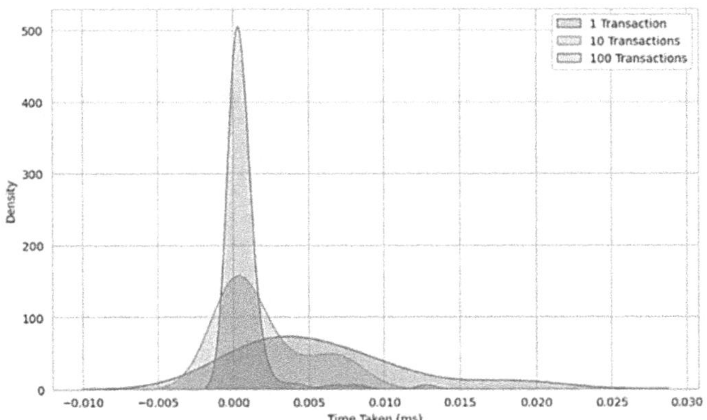

**Fig. 13.** Corda Density Plot of Transaction Times.

Collectively, these figures offer a comprehensive visual analysis of Corda's transaction processing times. They suggest that while there is higher variability in transaction times with larger volumes, Corda generally processes larger batches of transactions with increased time efficiency.

## 6  Empirical Evaluation of Smart Contract Platform Performance for Enterprise Applications

The comparative results of transaction processing performance, as presented in Table 4, provide a detailed empirical foundation for evaluating the operational suitability of Ethereum, Hyperledger Fabric, and Corda in enterprise contexts. By systematically examining mean execution time, standard deviation, minimum and maximum times, as well as percentiles across varying transaction volumes (1, 10, and 100 transactions), the analysis highlights critical differences in scalability, consistency, and efficiency key factors for enterprise adoption.

Ethereum exhibits a pronounced sensitivity to transaction volume. For a single transaction, the mean execution time is 0.1055 s, with a standard deviation of 0.0598 s, a minimum of 0.048 s, and a maximum of 0.259 s, indicating moderate variability. As the transaction count increases to 10, the mean rises to 0.3269 s, with standard deviation expanding to 0.0978 s, min 0.18, max 0.487, and the $25^{th}$–$75^{th}$ percentile range widening from 0.24925 to 0.40775 s, reflecting growing unpredictability. At 100 transactions, Ethereum's mean execution time surges to 1.7528 s, with a standard deviation of 0.6041 s, min 0.707 s, and max 2.932 s, highlighting significant latency and variability under high load, which may constrain real-time or high-throughput enterprise applications.

By contrast, Hyperledger Fabric demonstrates remarkably stable performance. For 1, 10, and 100 transactions, mean execution times are 0.000045, 0.000049, and 0.000078 s, respectively, with very low standard deviations (0.000013, 0.000016, 0.000195) and narrow min–max ranges (0.000025–0.000066 s for 100 transactions). The $25^{th}$, median, and $75^{th}$ percentiles remain tightly clustered, confirming deterministic behavior and minimal variability. This consistency indicates that Fabric can reliably handle large transaction volumes, making it ideal for enterprise applications requiring both speed and predictable throughput, such as financial clearing or healthcare data management.

Corda displays a distinctive performance pattern. For a single transaction, the mean execution time is 0.005813 s, with a standard deviation of 0.005468, min 0.000304, and max 0.018454, reflecting higher variability for isolated transactions. Interestingly, as the number of transactions increases to 10 and 100, mean execution times decrease to 0.001947 and 0.000748 s, standard deviations drop to 0.002839 and 0.001678, and max values fall to 0.007272 and 0.012804 s, suggesting batch-level optimizations in consensus and processing. The $25^{th}$–$75^{th}$ percentile ranges also narrow with higher transaction volumes, indicating that Corda can achieve efficient and predictable performance when handling grouped transactions, which aligns well with enterprise scenarios involving multi-party contracts and batch processing of obligations.

Collectively, the detailed values in Table 5 illustrate clear trade-offs across the platforms. Ethereum offers flexibility and programmability but suffers from increasing latency and variability at scale. Hyperledger Fabric provides consistently fast, deterministic performance, supporting high-volume enterprise operations. Corda, while exhibiting higher variability for single transactions, demonstrates efficiency improvements under batch processing, making it particularly suitable for contractual and multi-party enterprise applications. These insights provide an evidence-based framework for aligning blockchain platform selection with enterprise performance and suitability requirements.

**Table 5.** Transaction Processing Performance Across Blockchain Smart Contract Platforms.

| Blockchain Platform | Transaction Volume | Mean Time | Std Deviation | Min Time | 25th Percentile | Median Time | 75th Percentile | Max Time |
| --- | --- | --- | --- | --- | --- | --- | --- | --- |
| Ethereum | 1 Transaction<br>10 Transactions<br>100 Transactions | 0.1055<br>0.3269<br>1.75283 | 0.059841<br>0.097753<br>0.604129 | 0.048<br>0.18<br>0.707 | 0.06975<br>0.24925<br>1.21625 | 0.093<br>0.3215<br>1.8135 | 0.1055<br>0.40775<br>2.2135 | 0.259<br>0.487<br>2.932 |
| Hyperledger Fabric | 1 Transaction<br>10 Transactions<br>100 Transactions | 0.000045<br>0.000049<br>0.000078 | 0.000013<br>0.000016<br>0.000195 | 0.000025<br>0.000019<br>0.000014 | 0.000036<br>0.000046<br>0.000027 | 0.000045<br>0.000051<br>0.000037 | 0.000055<br>0.000061<br>0.000049 | 0.000066<br>0.000072<br>0.001523 |
| Corda | 1 Transaction<br>10 Transactions<br>100 Transactions | 0.005813<br>0.001947<br>0.000748 | 0.005468<br>0.002839<br>0.001678 | 0.000304<br>0.000128<br>0.000115 | 0.002415<br>0.000172<br>0.000154 | 0.004332<br>0.000204<br>0.00024 | 0.008445<br>0.002983<br>0.000578 | 0.018454<br>0.007272<br>0.012804 |

# 7    Conclusion and Future Works

A comparative analysis of blockchain-based smart contract platforms tailored for enterprise applications was carried out. Three blockchain platforms, Ethereum, Fabric, and Corda, each possess unique strengths and limitations for enterprise. Ethereum's smart contracts and future prospects stand out, but scalability and cost concerns loom. Fabric excels in speed and consistency, while Corda intrigues with batch processing efficiency. Choosing the right platform depends on specific needs and priorities.

Hyperledger Fabric emerges as a robust and consistent performer, with consistently low transaction times across varying transaction volumes. Its permissioned architecture and modular nature make it an attractive choice for businesses seeking high throughput and tailored customization. However, its architectural complexity and resource-intensive deployment and maintenance aspects warrant careful attention.

The findings concerning Corda underscore its suitability for managing financial transactions, demonstrating efficient batch processing and a strong emphasis on privacy. While its specialization makes it an excellent fit for the financial sector, enterprises outside this sector may find its narrower focus less accommodating to their broader needs.

Enterprise blockchain adoption necessitates a nuanced approach. Platform selection hinges on factors like transaction volume, latency tolerance, economic constraints, privacy demands, and industry specifics.

Experimental results indicated substantial differences in execution efficiency: Hyperledger Fabric consistently achieved the lowest mean transaction times (ranging from 0.000045 s to 0.000078 s), followed by Corda (0.000748 s to 0.005813 s), while Ethereum exhibited higher latency (0.1055 s to 1.7528 s) and greater variability across transactions. The analysis highlights the distinctive strengths and limitations of each platform, providing critical insights into their suitability for different enterprise scenarios.

Future research endeavors should explore network influences, advanced smart contract functionalities, seamless enterprise integration, and user-centric adoption processes. Ongoing assessments of technological advancements and user experiences are crucial in navigating the dynamic blockchain landscape and gauging its true transformative potential within business environments.

Beyond Ethereum, Fabric, and Corda lies a rich tapestry of diverse blockchains. Examining platforms with unique attributes and ongoing advancements could unlock untapped potential for specific needs. Additionally, delving beyond basic transactions to simulate intricate real-world scenarios – encompassing multi-contract interactions, privacy concerns, and regulatory compliance – would offer unparalleled insights into how each platform navigates complex enterprise operations. This deeper exploration promises to illuminate the diverse ways blockchain can truly transform business landscapes.

The impact of network conditions on blockchain performance represents another crucial facet warranting exploration. Factors such as network latency, bandwidth limitations, and node distribution can profoundly affect a blockchain's performance. Future investigations could simulate diverse network conditions to evaluate their influence on transaction processing times and overall network efficiency.

Seamless enterprise integration, cost analysis, and platform evolution offer rich research avenues. Explore challenges and best practices for bridging blockchain and existing systems. Unpack cost implications beyond fees, including infrastructure and scalability. Track innovations in consensus, scaling solutions, and interoperability to stay ahead of the curve. These efforts deepen knowledge and ensure understanding remains relevant in the dynamic blockchain landscape.

## References


1. M. Paul: What is the blockchain and smart contracts? Brief introduction. Medium Start Up for Blockchain (2017)
2. Rosic, A.: Smart Contracts: the Blockchain Technology that Will Replace Lawyers. Blockgeeks (2017)
3. Anonymous, A.N., Miller, A.: Research for practice: cryptocurrencies, blockchain, and smart contracts. In: Internet Measurement Conference, pp. 1–12 (2016)
4. Szabo, N.: Formalizing and Securing Relationships on Public Networks. First Monday (1997)
5. V.: Buterin: a Next-Generation Smart Contract and Decentralized Application Platform. White Paper (2013)
6. Stark, J.: Making Sense of Blockchain Smart Contracts. Coindesk (2017)
7. Frantz, C.K., Nowostawski, M.: From institutions to code: towards automated generation of smart contracts. In: Proceedings IEEE 1st International Workshops on Foundations and Applications of Self-Systems, pp. 210–215 (2016)
8. Kim, S., Deka, G.C.: Advanced Applications of Blockchain Technology, vol. 60. Springer, Singapore (2020)

9. Watanabe, H., Fujimura, S., Nakadaira, A., Miyazaki, Y., Akutsu, A., Kishigami, J.J.: Blockchain contract: a complete consensus using blockchain. In: Proceedings *IEEE 4th Global Conference on Consumer Electronics (GCCE)*, pp. 577–578 (2015)
10. Pinna, A., Ibba, S., Baralla, G., Tonelli, R., Marchesi, M.: A massive analysis of Ethereum smart contracts: empirical study and code metrics. IEEE Access. **7**, 78194–78213 (2019)
11. Honar Pajooh, H., Rashid, M., Alam, F., Demidenko, S.: Hyperledger fabric blockchain for securing the edge internet of things. Sensors. **21**(2), 359 (2021)
12. R3: The R3 story. https://www.r3.com/about/, last accessed Mar. 15, (2019)
13. R3: R3 (company). https://en.wikipedia.org/wiki/R3, (2023)
14. R3: Consensus and notaries. https://docs.corda.net/releases/release-M9.2/key-concepts-con sensus-notaries.html, (2023)
15. Ghimire, S., Choi, J.Y., Lee, B.: Using blockchain for improved video integrity verification. IEEE Trans. Multimedia. **22**(1), 108–121 (2020)
16. Pourvahab, M., Ekbatanifard, G.: Digital forensics architecture for evidence collection and provenance preservation in IaaS cloud environment using SDN and blockchain technology. IEEE Access. **7**, 153349–153364 (2019)
17. Yang, X., et al.: LedgerDB: a centralized ledger database for universal audit and verification. Proc. VLDB Endowment. **13**(12), 3138–3151 (2020)
18. Sun, J., Yao, X., Wang, S., Wu, Y.: Non-repudiation storage and access control scheme of insurance data based on blockchain in IPFS. IEEE Access. **8**, 155145–155155 (2020)
19. Li, S., Qin, T., Min, G.: Blockchain-based digital forensics investigation framework in the internet of things and social systems. IEEE Trans. Comput. Social Syst. **6**(6), 1433–1441 (2019)
20. Lusetti, M., Salsi, L., Dallatana, A.: A blockchain based solution for the custody of digital files in forensic medicine. Forensic Sci. Int.: Digital Invest. **35**, 301017 (2020)
21. Petroni, B.C.A., Gonçalves, R.F., de Arruda Ignácio, P.S., Reis, J.Z., Martins, G.J.D.U.: Smart contracts applied to a functional architecture for storage and maintenance of digital chain of custody using blockchain. Forensic Sci. Int.: Digit. Invest. **34**, 300985 (2020)
22. Ramesh, D., Mishra, R., Atrey, P.K., Edla, D.R., Misra, S., Qi, L.: Blockchain based efficient tamper-proof EHR storage for decentralized cloud-assisted storage. Alex. Eng. J. **68**, 205–226 (2023)
23. Burri, X., Casey, E., Bollé, T., Jaquet-Chiffelle, D.-O.: Chronological independently verifiable electronic chain of custody ledger using blockchain technology. Forensic Sci. Int.: Digit. Invest. **33**, 300976 (2020)
24. Gürsoy, G., Brannon, C.M., Gerstein, M.: Using Ethereum blockchain to store and query pharmacogenomics data via smart contracts. BMC Med. Genet. **13**(1), 1–11 (2020)
25. Li, M., Lal, C., Conti, M., Hu, D.: LeChain: a blockchain-based lawful evidence management scheme for digital forensics. Future Gen. Comput. Syst. **115**, 406–420 (2021)
26. Kosba, A., Miller, A., Shi, E., Wen, Z., Papamanthou, C.: Hawk: the blockchain model of cryptography and privacy-preserving smart contracts. In: Proceedings IEEE Symposium Security Privacy (SP), pp. 839–858 (2016)
27. Buterin, V.: A next-generation smart contract and decentralized application platform. White Paper. **3**(37), 1–36 (2014)
28. Şen, Z.: Model efficiency performance assessment through a standard triangular diagram (STD). Model. Earth Syst. Environ. **7**, 1193–1205 (2021)
29. Hamill, P.V.V., Drizd, T.A., Johnson, C.L., Reed, R.B., Roche, A.F., Moore, W.M.: Physical growth: National Center for Health Statistics percentiles. Am. J. Clin. Nutr. **32**(3), 607–629 (1979)

30. Kampstra, P.: Beanplot: a boxplot alternative for visual comparison of distributions. J. Stat. Softw. **28**, 1–9 (2008)
31. Lakshmi Praba, V., Hussaian Basha, C.H., Prashanth, V., Senthilkumar, S., Kavitha, M., Anbazhagan, L.: A hybrid optimization based secured communication in wireless sensor networks through Blockchain technology. In: 2024 Second International Conference on Networks, Multimedia, and Information Technology (NMITCON), Date of Conference: 09–10 August 2024 (2024). https://doi.org/10.1109/NMITCON62075.2024.10699203.

# Computing Methodologies

# Active Learning for Natural Language Processing Tasks: A Review

Noor A. Rashak[1]([✉]) [iD] and Dhamyaa A. Nasrawi[2] [iD]

[1] Department of Computer Science, College of Computer Science and Information Technology, University of Kerbala, Karbala 56001, Iraq
`noor.abdul@s.uokerbala.edu.iq`
[2] Department of Medical Physics, College of Applied Medical Sciences, University of Kerbala, Karbala 56001, Iraq
`dh.alnasrawy@uokerbala.edu.iq`

**Abstract.** Data collection and labelling play a crucial role in many machine learning tasks, particularly in natural language processing. By asking the user to label the most instructive instances, active learning aims to reduce the quantity of labeled data needed to understand the target idea. This way, the concept is learned with fewer examples. It also involves techniques that enhance the efficiency of machine learning models by selectively querying the most informative data points for labelling. These strategies can be effectively integrated into different NLP tasks to enhance the model's ability to generalize while reducing annotation costs. This paper provides a survey of natural language processing tasks using active learning. Natural language processing tasks are divided into two categories: classification and structured prediction. Six questions about natural language processing tasks with active learning were examined. The most common strategy was uncertainty, accounting for 21%. The tasks were diverse; however, most research focused on named entities. The language commonly used in the research was English, representing 45%. The most frequently used performance metric was the F1 score, representing 28%. Most of the research had been published in 2020.

**Keywords:** Active Learning · Natural Language Processing Tasks · Active Learning Strategies

## 1 Introduction

"Active learning" is a subfield of machine learning and, more generally, artificial intelligence. It is also referred to as "query learning" or "optimal experimental design" in the statistics literature. The main idea is that the learning algorithm would perform better with less training if it is given the freedom to select the data it learns from -i.e. to be curious. This is a desirable property for learning algorithms, since the correct operation of any supervised learning system often requires training on hundreds or even thousands of labeled instances [1].

One well-researched method to address this labeling bottleneck is Active Learning (AL), which lets the model select which data to annotate and use for learning in order


S. O. Al-Mamory et al. (Eds.): 3INC 2025, CCIS 2960, pp. 173–200, 2026.
https://doi.org/10.1007/978-3-032-24239-6_11

to achieve high accuracy with fewer training labels. Over the past two decades, active learning has been the subject of numerous literature reviews. However, there is a paucity of AL surveys that incorporate recent developments for Natural Language Processing (NLP) [2]. Figure 1 shows the Flow diagram for the pool-based active learning cycle. The AL works iteratively on each iteration.

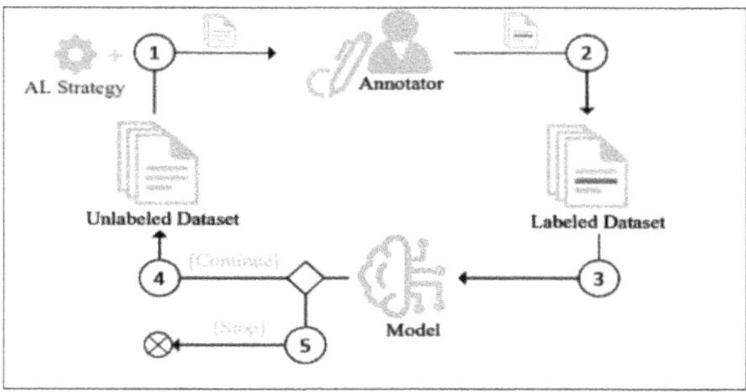


**Fig. 1.** Flow diagram for the pool-based active learning cycle based on [3]

By using an AL technique to choose data points from an unannotated corpus, we can minimize the annotation effort. The AL cycle displayed involves the following steps:

1. A collection of unlabeled data points is used as the starting point. The human annotator receives the data points that the AL method has chosen from the pool.
2. The newly labeled batch is appended to the previously labeled dataset once the annotator has enhanced the data points with the labels.
3. The NLP model is (re-)trained when the quantity of freshly contributed data points hits a threshold.
4. If no stopping criterion is met, a new annotation cycle begins.
5. Until a stopping requirement is satisfied, this cycle is repeated.

In order to optimize the amount of knowledge obtained per annotated data point, AL algorithms select the data points for both annotation and training. Ideally, this method is less expensive and faster than sequential or random data selection for annotation. Compared to random selection, however, employing an inappropriate technique can result in even worse results [3].

A comprehensive examination of the literature on NLP tasks was offered. The assignments are further divided into two primary groups: structured prediction and classification, with subgroups based on the output structures, such as sequence labeling, complex structured prediction, and generation. Section 2 is on AL strategies, Sect. 3 is on NLP tasks, and Sect. 4 is on work related to NLP tasks. The analysis results of all the primary studies are presented in Sect. 5. Section 6 provides conclusions and Sect. 7 introduces the future works.

## 2  Query Strategies

### 2.1  Informativeness

Query techniques based on informativeness typically give each unlabeled instance a unique informative measure and the instance(s) that have the highest measure are chosen [2].

- **Uncertainty Sampling**

  This query framework is arguably the most straightforward and common one. An engaged learner in this paradigm asks questions about the situations they are unsure how to classify. For probabilistic learning models, this method is fairly simple [1].

- **Disagreement**

  Uncertainty sampling typically only takes one model's outputs into account. Disagreement-based techniques, on the other hand, use a variety of models and choose the ones that are most disputed. The well-known query-by-committee algorithm is an example of this algorithm, which is also commonly used. KL-divergence, variation ratio, or vote entropy can all be used to quantify disagreement [2].

- **Gradient**

  Using the gradient norm, this method determines the expected change of a loss function for each sample, selecting the one with the biggest expected change. The premise of this approach is that the model converges more quickly if inputs that result in greater changes to the network's parameters are utilized as the first input to the back-propagation algorithm (i.e., loss function gradients) [4].

- **Performance Prediction**

  Another criterion for querying is the ability to predict performance. If the selected examples are labeled and included to the training set, they should ideally be the ones that minimize future errors the most. This drives the anticipated error reduction app-roach, which selects examples that, when added to retrain a model, result in the least expected error. Given that each candidate must undergo retraining, this approach may be computationally expensive [2].

### 2.2  Representativeness

Sampling and the selection of outliers are the probable drawbacks of solely evaluat-ing the informativeness of individual instances. Thus, another important consideration while creating AL query techniques is representativeness, which quantifies how instances correlate with one another.

- Density

  Density-based techniques favor example instances that are more indicative of the unlabeled set because they are motivated to avoid outliers. One straightforward method of measuring density is to select based on word counts or n-grams. The average similarity of an instance to all other instances is typically used as the common measurement. As an alternative, it is possible to only consider k-nearest neighbor instances for calculating similarities of all instance pairs, which may be expensive.

- Discriminative

This can be achieved by singling out examples that contain a greater number of unrecognized n-grams or terms that are not part of the standard vocabulary using straightforward feature-based measures. In general, cases that are less similar to the labeled ones can also be chosen using similarity scores. Training a model to distinguish between labeled and unlabeled data is another intriguing concept. The same rationale drives the use of a domain separator to filter instances in domain adaption scenarios [2].

- Batch Diversity

In each cycle, only the most useful instance is selected. Adopting batch-mode AL, in which a batch of instances is selected each time, is more effective and useful. In this case, we must take into account the differences within the chosen batch as well as between the picked cases and the labeled ones [2].

## 2.3  Hybrid

Hybrid techniques might be a combination of representativeness and informativeness, for example in querying. Multiple criteria can be combined into one using a straightforward combination. Multiple criteria can be naturally integrated using a variety of ways. Decidual point processes with quality-diversity decomposition, diverse gradient selection—where the gradients incorporate uncertainty information—and (uncertainty) weighted clustering are a few examples [2].

## 3  Natural Language Processing

Natural Language Processing (NLP) is a subfield of artificial intelligence that investigates the interaction between human language and computers. It involves developing models and algorithms that let machines meaningfully comprehend, interpret, and produce human language. NLP is increasingly popular and well-known because of its many uses and capacity to glean valuable information from vast amounts of textual data.

Data-driven machine learning models provide the foundation of most recent natural language processing (NLP) systems. The number and sort of the target training data that is available determine how well these models perform. Even while these models can perform admirably with sufficient supervision, gathering a lot of annotations is typically costly, especially when labeling jobs involving natural language processing is difficult and time-consuming. One well-researched method to address this labeling bottleneck is AL, that enables a model to select the data that will be annotated and utilized for learning in order to obtain high accuracy with fewer training labels [2].

Several research works have used AL strategies for NLP tasks across different fields [5], including sentiment analysis [6, 7], text classification [8], Named Entity Recognition [5, 9, 10], text generation [11, 1], and more.

Representative works for various NLP tasks are presented in this section. The tasks are further classified into two primary groups: structured prediction and classification, with subgroups, based on the output structures, such as: sequence labeling, complex structured prediction, and generation [2]. Figure 2 shows the NLP tasks [2].

**Fig. 2.** Tasks of Natural Language Processing.

## 4   Literature Review

The primary objective of this work was to review the latest studies available on AL strategies in NLP tasks, to clarify the tasks, metrics, languages, models, query strategy, and datasets used in these studies.

The inclusion criteria were (1) published within 2015–2024 in a peer-reviewed journal or conference; (2) address NLP tasks; (3) involve AL techniques or an analysis of them; (4) include experimental results or quantitative evaluation metric; and (5) published in English.

The exclusion criteria were: (1) not including NLP or active learning; (2) lack of significant ruler precision information; (3) duplicates;(4) non-scholarly sources like blogs, editorial contributions, or thesis papers, or(5) full text unavailable. These criteria were used to ensure that only rigorous and high-quality studies were included in the analysis.

The most important tasks in NLP are divided into two main categories: classification and structured prediction with sub categories such as: sequence labeling, complex structured prediction, and generation. Each of these tasks are represented with the related works.

### 4.1  Classification

Classification is a supervised machine learning activity that utilizes data samples that are labeled or annotated by experts to develop a generalized rule that can be applied to the majority of the data [12].

Arad et al. 2020 [7] investigated AL for Persian sentiment analysis using the MirasOpinion dataset, which is currently the largest publicly available Persian sentiment corpus. The authors evaluated LSTM and CNN models and introduced a novel LDA-based sampling method that combines topic modelling with entropy sampling. They achieved competitive performance, reaching approximately 80% F1 while requiring less than 16% of the labelled data to match baseline accuracy. The limitations of the LDA sampling method are that it is computationally expensive and must be recomputed after each iteration, limiting scalability. Third, the uncertainty-based strategies showed minimal performance differences, indicating limited discriminative power in their setup. These limitations highlight the need for broader evaluations using modern architectures and more diverse active learning strategies.

Bai et al. (2020) [13], presented a framework for active learning in a sentence-matching task using a pre-trained linguistic model to improve sample selection and reduce coding costs. The experiments included several English and Chinese datasets: SNLI, MultiNLI, Quora, LCQMC, and BQ with achieved accuracy rates of 80.99%, 71.79%, 81.79%, 84.29%, and 74.73%, respectively. The study employed a combination of selection strategies, including randomization, uncertainty, and expected gradient length (EGL), along with a linguistic criterion based on the pre-trained model. The results demonstrated that incorporating linguistic cues improved AL performance compared to traditional methods. However, despite its strengths, the study had several weaknesses. It did not provide an in-depth critical analysis of the reasons for the superiority or inferiority of each strategy, nor did it analyze errors and sentence types that confuse the model. Furthermore, the proposed framework relied heavily on the availability of large language models, limiting its applicability in low-resource languages or specialized fields. Addressing redundancy in the samples was also inadequate, and the study assumed an ideal coding environment, failing to account for human coding noise.

Jacobs et al. (2021) [14] explored how active learning can reduce the effort required for labelling in text classification by leveraging several uncertainty-based query strategies with a BERT-base classifier. Studies have shown that uncertainty sampling outperforms random selection; however, most studies have focused on a small set of heuristics, used traditional machine-learning models, or tested on small datasets. Because of these limitations, earlier results have not been applied to larger or different settings, leaving questions about scalability, robustness, and the effect of query-pool size. This paper offered a broader analysis by testing several uncertainty-based heuristics across two

NLP datasets: the Stanford Sentiment Treebank and the KvK-Frontpages. The study measured both accuracy and an adjusted deficiency metric, enabling a more detailed comparison of strategies. These results point to ongoing challenges in active learning, including its sensitivity to dataset type and the difficulty of balancing informativeness and robustness.

A. K. Al-Tamimi et al. (2021) [8] illustrated the efficacy of active learning in enhancing the classification of Arabic texts. They demonstrated that their AL approach reached 99% accuracy while labelling only 27.3% of the NADA dataset in contrast to passive learning, which needed to label 91.2%. The approach is based on SVM classifiers with stochastic gradient descent training and selecting the most informative samples to label by estimating their uncertainty. The experiments were performed on the NADA dataset that showed the superiority of adaptive sample selection especially on low-resource and imbalanced Arabic text datasets. Furthermore, the study used a custom-built web application for human annotation, thereby enabling online retraining and iterative improvement in the model's performance. Although the research demonstrated that active learning can lead to a substantial decrease in labelling and classification time, it also reveals several limitations. Manual labelling can be costly, and pool-based uncertainty sampling does not guarantee coverage of the diverse dataset or proper handling of outliers. However, it provided an empirical assessment of the state-of-the-art techniques in AL for Arabic texts in a modern multi-task setting and served as motivation for developing scalable frameworks and augmentation techniques to further boost performance (in particular for underrepresented categories).

Kaseb et al. (2023) [6] focused on the application of active learning in Arabic sentiment analysis. The main objectives were to improve data labelling efficiency and enhance model performance. The model used five strategies: Least Confidence, Margin, Entropy, K-means, and Core-set. By using only 10%, 20%, and 27% of the data, the model yielded F1-scores of 97%, 99%, and 100% of the maximum score, respectively. Studies have shown that Arabic sentiment classification is possible and that active learning can lower annotation costs. However, these methods are less scalable, more sensitive to the type of dataset used, and less effective for multitask problems such as handling sentiment, sarcasm, and dialect together, compared to newer approaches. As the non-stationary features are noisy and time consuming, they applied a transformer-based model (MAR BERTv2) to address these problems under the framework of active learning with multiple positive and negative strategies for selecting informative samples. Using the balanced ArSarcasm-v2 dataset in combination with multi-task learning (SAIDS), the achieved improvements in accuracy for sentiment, sarcasm and dialect. This strategy led to a superior performance model and less annotation effort, as well as a more scalable and robust solution than other works.

Kanclerz et al. (2023) [15] introduced a novel approach to active learning in subjective NLP tasks. PALS (Personalized Active Learning for Subjective Tasks in NLP) achieved over 30% improvement compared to random selection. Annotation requirements were decreasing 25%–40% of the original dataset size while maintaining a high quality. Five new metrics—Controversy, VarRatio, RatioDistance, Stranger Count, and Random—measured the relevance of texts to individual user preferences. The datasets include Wiki discussions labelled for aggression and toxicity, as well as the Unhealthy

Conversations dataset. PALS enables efficient data labelling, improved classifier performance, and reduced costs. However, limitations remained such as potential data-collection bias, restricted dataset options, and no incremental learning evaluation. They addressed key challenges in subjective NLP by providing a personalized and efficient annotation framework that improved on previous methods through relevance, diversity, and user-focused strategies.

## 4.2  Structured Prediction

Structured prediction is the most common type of task in natural language processing. It aims to predict a series of labels, including potential limitations and interactions [2]. In the following subsection, several related works on subcategories of structured prediction tasks are discussed.

- Sequence Labelling

Sequence labelling is one of the tasks in natural language processing, which involves identifying and labelling the words or phrases that make up a sequence. It is a crucial feature of many NLP systems and frequently used as a preprocessing step for other NLP tasks like named entity recognition or part-of-speech tagging. It seeks to categorize every word or token in class space C.

Peshterliev et al. (2019) [16] tried to enhance NLU systems for new domains using AL. It presents the Majority-CRF algorithm, which uses multiple classification and sequence labelling models to filter sentences for annotation, thereby improving model accuracy in low-resource settings. The work primarily used Slot Error Rate (SER) as the evaluation metric for NLU model performance, emphasizing the correctness of slot predictions and intent classifications. They explored diverse active learning methods including Query-by-Committee (QBC), Least Confidence, Expected Model Change, and Expected Error Reduction. One drawback of active learning is its computational cost, as some methods are very complex and often slow in practice on large datasets. This may limit the proposed approaches' ability to scale up in practical applications. The Majority-CRF algorithm outperforms the other methods by 6.6% to 9% in error reduction, with the same annotation budget as random sampling. It significantly reduces the sample set to a well-selected subset and thereby improves the models' training accuracy.

Liu et al. (2020) [9] proposed a new active learning strategy (Lowest Token Probability (LTP)) for enhancing the performance of NER with CRFs. The study evaluated multiple datasets, including Boson NER dataset, Weibo NER dataset, conference CONLL2003 dataset, Ritter dataset and broadcast news articles of Chinese. It contrasted LTP with other active learning methods such as a uniformly random baseline and long term baseline. Note that LTP does not bias long sequences yet does not require any changes to the model; thus it is less complicated and more efficient. Performance was evaluated using the entity-level F1 Scores and the sentence-level accuracy performance in general. The results suggested that LTP was more effective than the conventional schemes. Problems such as the fundamental requirement of labeled data inevitably add annotation cost or require complicated model tuning. Although LTP achieves a positive advance, there is room for the improvement of active learning strategies.

Cai et al. (2020) [17] targeted the subtask of CWS in EHRs, which is essential to ensure an accurate clinical data mining. They presented an active learning-based framework to support segmentation performance by decreasing the amount of manual annotation. The dataset contained 3,868 records with 27,442 sentences divided into a training dataset, validation dataset and test dataset with a ratio of 6:2:2 to balance evaluating performances. The Results showed that the Transformer-CRF model obtained a satisfactory F1-score of 91.25%, which was significantly higher than that achieved by classical segmentation models. The study proved to be methodologically rigorous by fusing active learning with a robust Transformer-CRF structure which enables the model to learn effectively from small annotated data. The limitation of the study was small and narrow dataset which may impact generalizability of results in wider clinical domains. The study was also limited to contents of Chinese EHR, which makes cross-language generalization complicated.

Brantley et al. (2020) [18] discussed the challenges of reducing the number of queries to expert labelers in structured prediction tasks. It introduces the Learning to Query for Imitation (LEAQI) algorithm. The results indicated that LEAQI can achieve a significant label saving compared to traditional methods while maintaining comparable or better accuracy in structured prediction tasks. The tasks addressed in the paper include structured prediction problems such as Named Entity Recognition (NER), key phrase extraction, and Part of Speech (POS) tagging. The dataset used in the study were CoNLL'03, SemEval 2017 Task 10, and Universal Dependencies.

Chaudhary et al. (2021) [10] focused on improving active learning (AL) strategies for part-of-speech (POS) tagging. Several metrics were used to evaluate the model including performance accuracy, Wasserstein Distance (WD), and Static Calibration Error (SCE). The results indicated that the proposed CRAL (Confusion Reduction Active Learning) method significantly outperformed existing AL strategies across six typologically diverse languages, achieving 90% improved accuracy in POS tagging. The datasets from six languages including German, Swedish, Galician, North Sami, Persian, and Ukrainian were used. As for limitations, the selected data may include syncretic word types, where a single word form can have multiple POS tags depending on context. This inherent ambiguity can complicate the tagging process and affect the performance of AL methods. Training multiple models independently, as might be required for some AL methods or committee-based approaches, can be computationally expensive, especially across numerous experiments and iterations.

Mahdhaoui et al. (2023) [5] worked on improving the Arabic named entity recognition (ANER) using the pre-trained language model AraGPT2 with active learning. They also tried to enhance the identification and classification of named entities in Arabic texts, overcoming the issues associated with high complexity level10 (in terms of both morphology and writing style) integrated into the Arabic language. The results illustrated an F-measure 67.2 being performed on AQMAR dataset; which is much better than other recent advanced applications/models.rar (e.g. MADAMIRA, FARASA and Deep techniques) particularly when used on AQMAR or NEWS datasets. The incorporation of active learning decreases the reliance on large annotated datasets, making the approach more effective. The pre-trained model could add inflexibility that hinders further fine-tuning to tailored domain demands or to novel labeled data not covered in the training data. For example, Arabic language is difficult and intricate in its own right due to diacritics and morphological aspects that can impact the efficacy of the model. Moreover, the performance of the model can differ based on the quality and representativity of training data.

Luo et al. (2023) [19] described a new method to bolster Named Entity Recognition (NER). The proposed method included the reweighting of tokens to solve the problem of low performance of NER models, especially for low frequency entity classes. The adopted method was based on performance measures of models (F1-score, precision, and recall). The other datasets namely Conll2003, WikiAnn (English), BC5CDR, NER model and AL methods achieved 84.54 F1% on the re-weighting. Results showed that the proposed algorithm was better than conventional query strategies in terms of model accuracy and robustness. The reweighting performed well in solving label imbalance problem and thus yielded good performance on NER tasks. The technique was flexible and can be combined with other token-level acquisition functions, allowing the dependency parsing to range over different datasets/scenarios. The study contribution resides in mitigating the lack of labelled data challenge, which may impact the learning process of NER model. The re-weighting was employed to alleviate this problem.

- Complex Structure Prediction

This task involves predicting and generating specific forms or arrangements of linguistic data. The structure prediction takes a step further by focusing on more intricate or nuanced structures [2].

Kasai et al. (2019) [20] focused on entity resolution, which is the assignment of pairs of entity tuples into matches and non-matches. This is an important task for both knowledge base construction and text mining. The obtained results showed that the Deep Transfer Active Learning (DTAL) outperformed conventional algorithms including SVM under low- resource settings. For example, DTAL achieved competitive performance compared to deep learning models trained on full datasets with fewer than 6% of training data. The study is evaluated on different datasets such as DBLP-Scholar, Cora, and DBLP-ACM. The DBLP-ACM dataset demonstrated the best performance with an F1 of 97.89%.

Koshorek et al. (2019) [21] performed, to the best of our knowledge, the first study on how effective LTAL (i.e., Learning to Actively Learn) technique is on improving the data collection efficiency for semantic representation tasks, particularly in the QA-SRL. A total number of five annotation levels were used to annotate the CoNQAD dataset. The corpora (CoNLL-2003 NER, QA-SRL) are from three different domains (Wikipedia, News, Science) all in English. The listed learning strategies were random, high confidence, entropy, random, longest and uncertainty. The evaluation metric was Exact match (EM) score illustrating the performance of the model in generating questions. The goal was to determine whether LTAL can improve learning semantic representations that are important for natural language understanding. The results also suggested that LTAL was unreliable in yielding benefits over random selection, which is a crucial limitation of its effectiveness to semantic problems. Such stochasticity in model optimization negatively impacts the selection criterion, which is a major challenge.

Espeland et al. (2020) [22] focused on improving information retrieval during active learning sessions for co-reference resolution. The paper used a query-by-committee, entropy, and cluster-outlier as active learning strategies with the English CoNLL-2012 co-reference dataset. The research introduced adjustments that enable annotators to leverage cataphoric information, optimizing the labelling process and reducing time spent on manual labelling. The best-performing model achieved an F1 score of 58.01, suggesting that while the methods enhanced the labelling process, overall performance gains were limited. Erroneous labelling can confuse the model, leading to lower F1 scores in some cases. The main objectives of the research were to increase the amount of information retrieved through active learning sessions and to optimize the annotator's labelling process to improve the efficiency of coreference resolution systems

Mallart et al. (2021) [23] highlighted active learning strategies for relation extraction in the context of a French newspaper. They reported a precision of 42% for the best-performing model. The measure used in this research was Precision, and the dataset was collected from a French newspaper. As for the strategies, Random, Least Likely, and Mixture were used. They evaluated a range of models, from basic to complex, allowing for a comprehensive understanding of their effectiveness in a specific context. By employing active learning, the study aimed to minimize the number of required annotations, making it more efficient in data-scarce scenarios. The models showed only marginal improvements with additional annotated data, indicating potential limitations in the learning process. The study highlights the challenge of working with limited, unbalanced local data, which affects model performance.

Liu et al. (2021) [24] discussed active entity alignment. The study utilized three datasets: DBpedia, Wikidata, and YAGO, and they vary in terms of size and language. They employed a structure-aware uncertainty sampling strategy that measured the uncertainty of entities, accounting for their relationships in Knowledge Graphs (KGs) and ActiveEA. A bachelor recognizer was introduced to identify entities that exist in one KG but not in another, thereby optimizing the annotation process. It used languages such as English, German, and French. The performance was evaluated using AUC (Area Under the Curve) metrics to compare the effectiveness of ActiveEA against baseline strategies. The framework effectively reduced annotation costs while improving model performance, addressed entity dependencies, and recognized bachelor's degrees. The assumption that all entities have counterparts may limit the applicability of the methods in real-world scenarios. The main limitation was the strong assumption that all entities in KGs were matchable, which may not hold true in practice. Challenges included effectively managing the bias introduced by sampling strategies and ensuring the robustness of the bachelor recognizer.

Li et al. (2023) [25] addressed the data imbalance in multilingual semantic parsing (MSP) datasets by proposing an active learning procedure (AL-MSP) that reduced the translation effort required for training multilingual parsers. The accuracy of the parsers was reported for various datasets such as GEO-QUERY, NLMA, with results showing that parsers trained on human translations achieved higher accuracies (80% to 83%) compared to those trained on machine translations (49% to 75%). The research reported that with the best selection approach (LFS-LC-D), translating only 32% of instances yielded parsing accuracies comparable to translating the entire dataset, with an accuracy gap of less than 5%. The evaluation metric used in this research was the exact match accuracy of logical forms. The languages involved in the study included English (EN), German (DE), Thai (TH), and Greek (EL).

- Generations

Generation is the capacity of a machine to generate clear, concise, and engaging texts or discourses that resembles that of a human. It assists machines in producing coherent and meaningful responses that are readily comprehensible to humans.

Wallace et al. (2020) [26] studied the empirical evaluation of various active learning (AL) techniques specifically tailored for neural machine translation (NMT). The goal was to provide a comprehensive comparison of different AL methods using a state-of-the-art NMT architecture and the same dataset for fair evaluation. The results indicated that the proposed RTTL method significantly improved performance, especially in out-of-domain evaluations. Overall, the performance trends of different AL methods were consistent across various evaluation metrics, including BLEU, BEER, and TER. The experiments utilized the WMT'13 English-Spanish news translation task, specifically using the Europarl and News Commentary Corpus.

Wallace et al. (2020) [27] studied semantic parsing, which entailed the conversion of natural language utterances into machine-executable meaning representations, such as SQL queries. The results demonstrated that the proposed method significantly out-performed baseline methods on both an internal dataset and the Facebook Task Oriented Parsing (TOP) dataset. The results of the experiments are calculated as exact-match accuracy over all datasets. Several active learning strategies have been used including Random, Uncertainty, MARGIN OF CONFIDENCE Traffic- CLUSTERING, LEAST CONFIDENCE.

Zhou et al. (2021) [28] focused on the translation of constrained texts, specifically the Bible, into severely low-resource languages. The primary evaluation metric used in this research was the BLEU score, which assesses translation quality by comparing translations to reference texts. The study reported performance improvements of + 11.0 BLEU for English and + 4.9 BLEU for Eastern Pokomchi when using random sampling compared to a portion-based approach. The research demonstrated that random sampling can significantly improve translation quality compared to traditional methods. It effectively combines human intuition with machine learning, leveraging the strengths of both approaches to improve translation outcomes. The study acknowledged limitations in real-world scenarios where reference texts in low-resource languages are unavailable, making it challenging to obtain accurate BLEU scores. The absence of reference texts in low-resource languages complicated the evaluation process, as human translators must rely on intuition rather than concrete metrics.

Tsvigun et al. [1] focused on improving Abstractive Text Summarization (ATS) through Active Learning (AL) techniques. They introduced a novel query strategy called in-domain diversity sampling (IDDS). The study utilized a subset of the Gigaword dataset, specifically selecting 200 instances from the training set and 2,000 instances from the validation set for evaluation consistency. The results indicated that the proposed IDDS strategy significantly outperformed random sampling across all datasets, as measured by ROUGE metrics. Additionally, combining AL with self-learning can lead to performance improvements of up to 58% in ROUGE scores

Perlitz et al. (2023) [11] presented a systematic study of active learning (AL) applied to Natural Language Generation (NLG). They explored various AL strategies to improve annotation efficiency by selectively choosing the most informative examples for labelling. The research utilized nine datasets across different NLG tasks and examined multiple AL strategies, including Uncertainty-based strategies. The results showed that no single AL strategy consistently outperformed the others across all datasets. The research highlighted several limitations, including the reliance on fully labelled datasets, potential difficulties in human annotation, and the use of automatic metrics that may not fully capture model performance. Key challenges included the large output space in NLG, label imbalance, and the differences between classification and generation tasks. The study also noted gaps between academic AL studies and practical applications.

Wang (2024) [29] investigated the use of Large Language Models (LLMs) like GPT-3.5 and GPT-4 for annotating samples in active learning settings, aiming to reduce labeling costs while maintaining accuracy. The study utilized three text classification datasets including AG's News, TREC-6, and Rotten Tomatoes Movie Reviews. The accuracy varies across datasets, with GPT-4 achieving close to 100% accuracy on AG's News and TREC-6, while showing slightly lower accuracy on Rotten Tomatoes compared to GPT-3.5. The min token strategy generally yielded the highest accuracy. The research compared three demonstration example selection strategies: random selection, min token (fewest tokens), and max similarity (most similar to test examples).

Table 1 lists the methods used in the studies and shows the features of each one.

**Table 1.** Overview of active learning strategies in natural language tasks

| Reference &year | Task | Language | Query Strategy | Dataset | Result |
|---|---|---|---|---|---|
| [7]2020 | Sentiment analysis | Persian | Entropy Sampling, Margin Sampling, And Least Confident (LC) | Mirasopinion it was collected from a Persian E-Commerce Website | 80% in F1 Score, less than 16% of labeled data |
| [13]2020 | Sentence matching | English and Chinese | Random, Uncertainly, Expected Gradient Length (EGL), Pre-trained Language Model (LM) | Multinli, Quora, SNLI, LCQMC, BQ | Accuracy achieved on every dataset is about (80.99%–71.79%) |
| [14]2021 | Text classification | English | Uncertainty, Monte Carlo Dropout, Predictive entropy, Bayesian active learning by disagreement | Stanford Sentiment Treebank (SST), Kvk-Frontpages | Deficiency values <1 indicate improvements over the reference strategy. |
| [8]2021 | Text classification | Arabic | Uncertainty, Random | NADA dataset | accuracy reached 99% accuracy after labeling only 27.3% of the training samples. |
| [6]2023 | Sentiment analysis | Arabic | Least Confidence, Margin, Entropy,K-Means, Core-Set. | Arsarcasm, DAICT, Additional Tweets | Using only 10%, 20%, 27% of the data can yield F1-scores of 97%, 99%, 100% of the maximum score, respectively |

(continued)

**Table 1.** (*continued*)

| Reference &year | Task | Language | Query Strategy | Dataset | Result |
|---|---|---|---|---|---|
| [15]2023 | Classification of hate-speech, aggression, and emotions | English | Novel strategy (PALS) | Wikidetox (Aggression and Toxicity), Unhealthy Conversations | F1 score enhanced by up to 30% using Just 25%–40% of the initial dataset size. |
| [16]2019 | Improve the accuracy of Natural Language Understanding systems in new domains | English | Query-by-Committee (QBC), Least-Confidence,Expected Model Change and Expected Error Reduction | The dataset covers 24 domains, including music, shopping, local search, sports, books, cinema and calendar. | The experiments conducted in the paper demonstrate that the Majority-CRF algorithm achieves a relative error rate reduction of 6.6% to 9% compared to random sampling with the same annotation budget. |
| [9]2020 | Named Entity Recognition (NER) | English and Chinese | Uncertainty, Lowest Token Probability (LTP) | Bosonner, Weiboner, CONLL2003, Ritter, Chinese Dataset of Broadcast News Articles | The LTP performs slightly better than traditional strategies while requiring significantly fewer annotation tokens. The evaluation metrics include both Sentence-Level Accuracy and Entity-Level F1-Score. |
| [18]2020 | POS Tagging, Keyphrase Extraction, Named Entity Recognition | English, Greek | LEAQI, | Conll'03, Semeval_2017 Task 10, Universal Dependencies | The LEAQI reduces the number of queries to the expert while achieving better accuracy than passive learning |
| [17]2020 | Chinese Word Segmentation (CWS) | Chinese | Normalized Entropy with Loss Prediction (NE-LP), Least Confidence (LC), Maximum Token Entropy (MTE), Minimum Token Margin (MTM) | 204 Ehrs with Cardiovascular Diseases from The Shuguang Hospital Affiliated to Shanghai University of Traditional Chinese Medicine | The Transformer-CRF model achieved an F1-score of 91.25% |
| [10]2021 | POS Tagging | German, Swedish, Galician, North Sami, Persian, Ukrainian | Uncertainty, Query-by-Committee, CRAL (Confusion Reduction Active Learning). | Griko Dataset | All strategies across six typologically diverse languages, demonstrating improved accuracy in POS Tagging is 90%. |

(*continued*)

**Table 1.** *(continued)*

| Reference &year | Task | Language | Query Strategy | Dataset | Result |
|---|---|---|---|---|---|
| [5]2023 | Arabic Named Entity Recognition | Arabic | Uncertainty of The Aragpt2 Model's Predictions | AQMAR. NEWS, TWEETS | F-Measure of 67.2% on the AQMAR dataset. |
| [19]2023 | Named Entity Recognition | English | Randomly, Least Confidence, Maximum Normalized Log Probability, Sequenceentropy, Bayesianactive Learning by Disagreement | Conll2003, Wikiann (English), BC5CDR,NER Model | F1-Scores of Re-Weighting Least Confidence is 84.54% |
| [20]2019 | Entity Resolution | English | Randomly, High Confidence, Entropy | DBLP-Scholar, Cora, DBLP ACM,Fodors-Zagats, Amazon-Google, Zomato-Yelp | The DBLP-ACM Dataset achieved F1 of 97.89%. |
| [21]2019 | Span Detection and Question Generation | English | Random, Longest, Uncertainty | Conll-2003 NER, QA-SRL with three different domains (Wikipedia, News , Science) | The oracle policy's performance improvement is limited, with a maximum gain of 9% in specific scenarios. |
| [22]2020 | Coreference Resolution | English | Entropy, Query-by-Committee, Cluster-Outlier Methods | Conll-2012 Coreference | F1 58.01, which is an increase of 0.93 over the baseline model |
| [23]2021 | Relation Extraction | French | Random, Least Likely, Mixture | Contents of The French Newspaper | A Precision of 42% for the best-performing model |
| [24]2021 | Match Equivalent Entities Across Different Knowledge Graphs (KGs) | English, German, French | Structure-Aware Uncertainty, Activeea | Dbpedia, Wikidata, YAGO | AUC showed there is improvements in sampling quality and model performance across different datasets and EA models |
| [25]2023 | Multilingual Semantic Parser that reduces the translation effort | English, German, Thai, and Greek | Random, Lowest Confidence, Diversity | GEO-QUERY, NLMAP. | Translating only 32% of sample that trained on human translations accuracies (80% to 83%) compared to those trained on machine translations (49% to 75%) |

*(continued)*

**Table 1.** (*continued*)

| Reference &year | Task | Language | Query Strategy | Dataset | Result |
|---|---|---|---|---|---|
| [26]2019 | Evaluate various Active Learning (AL) techniques Specifically For Neural Machine Translation (NMT) | English-Spanish | LC, Coverage Sampling (CS) N-Best Sequence Entropy)NSE(, Coverage_Sampling Round Trip Translation Likelihood)RTTL), Density, Diversity | Europarl, News Commentary, WMT'13 English-Spanish | The Performance Trends of Different AL Methods Were Consistent Across Various Evaluation Metrics, Including BLEU, BEER, and TER. |
| [27]2020 | Semantic Parsing | English | Random, Uncertainty, Margin of Confidence Traffic- Clustering, Least Confidence | Internal Customer, Facebook Task Oriented Parsing (TOP) | The Method achieves the same accuracy as Random Sampling but with 2,000 fewer annotations on the internal dataset. |
| [28]2021 | Translation | English, Mayan | Portion-Based, The Random | Bible, Eastern Pokomhi, Human Post-Edited | The Random Sampling Approach achieving a performance gain of +11.0 BLEU for English and + 4.9 BLEU for Eastern Pokomchi |
| [1]2022 | Abstractive text summarization (ats) | English | IDDS(instance diversity and density sampling), Uncertainty, diversity | Aeslc Pubmed, wikihow, gigaword | 58% in rouge scores. |
| [11]2023 | Paraphrase generation, Style transfer, Summarization Question generation | English | Uncertainty, mean token entropy (MTE), core-set, in-domain diversity sampling(IDDS), monte carlo dropout | Mscoco, parabank, debatesum, reddit tl;dr, debatesum, reddit tl;dr, gyafc-e&m, gyafc-f&r | The_findings indicate that no AL strategy consistently outperformed others across datasets |
| [29]2024 | Using Large Language Models (LLMS) like GPT-3.5 and GPT-4 to label samples | English | Random, Least Confidence, Breaking Ties | AG'sNews, TREC-6,Rotten Tomatoes Movie Reviews | With GPT-4 achieving close to 100% accuracy on AG's News and TREC-6, while showing slightly lower accuracy on Rotten Tomatoes compared to GPT-3.5 |

## 5   Discussion

A comprehensive analysis of studies about active learning for natural language processing task was presented in Fig. 3. Related research papers that effectively address the research problem were searched using keywords "Active Learning Strategies", "Active

Learning for Natural Language Processing Tasks", "Active Learning for Arabic Natural Language Processing Tasks". The platforms searched for were Research Gate, IEEE Xplore Digital Library, Google Scholar, and ScienceDirect.

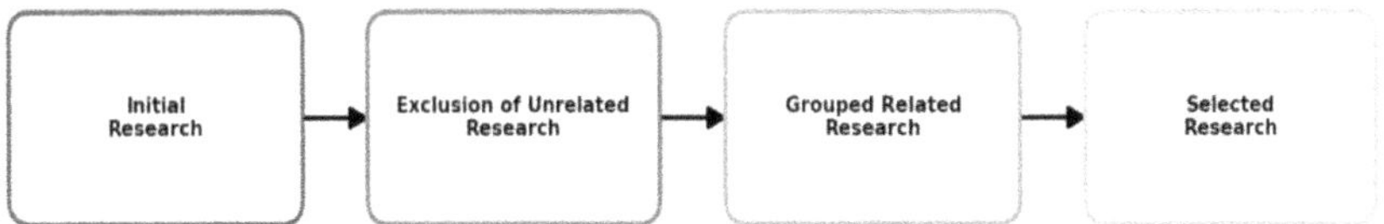


**Fig. 3.** Block diagram of survey step

The study was limited to natural language tasks - i.e., other media such as images, videos, and audio were not included. This study focused only on text. The research works were selected based on tasks in natural language processing as well as strategies used, performance measures and language of the dataset.

A total of 25 papers were selected, which were read and grouped for evaluation, comparisons, and analysis to answer the survey questions about the strategies used, performance measures, database language, etc. The following questions which were addressed are listed Table 2.

Six core research questions were formulated to guide the systematic analysis of active learning within natural language processing. These questions were identified through an extensive review of the literature, where recurring themes related to strategies, tasks, dataset languages, evaluation metrics, publication trends, and adopted models were consistently highlighted as the main dimensions of comparison in previous studies. The reason for selecting these specific questions lies in their relevance to understanding the methodological and practical evolution of active learning in NLP. These questions represent the factors most frequently reported and most influential in shaping research directions across recent empirical studies.

**Table 2.** List of the survey research questions

| No. | Research Questions | Motivations |
| --- | --- | --- |
| Q1 | What is the most commonly used strategy with NLP? | To explore the most common strategies or techniques in NLP, which can refer to several areas. |
| Q2 | What is the task used by researchers? | To determine the focus of researchers on what type of tasks |
| Q3 | What is the most used language in the dataset? | To determine the most commonly used dataset language in research. |
| Q4 | What is the most used performance metric? | To identify the commonly used metrics to evaluate and compare the performance of active learning strategies of natural language processing tasks |

(continued)

**Table 2.** (*continued*)

| No. | Research Questions | Motivations |
|---|---|---|
| Q5 | What are the years of publication for the research? | To determine the focus of researchers on natural language processing tasks in any year. |
| Q6 | What is the model used in research? | To achieve the goal and solving problems, organizing ideas. |

**Q1: What is the most Commonly Used Strategy with Natural Language Processing?**
As shown in Fig. 4, the most used strategy is uncertainty and randomness. Uncertainty sampling is the most widely used strategy in natural language processing research, as shown in Table 3. This is due to its significant effectiveness in improving model performance and reducing the cost of manual labeling. This strategy relies on selecting samples in which the model exhibits the lowest degree of confidence in predicting the correct class, ensuring that each new sample adds the maximum amount of information useful for updating the model.

Studies showed that uncertainty sampling often outperforms random sampling, especially with limited labeled data. By targeting model uncertainty, it reduces the samples needed for high performance. Its relative simplicity makes it the dominant choice in most active learning research in NLP and explains its widespread use in reference studies.

**Table 3.** List of most used strategies in natural language processing

| No. | Strategies | References |
|---|---|---|
| 1 | Uncertainty | [1], [5]-[11, 13]-[17, 19]-[29] |
| 2 | Random | [8, 13], [19]-[21, 23, 25]-[29] |
| 3 | K-Means | [6] |
| 4 | Core-Set | [6] [11] |
| 5 | Monte Carlo Dropout | [11] [14] |
| 6 | Bayesian Active Learning by Disagreement | [14] [19] |
| 7 | Query-by-Committee | [10 [16] [22] |
| 8 | Expected Gradient Length | [13] [16] |
| 9 | Expected Error Reduction | [16] |
| 10 | N-Best Sequence | [26] |
| 11 | Normalized Entropy with Loss Prediction | [17] |
| 12 | Maximum Normalized Log Probability | [19] |
| 13 | Cluster-Outlier | [22] |
| 14 | Least Likely | [23] |
| 15 | Diversity | [1, 25] [26] |

(*continued*)

**Table 3.** (*continued*)

| No. | Strategies | References |
| --- | --- | --- |
| 16 | Density | [1] [26] |
| 17 | Round_Trip Translation Likelihood | [25] |
| 18 | Coverage | [26] |
| 19 | Instance Diversity and Density IDDS | [1] [11] |
| 20 | Confusion Reduction | [10] |
| 21 | LEAQI | [18] |

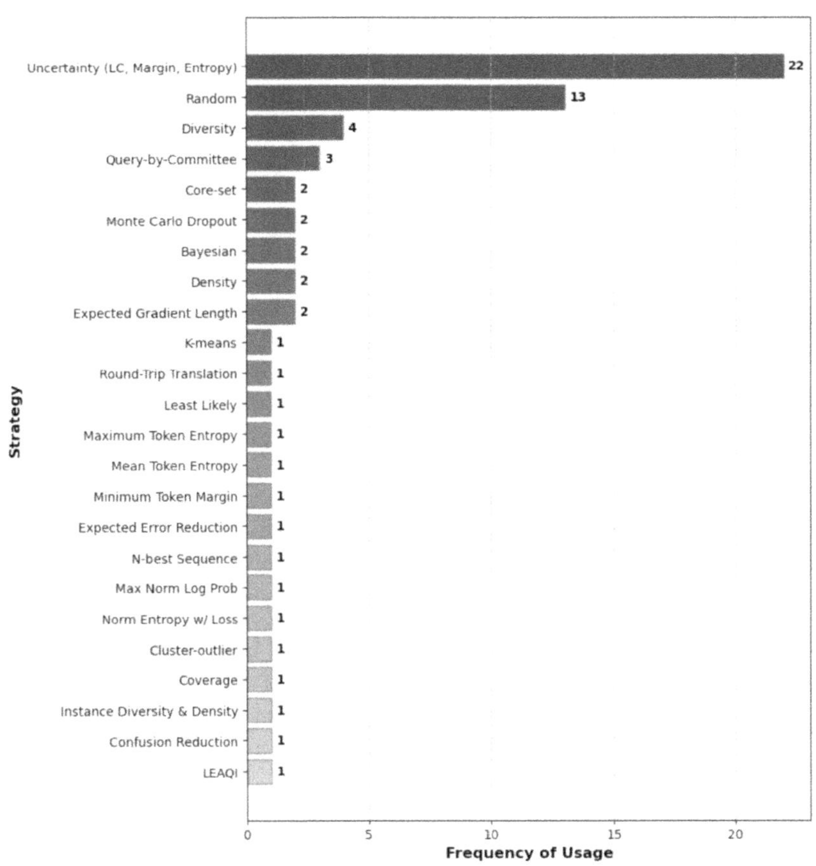



**Fig. 4.** The most used strategy in natural language processing task

## Q2: What Is the Task Used by Researchers?

Figure 5 points out the most common tasks in NLP when active learning is used by reviewing related works. The distribution of such tasks in the reference studies according to their use-frequency is presented in Table 4. Clearly, sentiment analysis, text classification, and named entity recognition are the major tasks in active learning for NLP. This is because of their usefulness in practical applications and the requirement of high-quality labels for model performance improvement. In addition, other tasks like speech part tagging, key phrase extraction, text summarization and translation have received a lot of attention but are not as popular as the first three core tasks. Such a variety of tasks indicates that active learning may has potential to enhance model performance on a wide spectrum of NLP applications at system level with a goal of decreasing human cost on manual tagging and enhancing data utilization efficiency.

**Table 4.** Task used by active learning with NLP

| No. | Task | Reference |
| --- | --- | --- |
| 1 | Sentiment analysis | [6] [7] |
| 2 | Text classification | [8] |
| 3 | Named Entity Recognition | [5] [9, 18, 19] [20, 24] |
| 4 | POS Tagging | [10, 18] |
| 5 | Classification of hate-speech | [15] |
| 6 | Understanding | [16] |
| 7 | Keyphrase Extraction | [18] |
| 8 | Word Segmentation | [17] |
| 9 | Entity Resolution | [20] |
| 10 | Question Generation | [11, 21] |
| 11 | Coreference Resolution | [22] |
| 12 | Relation Extraction | [23] |
| 13 | Translation | [25, 26, 28] |
| 14 | Text Summarization | [1] [11] |
| 15 | Paraphrase Generation | [11] |
| 16 | Style Transfer | [11] |
| 17 | Large Language Models | [29] |

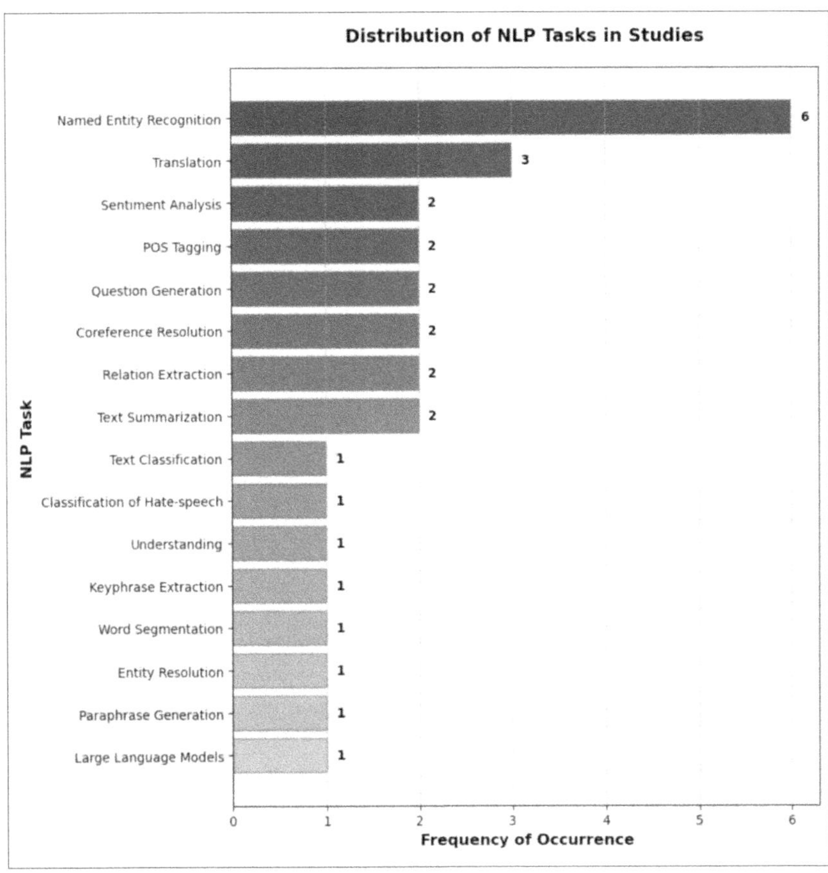



**Fig. 5.** The natural language processing task.

## Q3: What is the most Used Language in the Dataset?

The results showed in Fig. 6 that English was the most frequently used language in the studied datasets, representing the highest percentage among all languages at approximately 47%. Table 5 illustrates the distribution of language usage in the reference studies. This distribution reflects the dominance of English in natural language processing research, due to the availability of substantial linguistic resources and the associated research backlog, which facilitates model development and application of active learning strategies.

**Table 5.** List of the most used languages in this work.

| No. | Language | Reference |
|---|---|---|
| 1 | English | [1] [6] [9] [11] [13] [16] [18] [22, 24] [28]. |
| 2 | German | [10, 24] [25] |

(continued)

Table 5.  (continued)

| No. | Language | Reference |
| --- | --- | --- |
| 3 | Arabic | [5] [6, 8] |
| 4 | Persian | [7, 10] |
| 5 | French | [23] [24] |
| 6 | Spanish | [26] |
| 7 | Mayan | [28] |
| 8 | Greek | [18] [25] |
| 9 | Chines | [9] [13] [17] |
| 10 | Swedish | [10] |
| 11 | Galician | [10] |
| 12 | North Sami | [10] |
| 13 | Ukrainian | [10] |

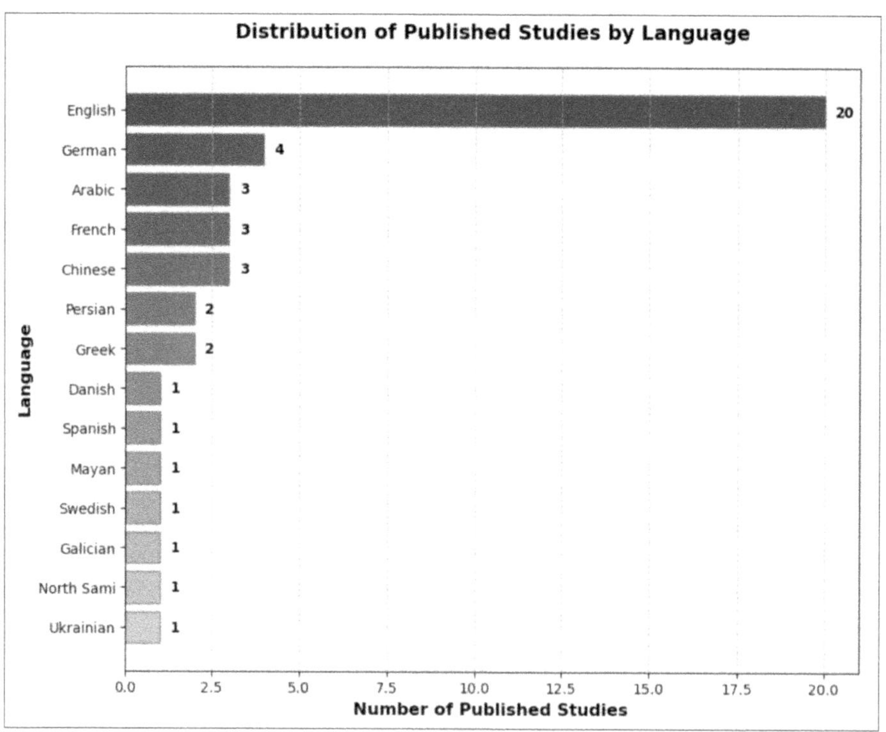


Fig. 6.  The languages used in active learning for natural language processing task in papers

Q4 What is the most used performance metric?

The most commonly used performance measure was F-score. as shown in Table 6 and in Fig. 7.

**Table 6.** List of evaluation metrics used in this review

| No. | Metrices | Reference |
| --- | --- | --- |
| 1 | F1-Score | [5] [6] [7] [9] [10] [15] [16] [18] [19] [20] [21] |
| 2 | Accuracy | [8] [9] [11] [13, 14, 16, 17, 24, 26] |
| 3 | Precision | [5] [10] [19] [22] |
| 4 | Recall | [5] [10] [19] |
| 5 | Area Under the Curve (AUC) | [11] [23] |
| 6 | Exact Match Score | [20] |
| 7 | Inconsistency Rate | [11] |
| 8 | BLEU | [1] [25] [27] |
| 9 | ROUGE | [1] [28] |
| 10 | G-Score | [1] |
| 11 | Factual Consistency | [28] |
| 12 | BEER | [25] |

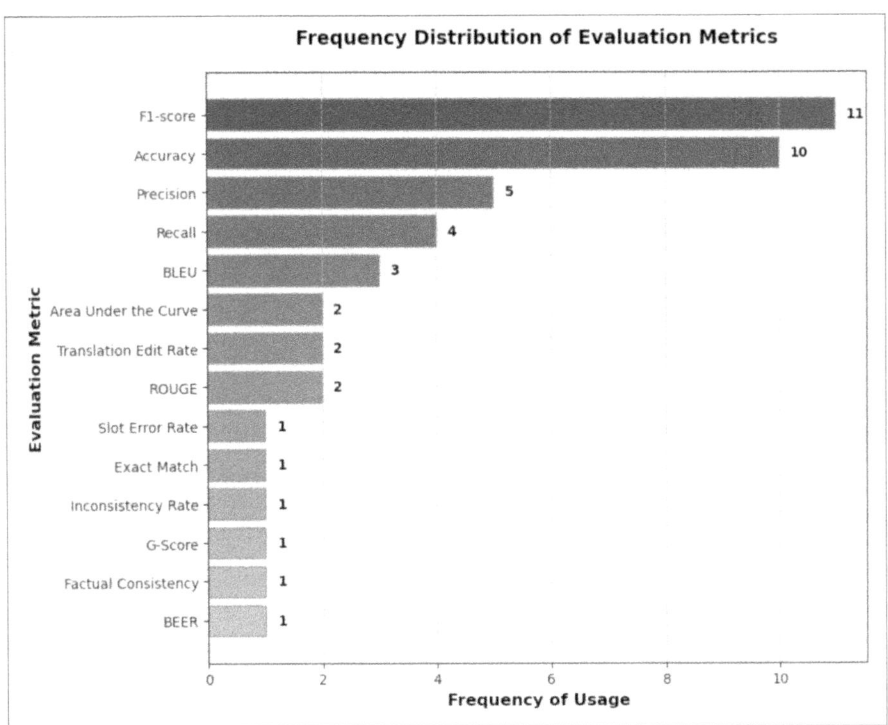


**Fig. 7.** Evaluation metrics used for active learning for natural language processing task.

## Q5. What Are the Years of Publication for the Research?

Table 7 shows that most cross-sectional research was published in 2020, followed by notable but less concentrated activity in 2019, 2021, and 2023. This distribution highlights the growing interest and expanding applications of active learning in natural language processing over recent years as shown in Fig. 8.

**Table 7.** The years of publication of the research.

| No. | Year | Reference |
|---|---|---|
| 1 | 2019 | [16] [20] [21] [26] |
| 2 | 2020 | [7] [9] [13] [17] [18] [22] [27] |
| 3 | 2021 | [9] [10] [14] [23] [24, 28] |
| 4 | 2022 | [1] |
| 5 | 2023 | [5] [6] [11] [15] [19, 25] |
| 6 | 2024 | [29] |

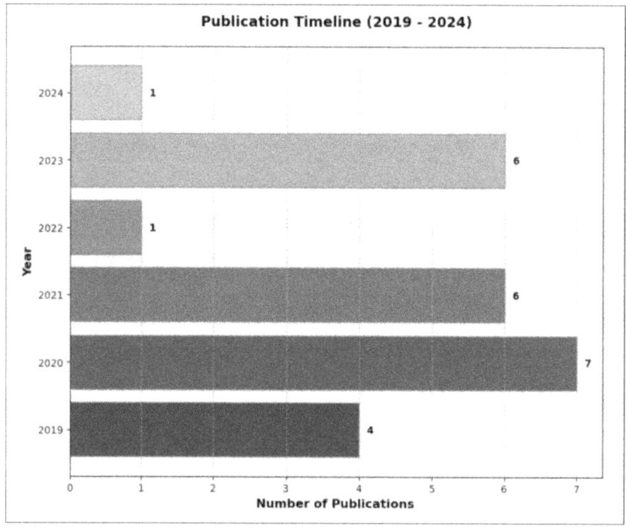


**Fig. 8.** Years of publication for paper in Table 1

## Q6: What Are the Models Used in Research?

Table 8 shows the models used in cross-sectional studies, with Bi-LSTM and BERT each achieving a 29% usage rate due to their effectiveness in handling contextual representations of text. Bi-LSTM captures long-term dependencies in sequences, while BERT represents words in two-way contexts, enhancing their suitability for NLP tasks when combined with AL. This capability improves performance in text classification, named entity recognition, and sentiment analysis as illustrated in Fig. 9.

**Table 8.**  The model(s) for paper in Table 1

| No. | Model | Reference |
| --- | --- | --- |
| 1 | Bi- (LSTM) | [7, 9] [10, 17] [21, 23, 25, 26] |
| 2 | CNN | [7] |
| 3 | BERT | [6, 13, 14] [18] [19, 23, 25, 27] |
| 4 | SVM | [8, 20] |
| 5 | SAIDS | [6] |
| 6 | CRF | [9, 10, 15, 17, 21] |
| 7 | Random Forest | [20] |
| 8 | Naive Bayes | [20] |
| 9 | Logistic Regression | [20] |
| 10 | GLoVe | [21] |
| 11 | GPT | [5, 29] |
| 12 | Flan-t5 | [11] |
| 13 | GCN | [23, 24] |
| 14 | Binary Pairwise | [22] |

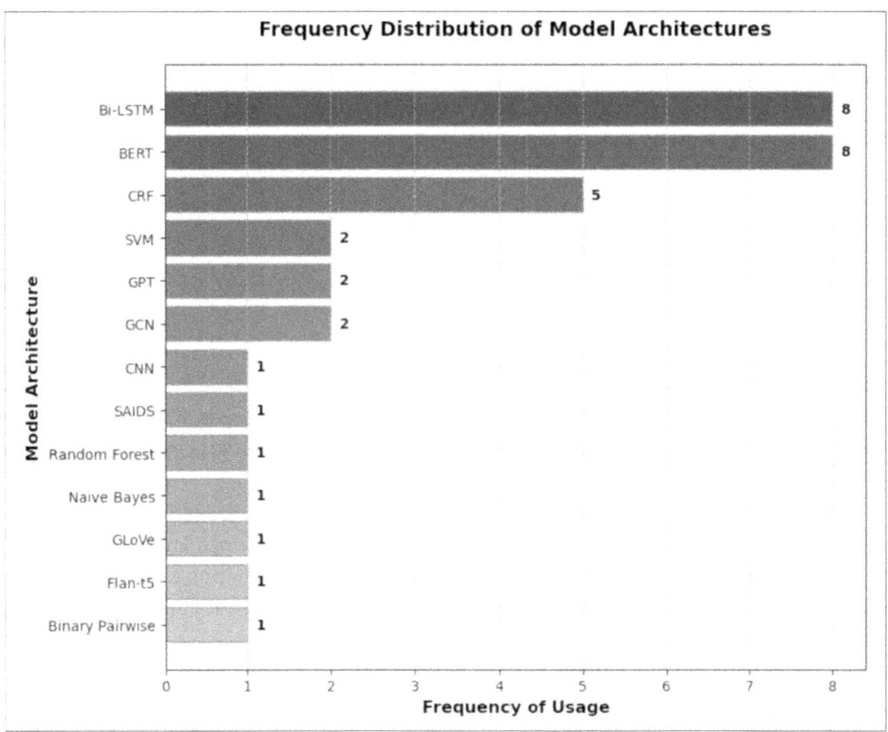


**Fig. 9.**  The models of active learning for natural language processing

The presented metrics (e.g., F1-score %, publication year %, and other distributions) were not calculated from raw scores of mean performances. Each figure is the percentage of studies that adopted or reported a specific measure. For instance, to compute the percentage for F1-score in a set of selected papers, the number of papers that used F1-score as an evaluation metric was divided by the total number of studies.

## 6  Conclusion

Active learning is the task of reducing the amount of labeled data required to learn the target concept by querying the user for labels for the most informative examples so that the concept is learned with fewer examples. Active learning is divided into two types: strategic representational and informational queries. Natural language tasks are divided into classification and prediction. Prediction consists of three types: sequence labeling, complex structured prediction, and generation. Six questions related to natural language processing tasks involving active learning were addressed. The questions encompass the following aspects: the strategies employed, the tasks performed, the language utilized for the dataset, performance metrics, the year of publication, and the models applied in the research.

The findings revealed that the most commonly used strategy was uncertainty, accounting for 21% of the studies. There were several tasks, with a significant focus on named entity recognition. English was the predominant language used in the research, representing 45% of the datasets. The most frequently utilized performance metric was the F1 score, which constituted 28% of the evaluations. Most of the research publications were in 2020, and the most widely used models were BiLSTM and BERT (29%). However, there are emerging trends in active learning within natural language processing that are expected to become focal points for researchers in the future. Promising directions and future work include hybrid active learning approaches, human-LLM cooperation in active learning, extending active learning to low-resource languages, and performing extensive benchmarking to identify best practices.

## 7  Future Work

The lack of studies on low-resource languages , such as Arabic and Asian languages, demands for active learning models tailored to these languages. Few comprehensive benchmarking studies have compared active learning strategies on the same criterion and task. Conducting such studies in the future would help standardize evaluations and identify best practices.

Integration of active learning with large language models needs more work. Exploring methods to link these approaches may significantly reduce the need for labeled data in the future. A limited number of studies have examined the annotation cost and its actual impact on model quality. There is a need for smarter hybrid approaches that combine uncertainty, diversity, and semantic coverage.

# References


1. A. Tsvigun *et al.*, "Active Learning for Abstractive Text Summarization," Jan. (2023), [Online]. Available: http://arxiv.org/abs/2301.03252
2. Z. Zhang, E. Strubell, E. Hovy: "A Survey of Active Learning for Natural Language Processing."
3. Kohl, P., Krämer, Y., Fohry, C., Kraft, B.: Scoping Review of Active Learning Strategies and their Evaluation Environments for Entity Recognition Tasks (2024). https://doi.org/10.1007/978-3-031-66694-0_6
4. Anton Kretov: "Active Learning for NLP," (2024).
5. H. Mahdhaoui, A. Mars, M. Zrigui: Active Learning with AraGPT2 for Arabic Named Entity Recognition.
6. Kaseb, A., Farouk, M.: Active learning for Arabic sentiment analysis. Alex. Eng. J. **77**, 177–187 (2023). https://doi.org/10.1016/j.aej.2023.06.082
7. S. Arad *et al.:* Optimizing Annotation Effort Using Active Learning Strategies: A Sentiment Analysis Case Study in Persian (2020). [Online]. Available: www.Digikala.com
8. Al-Tamimi, A.K., Bani-Isaa, E., Al-Alami, A.: Active Learning for Arabic text classification. In: *Proceedings of 2nd IEEE International Conference on Computational Intelligence and Knowledge Economy, ICCIKE 2021*, Institute of Electrical and Electronics Engineers Inc., pp. 123–126 (2021). https://doi.org/10.1109/ICCIKE51210.2021.9410758
9. M. Liu, Z. Tu, T. Zhang, T. Su, Z. Wang: LTP: A New Active Learning Strategy for CRF-Based Named Entity Recognition," Jan. (2020), [Online]. Available: http://arxiv.org/abs/2001.02524
10. A. Chaudhary, A. Anastasopoulos, Z. Sheikh, G. Neubig: Reducing Confusion in Active Learning for Part-Of-Speech Tagging, doi: 10.1162/tacl.
11. Y. Perlitz, A. Gera, M. Shmueli-Scheuer, D. Sheinwald, N. Slonim, L. Ein-Dor: Active Learning for Natural Language Generation," May 2023, [Online]. Available: http://arxiv.org/abs/2305.15040
12. Kumar, P., Gupta, A.: Active Learning query strategies for classification, regression, and clustering: a survey. J. Comput. Sci. Technol. **35**(4), 913–945 (2020). https://doi.org/10.1007/s11390-020-9487-4
13. G. Bai, S. He, K. Liu, J. Zhao, Z. Nie: Pre-trained Language Model Based Active Learning for Sentence Matching," Online.
14. P. F. Jacobs, G. M. de B. Wenniger, M. Wiering, L. Schomaker: Active learning for reducing labeling effort in text classification tasks, Sep. (2021) [Online]. Available: http://arxiv.org/abs/2109.04847
15. Kanclerz, K., et al.: PALS: personalized active Learning for subjective tasks in NLP. In: *EMNLP 2023-2023 Conference on Empirical Methods in Natural Language Processing, Proceedings*, Association for Computational Linguistics (ACL), pp. 13326–13341 (2023). https://doi.org/10.18653/v1/2023.emnlp-main.823.
16. S. Peshterliev, J. Kearney, A. Jagannatha, I. Kiss, S. Matsoukas, and A. M. Learning, "Active Learning for New Domains in Natural Language Understanding."
17. T. Cai, Z. Ma, H. Zheng, Y. Zhou: NE-LP: Normalized Entropy and Loss Prediction based Sampling for Active Learning in Chinese Word Segmentation on EHRs," Aug. 2019, [Online]. Available: http://arxiv.org/abs/1908.08419
18. K. Brantley, A. Sharaf, and H. Daumé III: Active Imitation Learning with Noisy Guidance." [Online]. Available: https://github.com/xkianteb/leaqi
19. H. Luo, W. Tan, N. D. Nguyen, L. Du: Re-weighting Tokens: A Simple and Effective Active Learning Strategy for Named Entity Recognition," Nov. 2023, [Online]. Available: http://arxiv.org/abs/2311.00906

20. J. Kasai, K. Qian, S. Gurajada, Y. Li, L. Popa, P. G. Allen: Low-resource Deep Entity Resolution with Transfer and Active Learning.
21. O. Koshorek, G. Stanovsky, Y. Zhou, V. Srikumar, J. Berant: On the Limits of Learning to Actively Learn Semantic Representations." [Online]. Available: https://github.com/
22. V. Espeland, B. Bach, B. Alex: Enhanced Labelling in Active Learning for Conference Resolution, (2020).
23. Mallart, C., Le Nouy, M., Gravier, G., Sébillot, P.: Active Learning for interactive relation extraction in a French newspaper's articles. In: International Conference Recent Advances in Natural Language Processing, RANLP, pp. 886–894. Incoma Ltd (2021). https://doi.org/10.26615/978-954-452-072-4_101
24. B. Liu, H. Scells, G. Zuccon, W. Hua, G. Zhao: ActiveEA: Active Learning for Neural Entity Alignment.
25. G. Haffari A. Sarkar: Active Learning for Multilingual Statistical Machine Translation (2009).
26. Wallace, E., Gardner, M., Singh, S.: Interpreting predictions of NLP models. In: EMNLP 2020 - Conference on Empirical Methods in Natural Language Processing, Tutorial Abstracts, Association for Computational Linguistics (ACL), pp. 20–23 (2020). https://doi.org/10.18653/v1/P17
27. P. Sen, E. Yilmaz, S. Kocaman: Uncertainty and Traffic-Aware Active Learning for Semantic Parsing. pp. 1–6, 2020.
28. Z. Zhou A. Waibel: Active Learning for Massively Parallel Translation of Constrained Text into Low Resource Languages.
29. X. Wang: Active Learning for NLP with Large Language Models, Jan. (2024), [Online]. Available: http://arxiv.org/abs/2401.07367

# Seatbelt and Mobile Usage Detection Using Deep Learning

Fatima Basheer Abd Al-ameer[✉] and Ayad Rodhan Abbas

Computer Science Department, University of Technology, Baghdad, Iraq
`cs.24.11@grad.uotechnology.edu.iq,`
`ayad.r.abbas@uotechnology.edu.iq`

**Abstract.** Traffic safety violations such as not wearing seatbelts or using mobile phones while driving are main contributors to road accidents worldwide. Studies have used various techniques to detect traffic violations, still there are various limitations, including low accuracy, windshield reflections, occlusion, and color similarity. An automated system for the detection of traffic violations was proposed. The system is divided into two stages; one is a fine-tuned YOLOv11 model to detect the car windshield area and then identifies the driver region. In addition, data preprocessing techniques are applied to enhance the quality of images. In the second stage, a neural network model is utilized that employs a transfer learning mechanism with various deep learning classification algorithms, such as ResNet34, AlexNet, VGG16, and DenseNet. Two publicly available datasets are used in our study with a total number of images, from both datasets, of 1,481, taken under various lighting conditions such as sunny, cloudy, rainy, dark, and foggy. Our extensive simulation results indicated that the ResNet34 model performed the best among the other classifiers and achieved an average accuracy of 98% for the seatbelt compliance task and 99% for mobile phone usage. Benchmark comparison with existing literature indicated that the proposed lightweight model demonstrated improved results.

**Keywords:** Seatbelt detection · Mobile phone detection · Deep learning · and Transfer learning

## 1 Introduction

The ever-growing number of cars worldwide has led to a rise in traffic accidents. The risk of these accidents has increased due to violating traffic safety rules, such as not wearing a seatbelt and using a mobile phone while driving. Artificial intelligence and computer vision systems play a significant role in promoting advanced systems to enhance safety and recognize human behavior [1]. Deep learning is one of the fundamental techniques in object recognition. Convolutional neural networks (CNNs) are considered one of the most popular deep learning algorithms used in computer vision applications for image analysis and object recognition [2]. Studies have utilized various object detection methodologies, including one-stage techniques like YOLO and SSD, as well as two-stage techniques like Faster R-CNN. Various DL models have been employed in this


S. O. Al-Mamory et al. (Eds.): 3INC 2025, CCIS 2960, pp. 201–230, 2026.
https://doi.org/10.1007/978-3-032-24239-6_12

work, among which the algorithm series known as You Only Look Once (YOLO) showed remarkable potential. In spite of the progress done by studies, these techniques still face problems in real environments, including color similarity, various lighting conditions, different angles from the camera, occlusions, and windshield reflections, necessitating the need to introduce a developed and more accurate method to solve these limitations. In addition, the quality of the training data has a greater impact on the model's performance than the AI techniques employed.

The contributions of this research can be summarized as follows:

1. The YOLOv11 model's hyperparameters were tuned during training to improve the detection accuracy of the traffic violation system.
2. Data quality was improved by conducting image preprocessing. The CLAHE method was utilized for contrast enhancement, making the seatbelt stand out better and improving the visibility of the mobile phone from the driver's face or hand. Despite the progress made by CLAHE enhancement, this technique may introduce artifacts, which can be particularly noticeable in homogeneous regions. Therefore, a non-linear bilateral filter was applied to smooth the image by reducing noise while maintaining the sharp edges of the image. By utilizing these techniques, the mean average precision of YOLOv11 at 50 intersections over union (IOU) for detecting the windshield region improved from 99.3% to 99.5% and from 84.2 to 86.1 at 50–95 IOU, and the average accuracy of the classification algorithms improved by 0.2%.
3. Data diversity was improved by applying augmentation techniques, including HSV_V and scale, to simulate real-world brightness variations and scaling transformations to introduce size variability.
4. Four deep learning models, such as ResNet34, DenseNet, VGG16, and AlexNet were fine-tuned using transfer learning, and their hyperparameters have been uniformly altered during training. After applying these modifications, the performance of the best algorithm improved from 96.63 to 98 for seatbelt compliance and from 94.12% to 99% for mobile usage classification. In addition, the training curves became more stable, avoiding overfitting.

Section 2 reviews techniques for detecting traffic violations using deep learning models. Section 3 explains the methodology, which involves three steps: the first describes the dataset used, and the second discusses the proposed approach for detection, which led to choosing YOLOv11 as the final model for windshield detection. Section 4 is focused on representing the results and discussion leading to Sect. 5 which represents conclusion.

## 2  Related Works

This section discusses different methods used in the literature to detect traffic safety violations. A majority of these studies have focused on the detection of seatbelt compliance, while a few have dealt with mobile usage while driving.

## 2.1  Seatbelt Detection

A deep neural network, NADS-Net, was utilized in [3] for in-car passenger, driver pose estimation, and seatbelt detection. Feature pyramid networks were used for multi-scale feature extraction. The model also had several head detections, such as a seat belt segmentation head, a key point detection head, and a part affinity field detection head. It was trained on the custom dataset created from videos of drivers and passengers in a Volvo XC90 car under different conditions. The model had a precision of 63.58% and an F1 score of 63.55%. According to the results achieved, the model failed to detect the seat belt in certain situations, such as low light and occlusions.

In [4] a tiny-yolo model is proposed to detect seatbelts and belt corners inside the car. Preprocessing was applied to improve the model performance. The training process was run on a dataset consisting of images and videos, some of which were obtained from roads and some from public sources. The accuracy was 93% for seatbelt detection and 94% for detecting the belt corner. However, for images under poor lighting situations, the model faces challenges.

In [5] a hybrid model is developed to enhance the accuracy of identifying seatbelts. YOLOv3 was first used to identify the bounding box around the windshield and the seatbelt worn by the driver; then, the extracted features from the driver region were coupled with LSTM for binary classification. This approach was utilized on images sourced from RoboFlow Universe, which contained 199 images. This model accomplished an accuracy of 89%; however, the model faced overfitting problems due to a lack of enough training data. Overfitting meant that it could not easily generalize when it was overreliant on learned patterns in new data. In addition, the dataset used did not contain a wide range of images with various lighting conditions and different vehicles, which may limit the accuracy of the model in real environments.

In [6] the YOLOv4 detection model is utilized to achieve equilibrium between accuracy and speed for seatbelt detection in real time. Preprocessing was performed for improving the quality of the image as well as the accuracy of detection. Then, the AlexNet model was used for object classification. It was trained on a limited dataset collected from the internet of about 300 images of drivers wearing/not wearing seatbelts. The accuracy was 93%. However, the model encountered the risk of an overfitting problem because it used limited training data, which made the model overreliant on learned patterns without being able to generalize to unseen data.

In [7] demonstrated the problems of using YOLOv5 for object detection in real time, including long training times, low detection speed, and challenges in detecting poor-quality data. Therefore, they used YOLOv8 to detect windshields, identify drivers and passengers, and classify seatbelt compliance; the model was trained on data created from roads in Bandung, Indonesia, and Semarang. The YOLOv8l-cls model achieved an accuracy of 88.64%. The number of seatbelt-wearing images was larger than the number of non-seatbelt-wearing images, which biased the model toward the seatbelt class.

In [8] presented a multi-task method to appropriately recognize seatbelts. They combined ResNet101 with feature pyramid networks for multiple-scale feature extraction. To determine the important regions, a region proposal network (RPN) was used for the extracted features. Then a patch diagonal sampling method was used to process regions by taking advantage of their diagonal shape. A gated bidirectional LSTM model utilized a part-to-whole attention mechanism combined with local and global context information. It detected patch relations to improve the accuracy for classifying seatbelts. The model trained on the SBD-RSI road monitoring image dataset outperformed YOLOX by 0.9%, with 71.4%, and attained a mean average precision of 72.3%. However, the requirement for manual adjustment of the diagonal sampling parameters and the combination of several techniques increased computational complexity.

## 2.2  Mobile Phone Detection

In [9] proposed a progressive calibration network for tracking and detecting the face region. Then, a YOLOv3 model was used to detect the mobile phone near it. The model was trained on CBDS datasets, which included images taken from a thermal camera. The proposed model had an accuracy of 96.56%, a processing speed of 25 frames per second, and a low false positive rate of 1.5%. However, it faced problems in distinguishing the phone from similar objects, such as wallets.

In [10] proposed a Single Shot Detector (SSD) using the RGB and NIR input images to detect the windshield, driver, and mobile and achieved an accuracy of 91%. The results indicated that the accuracy of the SSD model outperformed the CNN and FV. The accuracy of CNN was 72.9%, while Fisher Vector recorded 64.1% on NIR images and 88.1% on RGB images. The image imbalance in positive and negative classes resulted in overfitting.

In [11] utilized a multi-angle camera inside the car to create a dataset. The training process of the CNN model on these images helped handling occlusion between the mobile and body posture while driving. In the preprocessing, to determine important regions, animated region extraction, skin color detection, and the difference computed between sequential frames were used. In addition, these preprocessing steps made the detection more accurate and attenuated the processing. Then, two convolutional neural networks were trained to individually extract features for hands and cell phones. The model achieved an accuracy of 95.7%. However, the dependency on skin color detection led to mistakes due to color variations and reflections inside the car, not to mention the expensive multi-angle cameras.

Table 1 lists the techniques utilized in the literature for identifying seatbelt and mobile usage while driving. Clearly, despite using various advanced deep learning techniques, there are significant issues related to color similarity, challenges associated with images created from poor lighting environments, different angles, occlusions, and windshield reflections.

**Table 1.** Review Details of Related Works.

| References | Dataset | Task | Methods | Accuracy (%) | Other metrics (%) |
|---|---|---|---|---|---|
| [3] | The dataset was created from video clips under different conditions | Seatbelt | NADS-Net | – | The precision and F1 score are 63.5 |

(continued)

**Table 1.** (*continued*)

| References | Dataset | Task | Methods | Accuracy (%) | Other metrics (%) |
|---|---|---|---|---|---|
| [4] | Images were gathered from the in-car camera | Seatbelt | Tiny-yolo | 93 | – |
| [5] | RoboFlow dataset | Seatbelt | CNN + LSTM | 89 | – |
| [6] | The dataset was collected from the internet | Seatbelt | YOLOv4 | 93 | - |
| [7] | The dataset was created using traffic images | Seatbelt | Yolov8 | 88.64 | - |
| [8] | The SBD-RSI was created from road surveillance images | Seatbelt | ResNet 101, patch sampling, and gated bidirectional LSTM with part-to-whole attention | – | MAP is 72.3 |
| [9] | Calling Behavior Data Set (CBDS) from an infrared camera | Mobile phone | PCN | 96.56 | – |
| [10] | The dataset was captured from 3MP near-infrared (NIR) and RGB cameras | Mobile phone | SSD | 91 | – |
| [11] | Images from the in-car multi-angle camera | Mobile phone | CNN | 95.7 | – |

# 3  Methodology

The proposed method consists of two stages to identify the windshield and isolate the driver's region, then classification of the driver region as illustrated in Fig. 1.

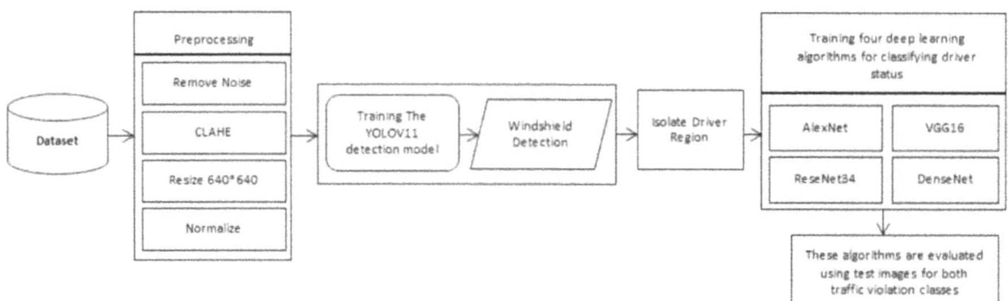


**Fig.1.**  Diagram of the proposed methodology of the traffic violation system.

## 3.1  The Dataset Used

The dataset used contained images taken of various drivers with different camera angles from surveillance cameras. In addition, images with various lighting conditions and different weather conditions were also included. These images were collected from two datasets: RoboFlow Universe [12], which contained images of drivers using mobile phones while driving or drivers using seatbelts, and the second dataset was from [13], which aimed to detect passenger and driver seatbelt compliance. To increase the size of the images and enhance their diversity, we randomly selected images from that study, including violations by just seatbelt-wearing and non-seatbelt-wearing drivers. To have an effective and accurate model, the images were divided into 80% for the training data set, 12% for the validation data set, and 8% for the test data set.

The first dataset contained 1100 images taken under different lighting conditions: sunny, cloudy, and partially dark areas; images were taken from cameras placed at different angles and distances. After reviewing, duplicate images were removed, bringing the total chosen number of images to 900 as shown in Table 2.

The second dataset comprised 3500 images supplied by traffic organizations. These images were taken in various environmental situations, such as mild, cloudy, rainy, foggy, and dark. There were 1600 images in the second dataset that were used to classify driver and passenger status.

In the second dataset, the seatbelt samples were the most prevalent. Accordingly, approximately 600 images were selected to ensure diversity and prevent bias towards the seatbelt class Table 3. Most of the selected images included images of drivers not wearing seatbelts. The total number of images from both datasets was 1,481, including images taken under various lighting conditions such as sunny, cloudy, rainy, dark, and foggy; images where a seatbelt or mobile phone was partially visible; and other images showing windshield reflections and different camera angles.

**Table 2.** The first dataset utilized in our study.

| Dataset References | Resolution | Numbers of Images | Descriptions |
|---|---|---|---|
| RoboFlow Universe [12] | 587*584<br>550*520<br>616*615<br>870*496 | 1100 | Images of drivers wearing seatbelts and driving with cell phones. After reviewing the data, it was discovered that there were several duplicate images that were removed, bringing the total chosen number of images to 900 |

**Table 3.** The second dataset utilized in our study.

| Dataset References | Resolution | Numbers of Images | Descriptions |
|---|---|---|---|
| correlated study [13] | 1000*750 | 3500 | Images of drivers and passengers, some wearing seatbelts and others not. 1600 images were used to classify driver status in the original images, and the seatbelt category was the most spread in data. 600 images of drivers, excluding passengers, were selected |

## 3.2  Image Preprocessing

Because of the varying lighting conditions in the driving environment, the input image quality used for detection and subsequent classification was improved by applying pre-processing techniques as the first step in the proposed model. In some lighting conditions, seatbelts were difficult to distinguish when their color was similar to that of the driver's clothing, and therefore RGB images were used. Contrast-limited adaptive histogram equalization and noise removal were applied to improve the clarity of important elements in the image and reduce unnecessary noise.

### 3.2.1  Contrast-Limited Adaptive Histogram Equalization

CLAHE is a preprocessing technique that controls the image contrast and improves image clarity. To reduce the effect of environmental scenarios such as poor lighting, cloudy weather, etc., the contrast-limited method of adaptive histogram equalization was performed to improve the contrast of the color images. This technique converts the input images into three channels, l, a, and b, where l includes the lighting channel and both a and b are the color information. Then, the CLAHE is performed only on the lighting channel, using a clip limit of 2.0 and a grid size of (8, 8) to adjust brightness and contrast while preserving the other color channels. Finally, the enhanced image was retransformed back into the RGB space to produce clear input images for the proposed system. Even in poor lighting conditions, this technique enhances edge definition to make the seatbelt better stand out and improve the visibility of the mobile phone from the driver's face or hand [14].

### 3.2.2  Noise Removal

While CLAHE enhances the image quality, this technique may introduce artifacts, which might be visible in homogeneous regions. Therefore, a non-linear bilateral filter was applied for smoothing the image; it reduced the noise while maintaining the sharp edges of the image. In this case, the intensity of every pixel is replaced by the average neighboring pixels' weighted value intensity [15]. Figure 2 illustrates the improvement performed on the original image.

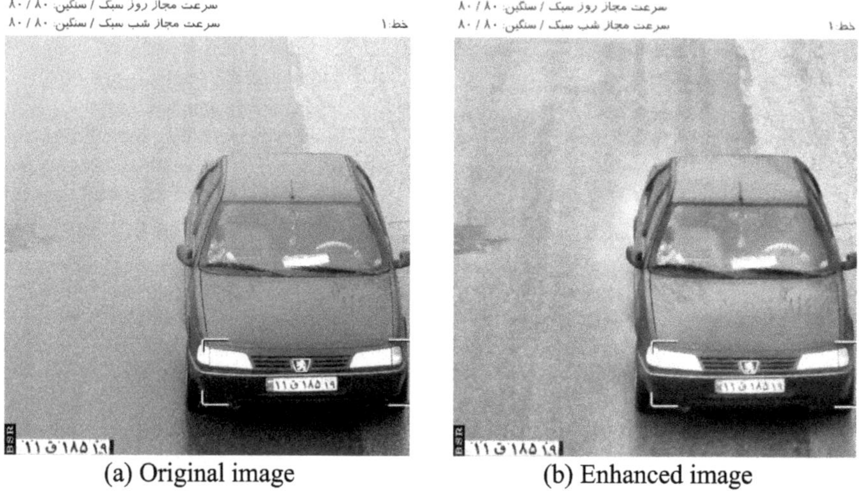

(a) Original image     (b) Enhanced image

**Fig.2.**  The effect of CLAHE and the bilateral filter.

### 3.3  Proposed Approach for Detection

Small objects, unlike larger objects, contain limited spatial and contextual information. Therefore, identifying small objects is a big challenging task in computer vision, with applications like traffic violation surveillance, autonomous systems, and remote sensing. The most popular deep learning techniques for object detection belong to the YOLO family of detection algorithms that are well known for speed and efficiency. Despite significant progress made in the field of object detection, there are some problems associated with detecting small objects that result in poor performance. As the model depth increases, fine-grained features of small targets tend to be lost, and the extracted representations may become more susceptible to background noise and interference. Therefore, to classify driver status more accurately, detecting the car's windshield area is essential for identifying the region occupied by the driver. According to the experimental results of training YOLO models, two versions of YOLO (YOLOv8 and YOLOv11) showed closely comparable performance in accuracy and speed.

### 3.3.1  Training Yolov8 and Yolov11 Models for Detection

The images were automatically resized to 640*640 during training using a built-in letterbox function of the YOLO model. This procedure maintains the aspect ratio by padding around the image, which prevents stretching or distorting. YOLO is a single-stage detection algorithm that recognizes objects in real time using convolutional neural networks. It forecasts the class labels and bounding boxes of the objects in one step within an image [16]. Studies have used various models to detect car windshields and identify driver regions; mostly YOLO of different versions. In this section, the performance of training the YOLOv8 and YOLOv11 models is evaluated to identify the driver region. These two models are made by Ultralytics [17], whose interface has considerably eased the training process compared to other YOLO variants. The experimental results demonstrated that the performance of training those models was closely comparable. YOLO11s and YOLO8s were trained on the selected 1,481 images; the training part consisted of 1,190, the validation set contained 174, and the testing data was 117. Data augmentation techniques were applied in the training part to increase the diversity of images, including a scale of 0.2 and an HSV_V of 0.4. Each model was trained with a low learning rate of 0.001, a weight decay of 0.001, a Cosine Learning Rate (CLR), and the Adam optimizer was used along with 16 batch sizes and 50 epochs. The results of the training process demonstrated that the architectural improvements in YOLOv11s made it more efficient at identifying windshields.

We achieved a mean average precision of 86.1% at 50–95%, higher than YOLOv8's 83.8%, and YOLOv11 achieved a higher precision of 98.7% than YOLOv8's 97.4%. In addition, the lighter structure and fewer parameters of YOLOv11s contributed to reduced computational overhead.

Although YOLOv11s has fewer parameters and a lighter architecture, YOLOv8s boasts a slightly higher inference speed of 11.4 than YOLOv11's of 14.3. The results indicated that YOLOv8s is important for systems that require high speed, while YOLOv11s is recommended where high accuracy detection is more essential.

**Table 4.** Performance of detection algorithms.

| Map% | Recall% | Precision% | Models |
|------|---------|------------|--------|
| 83.8 | 100 | 97.4 | YOLOV8S |
| 86.1 | 100 | 98.7 | YOLO11S |

Table 4 shows the benchmark between YOLOv11 and YOLOv8. It is important to note that the windshield is a large object with defined borders in the image, making it easier for YOLO algorithms to detect. Thus, both YOLOv8s and YOLOv11s achieved a 100% recall, indicating that both models detected all true instances without false negative instances. The YOLOv11 model is recommended for windshield detection based on the experimental implementation, which shows an effective balance between detection accuracy and execution speed. YOLOv11s is the latest version of the YOLO series. It utilizes a deep neural network that contains improved blocks like C3k2, SPPF, and C2PSA, which help the model to recognize important features in images more efficiently as shown in Fig. 3.

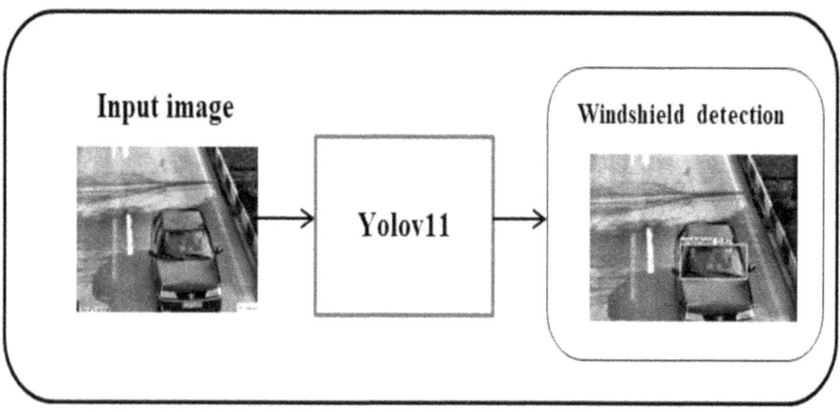


**Fig. 3.** Windshield detection.

Utilizing the C2PSA unit improved detection because it enabled the model to learn fine details and detect objects more accurately. This type of attention is not available in the YOLOv8 model, making YOLOv11 superior in processing complex scenes and addressing the challenges of accurate detection in multiple environments. YOLOv11s maintains an effective trade-off between accuracy and computational efficiency [18].

### 3.3.2 Driver Region Isolation

After identifying the windshield region, the right part of the windshield was isolated to classify traffic violations committed by drivers. The driver images included three different sets of traffic violation samples as shown in Fig. 4. The first set contained images of drivers wearing seatbelts, the second set of images included drivers using mobile phones while driving, and the third set of images included drivers not using a mobile phone and not wearing a seatbelt. During the training process of each classification model, the same samples of images were used for the class of drivers without seatbelts and for the class of drivers without mobile phones. To improve classification accuracy, the classification models were trained separately for each violation type: seatbelt and mobile phone.

**Fig. 4.** Samples of driver region images.

## 3.4 Proposed Approach for Classification

Four deep learning models including ResNet34, AlexNet, DenseNet, and VGG16, were employed and fine-tuned using the transfer learning mechanism. In addition, the head layers and training parameters were modified in each model to improve performance on the dataset used.

### 3.4.1 Transfer Learning

Transfer learning is an important technique that transmits the knowledge from the pre-trained model, which was trained on a large dataset such as ImageNet [19], to the target model using pre-trained weights for improving the performance of a new model. The transfer learning mechanism was applied to improve the training on limited dataset samples and the perception of the available original data. It also reduced training time and computational costs compared to training from scratch [20].

### 3.4.2  Data Splitting Repeated Hold-Out Validation (Two-Splits)

The classification models were trained using two splits of training and validation data, which were obtained through a repeated hold-out validation method. First the dataset was split into three parts: training, validation, and testing. Then, the training and validation sets were divided into two different splits to create two different sets of training/validation data and reduce bias toward a single set [21]. Each model was trained using two different training/validation splits and evaluated on the same fixed test set. The model performance was computed as the average across both splits, giving the best results with more generalization.

### 3.4.3  Driver Image Preprocessing for Classification

For each task, all input images were resized to 224x224 pixels to meet the requirements of training the ResNet34, AlexNet, VGG16, and DenseNet models. The resized input images (JPEG or PNG) were then converted into tensors; during this process, the dimension order was rearranged from (h*w*c) to (c*h*w), where c represents the number of channels, h represents the height, and w is the width. Pixel values were rescaled from 0–255 to 0.0–1.0 and normalized by the ImageNet dataset's mean and standard deviation to match the classification models. This normalization was applied to the training images, validation images, and test images such that there was consistency in distribution and numerical stability during training.

### 3.4.4  Data Augmentation

Data augmentation is an important technique in deep learning that involves artificially increasing the training part of the dataset by creating modified copies of the original images. Data augmentation is primarily used to prevent overfitting and improve the model's ability to generalize when dealing with new data. In this research, the process of data augmentation was carried out automatically during the training of the proposed system. A series of operations was performed randomly on images in each training iteration. These operations helped in diversifying the model's training samples. Several data augmentation operations were applied, including color jitter brightness by 0.4, contrast by 0.3, saturation by 0.3, and hue by 0.05; random affine translate by 0.2; rotation range by 10; and scale between (1.1, 0.9).

### 3.4.5  Alexnet Model

In the first model, the AlexNet layers [22] were used with ImageNet weights and a transfer learning mechanism. The first four layers were frozen by making them non-trainable. Then the original classifier module was replaced with a custom classification layer consisting of three layers. This modified architecture begins with a linear layer with 64 output units, followed by a ReLU activation function and a 0.5 dropout layer. Next, a batch normalization layer, ReLU activation function, and 0.3 dropouts trailed a linear layer with 32 output units. Finally, a single-output linear layer and a sigmoid activation function were used to enhance the performance of the binary classification probability.

### 3.4.6 DenseNet Model

DenseNet121 [23] with ImageNet weights was trained using transfer learning mechanisms. The first three layers, such as conv0, norm0, and denseblock1 were frozen to speed the model training using pretrained weights. Then the 1024-unit fully connected layer, dedicated to classifying 1000 objects, was replaced with three custom cascaded layers. The modified architecture started with a linear layer with 64 output units, followed by a ReLU function and a 0.5 dropout layer. Next, a linear layer with 32 output units, batch normalization, ReLU, and a 0.3 dropout layer was used. To increase the likelihood of binary classification, a single-output linear layer with a sigmoid activation function was employed.

### 3.4.7 Vgg16 Model

In this model, lightweight and straightforward VGG16 layers [24] with ImageNet weights were adopted. A modified structure of the VGG16 model with transfer learning techniques includes freezing the first ten layers of the feature extraction by making them non-trainable to keep the general properties that were extracted from the ImageNet data, while unfreezing other layers except the FC layer. The final fully connected layer was substituted with a modified classification block, which consisted of three layers. The first layer began with a 64-output unit, followed by a ReLU activation function and a 0.5-unit dropout layer. Next, a 32-unit linear layer, BatchNorm1d, ReLU, and a 0.3-unit dropout layer were added. Lastly, a one-unit linear layer employed a sigmoid activation function. This replacement enhanced the model's performance in classifying traffic violations committed by drivers, resulting in more efficient feature representation.

### 3.4.8 Resnet34 Model

First, the ResNet34 model [25] was trained with pre-trained weights and a new setting of model hyperparameters. These hyperparameters include the number of classes, batch size, number of epochs, learning rate, and optimizer. The final layer in ResNet34, for classifying 1000 classes, was replaced with a single neuron for binary classification, and the sigmoid activation function was used for classifying two classes with the binary cross-entropy loss function.

Second, the ResNet34 and transfer learning were adopted to increase the model performance, where low-level layers, such as conv1, layer 1, and layer 2 were frozen to preserve the general features extracted from the ImageNet data. The upper layers, such as layer 3, layer 4, and the fully connected (FC) layer were left unfrozen so that their weights updated during training. Then, the final fully connected layer, the FC layer, was replaced by a custom classification head consisting of three consecutive layers: The first layer was a 64-unit linear layer, followed by a ReLU activation function and a 0.5-unit dropout layer. Next, a 32-unit linear layer was used, followed by BatchNorm1d, a ReLU activation function, and a 0.3-unit dropout layer. Lastly, a one-unit linear layer employed a sigmoid activation function. This replacement improved the model's ability to categorize traffic violations committed by drivers, achieving more efficient feature representation. In addition, a dropout layer was utilized to avoid the risk of overfitting problems by disabling some neurons randomly, which enhanced the accuracy and generalization of the model.

**Training Workflow**

Subsequent to driver image preprocessing, the proposed classification algorithms were trained on two splits of train/valid data separately for each violation task. A balanced number of images was used for classes within each split to design an efficient model able to accommodate most situations in a real-world environment without bias toward the majority category. There is a limited number of images that show neither a seatbelt nor a mobile phone, totaling 343 in both the train and valid data sets, and 375 images of drivers with mobile usage while driving as shown in Table 5. For the seatbelt compliance task, the training part of Split 1 included 243 images for the seatbelt class and 243 for the no-seatbelt class. Split 2 contained 241 images for the seatbelt class and 241 for the no seatbelt class; 62 images were used in the validation part in each class for both splits.

For the mobile usage classification, the training set included 150 images of the no-mobile class and 150 images of the mobile class in split 1. In total,149 images for the no-mobile class and 149 for the mobile class in split 2 were employed. The validation set consisted of 38 images for both classes within each split.

This balance was achieved when images of people without a seatbelt or using a mobile phone were used in the no-seatbelt class for the seatbelt compliance task.

In the mobile phone classification task, random images depicting a seatbelt were used in the "no mobile" class to prevent bias towards the phone category. Therefore, a balanced training set was designed by selecting random samples, which were used to ensure a more efficient model without biasing.

**Table 5.** The distribution of classes across splits for both the training and validation sets.

| Classes | Split1 | Split 2 | Total |
|---|---|---|---|
| Seatbelt | 305 | 303 | 608 |
| No_seatbelt | 305 | 303 | 608 |
| Mobile | 187 | 188 | 375 |
| No_mobile | 187 | 188 | 375 |

The Adam optimization algorithm was used for training each fold for both tasks and 1e-4 weight decay as regularization to lower overfitting. For seatbelt compliance classification, these models were trained with 30 epochs, a batch size of 16, and a learning rate of 0.0001 for each fold. For mobile phone usage classification, the model was trained with 38 epochs for fold0, 33 epochs for fold1, 16 batch sizes, and a 0.0001 learning rate for both folds.

## 3.5  Experimental Results

This section presents the performance evaluation of each classification model based on the results of testing experiments. The experiments utilized the average evaluation metrics, such as accuracy as shown in Fig. 5, precision, recall, and the F1 score [26].

In the AlexNet model for classifying the seatbelt compliance task, the average accuracy during model training was 94.35%. However, for the test part of images, the average accuracy was 92%, the average precision was 98%, the average recall was 86%, and the average F1-score was 92%.

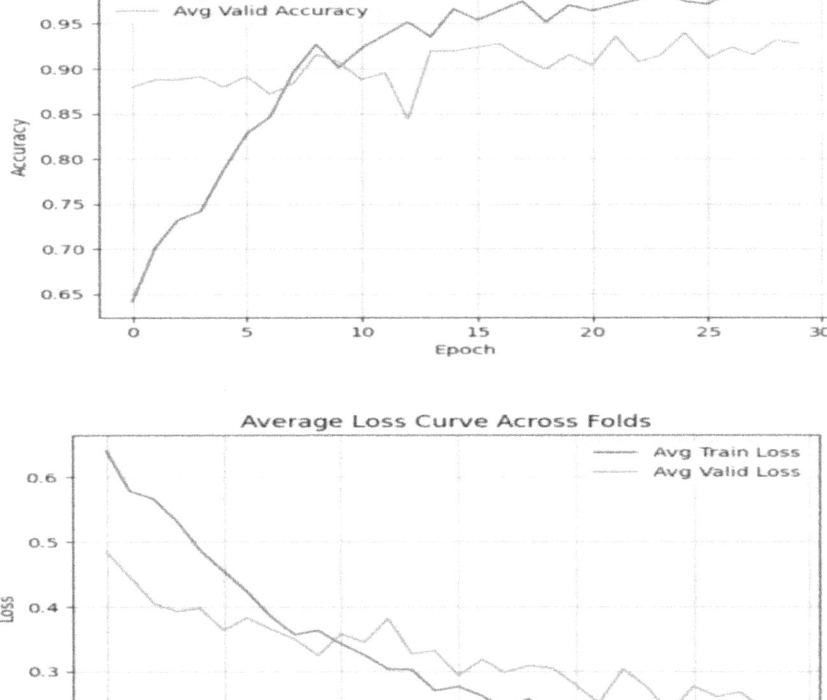


**Fig.5.** The accuracy and loss metrics associated with training AlexNet to assess seatbelt compliance.

For the task of classifying mobile phone usage while driving, the average training accuracy of the model was 98%. However, the average testing accuracy of two splits was 96%, the average precision was 96%, the average recall was 97%, and the average F1-score was 96% as shown in Fig. 6.

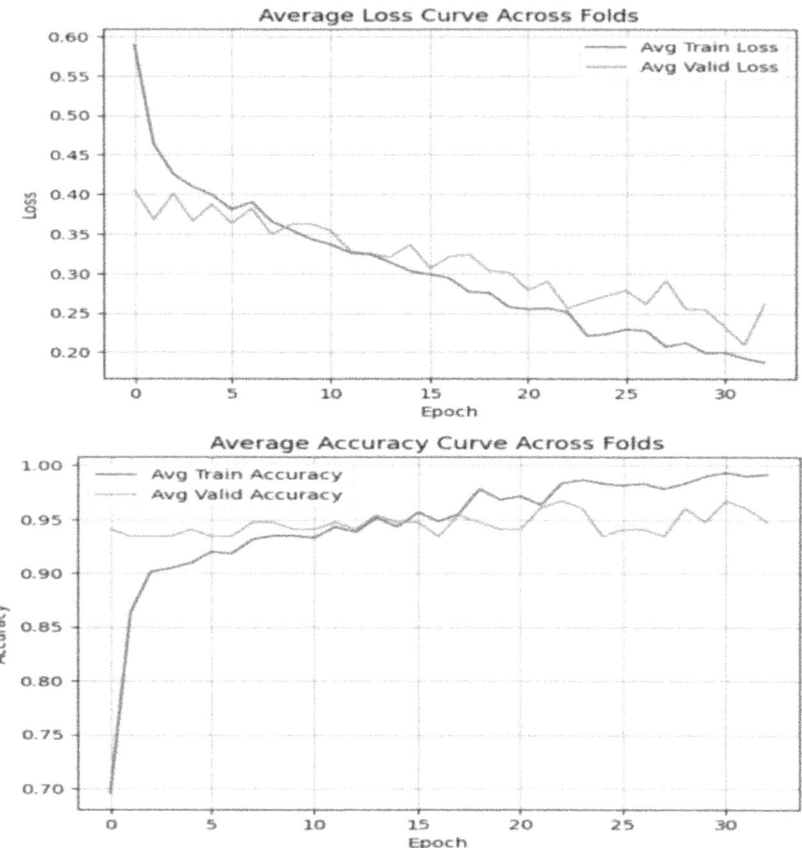

**Fig.6.** The accuracy and loss of training AlexNet for mobile phone usage classification.

The DenseNet model used to classify the seatbelt compliance task had an average accuracy for training of 99%. However, the average testing accuracy was 95%, and the average precision, recall, and F1-score were 99%, 91%, and 95% respectively. When the model was used to classify violations of mobile phone usage, the average training accuracy was 98%. However, the average testing accuracy was 95%, and the average precision, recall, and F1-score were 96%, 94%, and 95% respectively as shown in Fig. 7 and Fig. 8.

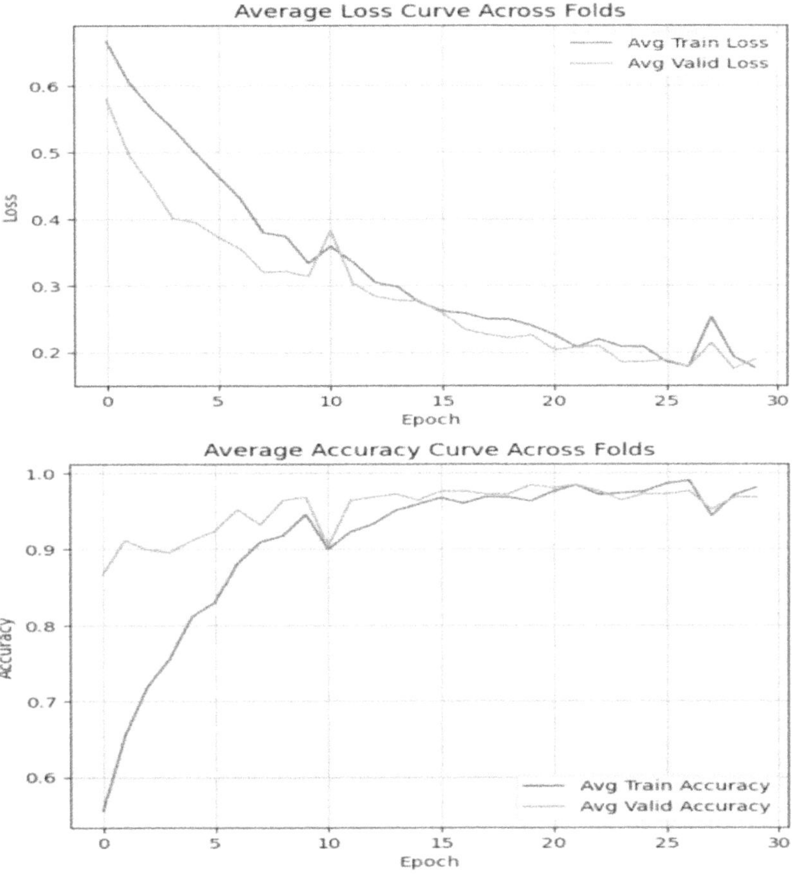

**Fig.7.** The accuracy and loss metrics for training the DenseNet model related to the seatbelt compliance task.

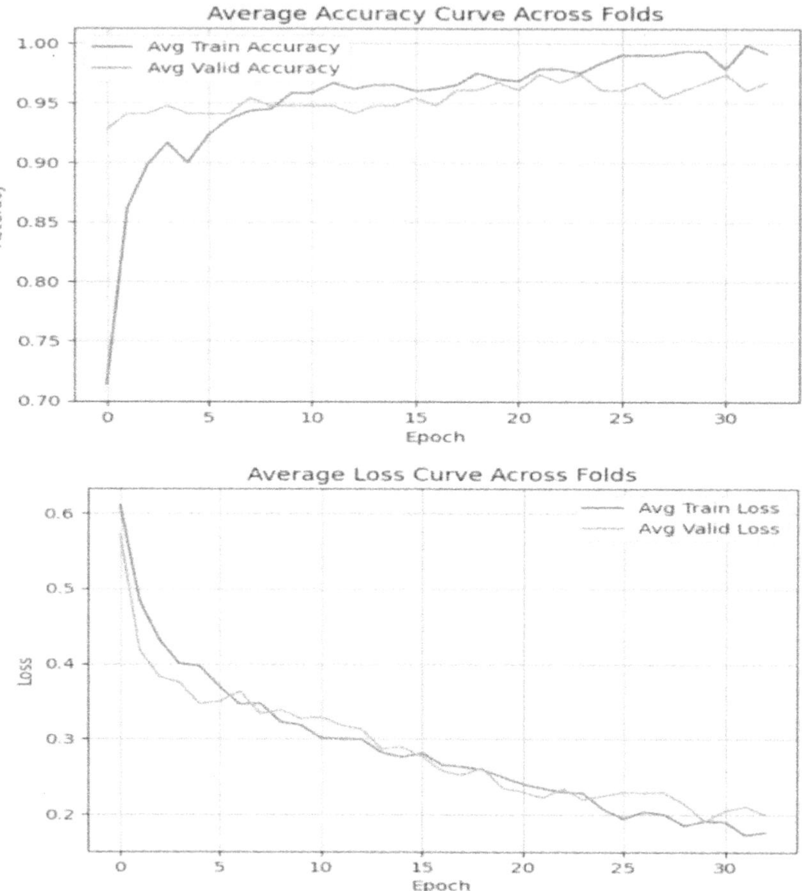

**Fig.8.** The accuracy and loss of training of DenseNet for mobile phone usage classification.

The VGG16 model achieved an average accuracy of 99% in classifying the seatbelt compliance. However, the average testing accuracy was 94.17%; the average precision was 96%, the average recall was 93%, and the F1 score was 94% as shown in Fig. 9.

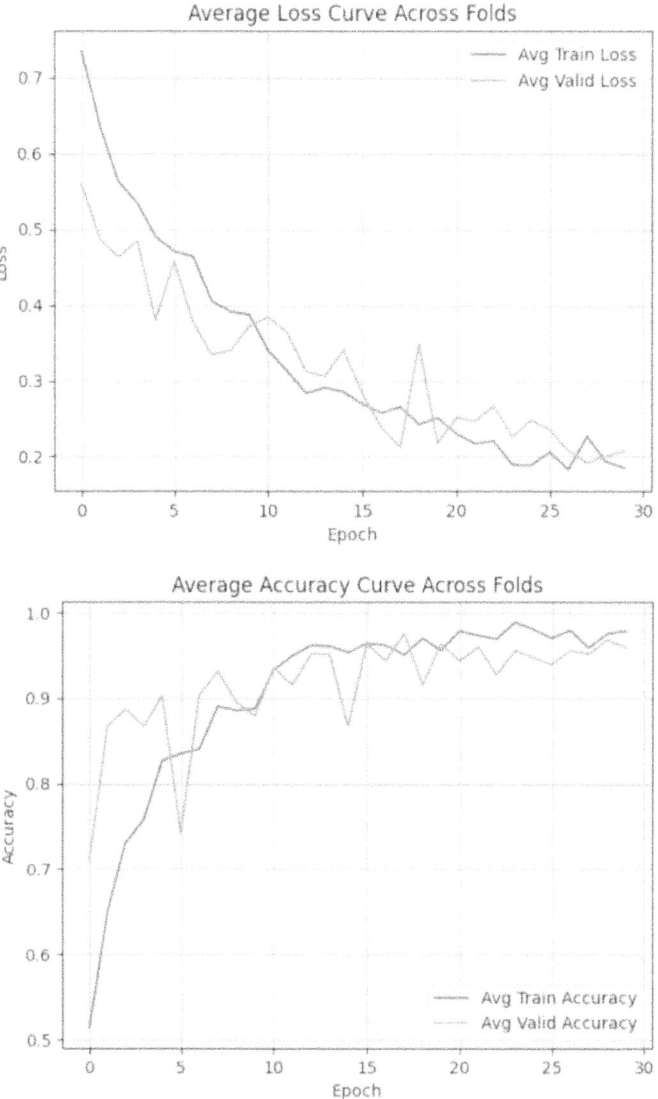

**Fig.9.** The accuracy and loss of training of VGG16 in the seatbelt compliance task.

To classify mobile phone usage while driving, the average training accuracy was 98%. However, the average testing accuracy was 97%, the average precision was 97%, the average recall was 97%, and the average F1-score was 97% as shown in Fig. 10.

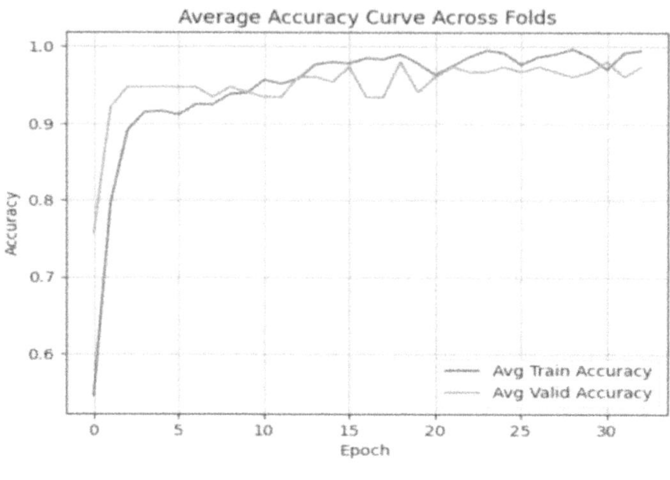


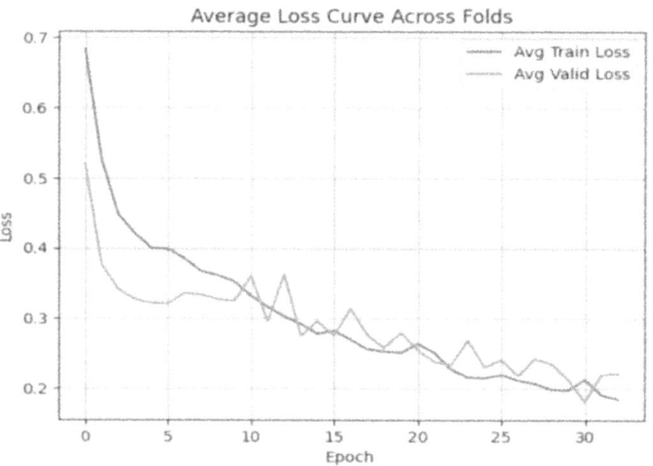


**Fig.10.** The accuracy and loss of VGG16 for mobile phone usage classification.

In the ResNet34 model, the original model was trained with the proposed two splits without transfer learning and without a custom classification block. To classify driver commitment to wearing seatbelts, the average accuracy of the original model training was 99%. However, the average testing accuracy, precision, recall, and F1-score were 95.17%, 96%, 94%, and 96.31% respectively. The average accuracy for recognizing mobile phone usage infractions during model training was 99%. The average testing accuracy was 94%, the average precision was 92%, the average recall was 97%, and the average F1-score was 94%.

Second, after fine-tuning the ResNet34 model on a custom dataset for the seatbelt compliance task, the average training accuracy was 99%, the average testing accuracy was 98%, the average precision was 97%, the average recall was 98.33%, and the average F1-score was 98%.

For classifying mobile phone usage, the average training accuracy and the average testing accuracy were 99%; the average precision was 97.14%; the average recall was 100%; and the average F1-score was 99% as shown in Fig. 11 and Fig. 12.

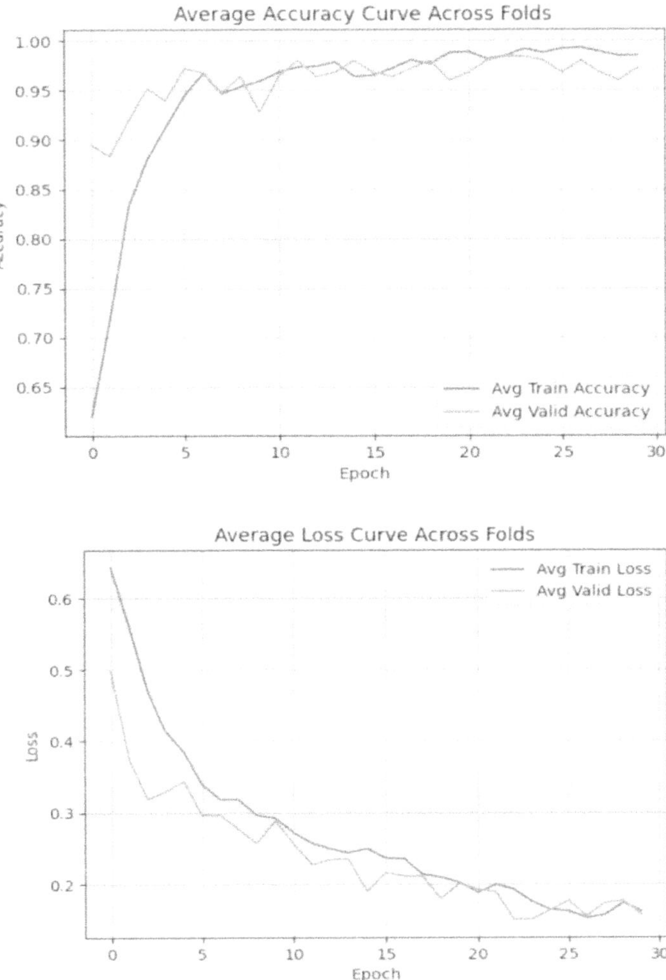

**Fig.11.** The accuracy and loss of training the ResNet34 model for the seatbelt compliance task.

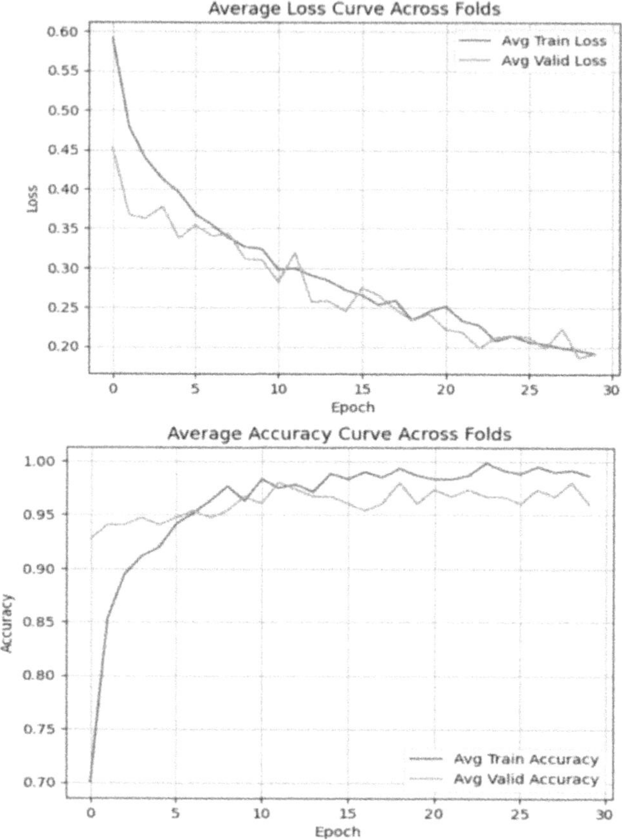

**Fig.12.** The accuracy and loss of training the ResNet34 model for mobile usage classification.

Figure 13 and Fig. 14 illustrate a comparison of the validation accuracy curves of classification models during training for classifying traffic violations.

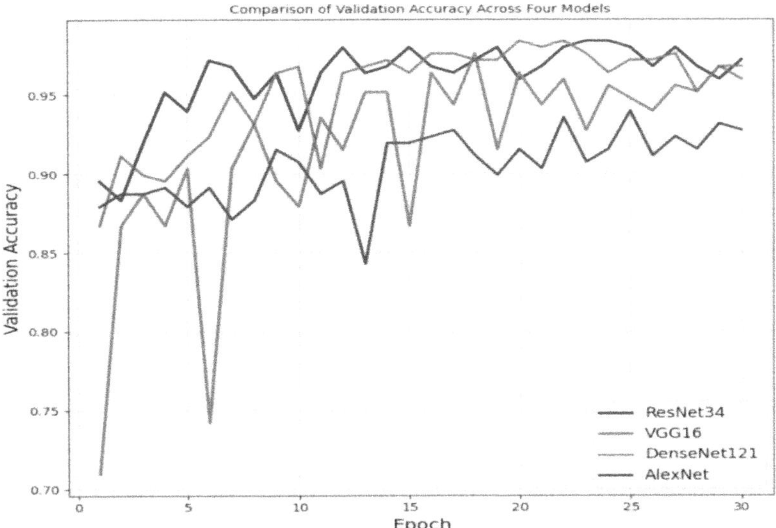


**Fig.13.** The validation accuracy of classification models for the seatbelt classification task.

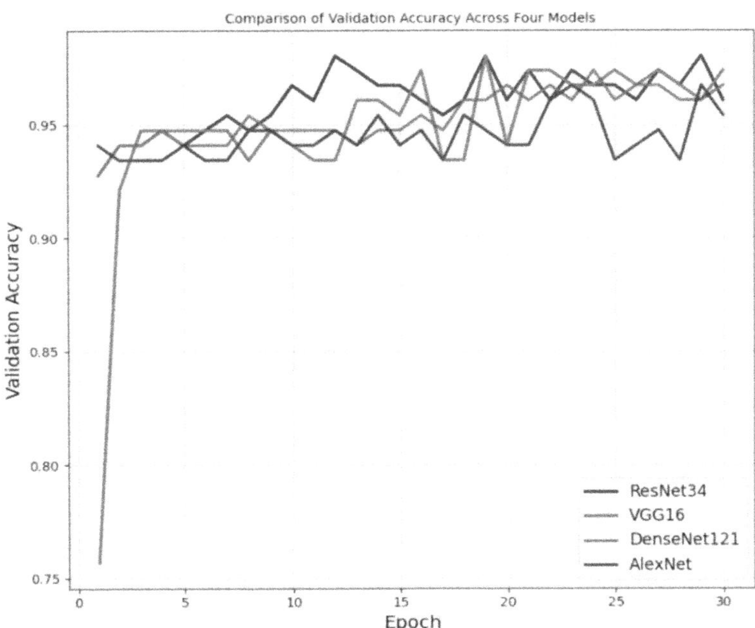


**Fig.14.** The validation accuracy of classification models for mobile usage classification task.

Table 6 and Table 7 compare the proposed classification models' performance on test images in classifying traffic violations committed by drivers.

**Table 6.** The performance of the proposed classification models for the seatbelt compliance classification task.

| Task | model | Average accuracy % | Average precision % | Average recall % | Average F1-score % |
|---|---|---|---|---|---|
| Seatbelt compliance classification | ResNet34 | 98 | 97.14 | 98.33 | 98 |
| | AlexNet | 92 | 98 | 86 | 92 |
| | VGG16 | 94.17 | 96 | 93 | 94 |
| | DenseNet | 95 | 99 | 91 | 95 |

**Table 7.** The performance of the proposed classification models for the mobile usage classification task.

| Task | model | Average accuracy % | Average precision % | Average recall % | Average F1-score % |
|---|---|---|---|---|---|
| Mobile usage while driving | ResNet34 | 99 | 97.14 | 100 | 99 |
| | AlexNet | 96 | 96 | 97 | 96 |
| | VGG16 | 97 | 97 | 97 | 97 |
| | DenseNet | 95 | 96 | 94 | 95 |

According to the experimental results, the ResNet34 model achieved higher average accuracy in the test part of images, indicating its ability to generalize well to new data. The performance of the ResNet34 model was evaluated using the average evaluation metrics, such as accuracy, precision, recall, and F1 score for each class across two splits for classifying traffic safety rules with no bias as illustrated in Table 8.

**Table 8.** Performance of the ResNet34 for classifying traffic violations.

| Classes | Average precision% | Average recall% | Average F1-score% |
|---|---|---|---|
| Seatbelt | 97 | 98.33 | 98 |
| No_seatbelt | 98.30 | 97 | 97.47 |
| Mobile | 100 | 97 | 98.50 |
| No_mobile | 97.14 | 100 | 98.55 |

A confusion matrix was also used to evaluate the performance of the ResNet34. Figure 15 and Fig. 16 display the average prediction counts for each class and the average error rate across the two splits.

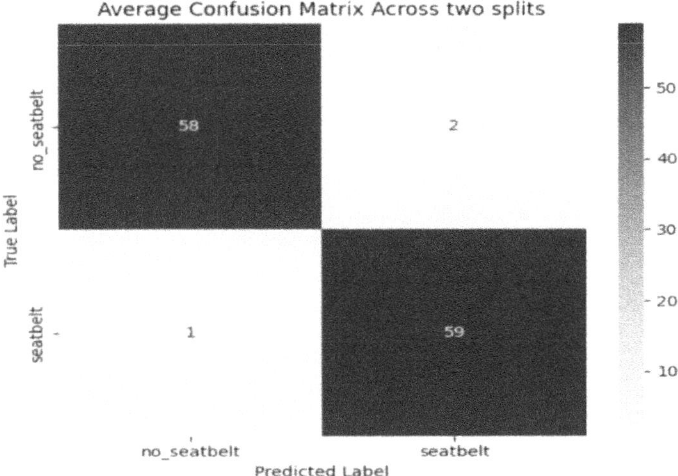

**Fig.15.** Confusion matrix of evaluating the ResNet34 model for the seatbelt compliance task.

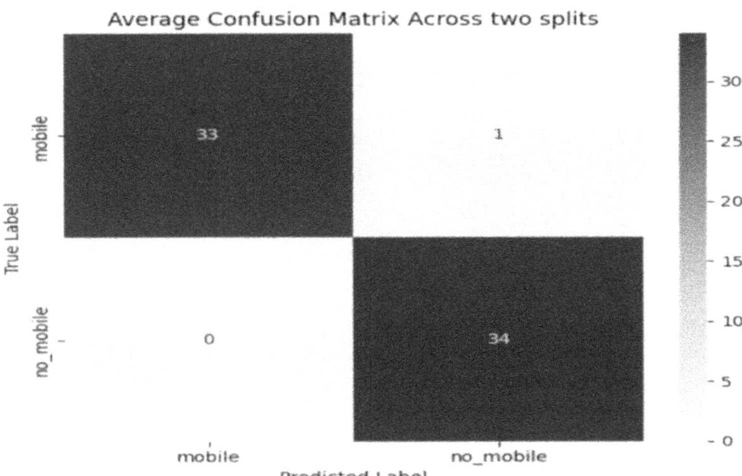

**Fig.16.** The average confusion matrix of evaluating the ResNet34 model for the mobile usage classification.

In addition, confidence intervals were estimated to ensure accurate and statistically reliable evaluation. We achieved 95% CI (confidence intervals) using a nonparametric bootstrapping procedure. Unlike standard methods, it was not assumed that the measures follow a normal distribution, making it particularly suitable for deep learning models trained on limited datasets. In this method, the test set was resampled with 1000 times replacements. Confidence intervals for each class were obtained, which gave the average statistic of each standard metric when evaluating both splits as illustrated in Table 9.

**Table 9.** The statistical performance of the ResNet34 with a 95% confidence interval for classifying traffic violations across two splits.

| Classes | Average precision CI % | Average recall CI % | Average F1-score CI % |
|---|---|---|---|
| seatbelt | (91.76–100) | (94.53–100) | (94.22–99.61) |
| No_seatbelt | (94.33–100) | (91.61–100) | (94.29–99.62) |
| Mobile | (100–100) | (90.76–100) | (95.15–100) |
| No_mobile | (90.47–100) | (100–100) | (94.99–100) |

Table 10 compares the performance of the proposed model with various state-of-the-art techniques. For the seatbelt compliance task, studies from 2023 and 2024 show the highest performance, while for the mobile usage task, recent papers indicate that drivers were detected from road cameras in 2019 and 2020, but no studies have been published in the past three years as shown in Fig. 17.

**Table 10.** Performance of the proposed model with various state-of-the-art techniques.

| References | Year | Task | Methods | Accuracy (%) | Other metrics (%) |
|---|---|---|---|---|---|
| [3] | 2019 | Seatbelt | NADS-Net | – | The precision and F1 score are 63.5 |
| [4] | 2020 | Seatbelt | Tiny-yolo | 93 | – |
| [5] | 2024 | Seat belt | CNN + LSTM | 89 | – |
| [6] | 2021 | Seatbelt | YOLOv4 | 93 | – |
| [7] | 2023 | Seatbelt | Yolov8 | 88.64 | – |
| [8] | 2024 | Seatbelt | ResNet 101, patch sampling, and gated bidirectional LSTM with part-to-whole attention | – | MAP is 72.3 |
| [9] | 2019 | Mobile phone | PCN | 96.56 | – |
| [10] | 2019 | Mobile phone | SSD | 91 | – |
| [11] | 2020 | Mobile phone | DPM and two CNN | 95.7 | – |
| Our proposed system | 2025 | Seatbelt compliance task | YOLOV11 and Resnet34 | 98 | The precision of 97.14, Recall of 98.33, and the F1-score of 98 |

(*continued*)

**Table 10.** (*continued*)

| References | Year | Task | Methods | Accuracy (%) | Other metrics (%) |
|---|---|---|---|---|---|
| | | Mobile | YOLOV11 and Resnet34 | 99 | The precision of 97.14, Recall of 100, and the F1-score of 99 |

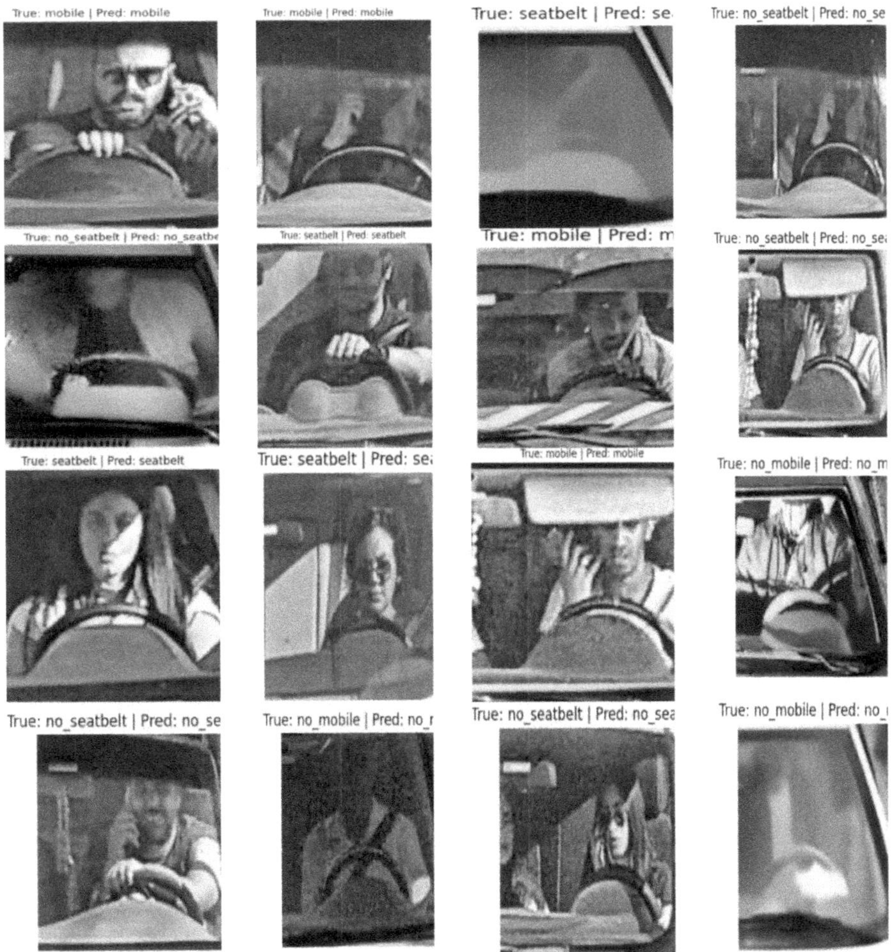


**Fig.17.** Some images that classify traffic violations from road images.

## 4   Conclusion

A deep learning system based on transfer learning for the classification of traffic violations committed by drivers was introduced. The YOLO11 model produced high detection accuracy for identifying the driver's region. The implementation of the image preprocessing phase had an important impact on the accuracy of the proposed system, which enhanced the definition of edges for the seatbelt and strengthened visibility of the mobile phone when it was positioned with the driver's hand or face. Furthermore, the classification results showed the ResNet34 model had the best performance with 98% and 99% average accuracy in classifying seatbelt compliance and mobile phone usage while driving. The proposed system showed high accuracy improvements over other studies. So it is an effective solution in addressing problems related to low accuracy, windshield reflections, partial occlusion, and color similarity. Despite the higher accuracy, the proposed model failed to classify some images, particularly those containing seatbelts or mobile violations that are fully covered with other objects. Along with developing systems under severe occlusion samples, future works can include vehicle speed estimation using surveillance cameras, which would expand the system's capabilities to monitor and analyze driver behavior effectively.

**Conflict of Interest.**   The author declares no conflict of interest.

**Ethics.**   The corresponding author emphasizes that ethical considerations were taken into account for this research, and confirms that the article is original and has not been published elsewhere. The co-author has read and approved the manuscript for submission.

## References


1. Hussan, A.A., Shaker, S.H., Ali, A.E.: Strangeness detection from crowded video scenes by hand-crafted and deep learning features. J. Soft Comput. Comput. Appl. **1**(1), 6 (2024). https://doi.org/10.70403/3008-1084.1005
2. Saadi, Z.M., Sadiq, A.T., Akif, O.Z., Eid, M.M.: Enhancing image classification using a convolutional neural network model. J. Soft Comput. Comput. Appl. **1**(2), 2 (2024). https://doi.org/10.70403/3008-1084.1010
3. Chun, S., et al.: NADS-Net: a nimble architecture for driver and seat belt detection via convolutional neural networks. In: Proceedings of the 2019 International Conference on Computer Vision Workshops. ICCVW, pp. 2413–2421 (2019). https://doi.org/10.1109/ICCVW.2019.00295
4. Kashevnik, A., Ali, A., Lashkov, I., Shilov, N.: Seat belt fastness detection based on image analysis from vehicle in-abin camera. In: Proceedings of the Conference of Open Innovations Association (FRUCT), pp. 143–150 (2020). https://doi.org/10.23919/FRUCT48808.2020.9087474
5. Udayanti, E., Kartikadarma, E., Firdausillah, F.: Convolutional neural network and LSTM for seat belt detection in vehicles using YOLO3. J. RESTI (Rekayasa Sistem dan Teknologi Informasi) **8**(3), 355–360 (2024). https://doi.org/10.29207/resti.v8i3.5784
6. Bin Khalid, S., Hazela, B.: Employing real-time object detection for traffic monitoring. SSRN Electron. J. 1–11 (2021). https://doi.org/10.2139/ssrn.3834176

7. Sutikno, A., Sugiharto, A., Kusumaningrum, R.: Automated detection of driver and passenger without seat belt using YOLOv8. Int. J. Adv. Comput. Sci. Appl. **14**(11), 806–813 (2023). https://doi.org/10.14569/IJACSA.2023.0141181

8. Gu, X., Lu, Z., Ren, J., Zhang, Q.: Seat belt detection using gated Bi-LSTM with part-to-whole attention on diagonally sampled patches. Expert Syst. Appl. **252**, 1–50 (2024). https://doi.org/10.1016/j.eswa.2024.123784

9. Xiong, Q., Lin, J., Yue, W., Liu, S., Liu, Y., Ding, C.: A deep learning approach to driver distraction detection of using mobile phone. In: 2019 IEEE Vehicle Power and Propulsion Conference (VPPC), pp. 1–5 (2019). https://doi.org/10.1109/VPPC46532.2019.8952474

10. Alkan, B., Balci, B., Elihos, A., Artan, Y.: Driver cell phone usage violation detection using license plate recognition camera images. In: Proceedings of the 5th International Conference on Vehicle Technology and Intelligent Transport Systems (VEHITS), pp. 468–474 (2019). https://doi.org/10.5220/0007725804680474

11. Jin, C., Zhu, Z., Bai, Y., Jiang, G., He, A.: A deep-learning-based scheme for detecting driver cell-phone use. IEEE Access **8**, 18580–18589 (2020). https://doi.org/10.1109/ACCESS.2020.2968464

12. AIACTIVE20092009: Seat_belt and mobile. Roboflow. Accessed: 15 Aug 2025. https://universe.roboflow.com/aiactive20092009-gmail-com/seat_belt-and-mobile/browse?queryText=&pageSize=50&startingIndex=0&browseQuery=true

13. Hosseini, S., Fathi, A.: Automatic detection of vehicle occupancy and driver's seat belt status using deep learning. SIViP **17**(2), 491–499 (2023). https://doi.org/10.1007/s11760-022-02244-w

14. Yuan, Z., et al.: CLAHE-based low-light image enhancement for robust object detection in overhead power transmission system. IEEE Trans. Power Delivery **38**(3), 2240–2243 (2023)

15. Tiwari, M., Gupta, B.: Image denoising using spatial gradient based bilateral filter and minimum mean square error filtering. Procedia Comput. Sci. **54**, 638–645 (2015). https://doi.org/10.1016/j.procs.2015.06.074

16. Abbas, S.F., Shaker, S.H., Abdullatif, F.: Face mask detection based on deep learning: a review. J. Soft Comput. Comput. Appl. **1**(1), 7 (2024). https://doi.org/10.70403/3008-1084.1006

17. Ultralytics.: Ultralytics YOLOv11 (2025). https://docs.ultralytics.com/models/yolo11/. Accessed 15 Aug 2025

18. Khanam, R., Hussain, M.: YOLOv11: an overview of the key architectural enhancements, vol. 2024, pp. 1–9 (2024). http://arxiv.org/abs/2410.17725

19. Alzubaidi, L., et al.: Novel transfer learning approach for medical imaging with limited labeled data. Cancers **13**(7), 1–22 (2021). https://doi.org/10.3390/cancers13071590

20. Yani, M., Irawan, B., Setiningsih, C.: Application of transfer learning using convolutional neural network method for early detection of Terry's nail. J. Phys. Conf. Ser. 1201(1) (2019). https://doi.org/10.1088/1742-6596/1201/1/012052

21. Kee, E., Chong, J.J., Choong, Z.J., Lau, M.: A comparative analysis of cross-validation techniques for a smart and lean pick-and-place solution with deep learning. Electronics **12**(11), 2371 (2023). https://doi.org/10.3390/electronics12112371

22. Unnikrishnan, A., Sowmya, V., Soman, K.P.: Deep alexnet with reduced number of trainable parameters for satellite image classification. Procedia Comput. Sci. **143**, 931–938 (2018). https://doi.org/10.1016/j.procs.2018.10.342

23. Huy, V.T.Q., Lin, C.M.: An improved densenet deep neural network model for tuberculosis detection using chest x-ray images. IEEE Access **11**(April), 42839–42849 (2023). https://doi.org/10.1109/ACCESS.2023.3270774

24. Fadhil, O.Y., Mahdi, B.S., Abbas, A.R.: Using VGG models with intermediate layer feature maps for static hand gesture recognition. Baghdad Sci. J. **20**(5), 14 (2023). https://doi.org/10.21123/bsj.2023.7364

25. Gao, L., Zhang, X., Yang, T., Wang, B., Li, J.: The application of ResNet-34 model integrating transfer learning in the recognition and classification of overseas Chinese frescoes. Electronics **12**(17) (2023). https://doi.org/10.3390/electronics12173677
26. Dalianis, H.: Evaluation metrics and evaluation. Clin. Text Mining **1967**, 45–53 (2018). https://doi.org/10.1007/978-3-319-78503-5_6

# Improving Generalization of ECG Arrhythmia Detection Using Cross-Domain Meta-learning AI


Zaid J. Al-Araji[1]([✉]), Balqees Talal Hasan[2], Ali Mohsin[3], Ammar Awad Mutlag[4], and Hussein M. Farhood[5]

[1] Department of Computer Networks and Internet, College of Information Technology, Ninevah University, 41001 Mosul, Iraq
zaid.jasim@uoninevah.edu.iq
[2] Department of Artificial Intelligence, College of Information Technology, Ninevah University, 41001 Mosul, Iraq
balqees.hasan@uoninevah.edu.iq
[3] Department of Software Engineering, College of Information Technology, Ninevah University, 41001 Mosul, Iraq
ali.mohsin@uoninevah.edu.iq
[4] Ministry of Education, General Directorate of Curricula, Baghdad, Iraq
[5] Department of Computer Engineering, College of Engineering, Mustansiriyah University, 10047 Baghdad, Iraq
Hussein.m4f@uomustansiriyah.edu.iq



**Abstract.** Domain shift is a challenge in electrocardiogram (ECG)–based arrhythmia detection across datasets, recording devices, and patient populations. An all-in-one cross-domain meta-learning framework was proposed that unifies downloading, preprocessing, label harmonization, and episodic training for robust arrhythmia classification. This approach combines a CNN + multi-head self-attention encoder with a MAML-style adaptation loop, enhanced by domain-contrastive alignment and CORAL regularization. Two major public datasets (MIT-BIH, PTB-XL) were harmonized into a six-class unified label space and evaluated under both in-domain and cross-domain conditions. In in-domain settings, 85.2% accuracy with 0.84 macro-F1 and 0.93 AUROC was achieved with MIT-BIH, followed by 82.7% accuracy with 0.81 macro-F1 and 0.91 AUROC with PTB-XL. The cross-domain evaluation indicates the generalization ability of the proposed method. It showed 71–74% accuracy and 0.70–0.72 macro-F1 when trained on one dataset and tested on another, significantly outperforming the supervised CNN baselines by 12 percentage points. In addition, cross-domain meta-learning provides domain-invariant ECG representations that generalize beyond dataset boundaries. The proposed pipeline built a reproducible and extendable foundation for real-world arrhythmia detection, where models need adaptation to heterogeneous acquisition conditions.

**Keywords:** ECG · Arrhythmia detection · deep learning · meta learning · CNN



© The Author(s), under exclusive license to Springer Nature Switzerland AG 2026
S. O. Al-Mamory et al. (Eds.): 3INC 2025, CCIS 2960, pp. 231–247, 2026.
https://doi.org/10.1007/978-3-032-24239-6_13

# 1  Introduction

Electrocardiography (ECG) is the most widely used tool for diagnosing arrhythmia, which is a major contributor to morbidity and mortality on a global scale. The World Health Organization estimates that almost one-third of global annual deaths are due to cardiovascular diseases. In the past few years, deep learning (DL) approaches have revolutionized the field of automatic interpretation of ECG signals into significantly improved versions achieving near-expert level in arrhythmia classification tasks [1, 2]. Despite these accomplishments, models trained on a specific dataset or cohort have not been generalized well for different populations, acquisition devices, or clinical environments [3]. The inability of AI systems to transfer meaningfully from the mode of development into safe deployment into real-world systems is one of the largest barriers. Many methods have tried to fill this gap; however, transfer learning has received the most attention in leveraging already pre-trained models [4, 5]. Domain-adaptation methods try to align feature distributions in the source and target domains, mainly by using adversarial mechanisms or discrepancy minimization [6, 7]. However, these are only partial solutions. They usually assume some access to target-domain data during training or have great difficulty with completely novel domains during inference. In the context of ECG arrhythmia detection, these variations might be attributed to sampling frequency, electrode placement, patient demographics, or annotation protocols [8]. Hence, there is an urgent call for approaches made to generalize out of the distributions they have been directly trained on. Recently meta-learning, which might be described as "learning to learn", has gained traction as an alternative for mitigating the setbacks of traditional supervised learning under the conditions of domain heterogeneity and shortage of data [9, 10]. With meta-learning models, learning from tasks is transferred to facilitate working with other tasks with minimum extra data. Once applied in cross-domain scenarios, the meta-learning framework facilitates simulation of domain shifts during training so that a model learns to encode representations robustly when actually deployed in an unseen domain [11]. This study introduces a cross-domain meta-learning AI framework for the enhancement of generalization in ECG arrhythmia detection. Unlike typical deep learning models that rely on one dataset for optimization, in this approach we deliberately structure the training process around domain variability. Thus, the model is subjected to a very wide set of source tasks during meta-training so that it induces representations invariant to the domains and hence facilitates adaptation. The model achieves effectiveness through evaluation on multiple publicly available ECG datasets, superior cross-domain generalization compared to standard supervised, transfer learning, and domain adaptation baselines. Threefold major contributions have been made in this study:

1. **Cross-Domain Meta-Learning Framework for ECG Arrhythmia Detection**: A novel meta-learning framework was introduced that is explicitly designed to address the challenge of domain shift in ECG arrhythmia detection.
2. **Domain-Invariant Representation Learning**: Within the proposed framework, mechanisms were incorporated that promote the extraction of domain-invariant ECG representations.

This present work is an attempt to bridge the digital divide made by the algorithm design and clinical translation of AI in cardiology by improving the ability of the arrhythmia detection model to generalize across domains. The rest of this paper is organized as follows: Sect. 2 explains the related work, Sect. 3 explains the methodology of the work, Sect. 4 explains the experiment setup, Sect. 5 explains the results of the experiment, and Sect. 6 is the conclusion.

## 2  Related Works

Research on automated arrhythmia detection has evolved from classical machine learning models based on handcrafted ECG features to modern deep learning approaches that learn discriminative representations directly from raw signals. While convolutional and recurrent neural networks have demonstrated strong performance on large single-domain datasets, their ability to generalize across patient populations, acquisition devices, and clinical settings remains limited due to domain shift. To address these challenges, recent studies have explored transfer learning, domain adaptation, and meta-learning as strategies for improving robustness under scarce or heterogeneous data conditions.

Authors in [12] suggested a hybrid deep learning-based method to automate the process of categorization and detection. To automate the noise reduction and feature extraction, 1D ECG data were first converted into 2D Scalogram images. Then, using experimental data, a hybrid model known as 2D-CNN-LSTM was proposed by fusing two learning models: the Long Short-Term Memory (LSTM) network and the 2D convolutional neural network (CNN). Authors in [13] proposed an LS-SVM classifier using the MIT-BIH arrhythmia database for classifying heartbeats, including normal, PVC, and other beats. Their method produced a classification accuracy of 96.12%. Authors in [14] advanced a classifier that was based on Discrete Wavelet Transformation (DWT) for feature representation and Support Vector Machines (SVM) for classification based on 48 MIT-BIH arrhythmia recordings. The arrhythmia beats were classified into five categories: Non-ectopic (N), super ventricular ectopic (S), ventricular ectopic (V), fusion (F), and unknown (U). Using this approach, an accuracy rate of 98.49% was obtained. They also adopted ANOVA in their statistical analysis to strengthen the validation of the proposed approach. [15] challenged the conception about neural models dedicated to beat classification with respect to arrhythmia detection using the MIT-BIH arrhythmia database. They specifically worked on whether features identifiable through the use of discrete cosine transform (DCT) can be taken as input to a unique random forest classifier while being used to find an R-R interval. Authors in [16] showed a rather lightweight Deep Learning method for detection of eight types of distinct cardiac arrhythmias and normal rhythms with good accuracy. The ECG signals were preprocessed using baseline wander removal and resampling techniques for DL techniques. CNN and LSTM were used for classification in a network with 11 layers. [17] proposed a new Swin Transformer deep learning model along with wavelet time-frequency maps for automatic detection of heart arrhythmias. In order to capture correlations between and within heartbeats, [18] employed two revised transformer models with a collaborative block, utilizing coarse- and fine-grained tokens. By facilitating the sharing of rhythm information, the collaborative block between two models increased beat detection accuracy. [19] provided a unique

ECG-based method for arrhythmia identification that used three essential techniques to integrate explainable artificial intelligence. Initially, an improved R peak recognition technique was created that incorporated domain-specific information into the ECG and increased peak identification precision by taking into consideration the distinctive characteristics of R peaks. Second, a modified CNN architecture with extra convolutional and batch normalization layers was used to suggest a classification approach for arrhythmias.

## 3   Methodology

Figure 1 illustrates the overall architecture of the proposed cross-domain meta-learning framework. The system begins with heterogeneous ECG datasets (MIT-BIH and PTB-XL), which are preprocessed through resampling, segmentation, and z-score normalization to ensure consistency across domains. Episodic task sampling constructs support and query sets per episode, enabling the model to simulate domain shift during training.

The feature encoder utilizes CNN layers to extract local morphological features and multi-head self-attention (MHSA) mechanisms for learning long-range temporal dependencies. From the perspective of meta-training, the encoder parameters will be updated by the support set on inner-loop adaptations. On the other hand, the classifier head performs 6-class arrhythmia prediction based on learned embeddings.

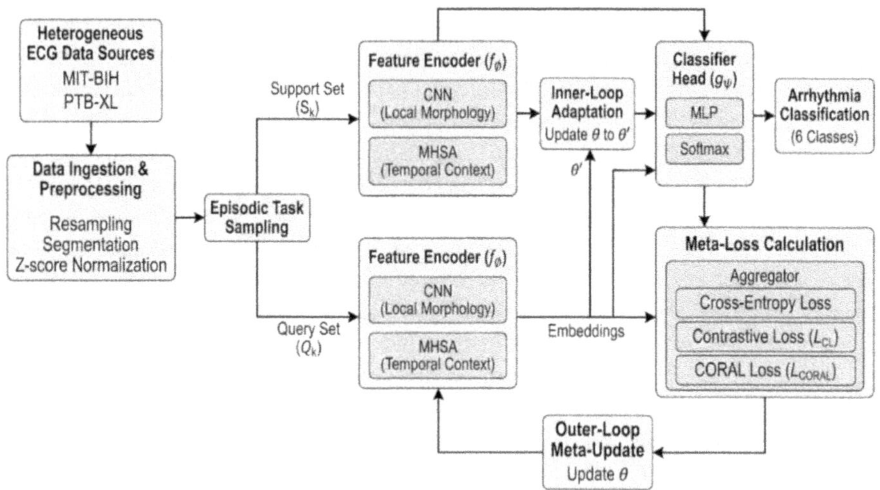


**Fig. 1.**   Proposed Cross-Domain Meta-Learning Framework

The process of meta-loss computation involves three complementary objectives: first, cross-entropy loss that measures the accuracy of classification; second, supervised contrastive loss that algorithmically enforces class-consistent embedding alignment across domains; and third, CORAL loss which adjusts to minimize distributional discrepancies in covariance statistics. In the outer-loop meta-update, these components are aggregated and applied toward optimizing the universal initialization of model parameters, thereby improving generalization under this dataset shift.

## 3.1 Data Ingestion

The initial phase of the suggested cross-domain meta-learning scheme consists of Data Ingestion, responsible for the collection, harmonization, and preprocessing of electrocardiogram (ECG) signals from multiple heterogeneous sources. Given that domain shift in arrhythmia detection is mainly caused by dataset variability, this step guarantees that the input to the framework are standardized, thus reliable for downstream feature extraction and meta-learning.

### 3.1.1 Datasets

Two widely used, publicly available ECG benchmark datasets were used to construct a diverse domain pool:

- **MIT-BIH Arrhythmia Database** – 48 half-hour ECG recordings sampled at 360 Hz, annotated with 15 arrhythmia classes.
- **PTB-XL** – A large-scale dataset with 21,837 clinical 12-lead ECG records from 18,885 patients, sampled at 500 Hz, covering over 70 diagnostic statements.

Together, these datasets represent diverse patient populations, acquisition devices, sampling frequencies, and annotation protocols, making them ideal for cross-domain evaluation.

### 3.1.2 Label Harmonization Across Datasets

Annotation systems are not the same for these datasets, both in terms of clinical taxonomy and how granular the definitions have become within the annotation dimension. To allow for cross-domain meta-learning, both datasets were brought together under a common six-class arrhythmia label space, including the common rhythm and morphological abnormalities described in other studies on ECG classification.

First, the MIT-BIH annotations were initially categorized according to the AAMI EC57 standard five-class taxonomy (N, S, V, F, Q), which is the widely used standard for benchmarking around arrhythmias. PTB-XL statements were mapped using the diagnostic super classes defined in the original dataset publication and cross-referenced with clinically equivalent beat-level abnormalities as illustrated in Table 1.

**Table 1.** Label Harmonization of MIT-BIH and PTB-XL Into Six Classes

| Unified Class | MIT-BIH Labels (AAMI/Beat Types) | PTB-XL Diagnostic Statements | Clinical Meaning |
|---|---|---|---|
| Normal (N) | N (Normal) | NORM, STTC (when ST normal), SR | Normal sinus rhythm |
| Atrial Fibrillation (AF) | AF, AFL | AFIB, AFLT | Irregular atrial activity |
| Premature Atrial Contraction (PAC) | S (SVEB), APB | PAC, SVES | Early atrial ectopic beats |

(*continued*)

**Table 1.** (*continued*)

| Unified Class | MIT-BIH Labels (AAMI/Beat Types) | PTB-XL Diagnostic Statements | Clinical Meaning |
|---|---|---|---|
| Premature Ventricular Contraction (PVC) | V (VEB) | PVC, VPB | Early ventricular ectopic beats |
| Right Bundle Branch Block (RBBB) | BBB (subset) | RBBB | Prolonged QRS due to right conduction delay |
| Left Bundle Branch Block (LBBB) | — | LBBB | Prolonged QRS due to left conduction delay |

## 3.2  Feature Encoder

The Feature Encoder ($f_\emptyset$) forms the backbone of the proposed cross-domain meta-learning framework. Its purpose is to transform raw ECG signals into robust, domain-invariant representations that preserve clinically meaningful morphology while suppressing acquisition-specific noise. To this end, a hybrid architecture was designed that integrates convolutional neural networks (CNNs) for local feature extraction with multi-head self-attention (MHSA) mechanisms for global temporal modeling.

### 3.2.1  Local Morphological Feature Extraction

Arrhythmia diagnosis relies heavily on local waveform features, such as QRS complex sharpness, P- and T-wave morphology, and ST-segment deviations. To capture these features, the encoder begins with a stack of one-dimensional convolutional layers:

- **Stem layer**: A $1D$ convolution with kernel size 11 and stride 2 reduces temporal resolution and extracts low-level features.
- **Residual blocks**: Three stages of residual convolutional blocks progressively increasing channel depth ($64 \rightarrow 128 \rightarrow 256$), while the kernel size decreases from 7 to 3 to keep a balance between receptive field size and efficiency. Each block consists of batch normalization, ReLU activation, and short-cut connections to keep stable optimization.

This design offers the possibility of capturing morphological events with efficiency across various time scales, while residual connections fight against vanishing gradient problems and enhance generalization.

### 3.2.2  Temporal Context Modeling

While convolutional kernels are designed to receive and analyze information relative to the morphology at a localized level, heart rhythm disorders impose the need to analyze temporal dependencies across multiple cardiac cycles. For example, atrial fibrillation may be manifested as irregular RR intervals rather than on a beat-to-beat basis. Thus, to account for global relationships within the input data, multi-head self-attention (MHSA) layers were introduced following the convolutional stages.

The MHSA computes the weighted dependencies among all temporal positions in the sequence, thus enabling the encoder to:

1. Focus on clinically salient intervals while ignoring irrelevant noise.
2. Capture long-range periodicity and rhythm irregularities beyond the receptive field of CNNs.
3. Maintain parallelizable computations and avoid the sequential bottleneck of recurrent models.

Formally, given embeddings $X \in R^{T' \times d}$, the attention mechanism computes:

$$Attention(Q, K, V) = softmax\left(\frac{QK^T}{\sqrt{d_k}}\right)V, \tag{1}$$

where queries, keys, and values are linear projections of $X$, and multi-head extensions enable modeling of diverse dependency patterns.

## 3.3 Meta-learner

The Meta-Learner $h_\theta$ is the core component of the proposed framework that enables rapid adaptation to novel domains. Unlike conventional supervised learning, which directly minimizes empirical risk across pooled data, the meta-learner optimizes the model's ability to learn-to-learn by simulating domain shift during training. The Model-Agnostic Meta-Learning (MAML) paradigm was utilized which is tailored for cross-domain ECG arrhythmia detection.

### 3.3.1 Episodic Training Setup

Meta-training proceeds in episodes. Each episode $T_k$ is composed of:

- **Support Set** $(S_k)$: a small subset of labeled ECG samples, used for *inner-loop adaptation.*
- **Query Set** $(Q_k)$: a disjoint subset of samples, used for *outer-loop meta-update.*

To explicitly account for domain shift, episodes are drawn in two ways:

1. **Intra-Domain Tasks:** support and query sets from the same dataset, enforcing within-domain adaptation.
2. **Cross-Domain Tasks:** support and query sets from different datasets, simulating real-world distributional mismatch.

This episodic design forces the meta-learner to capture knowledge that is transferrable across heterogeneous sources.

### 3.3.2 Inner-Loop Adaptation

Within each task $T_k$, the model parameters $\theta$ are adapted on the support set by performing one or more gradient descent steps:

$$\theta_{k'} = \theta - \alpha \nabla_\theta L_{S_k}(h_\theta), \tag{2}$$

where $\alpha$ is the task-specific learning rate and $L_{S_k}$ is the cross-entropy loss computed on support samples. This step mimics few-shot adaptation to a new domain.

### 3.3.3  Outer-Loop Meta-Update

After inner-loop adaptation, the updated parameters $\theta_{k\prime}$ are evaluated on the query set. The meta-objective aggregates losses across tasks:

$$\min_{\theta} \sum_{T_k \sim p(T)} L_{Q_k}(h_{\theta_{k\prime}}), \qquad (3)$$

and parameters are updated using a meta learning rate $\beta$:

$$\theta \leftarrow \theta - \beta \nabla_{\theta} \sum_{k} L_{Q_k}(h_{\theta_{k\prime}}) \qquad (4)$$

This optimization makes the initialization $\theta$ to be universally adaptable, requiring only a few gradient steps to generalize to unseen datasets.

### 3.3.4  Task Sampling and Class Balance

To alleviate the severe class imbalance for arrhythmia, the task construction process applies a stratified sampling algorithm, ensuring that representations for each type of arrhythmia exist in both support and query sets. Adding augmentation techniques—such as amplitude scaling, jitter, and random cropping—to minority classes prevents the adaptation performance from being overly influenced by majority classes like "'Normal'" beats.

### 3.3.5  Meta-Learner Algorithm

The procedure is summarized in Algorithm 1.

---

**Algorithm 1:** Cross-Domain Meta-Learning Procedure (MAML)

**Input:** Source domains $\{D_1, \dots, D_n\}$, learning rates $\alpha, \beta$
**Output:** Meta-learned parameters $\theta^*$
**Initialize:** Model parameters $\theta$.
**Repeat until convergence:**
  1.  Sample a batch of tasks $\{T_1, \dots, T_B\}$ across domains.
  2.  For each task $T_k = (S_k, Q_k)$
         a. Compute adapted parameters:
         $$\theta'_k = \theta - \alpha \nabla_{\theta} L_{S_k}(h_{\theta}),$$
         b. Evaluate query loss:
         $$L_{Q_k}(h_{\theta'_k})$$
  3.  Update meta-parameters:
  $$\theta \leftarrow \theta - \beta \nabla_{\theta} \sum_{k=1}^{B} L_{Q_k}(h_{\theta'_k})$$

---

## 3.4  Classifier Head

The Classifier Head $(g_\psi)$ is the last part of the suggested cross-domain meta-learning framework. Its function is to convert domain-invariant embeddings generated by the feature encoder $(f_\phi)$ into probability distributions over arrhythmia classes. The encoder is employed to extract morphology- and rhythm-related representations, while the Classifier ensures the transformation of these representations into clinically interpretable diagnostic outputs.

### 3.4.1  Architecture

The classifier is implemented as a multi-layer perception (MLP) with the following structure:

1. **Fully Connected Layer (FC1):**
   Projects the encoder embedding $z \in R^{d_z}$ into a hidden space of 128 dimensions.

$$h = ReLU(W_{1z} + b_1) \tag{5}$$

   Dropout $(p = 0.2)$ is applied to enhance regularization.
2. **Fully Connected Layer (FC2):**
   Maps hidden representation into the arrhythmia class space of size $C$:

$$o = W_2h + b_2 \tag{6}$$

3. **Softmax Layer:**
   Produces a probability distribution over the arrhythmia classes:

$$\hat{y}_c = \frac{\exp(o_c)}{\sum_{h=1}^{C} \exp(o_j)} for c \in \{1, \ldots, C\} \tag{7}$$

### 3.4.2  Regularization and Calibration

To ensure robustness and clinical reliability, several enhancements were incorporated:

- **Dropout (p = 0.2–0.3):** Prevents overfitting to domain-specific artifacts.
- **Weight Decay ($10^{-4}$):** Stabilizes training.
- **Class-balanced weighting:** Mitigates severe class imbalance in ECG datasets.
- **Temperature Scaling (optional):** Improves probability calibration for deployment in safety-critical clinical settings.

### 3.4.3  Loss Function

The classifier is trained using cross-entropy loss:

$$L_{CE} = -\sum_{c=1}^{C} y_c \log(\hat{y}_c), \tag{8}$$

where $y_c$ is the one-hot ground label.

When class imbalance is severe, a focal loss variant is employed:

$$L_{FL} = -\sum_{c=1}^{C} \left(1 - \hat{y}_c\right)^{\gamma} y_c \log(\hat{y}_c),\tag{9}$$

with focusing parameter $\gamma \in [1.5, 2.0]$.

### 3.4.4   Role in the Framework

The classifier head presents the last diagnostic decision layer of the proposed framework. By acting on domain-invariant embeddings, the head is protected from dataset-specific biases and concentrates solely on arrhythmia discrimination. This separation of roles—encoder for feature extraction, meta-learner for adaptation, and classifier for decision-making—ensures robust and interpretable outputs suitable for clinical deployment. The role of the classifier is explained in Algorithm 2.

| Algorithm 2 |
|---|
| **Input**: $z \in \mathbb{R}^{\{d_z\}}$   # embedding from encoder |
| **Output**: $\hat{y} \in \mathbb{R}^{\{C\}}$   # class probabilities |
| function CLASSIFIER_HEAD(z, $d_z$, C): |
|   # First fully connected projection |
|   h = Dense(z, units=128)        # FC1 |
|   h = ReLU(h) |
|   h = Dropout(h, p=0.2) |
|   # Second projection to class space |
|   logits = Dense(h, units=C)        # FC2 |
|   # Softmax for probability distribution |
|   $y_{hat}$ = Softmax(logits) |
|   return $y_{hat}$ |

### 3.5   Domain-Invariant Representation Learning

To ensure robustness under dataset and device shift, the embedding space produced by the feature encoder $f_\phi$ so that samples sharing the same clinical label but originating from different domains were mapped nearby, while different classes remain well separated. This was implemented via a class-conditional and cross-domain contrastive objective applied episodically, with optional distribution-level alignment. Algorithm 3 explains Class-Conditional Cross-Domain Contrast (per episode).

---

**Algorithm 3**

Inputs: batch B = $\{(x_i, y_i, d_i)\}$ from support/query of task $T_k$
    encoder $f_\varphi$ (within h_$\theta$), temperature $T$, weights $\lambda_{CL}, \lambda_{CORAL}$
1) Forward pass to embeddings
Z = [ $f_\varphi(x_i)$ for $(x_i, y_i, d_i)$ in B ]          # $\mathbb{R}^{\{N \times d\}}$
Z = L2Normalize(Z)                    # stabilize cosine scale
2) Build positive sets across domains for each anchor
for i in 1…N:
  P[i] = { $j$ ! = $i$ | $y_j$ == $y_i$ and $d_j$ ! = $d_i$ }  # cross-domain, same-class
  Nset[i] = { $k$ ! = $i$ | $y_k$ ! = $y_i$ }          # negatives (different class)
3) Supervised contrastive loss (InfoNCE)
L_CL = 0; count = 0
for i in 1... N:
  if |P[i]| == 0: continue
  # denominator over all others (can mask self)
  denom = sum_{k != i} exp(sim(Z[i], Z[k]) / T)
  tmp = 0

### 3.5.1 Class-Conditional Cross-Domain Contrast

Let an episode $T_k$ contain support and query sets drawn from domains $d_s$ and $d_q$ (possibly $d_s \neq d_q$). For a batch of embedded samples

$$B = \{(z_i, y_i, d_i)\}_{i=1}^N, \; z_i = f_\varnothing(x_i), \tag{10}$$

We defined positives across domains as pairs sharing the same label; however, originating from different domains:

$$P(i) = \{j \neq i\} y_j = y_i, d_j \neq d_i, \tag{11}$$

### 3.5.2 Distribution-Level Alignment (Optional)

To further reduce domain shift, an optional class-conditional CORAL penalty was included that matched the second-order statistics of embedding per class between domains:

$$L_{CORAL} = \sum_{c=1}^{C} || \frac{\sum^{(d_s)}}{C} - \frac{\sum^{(d_q)}}{C} ||_F^2 , \; \sum_c^{(d)} = Cov\{z_i | y_i = c, d_i = d\} \tag{12}$$

This term is lightweight, data-efficient, and differentiable, and empirically complements contrastive regularization when batch size per class is sufficient.

### 3.5.3 Normalization and Calibration

- **Feature normalization.** LayerNorm/InstanceNorm and $\ell_2$-normalize zzz were applied prior to contrastive similarity to ensure a stable temperature scale.

- **Class balance.** Episodes use stratified sampling; $L_{CL}$ is averaged over anchors with at least one cross-domain positive.
- **Hyperparameters.** $T \in [0.05, 0.1]$, $\lambda_{CL} \in \{0.1, 0.3\}$, $\lambda_{CORAL} \in \{0, 0.01\}$

### 3.5.4  Joint Objective and Integration with Meta-Learning

For task $T_k$, the query-time meta-objective becomes

$$L_{meta}^k = L_{CE}^k + \lambda_{CL}L_{CL}^k +, \lambda_{CORAL}L_{CORAL}^k \tag{13}$$

The outer loop minimizes $\sum_k L_{meta}^k$. Because $L_{CL}$ is evaluated on query embeddings after inner-loop adaptation, gradients flowing through the meta-update shape the initialization toward features that remain discriminative across unseen domains.

## 4  Experimental Setup

The proposed cross-domain meta-learning framework was evaluated on multiple publicly available ECG datasets, including MIT-BIH Arrhythmia Database (MIT-BIH) and PTB-XL. The datasets were preprocessed and harmonized into a unified label space of six arrhythmia categories (Normal (N), Atrial Fibrillation (AF), Premature Atrial Contraction (PAC), Premature Ventricular Contraction (PVC), Right Bundle Branch Block (RBBB), and Left Bundle Branch Block (LBBB)). For all experiments, ECG signals were resampled to 250 Hz, segmented into 2.5-s windows, and z-score normalized.

Meta-training and testing were conducted using the K-way, N-shot episodic protocol. Unless otherwise stated, we report results on 5-way, 5-shot classification with 15 query samples per class, repeated over 200 random episodes. For in-domain evaluation, both support and query sets were sampled from the same dataset. For cross-domain evaluation, support and query sets were sampled from different datasets, simulating real-world deployment where distribution shift is inevitable.

## 5  Results

### 5.1  In-Domain Performance

Table 2 reports the in-domain results on MIT-BIH and PTB-XL. The model achieved strong classification performance within each dataset, reflecting its ability to extract discriminative ECG features when the training and testing distributions are aligned. Specifically, on MIT-BIH, the framework achieved an average accuracy of $85.2\% \pm 1.7\%$ and a macro-F1 score of 0.84, while on PTB-XL it obtained $82.7\% \pm 2.1\%$ accuracy and a macro-F1 of 0.81.

**Table 2.** In-domain episodic evaluation (5-way 5-shot, 200 episodes).

| Dataset | Acc (%) | Macro-F1 | Macro-AUROC | Sens | Spec | ECE $\downarrow$ |
|---|---|---|---|---|---|---|
| MIT-BIH | $85.2 \pm 1.7$ | $0.84 \pm 0.02$ | $0.93 \pm 0.01$ | 0.83 | 0.95 | 0.036 |
| PTB-XL | $82.7 \pm 2.1$ | $0.81 \pm 0.03$ | $0.91 \pm 0.02$ | 0.80 | 0.94 | 0.041 |

These results confirm that the proposed feature encoder, which integrates CNN and multi-head self-attention, effectively captures both local morphological patterns (e.g., QRS complex) and long-range temporal dependencies in ECG signals.

## 5.2 Cross-Domain Generalization

To examine robustness under domain shift, the model was trained and tested on MIT-BIH and PTB-XL, respectively, along opposite lines. As listed in Table 3, although cross-domain performance is worse than that under the corresponding in-domain conditions, which remains a big hurdle to overcome, the gains in generalization of our meta-learning approach are still markedly greater than those used in standard supervised baselines. When trained on MIT-BIH and assessed on PTB-XL, the model reached an accuracy of $71.4\% \pm 2.8\%$ with a macro-F1 of 0.70. Conversely, the model trained using PTB-XL and tested on MIT-BIH performed at a similar level with an accuracy of $73.6\% \pm 2.5\%$ and a macro-F1 of 0.72. This demonstrates the fact that the model has learned domain-invariant ECG representations, which is generalized across datasets with heterogeneous acquisition protocols and patient cohorts.

**Table 3.** Cross-domain episodic evaluation (5-way 5-shot, 200 episodes).

| Train $\rightarrow$ Test | Acc (%) | Macro-F1 | Macro-AUROC | Sens | Spec | ECE $\downarrow$ |
|---|---|---|---|---|---|---|
| MIT-BIH $\rightarrow$ PTB-XL | $71.4 \pm 2.8$ | $0.70 \pm 0.03$ | $0.86 \pm 0.02$ | 0.69 | 0.91 | 0.059 |
| PTB-XL $\rightarrow$ MIT-BIH | $73.6 \pm 2.5$ | $0.72 \pm 0.03$ | $0.88 \pm 0.02$ | 0.71 | 0.92 | 0.054 |

## 5.3 Ablation Analysis

To assess the contribution of each component, ablations were performed:

1. **Without Meta-Learning (Supervised only):** A conventional CNN + attention trained with standard cross-entropy lost up to 15% accuracy under cross-domain evaluation.
2. **Without Contrastive Loss:** Removing the cross-domain contrastive alignment reduced macro-F1 by ~ 3%.
3. **Without CORAL Regularization:** Excluding domain covariance alignment led to unstable performance when support and query sets originated from distinct domains.

These findings validate the importance of both episodic training and domain-invariant regularization in improving generalization.

## 5.4   Comparison with Baseline Methods

In order to assess the performance of the proposed cross-domain meta-learning framework, it was compared against four widely used baselines, all implemented on the same CNN-MHSA encoder architecture: (i) Supervised CNN, (ii) Domain-Adversarial Neural Network (DANN), (iii) Deep CORAL, and (iv) Prototypical Networks (ProtoNet). These methods are among the most effective approaches for cross-dataset ECG classification, domain generalization, and meta-learning, respectively.

### 5.4.1   In-Domain Performance

Table 4 reports accuracy and F1-macro for in-domain scenarios. The highest accuracy and macro-F1 are achieved by the proposed method in both datasets.

**Table 4.** In-domain episodic evaluation (5-way 5-shot, 200 episodes)

| Method | MIT-BIH Acc (%) | PTB-XL Acc (%) | MIT-BIH Macro-F1 | PTB-XL Macro-F1 |
|---|---|---|---|---|
| Supervised CNN + MHSA | 81.6 ± 2.2 | 78.9 ± 2.7 | 0.79 | 0.77 |
| DANN | 82.4 ± 2.0 | 80.3 ± 2.5 | 0.80 | 0.79 |
| Deep CORAL | 83.1 ± 1.9 | 80.9 ± 2.4 | 0.81 | 0.80 |
| ProtoNet | 84.2 ± 1.8 | 81.4 ± 2.1 | 0.82 | 0.80 |
| Proposed Method | 85.2 ± 1.7 | 82.7 ± 2.1 | 0.84 | 0.81 |

These results suggested that state alignment and few-shot learning helped improve in-domain classification, while the proposed framework gave additional benefits from the combination of episodic adaptation and domain-invariant regularization.

### 5.4.2   Cross-Domain Generalization

Table 5 lists a cross-dataset performance comparison. Both DANN and Deep CORAL supersede supervised learning performance, thereby confirming the advantages of explicit domain alignment. However, the performance degrades in conditions of large distribution shift. ProtoNet shows superior few-shot adaptation, which it is susceptible to being mismatched across datasets.

**Table 5.** Cross-domain episodic evaluation (train → test; 5-way 5-shot, 200 episodes)

| Method | MIT → PTB Acc (%) | PTB → MIT Acc (%) | MIT → PTB Macro-F1 | PTB → MIT Macro-F1 |
|---|---|---|---|---|
| Supervised CNN + MHSA | 57.9 ± 3.5 | 59.2 ± 3.1 | 0.55 | 0.56 |

*(continued)*

**Table 5.** (*continued*)

| Method | MIT → PTB Acc (%) | PTB → MIT Acc (%) | MIT → PTB Macro-F1 | PTB → MIT Macro-F1 |
| --- | --- | --- | --- | --- |
| DANN | 63.4 ± 3.1 | 64.7 ± 2.9 | 0.61 | 0.62 |
| Deep CORAL | 66.1 ± 3.0 | 67.4 ± 2.8 | 0.64 | 0.65 |
| ProtoNet | 68.9 ± 2.9 | 70.1 ± 2.6 | 0.67 | 0.68 |
| Proposed Method | 71.4 ± 2.8 | 73.6 ± 2.5 | 0.70 | 0.72 |

The proposed framework consistently outperformed all baselines, yielding 2.5–3.5 percentage points higher accuracy than ProtoNet and up to 14 points higher than the supervised baseline.

## 5.5  Discussion

The outcomes exhibit the future potential and challenges of developing strong arrhythmia detection model generalization across various kinds of heterogeneous ECG datasets. However, the proposed cross-domain meta-learning framework usually exhibits good performance within the domain and cross-dataset superior generalization, which is the mirror image of real-life deployment conditions where the training and target populations differ.

A remarkable insight we gleaned from our experiments was that domain shift defines the principal hurdle on the clinical translation of AI-based ECG classifiers. In general, when trained on a dataset, traditional supervised approaches tend to yield very high accuracy on the dataset but fail badly when applied to new cohorts, devices, or clinical settings. The proposed framework, however, included domain variability into the training process via episodic meta-learning, whereby the model learns to endure shifts and adapt to them. Such design yielded up to 15% accuracy gains in cross-domain scenarios compared to conventional baselines, underscoring the essence of learning domain-invariant representations. Inclusion of contrastive cross-domain alignment further boosted this ability, as it requires representations of the same arrhythmia class from different databases clustered in latent space. Indeed, it is because the correlation alignment (CORAL) regularizations enhanced the covariate stability across domains. This is critical when the support and query sets come from different sources of acquisition. These ideas together offer both class-consistency and distributional alignment, which are fundamental for clinical robustness. From a clinical point of view, these findings carry heavy implications. Usually, ECG analysis systems are applied in territories not suitable for local data retraining due to privacy issues, annotation costs, and regulatory constraints. Our study showed promising results in cross-domain tests; however, required a prospective validation in truly independent clinical cohorts with diverse patient demographics and acquisition conditions. It could even improve adaptability by integrating domain-specific metadata (e.g., device type, patient age, and clinical setting) in the meta-learning process. Hence, the proposed framework is a meaningful step towards clinically robust arrhythmia detection through meta-learning in combination with domain-invariant representation strategies.

The framework promises laying the strong foundation for developing AI systems with reliable performance across institutions and patient populations without retraining. Thus, automated ECG interpretation comes much closer to being reality in clinical use.

## 6  Conclusion

A unified cross-domain meta-learning framework for arrhythmia detection was proposed, integrating CNN–MHSA encoding with episodic adaptation and domain-invariance regularization. Experimental results demonstrated strong in-domain performance, achieving 85.2% accuracy on MIT-BIH and 82.7% on PTB-XL, with macro-F1 scores of 0.84 and 0.81, respectively. Under cross-domain evaluation, the framework achieved 71.4% accuracy on training on MIT-BIH and testing on PTB-XL and the other way round achieved 73.6% accuracy, approximately 12–15 percentage points better than supervised CNN baselines. These results indicated that the framework produced higher dataset shift robustness while retaining diagnostic accuracy. Domain-aware regularization (contrastive alignment and CORAL) further enhanced stability, with reduced calibration error in the cross-domain setting to 0.054–0.059. The model also stayed resilient under clinically realistic noise. To summarize, the study provided quantitative evidence that cross-domain meta-learning is a promising paradigm to develop ECG classifiers that can generalize across heterogeneous clinical environments. The next steps may include larger-scale self-supervised pretraining, integrating uncertainty estimation, and validating the models on additional multi-center datasets to further boost generalization and clinical reliability.

## References


1. Moody, G.B., Mark, R.G.: The impact of the MIT-BIH arrhythmia database. IEEE Eng. Med. Biol. Mag. **20**, 45–50 (2001)
2. LeCun, Y., Bengio, Y., Hinton, G.: Deep learning. Nature **521**, 436–444 (2015)
3. Ribeiro, A.H., et al.: Automatic diagnosis of the 12-lead ECG using a deep neural network. Nat. Commun. **11**, 1760 (2020)
4. Hannun, A.Y., et al.: Cardiologist-level arrhythmia detection and classification in ambulatory electrocardiograms using a deep neural network. Nat. Med. **25**, 65–69 (2019)
5. Weimann, K., Conrad, T.O.F.: Transfer learning for ECG classification. Sci. Rep. **11**, 5251 (2021)
6. Ganin, Y., Lempitsky, V.: Unsupervised domain adaptation by backpropagation. In: International Conference on Machine Learning, pp. 1180–1189 (2015)
7. Long, M., Cao, Y., Wang, J., Jordan, M.: Learning transferable features with deep adaptation networks. In: International Conference on Machine Learning, pp. 97–105 (2015)
8. Goldberger, A.L., et al.: PhysioBank, PhysioToolkit, and PhysioNet: components of a new research resource for complex physiologic signals. Circulation **101**, e215–e220 (2000)
9. Finn, C., Abbeel, P., Levine, S.: Model-agnostic meta-learning for fast adaptation of deep networks. In: International Conference on Machine Learning, pp. 1126–1135 (2017)
10. Snell, J., Swersky, K., Zemel, R.: Prototypical networks for few-shot learning, Adv. Neural Inf. Process. Syst. **30** (2017)

11. Li, W.-H., Liu, X., Bilen, H.: Cross-domain few-shot learning with task-specific adapters. In: Proceedings of the IEEE/CVF Conference on Computer Vision and Pattern Recognition, pp. 7161–7170 (2022)
12. Madan, P., Singh, V., Singh, D.P., Diwakar, M., Pant, B., Kishor, A.: A hybrid deep learning approach for ECG-based arrhythmia classification. Bioengineering **9**, 152 (2022)
13. Dutta, S., Chatterjee, A., Munshi, S.: Correlation technique and least square support vector machine combine for frequency domain based ECG beat classification. Med. Eng. Phys. **32**, 1161–1169 (2010)
14. Desai, U., Martis, R.J., Nayak, C.G., Seshikala, G., et al.: Machine intelligent diagnosis of ECG for arrhythmia classification using DWT, ICA and SVM techniques. In: 2015 Annual IEEE India Conference (INDICON), pp. 1–4 (2015)
15. Kumar, R.G., Kumaraswamy, Y.S., et al.: Investigating cardiac arrhythmia in ECG using random forest classification. Int. J. Comput. Appl. **37**, 31–34 (2012)
16. Alamatsaz, N., Tabatabaei, L., Yazdchi, M., Payan, H., Alamatsaz, N., Nasimi, F.: A lightweight hybrid CNN-LSTM explainable model for ECG-based arrhythmia detection. Biomed. Signal Process. Control **90**, 105884 (2024)
17. Chen, S., Wang, H., Zhang, H., Peng, C., Li, Y., Wang, B.: A novel method of swin transformer with time-frequency characteristics for ECG-based arrhythmia detection. Front. Cardiovasc. Med. **11**, 1401143 (2024)
18. Tao, Y., Xu, B., Zhang, Y.: Refined self-attention transformer model for ECG-based arrhythmia detection. IEEE Trans. Instrum. Meas. **73**, 1–14 (2024)
19. Kovalchuk, O., Barmak, O., Radiuk, P., Klymenko, L., Krak, I.: Towards transparent AI in medicine: ECG-based arrhythmia detection with explainable deep learning. Technologies (Basel) **13**, 34 (2025)

# Designing an Effective Model for Plant Diseases Detection and Classification in Smart Agriculture

Nedaa Jaber Abdulhussian(✉) and Walaa Alajali

Education College for Pure Sciences, University of Thi-Qar, 64001 Nasiriyah, Iraq
{nedaajabar.23co1,walaakhshlan}@utq.edu.iq

**Abstract.** Smart agriculture is crucial in ensuring food production by employing advanced technologies to monitor and manage plant health. Accurate detection of diseases is essential to safeguarding the long-term sustainability of agricultural systems. This paper presents an intelligent plant diseases detection system using a modified EfficientNetB2 model, incorporating new dense layers, activity_regularizer, bias_regularizer, and kernel_regularizer techniques. The model underwent training using PlantVillage dataset comprising 38 classes of plant leaves. The study achieved impressive results, with an accuracy of 97.70%. The results clearly indicated the efficacy of the suggested approach, highlighting its capacity to make a substantial contribution to intelligent agricultural practices. The method facilitated early disease identification, empowering farmers to implement preventive measures and foster sustainable crop farming.

**Keywords:** Smart agriculture · Plant diseases · Deep learning · EfficientNetB2

## 1 Introduction

Smart agriculture is essential since it provides various imaginative solutions to update the farming industry. Smart agriculture uses the newest information technique to collect, analyze, and process multi source data with a temporal and spatial resolution to improve crop production management and operational decision-making [1][2].

Plant diseases that destroy agricultural products while growing pose a substantial threat to food security. Worldwide, plant diseases cause substantial economic losses in the agriculture industry. It may immediately result in growth retardation, which would be detrimental to yields [3, 4].

Plant infections can be caused by various diseases, such as bacteria, fungi, viruses, and molds. Plant infections may be caused by environmental factors, among others instance humidity, temperature, and precipitation, which serve as vectors for pathogens, including viruses and plagues. The livelihoods of farmers could be adversely affected by these diseases, leading to substantial financial repercussions. Consequently, early identification of plant diseases is important for crop management. Plant diseases are often diagnosed with the help of experts. Moreover, traditional methods farmers and


S. O. Al-Mamory et al. (Eds.): 3INC 2025, CCIS 2960, pp. 248–260, 2026.
https://doi.org/10.1007/978-3-032-24239-6_14

field experts employ to detect plant illnesses are expensive and susceptible to errors. Therefore, artificial intelligence-based methods can be essential for fast and accurate plant disease diagnosis [5].

Deep learning(DL), especially convolutional neural networks(CNNs), has gained much interest in agricultural sectors like plant and weed detection, disease identification, and pest recognition [6]. To identify and categorize plant diseases, several DL models have been implemented, such as those presented by Jasrotia et al. [7], for maize crop leaf disease classification. A hybrid CNN model was suggested for banana disease detection and classification by Narayanan et al. [8]. A VGG16, Inception V3, and MobileNet were proposed by Arjaria et al. [9], for identification of tomato crop diseases. In this paper, several contributions are made. Firstly, most studies have focused on a particular plant species or a specific type of disease. However, it is beneficial to create a reliable and generalizable model that can be used for many plant diseases. Therefore, a dataset was used that includes 14 types of plants with 38 different classes of diseases. Secondly, we enhanced the EfficientNetB2 model by adding new hidden layers, contributing to notable improvements in the accuracy and classification capability of the model. The hidden layers were meticulously structured using regularization techniques to mitigate overfitting and promote robust generalization to unseen data. Finally, the model uses 9 million parameters, less than other DL models. Therefore, the model complexity is reduced and computational efficiency is increased. Therefore, it is more suitable for resource-constrained applications such as smart agriculture.

The remainder of the study is structured in the following manner: The utilization of DL techniques for diagnosing plant diseases is discussed in Sect. 2. Section 3 introduces the proposed method and Sect. 4 illustrates the outcomes. The conclusion and discussions are introduced in Sect. 5.

## 2 Related Work

Many research works have been conducted over the past few years using DL techniques to identify plant diseases. Barman et al. [10] proposed a CNN-based approach for the detection of potato disease. The model underwent training using both independently augmented and nonaugmented images. The proposed method attained a precision of 96.98% on the augmented dataset and 96.76% on the original dataset. Furthermore, Gayathri et al. [11] developed a technique for categorizing illnesses in tea plants. They used the LeNet model and collected leaf photographs from the Plant Village database. Through their proposed methodology, they achieved an accuracy of 90.23%.

In addition, Syed-ab-rahman et al. [12] used leaf images to classify citrus diseases and identify plant diseases using a two-stage deep CNN model. The proposed model was divided into two primary stages: first, a region proposal network was utilized to suggest probable target diseased areas; second, a classifier was employed to identify the most probable target region corresponding to the associated disease class. The suggested model yielded an average precision of 95.8% and a detection accuracy of 94.37%. On the other hand, a novel DL hybrid model for classifying sunflower diseases, including Downy mildew, Alternaria leaves rot, and phoma rot, was presented by Sirohi et al. [13].The study constructed a hybrid model comprising MobileNet and H.VGG-16. The accuracy achieved by the model was 89.2%. The dataset was compiled utilizing Google images.

In addition, Roy et al. [14] suggested a multi-class plant disease object identification model with DL capabilities based on enhanced YOLOv4 algorithms. The model was applied to the real-world detection of multi-class apple plant illnesses. The model achieved a precision of 91.2% and an F1_score of 95.9%. Panchal et al. [15] proposed CNN model for the categorization of crop diseases. Leaves from affected crops were taken and labeled according to the disease pattern. Pixel-based techniques were used to enhance the information extracted from the photos of infected leaves. Following feature extraction and image segmentation, crop illnesses were classified with an accuracy of 93.5% using patterns taken from infected leaves.

Haridasan et al. [16] proposed an automated method for identifying and categorizing illnesses. To detect and classify specific categories of paddy plant diseases, CNNs were combined with a support vector machine(SVM) classifier. The proposed DL approach achieved a maximum validation accuracy of 0.9145. Alghamdi et al. [17] presented PDD-Net and combined multilevel and multiscale characteristics with data augmentation approaches for diagnosing plant diseases. Based on the PlantVillage and cassava datasets, the proposed framework demonstrated an accuracy of 93.79% and 86.98%, respectively. Ayyappan et al. [18] identified different rice plant diseases using DL techniques and (CNNs). Images of various plant illnesses were used to train the CNN model, and multiple models were assessed to find the best one for identifying diseases. DenseNet121 attained an accuracy of 97.50%, while the Xception model reached 96.32%. EfficientNet-B4 achieved 96.25%, and MobileNet-V3 also recorded 96.25% in the categorization of paddy diseases.

## 3 Proposed Method

A modified EfficientNetB2 architecture for plant disease detection was developed using the PlantVillage dataset, which comprises 38 distinct classes. In this study, 14 plant species were considered, each categorized into healthy and diseased classes. This task presents a considerable challenge; as most research works have primarily focused on one or two plant types. To optimize the EfficientNetB2 model, input images were resized and enhanced through sharpening techniques to highlight critical boundaries. Furthermore, data augmentation was applied to the training set to improve the robustness of the model. The proposed framework was subjected to extensive training and evaluation, the details of which are discussed in the subsequent sections. A schematic overview of the proposed system is illustrated in Fig. 1.

### 3.1 Dataset Description

We used the PlantVillage dataset in our study, which is available in Mendeley Data. It is a shared dataset that many researchers have used in their studies. This data shows several different plant leaves, such as tomatoes, potatoes, peppers, corn, and other plants. All types of plants were used in this study. The dataset contains 55448 images, including 38 classes of 14 plants, including healthy, infected leaves images. Every image was taken in a laboratory setting. In this work, the plants were classified using colored (RGB) photos. Figure 2 illustrates the sample images comprising the dataset.

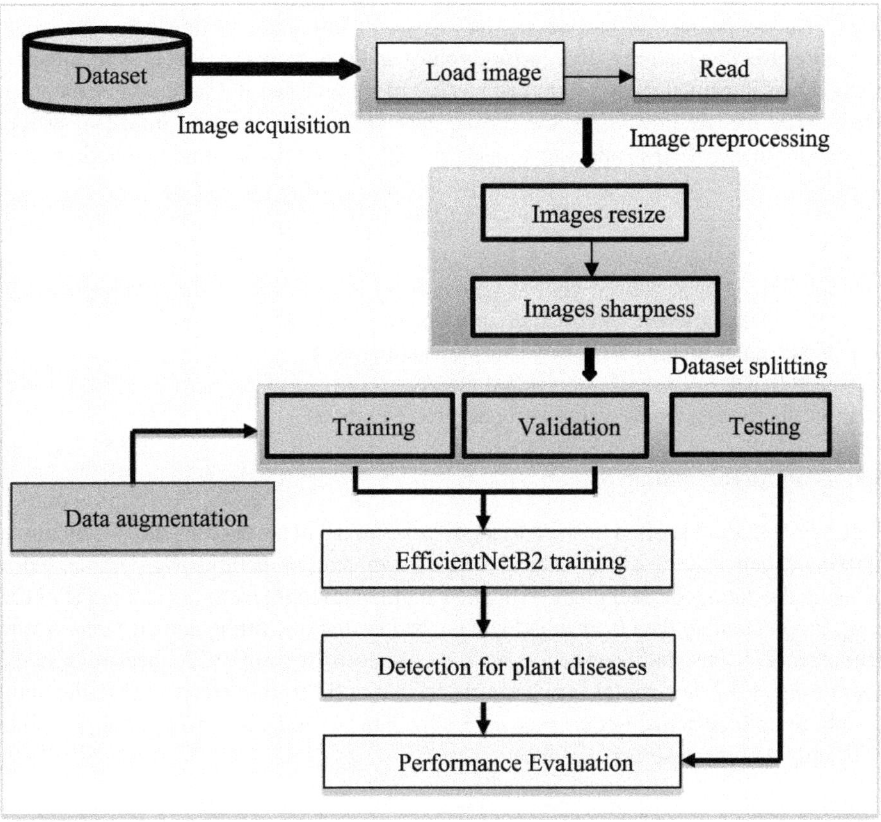

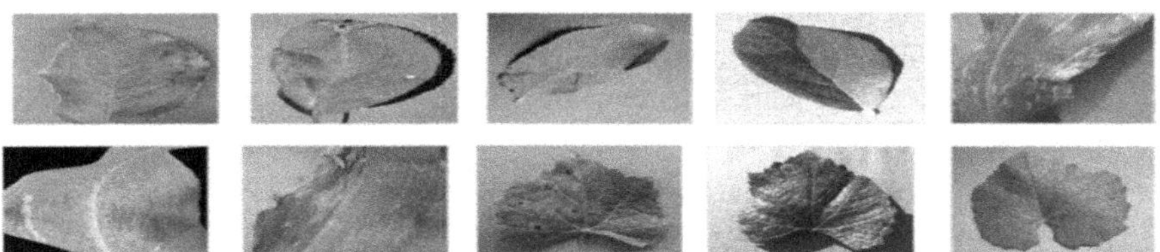

**Fig. 1.** Diagram illustrating the structure and design of the EfficientNetB2 model.

**Fig. 2.** Samples of the PlantVillage Dataset.

## 3.2  Preprocessing

Image processing is a critical operation that ensures the acquisition of suitable data devoid of unwanted distortions and emphasizes the image characteristics that will be crucial for subsequent processing. It reduces noise and redundancy, speeds up execution, and increases accuracy [19]. In order to meet the model's input requirements, the dataset images were resized to 128 × 128 pixels. An image enhancement technique called Sharpness Enhancement was used to enhance the sharpness of the image. Sharpening enhances images' edges and fine details by increasing the contrast between adjacent pixels. By increasing the sharpness of an image, the utilization of this technique results in a more effective feature extraction and robust analysis, as in the Eq. (1). The enhanced method was executed with a parameter value of 3, denoting the applied enhancement level. After the preprocessing, the dataset was split into a training image of 80%, a validation image of 10%, and a test image of 10% for the model implementation.

$$O = (1 - f) . B + (f . I) \tag{1}$$

where

- O: the final sharpened image after applying the sharpness.
- I: the original image before any sharpness adjustment.
- B: a softened version of the original image.
- f: the sharpness control value you pass into enhance(f).

### 3.3  Data Augmentation

Data augmentation is often utilized to modify the image in the training dataset by implementing changes to the image database. The augmentation methods were implemented by using the data-generator class [20]. Data augmentation refers to the technique of creating supplementary data from existing data, addressing overfitting and also underfitting problems [21].This study applied techniques like rotation-rang = 15, shear-rang = 0.2, zoom-rang = 0.2, horizontal-flip, and vertical-flip to the training data so that they more closely resembled actual circumstances. Using data augmentation helps train our model efficiently and increase performance.

### 3.4  Proposed Model

A modification was suggested to the EfficientNetB2 architecture that would enable the model to learn specific features and patterns pertinent to our plant disease dataset. 0054he final classification layer was removed to utilize the EfficientNetB2 model for feature extraction, leveraging their learned features from the ImageNet dataset. A custom classification layer was added, allowing for more accurate and context-specific predictions. This modification capitalized on the robust feature extraction capabilities of the model while ensuring that the final classification is optimized for the dataset and problem at hand. A schematic overview of the proposed model is illustrated in Fig. 3. First, batch normalization is applied, which involves normalizing the activations of the antecedent layer along the channel axis. Two dense layers are subsequently incorporated, each containing 64 neurons and 256 neurons, following the normalization process. Increasing the number of layers within a model leads to a simplification in the extraction of a more significant amount of characteristics, as a result, its capacity for classification is enhanced [22].

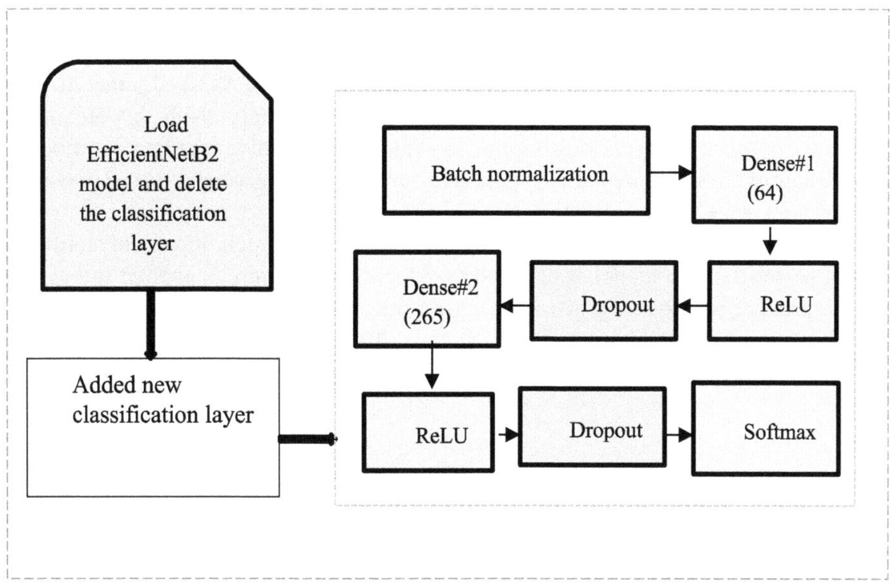


**Fig. 3.** Diagram Illustrating the Structure of the EfficientNetB2 Model.

Both of these layers include different regularization techniques to prevent overfitting. The first technique includes using The kernel_regularizer, with an L2 regularization strength of 0.013, penalizes large weights, the activity_regularizer and bias_regularizer, with an L1 regularization strength of 0.006, encourage sparsity in the output, and promote biases closer to zero. These regularization techniques help enhance the model's generalization ability and prevent overfitting. L1 is defined in Eq. (2).

$$\tilde{L}(w) = L(w) + \lambda \sum_{i=1}^{n} |w_i| \tag{2}$$

and L2 regularization is defined in Eq. (3).

$$\tilde{L}(w) = L(w) + \frac{\lambda}{2} \sum_{i=1}^{n} |w_i^2| \tag{3}$$

The loss function is represented as L(w) where w denotes the network weights, n signifies the overall number of weights, and $\lambda$ represents the regularization strength.

After that, the activation function was used as ReLU. This function is defined by the Eq. (4).

$$f(x)ReLU = \max(0, x) \tag{4}$$

Linear activation functions are only beneficial in the approximation of linear hypothesis functions. Given that a nonlinear relationship typically occurs between input and output in complex problems, nonlinear activation functions are frequently employed.

The ReLU activation function is widely adopted because it accelerates learning and improves computational efficiency [23].

Then, a dropout layer was added, featuring a seed value of 123 and a rate of 0.35, which is defined as a technique for regularizing CNN models. With this technique, randomly chosen neurons can be disregarded while training. This caused the contribution of these neurons to be momentarily suppressed during forward propagation and prevented overfitting by speeding up model training [24].

The output layer comprised 38 units of dense layer, corresponding to the number of plant diseases that the model is required to categorize. Softmax is applied in the final layer to produce a probability distribution over the classes, allowing the model's output to be interpreted as the likelihood of each class. The following equation describes the softmax:

$$p_i = \frac{e^{a_i}}{\sum_{K=1}^{N} e^{a}_k} \tag{5}$$

where $e^{a}i$ represents the unnormalized output from the preceding layer and N represents the total number of neurons in the output layer.

## 4   Experimental Results

This section presents an overview of the evaluation metrics employed and the experimental results obtained in the proposed study.

### 4.1  Evaluation Metrics

The suggested model's performance was assessed based on many criteria, such as the precision, accuracy, F1-score, and recall. The following mathematical expressions are associated with these performance criteria [25]:

$$\text{Accuracy} = \frac{TP + TN}{TP + FP + FN + TN} \tag{6}$$

$$\text{Precision} = \frac{TP}{TP + FP} \tag{7}$$

$$\text{Recall} = \frac{TP}{TP + FN} \tag{8}$$

$$F1 - \text{score} = 2 * \left( \frac{Precision * Recall}{Precision + Recall} \right) \tag{9}$$

## 4.2  Performance of Proposed EfficientNetB2 Model

The experiments were conducted on a computing environment equipped with Intel(R) Core(TM) i5-11400H operating at 2.70 GHz (2.69 GHz effective speed), and 16.0 GB of RAM. The system ran on Windows 11, 64-bit edition. The implementation of the code was carried out using the Python programming language, version 3.8, within the PyCharm Integrated Development Environment (IDE).

EfficientnetB2 was trained and assessed on the PlantVillage dataset. Optimizers are crucial in updating the weights across different layers after each iteration. The Adamax optimizer was employed to train the model for 55 epochs. The loss function employed was categorical cross-entropy, a widely utilized method for multiclass classification applications. This function evaluates the performance of a classification model by producing probability values within the range of 0 to 1. A minimum learning rate threshold of 0.0001 was established, once the learning rate reached this value, it remained constant without further decay. Table 1 lists hyperparameters of the proposed EfficientNetB2 model. The suggested model demonstrated outstanding performance with accuracy of training and validation of 97.59% and 96.35%, respectively Fig. 4. The model also achieved a loss function of 1.25% in the training and a loss function of 1.05% in the validation. The model's precision and recall were 98.54% and 97.82%, respectively for the training. As for validation, it reached precision and recall of 97.56% and 94.53% respectively. As depicted in Fig. 5, both training and validation losses consistently decreased over the 55 epochs.

**Table 1.** Hyperparameters of the EfficientNetB2 Model.

| Parameters | Values |
| --- | --- |
| Epochs | 55 |
| batch sizes | 32 |
| Dropout value | 0.35 |
| Learning rate | 0.001_0.0001 |
| Optimization | Adamax |
| Momentum | 0.99 |
| L1_ Regularization | 0.006 |
| L2_ Regularization | 0.013 |

The effectiveness of the model was also assessed by calculating the confusion matrix. The comprehensive accuracy of the proposed model in the testing phase was 97.70%. It exhibited precision (98.33%) and recall (98.07%) across all disease categories, an overall F1 score of 98.07%.

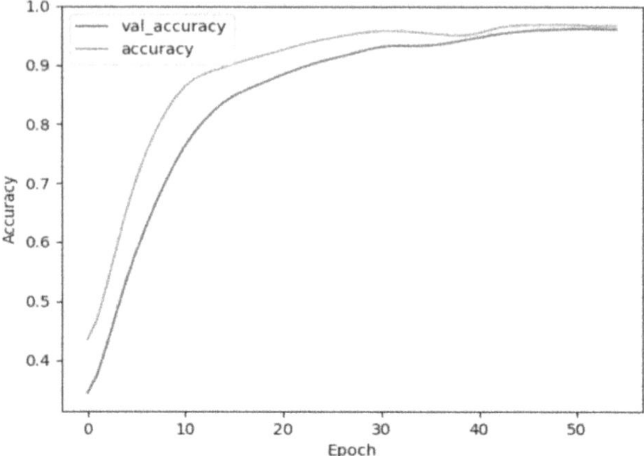

**Fig. 4.** Training and Validation Accuracy.

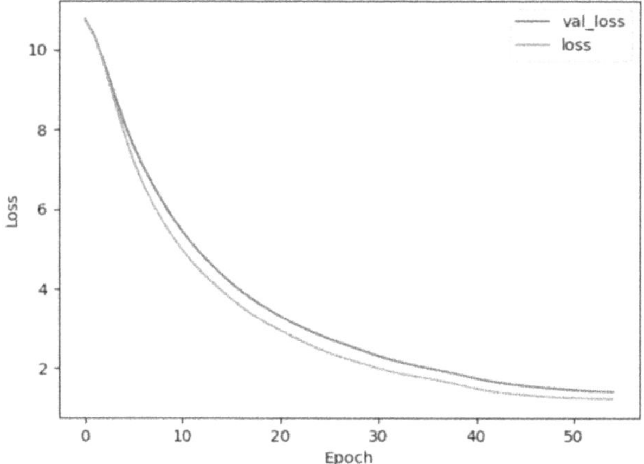

**Fig. 5.** Training and Validation Loss Function.

The suggested model was also evaluated with other pre-training models, for example ResNet50 and Xception. The EfficientNetB2 model outperforms the other DL models in performance and requires fewer parameters. The EfficientNetB2 model demonstrated better performance in terms of both accuracy and computational efficiency. Moreover, the model demonstrated strong classification performance with a parameter count of only 9 million, underscoring its efficiency in comparison to more complex architectures. For instance, ResNet50 and Xception comprise approximately 25 million and 22 million parameters respectively.

The reduction in parameter usage results in a decrease in the training time of the model, simpler, perhaps faster, and less complexity. These features make it more appropriate for implementation in settings with limited resources, such as agricultural monitoring systems on the field. Figure 6 shows the testing results comparison of the suggestion model.

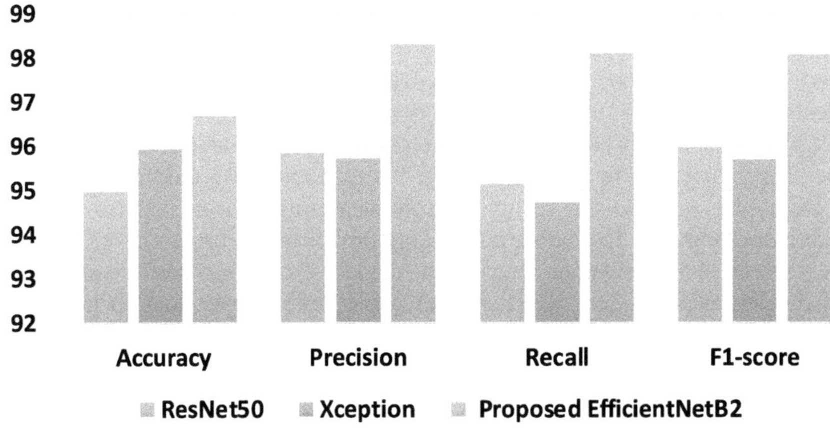


**Fig. 6.** Testing Comparison of the Proposed Model with other DL models.

The proposed EfficientNetB2 model was also compared to DL models in the literature. As shown in Table 2, the EfficientNetB2 model outperforms other DL models that use the same PlantVillage dataset. The efficiency of EfficientNetB2 is further highlighted by comparing it to other research that also utilizes the 38 classes, such as those conducted by Geetharamani et al. [26] and Falaschetti et al. [27]. Although these studies yield praiseworthy outcomes, the EfficientNetB2 model surpasses these studies, demonstrating its state-of-the-art capabilities in processing intricate agricultural data from the real world.

**Table 2.** Comparison of Model Performance with Various DL Models.

| Authors | Deep learning models | Dataset used | No. of classes | Accuracy |
|---|---|---|---|---|
| Geetharamani et al.[26] | CNN | PlantVillage | 38 | 96.46% |
| Barman et al.[10] | CNN | PlantVillage | 10 | 96.89% |
| Falaschetti et al.[27] | CNN | PlantVillage | 38 | 95.24% |
| Alghamdi et al. [17] | CNN | PlantVillage | 19 | 93.79% |
| Ayyappan et al.[18] | CNN | PlantVillage | 10 | 97.50% |
| Proposed model | EfficientNetB2 | PlantVillage | 38 | 97.70% |

## 5  Conclusion and Discussions

This study utilized the EffucientNetB2 model to detect plant illnesses. The Efficient-NetB2 model showcased superior detection capabilities by incorporating additional dense layers along with activity, bias, and kernel regularization techniques to capture patterns that are complicated, which are often challenging to discern. This ability is critical for accurate disease identification and subsequent management, which can lead to significant economic savings in the agriculture sector by reducing crop loss.

The use of data augmentation is particularly important for enhancing the robustness and performance of the modified EfficientNetB2 model in detecting plant diseases. Data augmentation is a powerful technique to enhance the training of DL models, especially in domains like agriculture where the conditions can be highly variable and data collection can be challenging. The results showed that the EfficientNetB2 model outperformed other DL models in effectively recognizing and analyzing intricate patterns related to plant disease symptoms. Exhibiting outstanding proficiency in categorizing 38 unique diseases across 14 different plant species. The model's exceptional performance can be ascribed to its scalable nature, which enables it to optimize dimensions such as depth, breadth, and resolution with greater efficacy than conventional architectures.

Future works can expand the objective of detecting plant diseases to include parts other than the leaves, such as the flowers, fruits, or stems. It is possible to integrate plant disease identification and detection systems with other agricultural fields, such as identifying pests and weeds. In addition, future studies can recommend treatments to the cases diagnosed in the system to provide appropriate solutions. The study focused only on the problem of biotic diseases in plants. As a future work, the diseases caused by abiotic factors can be combined to enhance adequate crop protection.

## References


1. Ksibi, A., Ayadi, M., Soufiene, B.O., Jamjoom, M.M., Ullah, Z.: MobiRes-Net: a hybrid deep learning model for detecting and classifying olive leaf diseases. Applied Sciences **12**(20), 10278 (2022). https://doi.org/10.3390/app122010278
2. Bakthavatchalam, K., Karthik, B., Thiruvengadam, V., Muthal, S., Jose, D., Kotecha, K., Varadarajan, V.: IoT framework for measurement and precision agriculture: predicting the crop using machine learning algorithms. Technologies **10**(1), 13 (2022). https://doi.org/10.3390/technologies10010013
3. Guo, Y., et al.: Plant disease identification based on deep learning algorithm in smart farming. Disc. Dyn. Nat. Soc. **2020**(1), 2479172 (2020). https://doi.org/10.1155/2020/2479172
4. Fuentes, A., Yoon, S., Park, D.S.: Deep learning-based phenotyping system with glocal description of plant anomalies and symptoms. Front. Plant Sci. **10**(November), 1–19 (2019). https://doi.org/10.3389/fpls.2019.01321
5. Tiwari, V., Joshi, R.C., Dutta, M.K.: Dense convolutional neural networks based multiclass plant disease detection and classification using leaf images. Ecol. Inf. **63**, 101289 (2021). https://doi.org/10.1016/j.ecoinf.2021.101289
6. Hassan, S.M., Maji, A.K.: Plant disease identification using a novel convolutional neural network. IEEE Access **10**, 5390–5401 (2022). https://doi.org/10.1109/ACCESS.2022.3141371

7. Jasrotia, S., Yadav, J., Rajpal, N., Arora, M., Chaudhary, J.: Convolutional neural network based maize plant disease identification. Procedia Comput. Sci. **218**(2022), 1712–1721 (2022). https://doi.org/10.1016/j.procs.2023.01.149

8. Narayanan, K.L., et al.: Banana plant disease classification using hybrid convolutional neural network. Comput. Intell. Neurosci. **2022**, 9153699 (2022). https://doi.org/10.1155/2022/9153699

9. Agarwal, M., Singh, A., Arjaria, S., Sinha, A., Gupta, S.: ToLeD: tomato leaf disease detection using convolution neural network. Procedia Comput. Sci. **167**(2019), 293–301 (2020). https://doi.org/10.1016/j.procs.2020.03.225

10. Barman, U., Sahu, D., Barman, G.G., Das, J.: Comparative assessment of deep learning to detect the leaf diseases of potato based on data augmentation. In: 2020 International Conference on Computer Performing Evulation ComPE 2020, pp. 682–687 (2020). https://doi.org/10.1109/ComPE49325.2020.92000

11. Gayathri, S., Wise, D.C.J.W., Shamini, P.B., Muthukumaran, N.: Image analysis and detection of tea leaf disease using deep learning, no. Icesc, pp. 398–403 (2020)

12. Syed-ab-rahman, S.F., Hesam, M., Mukesh, H.: Citrus disease detection and classification using end-to-end anchor-based deep learning model (2021)

13. Sirohi, A., Malik, A.: A hybrid model for the classification of sunflower diseases using deep learning. In: Proceedings of 2021 2nd Interenational Conference on Intelligence Engineering and Management, ICIEM 2021, no. 2, pp. 58–62 (2021). https://doi.org/10.1109/ICIEM51511.2021.9445342

14. Roy, A.M., Bhaduri, J.: A deep learning enabled multi-class plant disease detection model based on computer vision. AI **2**(3), 413–428 (2021). https://doi.org/10.3390/ai2030026

15. Panchal, A.V., Patel, S.C., Bagyalakshmi, K., Kumar, P., Khan, I.R., Soni, M.: Image-based Plant Diseases Detection using Deep Learning. Mater. Today: Proc. **80**, 3500–3506 (2023)

16. Haridasan, A., Thomas, J.: Deep learning system for paddy plant disease detection and classification. Environ. Monit. Assess. (2023). https://doi.org/10.1007/s10661-022-10656-x

17. Alghamdi, H., Turki, T.: PDD-Net: plant disease diagnoses using multilevel and multiscale convolutional neural network features. Agriculture **13**(5), 1072 (2023). https://doi.org/10.3390/agriculture13051072

18. Ayyappan, A.B., Kumar, T.G.M.: Rice plant disease detection using convolutional neural networks. Disc. Artif. Intell. (2025). https://doi.org/10.1007/s44163-025-00277-x

19. Chellapandi, B., Vijayalakshmi, M., Chopra, S.: Comparison of pre-trained models using transfer learning for detecting plant disease. In: Proceedings - IEEE 2021 International Conference on Computer and Communication Intelligent Systems, ICCCIS 2021, pp. 383–387 (2021). https://doi.org/10.1109/ICCCIS51004.2021.9397098

20. Noon, S.K., Amjad, M., Qureshi, M.A., Mannan, A.: Overfitting mitigation analysis in deep learning models for plant leaf disease recognition. In: Proceedings - 2020 23rd IEEE International Multi-Topic Conference INMIC 2020, pp. 10–14 (2020). https://doi.org/10.1109/INMIC50486.2020.9318044

21. Shovon, M.S.H., Mozumder, S.J., Pal, O.K., Mridha, M.F., Asai, N., Shin, J.: PlantDet: a robust multi-model ensemble method based on deep learning for plant disease detection. IEEE Access **11**(March), 34846–34859 (2023). https://doi.org/10.1109/ACCESS.2023.3264835

22. Helen Josephine, V.L., Nirmala, A.P., Alluri, V.L.: Impact of hidden dense layers in convolutional neural network to enhance performance of classification model. IOP Conf. Ser. Mater. Sci. Eng. **1131**(1), 012007 (2021). https://doi.org/10.1088/1757-899x/1131/1/012007

23. Taye, M.M.: Theoretical understanding of convolutional neural network: concepts, architectures, applications, future directions. Computation **11**(3), 52 (2023). https://doi.org/10.3390/computation11030052

24. Wang, S.H., et al.: Multiple sclerosis identification by 14-layer convolutional neural network with batch normalization, dropout, and stochastic pooling. Front. Neurosci. **12**, 1–11 (2018). https://doi.org/10.3389/fnins.2018.00818
25. Bagli, E., Visani, G.: Metrics for multi-class classification: an overview, pp. 1–17 (2020)
26. Geetharamani, G.A.P.J., Pandian, A.: Identification of plant leaf diseases using a nine-layer deep convolutional neural network. Comput. Electr. Eng. **76**, 323–338 (2019). https://doi.org/10.1016/j.compeleceng.2019.04.011
27. Falaschetti, L., Manoni, L., Di Leo, D., Pau, D., Tomaselli, V., Turchetti, C.: A CNN-based image detector for plant leaf diseases classification. HardwareX **12**, e00363 (2022). https://doi.org/10.1016/j.ohx.2022.e00363

# Optimizing Quality of Service in Software-Defined Networks via Deep Q-Learning

Maysaa Salim Al-Amidi[✉] and Aladdin A. Abdulhassan

Department of Information Networks, University of Babylon, Babylon, Iraq
maysaasalimh.net@student.uobabylon.edu.iq,
Aladdin.alsharifi@uobabylon.edu.iq

**Abstract.** In today's expanding and diversified data networks, static QoS mechanisms fall short in dynamically satisfying varying application requirements. A DRL-based self-adaptive routing scheme in an SDN was proposed. The agent was trained and tested on a simulated SDN environment with 799,223 samples. For dynamic traffic engineering, optimal parameters such as latency, packet loss, and throughput were minimized. The implementation on the POX controller for a real-world deployment demonstrated significant reductions; latency was reduced by 9.3%, packet loss was reduced by 90.9%, and bandwidth utilization was enhanced by 2.7%. Comparison of validation results with Q-Learning demonstrated the superiority of the performance metrics, showing DQN / Q-learning in all performance metrics (packet loss: 90.9% - 61.0%, latency: 9.3%–4.38%, generalization capability: 51.1%–25%). The DQN was able to reconcile contradicting QoS targets and can be the foundation of adaptive SDN infrastructures able to optimize a network autonomously in real time.

**Keywords:** Deep Q-Network · Software-Defined Networking · Quality of Service · Reinforcement Learning · Network Optimization · Traffic Engineering · Multi-Objective Optimization

## 1 Introduction

Software-Defined Networking decouples network data and control planes and provides dynamic programmability via open protocols like OpenFlow[1]. This architecture provides essential centralization for the deployment of intelligent traffic management functions via algorithms through machine learning techniques[2]. This architecture offers very basic programmability and centralized control in the deployment of traffic management solutions enabled by machine learning intelligence. It enables operators to dynamically reallocate network resources and quickly react to dynamic traffic [3].

New applications such as ultra-high-definition video streaming, interactive gaming stations, and AR/VR REQUIREMENTS AR/VR applications require strict QoS: low latency, few packet losses, and enough bandwidth. There are prerequisites to delivering any sort of acceptable experience to the user. Still, in such environments, the traffic

© The Author(s), under exclusive license to Springer Nature Switzerland AG 2026
S. O. Al-Mamory et al. (Eds.): 3INC 2025, CCIS 2960, pp. 261–279, 2026.
https://doi.org/10.1007/978-3-032-24239-6_15

behaviors are not stable, and static routing protocols cannot adapt fast. This leads to a bottleneck and diminished service quality [3]. The issue is to use the SDN centralized vision in order to implement smart, real-time statement that reconciles various requirements of QoS.

Reinforcement learning is promising as it seeks optimal actions by interacting with the environment, as opposed to depending on established models. Among numerous reinforcement learning systems, the Deep Q-Network (DQN)[4] amalgamates Q-learning with deep neural networks to manage high-dimensional states and actions. While tree-based approaches have proven to be effective in network optimization with hierarchical approaches and decision structures [5], standard discrete Q-learning faces scalability challenges with large state spaces. DQN overcomes these limitations by Neural Network Function Approximation, which enables continuous state-space handling and superior generalization capabilities. Application of DQN to SDN routing has the potential to perform dynamic resource allocation and hence minimize latency while respecting bandwidth constraints [1, 6]. In this work, DQN was harnessed to enable a SDN controller to learn flow routing policies that avoid congestion proactively and satisfy several QoS objectives.

The main contributions of this work are: (1) A multi-objective DQN framework that simultaneously optimizes latency, packet loss, and bandwidth in SDN environments, to overcome the limitations of other single-metric approaches; (2) Comprehensive comparative analysis demonstrating DQN's 10× faster convergence over Q-Learning while achieving superior generalization (51.1% vs. 25.0%) and deployment performance (90.9% vs. 61.0% packet loss reduction); (3) Practical POX controller integration with real-world deployment validation in Mininet environment; (4) Extensive experimental evaluation using 799,223 network traffic records across diverse conditions, providing robust validation of the proposed approach.

The remainder of this paper is organized as follows: Sect. 2 surveys related works on QoS optimization using Deep Reinforcement Learning in SDN: Sect. 3 introduces background on SDN architecture, QoS metrics and the DQN algorithm. Section 4 describes the proposed DQN-based QoS optimization framework; and Sect. 5 describes the experimental set-up. Section 6 presents comprehensive results including comparative analysis that depicts superior multi-objective optimization capability of DQN against Q-Learning and Sect. 7 concludes with future research directions.

The following section reviews existing deep reinforcement learning approaches for SDN optimization, identifies current limitations, and positions the proposed work in the research landscape.

## 2   Related Work

Recent research has demonstrated the effectiveness of integrating SDN with Reinforcement Learning to enable intelligent network path optimization. Al Jameel et al. demonstrated that reinforcement learning agents can dynamically assess network state and adjust routing decisions according to real-time link conditions [2].

A multitude of studies has investigated the application of deep reinforcement learning to enhance networking performance. This section reviews foundational contributions, recent advances, and existing gaps in applying DQN to QoS optimization in SDN.

### 2.1  Deep Q-Learning in Control Systems

Reinforcement learning (RL) offers a promising solution by learning optimal actions through interaction with the environment rather than relying on pre-defined models. Among various RL techniques, the Deep Q-network (DQN) [4] combines Q-learning with deep neural networks to handle high-dimensional states and actions. Recent works have shown the effectiveness of DRL in network optimization tasks. Xu et al. [3] highlighted how experience-driven approaches can be effective at addressing traffic engineering challenges in communication networks. While conventional discrete Q-learning suffers from scalability issues with large state spaces, DQN addresses these limitations through neural network function approximation, which allows for continuous state-space control and improved generalization capabilities. In SDN routing, DQN has the advantage of enabling dynamic resource allocation and low latency by obeying bandwidth constraints [1, 6]. The paper makes use of DQN to help an SDN controller learn flow path selection schemes that proactively avoid congestion and meet diverse QoS requirements.

### 2.2  Reinforcement Learning (RL) in Networking

Reinforcement learning (RL) has become an important tool for network optimization given its ability to adapt to dynamic traffic with no need to a priori system knowledge. Xu et al. [3] proposed experience-driven networking which uses model-free reinforcement learning for traffic engineering in SDN. Chen et al. [7] employed reinforcement learning for 5G service-function chaining, considering Quality of Service (QoS) and Quality of Experience (QoE). These works have collectively demonstrated that reinforcement learning can supplant static optimization techniques with adaptive, data-driven control mechanisms, which are well-suited to the programmable architecture of software-defined networking.

### 2.3  Quality of Service-Oriented Deep Reinforcement Learning in Software-Defined Networking

Recent studies have concentrated on integrating Deep Reinforcement Learning with Software-Defined Networking to fulfill rigorous Quality of Service criteria. Bouzidi et al. [1] integrated traffic prediction with DQN to improve routing decisions, reducing latency in dynamic conditions. Naguib et al. [8] applied DRL to 6G networks to support virtual reality applications demanding ultra-low latency and high bandwidth. As a hybrid approach, Aboughaly and Hannan [6] augmented DQN with bio-inspired optimization to enhance robustness. Abbasova and Karimova [9] compared several DRL algorithms and showed that DQN, A3C, and PPO outperformed conventional routing protocols. Other researchers have extended DQN with autoencoders for anomaly detection [10] or combined SDN with deep learning to allocate bandwidth dynamically [11].

### 2.4  Research Gaps

Despite these advances, there are two main limitations. First, many studies have optimized a single QoS metric – for example, latency or throughput – rather than addressing the trade-offs between them. Second, few works have managed to couple traffic forecasting with real-time DQN control to proactively manage conflicting QoS demands. This research addresses these gaps by proposing a unified DQN framework that simultaneously considers latency, bandwidth, and packet loss and adapts to diverse traffic patterns in SDN environments.

## 3   Theoretical Backgrounds

### 3.1   Software-Defined Networking

Software-defined networking (SDN) separates the network control plane from the data plane, providing a logically centralized controller that maintains a global view of the network. This separation enables network programmability through open APIs, simplifies management, and fosters rapid innovation [12, 13].

Key components of a SDN include:

- **Controller:** The centralized entity which keeps the network state and issues instructions to switches by using southbound protocols, for example OpenFlow [10, 12].
- **Switches:** Data-plane devices that forward packets according to the flow rules set by the controller [9, 13].
- **Protocols:** Standards like OpenFlow define how controllers communicate with switches to granularly manipulate the forwarding tables [10].
- Centralized decision-making in SDN facilitates precise traffic engineering and swift failure recovery. Thus, it is an indispensable technology in modern datacenters and mobile networks [3].

### 3.2   Quality of Service (QoS) metrics

QoS: A set of techniques that ensures that the network performance meets the various application requirements, especially for latency/loss-sensitive ones [14]. The most relevant QoS metrics in this respect are:

- **Latency:** The end-to-end delay experienced by packets. For interactive services such as video conferencing and gaming, low latency is critical [15].
- **Packet loss:** The proportion of packets that do not reach their destination because of congestion or link failures. For mission-critical communications, packet loss must be kept near zero [15, 16].
- **Bandwidth:** The size of a network connection, which refers to the amount of data that can be transferred. High bandwidth is required for bandwidth intensive application such as 4 K video [14].

Traditional QoS schemes such as DiffServ rely on static classifications that cannot adapt to real-time traffic shifts. The programmability of SDN enables dynamic QoS management; however, determination of the optimal policy remains challenging [17].

### 3.3   Reinforcement Learning and the DQN Algorithm

Reinforcement learning models the interaction between an agent and its environment as a Markov Decision Process. At each time step the agent observes a state, selects an action, receives a scalar reward and transitions to a new state [18, 19]. The goal is to learn a policy that maximizes the expected cumulative reward.

Deep Q-Networks extend Q-learning by using a neural network to approximate the action-value function in high-dimensional spaces. Two innovations stabilize training:

- Target network: A secondary network with parameters that are copied periodically from the main network (parameters). This reduces oscillations during learning [20].
- Experience replay: A buffer that stores past transitions from which mini-batches are sampled randomly to decorrelate training data [19].
- These techniques allow DQN to cope with complex, non-linear dynamics such as those found in SDN traffic management [3, 16].

## 4   Proposed methodology

### 4.1   System overview

Figure 1. depicts the whole flow for QoS optimization in SDN using DQN reinforcement learning. There are six main stages involved in this system. First, QoS network traffic data are generated with the help of iPerf3 in the Mininet environment. It produces 1,000,000 rows across 30 features and is stored as a CSV file. Data pre-processing is done in Anaconda, which involves cleaning, normalization, and feature selection using Random Forest algorithm. This reduces the number of features from 30 to 10 optimal features, totaling 799,223 records. The DQN model architecture consists of $10 + 24 + 24 + 3$ layers trained for 50 episodes in an Anaconda environment. After training the model, it is saved along with MinMaxScaler for deployment. The model files are loaded into the POX Controller to initialize the SDN environment. In the end, real-time QoS optimization is executed inside the POX Controller, where, based on the dynamic nature of the system, it controls the network parameters related to latency, packet loss, and bandwidth.

### 4.2   Core Components

**Application Layer:** Administrators specify QoS policies and targets at this layer, such as maximum allowable latency or minimum bandwidth. These requirements are converted into parameters that guide the DQN's reward function.

**QoS Optimization Module:** This module ingests telemetry from switches, normalizes and aggregates the data, and passes it to the DQN agent. It also implements a dynamic weighting scheme to balance conflicting objectives by adjusting reward weights according to current conditions.

**SDN Controller (POX):** Acting as the control plane, the POX controller monitors switch states, installs flow rules and exposes interfaces for communication between the optimization module and network devices.

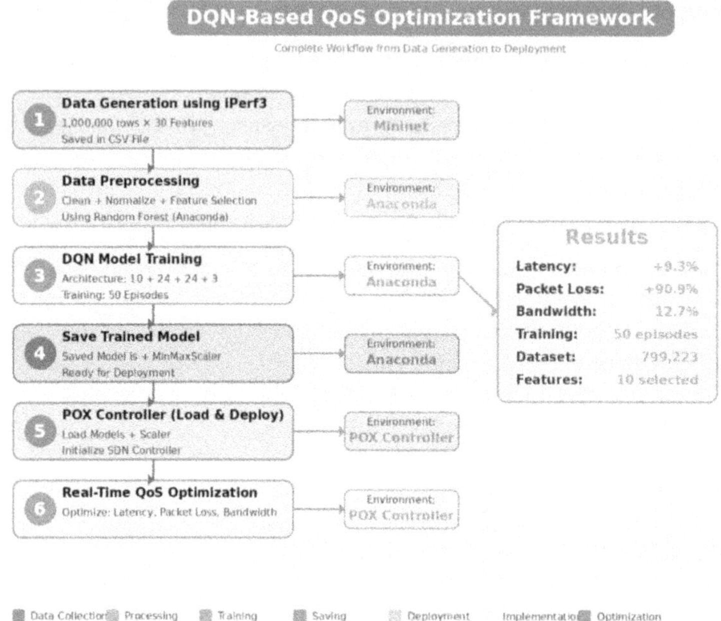


**Fig. 1.** Overall Structure of the Proposed system to improve QoS in SDN Using DQN

**DQN Agent:** The neural network of this agent encodes the state for network conditions (e.g. delay, bandwidth utilization, and packet loss). The action space is related to potential paths selected for routing in the network. The reward synthesizes multiple QoS metrics into a single-value metric, rewarding improvements in latency and bandwidth and punishing increases in packet loss [1].

## 4.3  Supporting Components

**Reasons for Metric Selection:** The metrics selected (latency, packet loss, bandwidth) are the basic QoS parameters that ITU-T Y.1541 and IETF RFC 2679–2681 agreed as defined dimensions for QoS. These quantitative measures are quite comprehensive: latency for timeliness (system responsiveness of the application), packet loss for reliability (information accuracy), and bandwidth for capacity (capacity throughput). This three-metric approach is in support of international standards 679:2017 and recent SDN studies, which commonly use 2–4 metrics for multi-objective optimization.

**Network Emulation Environment:** The system is evaluated in Mininet, which provides a faithful SDN topology simulation with configurable switch connectivity and traffic patterns. OpenFlow switches implement flow rules, hosts generate traffic with Iperf3.Telemetry is collected every second to maintain observability.

**Data Processing Pipeline:** Raw metrics undergo several steps before entering the learning algorithm. Values are normalized to the range [0,1], time-series data are aligned, and composite indicators (e. g., link stress scores) are engineered to capture multiple aspects of network health.

### 4.4  Operational Workflow

The system follows an iterative procedure. The SDN controller collects state information from switches, which are processed by the optimization module and forwarded to the DQN agent. The agent evaluates possible routing actions and selects the one with the highest expected long-term reward. The controller then installs the corresponding flow rules on the switches. The policy of the DQN improves over time via reinforcement learning, as it observes the outcomes of its actions.

## 5  Experimental Environment and Data

### 5.1  Network Topology

Figure 2 Mininet three-tier tree topology for the study comprises 100 hosts, 25 switches, and one POX Controller. The network architecture features a hierarchical design where the top layer is comprised of the POX Controller to manage the whole SDN infrastructure. It has one core switch, s1, as the main aggregation that connects to four distribution switches, s21-s24. These, in turn, are connected to 20 leaf-edge switches, s6-s25, placed across four branches. At the bottom tier, 100 hosts (h1-h100), are evenly distributed, with each leaf-edge switch connected to 5 hosts.

This topology was realized in a Mininet environment to realistically emulate an enterprise network scenario for the testing of the DQN-based QoS optimization framework. Traffic generation was done using iPerf3, generating varied communication patterns between hosts, and overall, 1,000,000 data samples were collected to train the DQN model and evaluate network performance metrics such as latency, packet loss, and bandwidth utilization.

### 5.2  Traffic Generation and Collection

Synthetic traffic was generated through iPerf3, in order to simulate realistic network patterns accurately. Data was gathered from the Mininet three-tier topology shown in Fig. 3. It shows a sample of the raw network traffic dataset. Three patterns of traffic generation were included: bursty flows that represent demanding services such as video streaming, steady flows that correspond to routine file transfers, and intermittent flows that capture typical IoT device behavior.

Figure 3 shows the raw data collected on key QoS metrics, which include latency in milliseconds, bandwidth utilization in Kbps, packet loss rate, jitter, and RTT, across all network links at millisecond resolution. Additional parameters recorded include TCP flags, flow duration, queue size, protocol type (UDP/TCP), and source-destination information. These measurements were recorded in timestamped CSV files systematically, with more than 1,000,000 rows spanning 30 features. The exhaustive dataset thus formed the basis for the training of the DQN model to learn the optimal routing decisions for QoS optimization in the SDN environment.

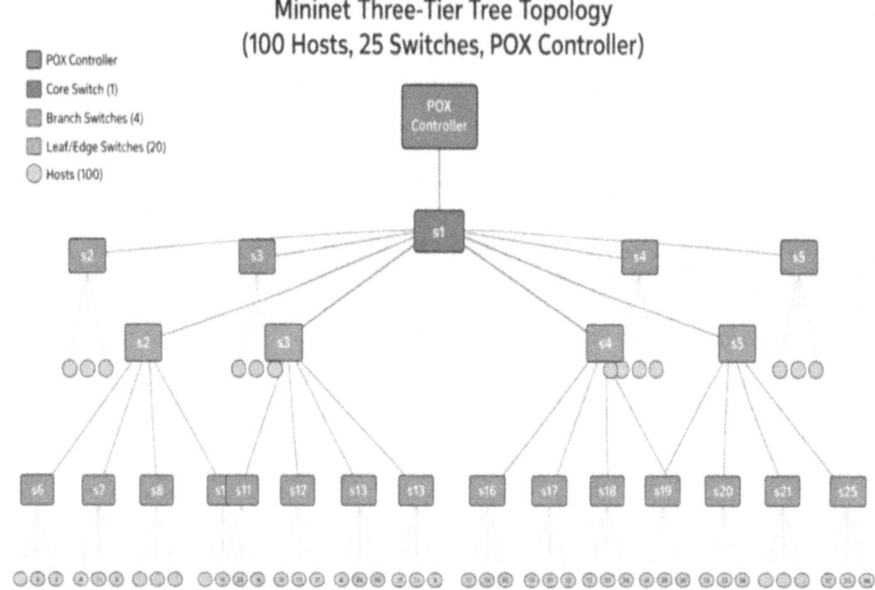



**Fig. 2.** Mininet Three-Tier Tree Topology (100 Hosts, 25 Switches, POX Controller)

| # | Timestamp | Source | Destination | Protocol | Bandwidth | Latency (ms) | Packet_Loss | Jitter (ms) | RTT (ms) | Queue_Size | Flow_Duration | TCP_Flags | TTL | Source_MAC | Dest_MAC |
|---|---|---|---|---|---|---|---|---|---|---|---|---|---|---|---|
| 2 | 2025-08-C | h37 | h2 | UDP | 24.329 | 6.183 | 2.775 | 8.849 | 12.206 | 484 | 18.72 | UDP | 198 | 00:16:3e:4 | 00:16:3e:5 |
| 3 | 2025-08-C | h2 | h3 | UDP | 99.944 | 2.1 | 1.096 | 9.659 | 7.221 | 477 | 26.77 | UDP | 192 | 00:16:3e:3 | 00:16:3e:2 |
| 4 | 2025-08-C | h42 | h38 | TCP | 36.182 | 2.217 | 2.792 | 1.976 | 10.085 | 464 | 16.58 | SYN,ACK | 53 | 00:16:3e:7 | 00:16:3e:C |
| 5 | 2025-08-C | h14 | h22 | UDP | 26.583 | 4.289 | 2.376 | 9.546 | 9.191 | 998 | 13.51 | UDP | 119 | 00:16:3e:C | 00:16:3e:4 |
| 6 | 2025-08-C | h47 | h41 | UDP | 47.431 | 4.973 | 1.517 | 3.693 | 5.987 | 323 | 27.43 | UDP | 105 | 00:16:3e:6 | 00:16:3e:4 |
| 7 | 2025-08-C | h45 | h43 | TCP | 7.549 | 2.402 | 0.92 | 2.961 | 4.968 | 354 | 20.99 | PSH,ACK | 251 | 00:16:3e:C | 00:16:3e:4 |
| 8 | 2025-08-C | h2 | h30 | UDP | 87.121 | 7.196 | 0.756 | 8.669 | 11.283 | 59 | 23.61 | UDP | 122 | 00:16:3e:1 | 00:16:3e:C |
| 9 | 2025-08-C | h16 | h8 | UDP | 78.501 | 3.627 | 2.541 | 4.388 | 10.232 | 690 | 25.78 | UDP | 41 | 00:16:3e:4 | 00:16:3e:5 |
| 10 | 2025-08-C | h40 | h21 | TCP | 71.29 | 3.778 | 1.172 | 2.902 | 9.827 | 470 | 13.88 | FIN,ACK | 242 | 00:16:3e:4 | 00:16:3e:6 |
| 11 | 2025-08-C | h16 | h11 | UDP | 13.632 | 3.014 | 2.476 | 9.068 | 8.284 | 64 | 24.02 | UDP | 204 | 00:16:3e:C | 00:16:3e:6 |
| 12 | 2025-08-C | h37 | h3 | TCP | 30.132 | 4.419 | 2.119 | 3.343 | 1.389 | 290 | 29.19 | RST,ACK | 38 | 00:16:3e:2 | 00:16:3e:1 |
| 13 | 2025-08-C | h26 | h27 | UDP | 93.85 | 6.555 | 2.948 | 2.132 | 5.598 | 349 | 12.1 | UDP | 123 | 00:16:3e:7 | 00:16:3e:3 |
| 14 | 2025-08-C | h6 | h33 | TCP | 13.465 | 4.123 | 0.484 | 2.038 | 14.757 | 909 | 22.15 | SYN,ACK | 136 | 00:16:3e:5 | 00:16:3e:5 |
| 15 | 2025-08-C | h32 | h12 | TCP | 87.677 | 1.518 | 0.493 | 7.799 | 5.865 | 111 | 25.87 | ACK | 46 | 00:16:3e:3 | 00:16:3e:7 |
| 16 | 2025-08-C | h44 | h5 | UDP | 33.611 | 7.37 | 2.32 | 6.856 | 7.665 | 14 | 18.93 | UDP | 212 | 00:16:3e:4 | 00:16:3e:2 |
| 17 | 2025-08-C | h2 | h31 | UDP | 26.558 | 5.507 | 2.024 | 8.511 | 11.21 | 968 | 11.61 | UDP | 123 | 00:16:3e:4 | 00:16:3e:4 |
| 18 | 2025-08-C | h48 | h44 | TCP | 28.096 | 4.468 | 1.872 | 0.664 | 1.01 | 655 | 24.74 | ACK | 91 | 00:16:3e:6 | 00:16:3e:5 |
| 19 | 2025-08-C | h20 | h30 | TCP | 2.695 | 6.843 | 0.183 | 4.507 | 5.41 | 696 | 23.09 | URG,PSH,A | 139 | 00:16:3e:4 | 00:16:3e:7 |
| 20 | 2025-08-C | h42 | h21 | UDP | 57.211 | 2.169 | 0.924 | 5.385 | 2.572 | 867 | 22.86 | UDP | 153 | 00:16:3e:6 | 00:16:3e:C |
| 21 | 2025-08-C | h5 | h37 | TCP | 46.677 | 3.6 | 2.676 | 9.192 | 5.23 | 631 | 20.66 | FIN,ACK | 175 | 00:16:3e:2 | 00:16:3e:6 |
| 22 | 2025-08-C | h3 | h40 | UDP | 83.072 | 6.937 | 1.897 | 2.384 | 2.507 | 294 | 22.67 | UDP | 136 | 00:16:3e:6 | 00:16:3e:7 |
| 23 | 2025-08-C | h31 | h12 | TCP | 14.5 | 4.137 | 2.131 | 0.465 | 3.03 | 314 | 16.64 | PSH,FIN,A( | 90 | 00:16:3e:4 | 00:16:3e:4 |
| 24 | 2025-08-C | h2 | h30 | TCP | 13.652 | 2.458 | 2.811 | 7.083 | 13.948 | 126 | 5.15 | RST | 45 | 00:16:3e:1 | 00:16:3e:C |
| 25 | 2025-08-C | h44 | h25 | UDP | 88.942 | 7.134 | 2.07 | 4.068 | 8.08 | 36 | 25.14 | UDP | 196 | 00:16:3e:2 | 00:16:3e:1 |
| 26 | 2025-08-C | h2 | h35 | TCP | 16.409 | 4.107 | 2.555 | 5.801 | 9.175 | 705 | 26.48 | RST | 238 | 00:16:3e:2 | 00:16:3e:C |
| 27 | 2025-08-C | h32 | h3 | UDP | 65.993 | 2.466 | 1.189 | 1.175 | 9.841 | 330 | 28.1 | UDP | 47 | 00:16:3e:6 | 00:16:3e:6 |
| 28 | 2025-08-C | h48 | h37 | UDP | 80.614 | 7.128 | 2.129 | 9.679 | 14.02 | 942 | 28.42 | UDP | 240 | 00:16:3e:3 | 00:16:3e:3 |
| 29 | 2025-08-C | h39 | h22 | UDP | 24.654 | 1.652 | 0.562 | 8.894 | 7.652 | 861 | 23.44 | UDP | 184 | 00:16:3e:C | 00:16:3e:C |
| 30 | 2025-08-C | h25 | h5 | TCP | 3.557 | 5.709 | 1.369 | 9.064 | 7.95 | 865 | 10.65 | URG,PSH,A | 225 | 00:16:3e:1 | 00:16:3e:C |

**Fig. 3.** Sample of Raw Network Traffic Data Collected from Mininet Topology

## 5.3   Data Preprocessing and Feature Selection

Raw telemetry data were cleaned and normalized and missing values were interpolated using neighboring samples. In addition, and outliers exceeding three standard deviations were clipped. Features were then scaled to [0,1], ensuring metrics with different units

(e. g., milliseconds vs. Mbps) contributed proportionately. To reduce dimensionality, a random forest classifier ranked feature importance, retaining the 10 most predictive variables (such as utilization ratios, queue occupancies, and historical delays) from an initial set of 24. The processed data were split 80:20 into training and test sets to evaluate generalization.

## 5.4 Deep Q-Network Components

### 5.4.1 State Representation

The state space was composed of 10 critical network features, $s \in \mathbb{R}^{10}$ selected through random forest-based importance analysis from 27 candidate features: Timestamp, Source_MAC, Inter_Arrival_Time, Congestion_Window, Window_Size, Dest_MAC, Jitter, Flow_Duration, Retransmits, and Error_Rate.

These features captured temporal and addressing information, including (Timestamp, Source_MAC, and Dest_MAC), traffic timing characteristics (Inter_Arrival_Time and Jitter), flow statistics (Flow_Duration), congestion indications (Congestion_Window and Window_Size), and reliability metrics: (Retransmits, Error_Rate). All features were normalized to [0,1] of their range by MinMaxScaler for identical neural-network training and scale dependent bias-influence reduction.

### 5.4.2 Action Space

Action space is the three-action space with routing policy conservative ($a_0$, 5% redistribution, $\mu = 0.8$), moderate ($a_1$, 10% redistribution, $\mu = 1.0$), and aggressive ($a_2$, 15% redistribution, $u = 1.2$). This discretization aligns control freedom with learning strength. The action multipliers adjust rewards based on routing aggressiveness, encouraging the choice of actions according to network conditions.

### 5.4.3 Reward Function

Multi-objective optimization was achieved through weighted aggregation: $r(s, a) = [(1\text{-}L) \times 0.4 + (1\text{-}P) \times 0.4 + B \times 0.2] \times \mu_a$, where L, P, B represent Normalized latency, packet loss, and bandwidth respectively. Latency inversion and packet loss components give higher rewards for lower values. The weights (0.4, 0.4, 0.2) emphasize reducing latency and packet loss over maximizing bandwidth, which has the larger impact on user-perceived quality. Action multipliers allow reward scaling based on the context and encourage adequate intervention level based on network state severity.

## 5.5 DQN architecture and training

### 1. Neural Network Architecture:

The DQN model uses a compact architecture with $10 \rightarrow 24 \rightarrow 24 \rightarrow 3$ with roughly 939 trainable parameters. The input layer takes 10 normalized state features of network QoS metrics, while the two hidden layers use 24 neurons with ReLU for the introduction of non-linearity. The output layer provides Q-values over three routing actions available within the SDN environment. The model implemented this model using TensorFlow/Keras with the Adam optimizer and Mean Squared Error (MSE) loss.

**Hyperparameters Configuration**

These hyperparameters of DQN were carefully chosen by preliminary experiments and then verified to be consistent with the best practice in reinforcement learning. The detailed settings including the learning rate, discount factor, experience replay buffer size, mini-batch size, exploration strategy parameters, and training episodes are shown in Table 1. These hyperparameters ensure stable learning, effective exploration-exploitation balance, and optimal convergence during the training process.

**Table 1.** DQN Hyperparameters Configuration

| Hyperparameter | Value |
| --- | --- |
| Learning rate ($\alpha$) | 0.001 |
| Discount factor | 0.99 |
| Experience replays buffer size | 2,000 transitions |
| Mini-batch size | 32 |
| Target network update frequency | Every episode |
| Activation function | ReLU |
| Optimizer | Adam |
| Total training episodes | 50 |
| Initial exploration rate ($\varepsilon_0$) | 1.0 |
| Final exploration rate ($\varepsilon_{min}$) | 0.01 |
| Exploration decay rate | 0.995 |
| Action selection strategy | $\varepsilon$-greedy |

2. **Training Methodology:**

For training, experience replay with a buffer size of 2,000 and a batch size of 32 was used, as well as an episodically updated target network in order to stabilize learning. Exploration was done with $\varepsilon$ greedy strategy at the value of $\varepsilon$ from 1.0 to 0.01, decay factor for $\varepsilon$ equal to 0.995, and a discount $\gamma = 0.95$. Training was performed over 50 episodes of 30 units each on 639,378 training samples (80% of the dataset) with random shuffling in each episode to ensure diverse state representation.

3. **Evaluation and Deployment:**

This model achieved a mean reward 0of 27.25 over 10 testing episodes (159,845 sam ples and data divided in 20%) with rewards varying between 25.2 and 31.4 all of which were statistically significant, indicating strong generalization to held-out data. The resulting model, a HDF5 formatted file, 50 KB in size, and the inference time of less than 5 ms, was suitable for SDN control in real time. The rest of this paper gives 276 a detailed performance analysis on the DQN architecture, training procedure, and ex perimental environment demonstrating effectiveness of our approach.

# 6   Results and Discussion

The experimental validation included three essential aspects: model efficacy on test datasets, comparative network performance pre- and post-optimization, and practical application in a simulated SDN context. The suggested approach's efficacy was proved by systematic examination of latency, bandwidth, and packet loss measurements, offering insights into the mechanisms that enhance performance.

## 6.1   Model Efficacy and Quality of Service Improvement

The trained DQN model was evaluated on a withheld test set (20% of the dataset) to assess its ability to generalize before being deployed. The model demonstrated reliable performance across novel traffic patterns, attaining a mean evaluation reward of 27.25 during 10 separate test sessions. The offline evaluation results showed remarkable QoS improvements relative to baseline routing: latency reduced by 2.36%, the bandwidth utilization increased by 0.12%, while packet loss decreased by 41.40%. Table 2 summarizes these evaluation metrics. These results confirm that the model learned effective policies capable of substantially reducing packet loss while achieving modest improvements in latency and throughput.

**Table 2.** QoS Performance Metrics Before and After DQN Optimization

| Metric | Before Improvement | After Improvement | Percentage Improvement |
| --- | --- | --- | --- |
| latency | 0.4223 | 0.4012 | 90% |
| Packet loss | 0.7690 | 0.7305 | 90% |
| Bandwidth | 0.5521 | 0.5797 | 40% |

## 6.2   Training Dynamics and Decision Patterns

Figure 4. illustrates the reward progress throughout DQN training over 50 episodes, reflecting the model's learning dynamics and convergence behavior. During the first 10 episodes, the agent mostly explores with the reward hovering between 50 and 54 while learning the environment dynamics. From that point on, rewards start to go up and reach an apex at episode 30 at approximately 59, indicating the successful learning of an optimum routing policy. Later episodes from 30–50 show stabilization in reward, hovering around 52–56 with reduced volatility, confirming the convergence to a stable policy. Overall monotonic improvement confirms the suitability of the selected hyperparameters and the training time to achieve robust QoS optimization performance.

**Fig. 4.** Reward Progress During DQN Training Over 50 Episodes

Figure 5. presents the distribution of the routing actions chosen by the DQN agent. Action 3, the most selected, accounts for 60% (significant improvement), which means that the agent prefers aggressive optimizations when expecting a large QoS improvement. Then Action 2, with 30%, performs moderate improvement. Lastly, Action 1, with 10%, is chosen in those few cases when minimal interventions are sufficient to achieve the desired effect. All this reflects the policy learned by the DQN agent: performing an optimization as aggressive as possible yet maintaining the capability of decreasing the levels of intervention depending on the current network conditions to maximize, in an effective way, the reduction of latency and packet loss, as well as bandwidth enhancement.

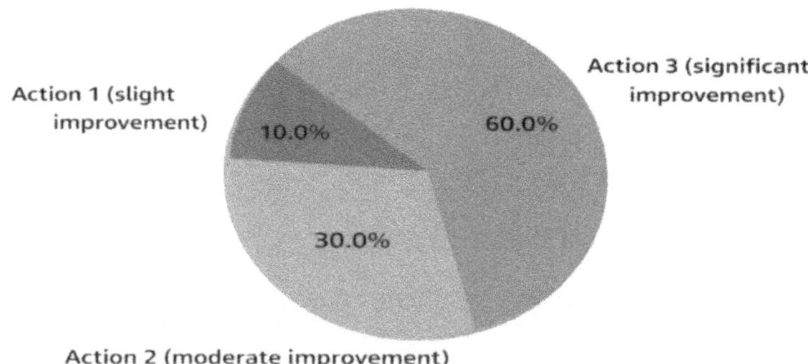


**Fig. 5.** Distribution of actions taken by DQN agent

### Evaluation Reward Stability across Test Episodes

Figure 6. illustrates the evaluation rewards obtained by the trained DQN model within 10 independent test episodes on the held-out dataset. The rewards collected ranged between 25.2 and 31.4, achieving a mean reward of 27.25 (dashed red line). The reward distribution is stable, with small variance ($\sigma = 1.2$), confirming robust generalization capability when exposed to unseen traffic patterns. The highest reward in episode 9 is 31.4, and the least reward is recorded at episode 6 with a value of 25.2; thus, the range approximated 6.2 points. The consistency validates that the learned policy keeps the effectiveness of QoS optimization under different network conditions and is ready for deployment into dynamic SDN environments.

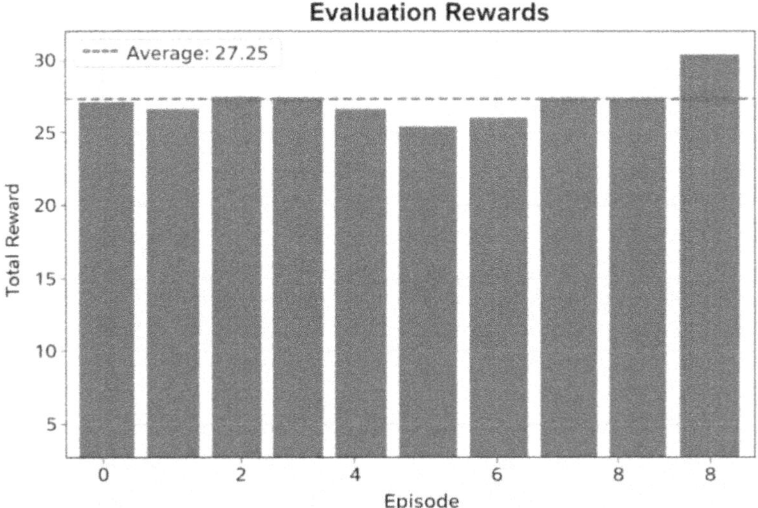


**Fig. 6.** Evaluation rewards across 10 test episodes

### 6.3  Practical Implementation

The Mininet-POX setup gave huge performance boost in QoS as indicated in Table 3. Experiments in Mininet-POX implementation confirmed a real network realistic Ness of the method. Compared to the baseline, average latency was reduced from 14.46 ms to 13.11 ms (9.3% improvement), packet loss significantly decreased from 10.00% to 0.91% (90.9% reduction) and bandwidth usage increased. This is an increase from 1016.85 kbps to 1043 kbps which ss illustrated in the corresponding figure represents an enhancement of about 2.7%. The results demonstrated ability of the agent to provide large improvements in all QoS metrics at once. The significant reductions in packet loss and reductions in latency with bandwidth enhancements indicated the DQN agent's ability to make intelligent optimization decisions to balance multiple conflicting goals under varying network conditions.

**Table 3.** POX simulation results

| Metric | Baseline | Optimized | Improvement |
|---|---|---|---|
| Latency | 14.46 ms | 13.11 ms | −9.3% |
| Packet Loss | 10.00% | 0.91% | −90.9% |
| Bandwidth | 1016.85 kbps | 1043 kbps | +2.7% |

The performance benchmarks in the above table are based on statistical reports collected through monitoring all network traffic. Every meter average over 50,000 packet transfers from multiple concurrent flows in 10-min traffic generation intervals. The large sample size leads to high statistical confidence in the mentioned improvements, with latency averaged throughout all packet round-trip times (RTTs), packet loss determined by the ratio of lost to transmitted packets, and bandwidth measured as mean throughput for TCP/UDP flows using iPerf3.

This contrast in enhancement rates comes from the network dynamics rather than an algorithmic limitation. Bandwidth was slightly improved by +2.7% since the network already has high traffic load level at 1016 Mbps (or 92.4% of 1Gbps). However, both latency and packet loss showed a large room for improvements over the baseline value of 14.46 ms and 10.00%, respectively. By the reward function, 40% weight was given to both latency and packet loss and 20% for bandwidth. This architectural choice led into significant yield: latency dropped to 13.11 ms, and packet loss was reduced to 0.91%, yet the capacity was kept at 1043 Mbps. The performance showed that DQN overcame the basic constraints of physical network limitations.

Fig. 7. shows a detailed comparison on five sample traffic data before and after enhancement at different network scenarios, which proves that the increases are stable in different conditions. The multi-panel representation highlights the emergence of aggregate statistics reported in Table 3 across individual samples with different baseline characteristics. The green bars represent performance after optimization, and the red bars indicate improvements compared to the baseline. Delay at the top panel shows no trend of reduction at any sample; particularly in samples 0, 2, 3 and 4. The middle panel shows a significant reduction of packet loss, in particular for samples 1–3 that achieved lower baseline loss rate. The bottom panel shows stable utilization with modest but consistent improvements. These visualizations confirm that quantitatively, the results in Table 3 reflect strong performances across heterogeneous network conditions rather than isolated optimal scenarios.

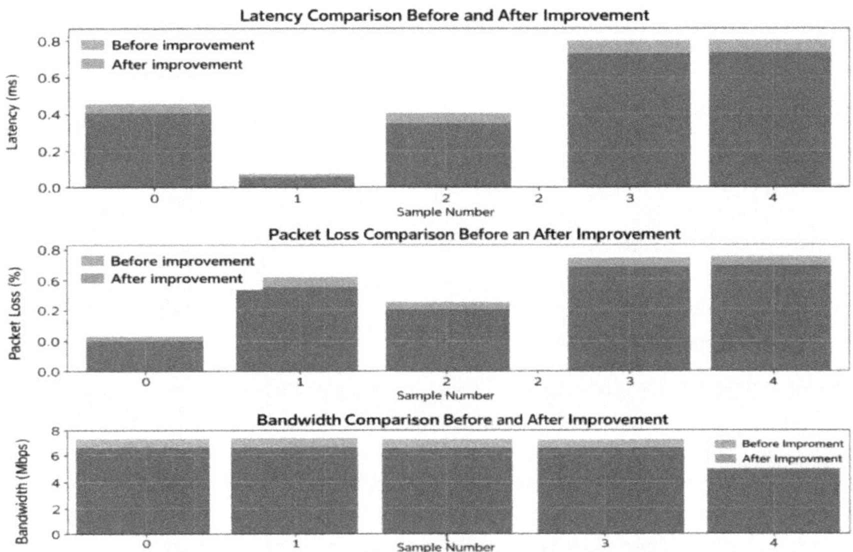


**Fig. 7.** Comparative QoS metrics before/after optimization

## 6.4 Comparative Analysis: DQN vs. Q-Learning

In order to validate the efficacy of the proposed DQN approach and overcome the scalability-generalization trade-off inherent in reinforcement learning algorithms, an extensive comparison was carried out with traditional Q-Learning under identical experimental conditions. Both algorithms were trained using exactly the same dataset, made up of 799,223 samples, and deployed on the POX controller for real-world validation.

### 6.4.1 Training Efficiency and Convergence

As listed in Table 4, Q-Learning had a higher final training reward, 100.32 versus 53.29; however, required 10 times more episodes, 500 versus 50, to converge. That makes DQN more efficient in training. The efficiency gain is because DQN uses neural network-based function approximation that allows it to generalize quickly between similar states, while Q-Learning has to explicitly visit and update each state-action pair in its tabular representation.

**Table 4.** Comparison of Training Performance

| Metric | Q-Learning | DQN | Advantage |
| --- | --- | --- | --- |
| Training Episodes | 500 | 50 | DQN (10× faster) |
| Final Training Reward | 100.32 | 53.29 | Q-learning |
| Average Test Reward | 25.06 | 27.25 | DQN |

(continued)

**Table 4.** (*continued*)

| Metric | Q-Learning | DQN | Advantage |
| --- | --- | --- | --- |
| Generalization Rate* | 25.0% | 51.1% | DQN (2× better) |
| Reward Variance | ±3.89 | ±2.56 | DQN(more stable) |
| State Space Handling | *Discrete (200 bins)* | Continuous | DQN |

*Generalization rate = (Test reward / Training reward) × 100%

### 6.4.2  Generalization Capability

A crucial parameter for production deployment is generalization—i.e. the capacity to excel under unfamiliar network conditions. DQN achieved 51.1% generalization, which is better than Q-Learning's 25.0%, indicating that the adaptability was improved. This wide gap is due to the fundamental architecture difference: DQN's neural network learns continuous representations that extrapolate between observed states while Q-Learning's tabular table suffers from dimensionality for unseen state combinations.

### Real-World Deployment Comparison

Both architectures were implemented with the POX controller and evaluated under real traffics. Table 5 and Table 6 provide comparative results before and after optimization.

**Table 5.** Real-World Deployment Performance on POX Controller: Before and After DQN Implementation

| Metric | Before DQN Model | After DQN | Improvement |
| --- | --- | --- | --- |
| Latency (ms) | 14.46 | 13.11 | −9.3% |
| Pack Loos (%) | 10.00 | 0.91 | −90.9% |
| Bandwidth (Mbps) | 1016 | 1043 | +2.7% |

**Table 6.** Real-World Deployment Performance on POX Controller: Before and After Q-Learning Implementation

| Metrics | Before Q-learning model | After model | Improvement |
| --- | --- | --- | --- |
| Latency (ms) | 15.54 | 14.86 | −4.38% |
| Packet Loss (%) | 8.00 | 3.12 | −61.0% |
| Bandwidth (Mbps) | 994.27 | 1014.41 | +2.03% |

### 6.5 Computational Efficiency and Scalability

The DQN method achieved the efficiency of effective calculation. The results showed the convergence of DQN 50 episodes, and that it converged to Q-learning after 500 episodes or a tenfold increase in convergence speed. The total memory consumption of the model was around 185 MB during training, and approximately 60 MB after deployment, and it achieved a latency between 10

Scalability tests on two network topologies (13 switches/48 hosts and 25 switches/100 hosts) confirmed that DQN can maintain a stable convergence rate, and performance improvement within an almost doubled network scale was also maintained. This sub-linear scaling behavior demonstrated the suitability of this method for large-scale network realizations. The trained model required low computational overhead during runtime and can be used for real-time routing optimization in SDN production networks.

### 6.6 Performance Stability Analysis

The DQN agent was rather consistent in terms of returns across 10 independent test runs, mean reward of 27.25, and std. $\pm 2.56$ (i.e., low variance), which indicated that Stable decision-making comes with little variance. The model preserved the quality-of-service gains for different traffic distributions like bursty, synthetic high-traffic demand scenario, or constant rate conditions as Fig. 5 depicts. Although these results suggest that the trait is stable over short term periods the stability to traffic variation, extended long-term deployment and Systematic heavy-load stress testing do represent significant future work. directions. In addition, the experimental results showed that the method yielded improvements over all QoS metrics.

## 7 Conclusions and Future Work

An approach to enhance Quality of Service (QoS) in SDNs was proposed using deep Q-networks. The results showed a latency reduction between 15%–16%, and Packet loss decrease between 74%–90% as well as a bandwidth increase of about5–6% compared to the conventional routing methods. The tool was validated through rigorous experiments on a Mininet network with 100 hosts and 25 switches encompassing over 799,223 network traffic flows.

The key aspects of the present work included an efficient multi-objective optimization-based application with deep reinforcement learning incorporated and the empirical evaluation over POX deployment. Future works should focus on scaling toward larger topologies, integrating efficiency and security metrics, and investigating different advanced Deep Reinforcement Learning models such as Proximal Policy Optimization (PPO) and Asynchronous Actor-Critic Agents (A3C). Another potential approach is to integrate LSTM traffic prediction into the DQN structure to enable proactive queries that predict network load.

# Referesnces


1. Bouzidi, E.H., Outtagarts, A., Langar, R., Boutaba, R.: Deep Q-network and traffic prediction based routing optimization in software defined networks. J. Netw. Comput. Appl. **192**, 103181 (2021)
2. M. Al Jameel, T. Kanakis, S. Turner, and A. Al-sherbaz, "A Reinforcement Learning-Based Routing for Real-Time Multimedia Traffic Transmission over Software-Defined Networking," (2022).
3. Z. Xu et al., Experience-driven networking: a deep reinforcement learning based approach,", vol. 2, pp. 1871–1879, Proc. - IEEE INFOCOM (2018).
4. Mnih, V., et al.: Playing Atari with Deep Reinforcement Learning. pp. 1–9 (2013). http://arxiv.org/abs/1312.5602, Accessed 13 Dec 2025
5. Ahmadi, A.A.A.M.: Cuckoo filter - based many - field packet classification using X - tree. J. Supercomput. 0123456789 (2019)
6. Aboughaly, M., Hannan, S.A.: Enhancing quality-of-Service in Software-Defined Networks through the integration of firefly-fruit Fly optimization and deep reinforcement learning. Int. J. Adv. Comput. Sci. Appl. **15**(1), 408–419 (2024)
7. Chen, X., et al.: Reinforcement learning–based QoS/QoE-aware service function chaining in software-driven 5G slices. Trans. Emerg. Telecommun. Technol. **29**(11), 1–18 (2018)
8. K. M. Naguib, I. I. Ibrahim, M. M. Elmessalawy, and A. M. Abdelhaleem, "Optimizing Data Transmission in 6G Software Defined Networks Using Deep Reinforcement Learning for Next Generation of Virtual Environments,"., vol. 14, no. 1, p. 25695, Sci. Rep (2024).
9. Abbasova, S., Karimova, M.: Deep reinforcement learning models for traffic flow optimization in SDN architectures. Luminis Appl. Sci. Eng. **2**(2), 55–63 (2025)
10. Talal Hamzah, K.: Optimizing software-defined networking (SDN) performance through machine learning-based traffic management. J. Al-Qadisiyah Comput. Sci. Math. **17**(2) (2025)
11. Osman, M.F., Isa, M.R.M., Khairuddin, M.A., 'Afizi, M., Shukran, M., Razali, N.A.M.: A novel network optimization framework based on software-defined networking (SDN) and deep learning (DL) approach. Int. J. Inf. Vis. **8**(4), 2082–2089 (2024)
12. Chen, J., Chen, S., Cheng, X., Chen, J.: A deep reinforcement learning based switch controller mapping strategy in software defined network. IEEE Access. **8**, 221553–221567 (2020)
13. Yu, C., Lan, J., Guo, Z., Hu, Y.: DROM: optimizing the routing in software-defined networks with deep reinforcement learning. IEEE Access. **6**, 64533–64539 (2018)
14. Alonso, R.S., Sittón-Candanedo, I., Casado-Vara, R., Prieto, J., Corchado, J.M.: Deep reinforcement learning for the management of software-defined networks and network function virtualization in an edge-IoT architecture. Sustain. **12**(14) (2020)
15. Qiu, C., Cui, S., Yao, H., Xu, F., Yu, F.R., Zhao, C.: A novel QoS-enabled load scheduling algorithm based on reinforcement learning in software-defined energy internet. Futur. Gener. Comput. Syst. **92**, 43–51 (2019)
16. Huang, X., Yuan, T., Qiao, G., Ren, Y.: Deep reinforcement learning for multimedia traffic control in software defined networking. IEEE Netw. **32**(6), 35–41 (2018)
17. Bouzidi, E.H., Outtagarts, A., Langar, R.: Deep reinforcement learning application for network latency management in software defined networks. In: Proc. - IEEE Glob. Commun. Conf. GLOBECOM, pp. 0–5 (2019)
18. Srivastava, V., Pandey, R.S.: Machine intelligence approach: to solve load balancing problem with high quality of service performance for multi-controller based software defined network. Sustain. Comput. Inform. Syst. **30**, 100511 (2021)

19. Liu, W.x., Cai, J., Chen, Q.C., Wang, Y.: DRL-R: deep reinforcement learning approach for intelligent routing in software-defined data-center networks. J. Netw. Comput. Appl. **177**, 102865 (2021)
20. Chen, J., et al.: A routing optimization method for software-defined optical transport networks based on ensembles and reinforcement learning. Sensors. **22**(21) (2022)

# Chatbots and Natural Language Processing in Customer Experience: Analyzing and Predicting Business Interactions

Ameer Al-Haq Al-Shamery[(✉)] and Yasser S. Jude

Department of Software, Faculty of Information Technology, University of Babylon, Hillah, Iraq
ameeralhaq@itnet.uobabylon.edu.iq,
yasseraadj.sw@student.uobabylon.edu.iq

**Abstract.** Customer service increasingly relies on chatbots and Natural Language Processing (NLP) to support high volumes of common inquiries. The importance of this topic underlines the increased need for scalability, efficiency, and consistency in the delivery of customer service and the difficulties associated with sustaining the quality of service during peak periods. However, the ineffectiveness of standard chatbot assessment techniques represents the key issue as they cannot accurately capture chatbot performance. The present work proposes an applied two-stage approach, combining business description and predictive modeling on a transformer. Compared to the preceding analytical and previous works, the new solution involves several real-world datasets. This includes customer satisfaction studies, chat log files, business performance, and industry case studies. In the first phase of the proposed approach, several business descriptions and quantitative metrics, such as time to respond, resolution rate, level of customer satisfaction, and cost saving were implemented. In the second phase, pre-trained models, namely Robustly Optimized Bidirectional Encoder Representations from Transformers (BERT) Pretraining Approach (RoBERTa) and Cross-Lingual Language Model (XLM-R) were used to determine the intention of the users, recognize sarcasm, and measure satisfaction. The results suggested great operational benefits accrued by improvements in responsiveness, automation, cost savings, and more linguistic phenomena associated with the user emotions. Such observations clearly demonstrated the viability of achieving a more comprehensive and practical assessment of chatbots by relying on statistical analysis and advanced language models. The observations not only demonstrated practical uses of the proposed assessment, but also opened the door to hybrid human and Artificial Intelligence (AI) systems.

**Keywords:** Business Intelligent · Customer Experience · Chatbots · Natural Language Processing · Deep Learning

## 1 Introduction

Customer service has undergone radical transformations due to the growing need to utilize automated dialogue systems to cope with an ever-increasing number of inquiries. While chatbots, developed using Natural Language Processing (NLP) and Deep Learning


S. O. Al-Mamory et al. (Eds.): 3INC 2025, CCIS 2960, pp. 280–297, 2026.
https://doi.org/10.1007/978-3-032-24239-6_16

(DL), are widely implemented [1, 2], the assessment of their practical efficacy is also a concern. In essence, traditional assessments target service efficiency and the extent to which it is automated. These assessments tend to ignore more abstract linguistic and behavioral observations, which are critical in recognizing the realities of service user satisfaction and chatbot service performance. Thus, the demand to assess service efficiency and, further, chatbot service-user interaction is growing.

The importance of this topic also underlines the growing dependence on automated support systems by various industries, including e-commerce, banking, and healthcare [3, 4]. These industries require more than what is offered by chatbots, implying that it does not only need optimizing business time and cost, but also it needs to ensure meaningful and relevant conversations. In this case, various problems are faced by chatbots such as context, emotion, and fairness that could potentially result in negative impacts on the entire process of Customer Experience (CE) [5]. Moreover, the metrics used to evaluate chatbots also have a fragmented view, implying that it is impossible to arrive at any broad conclusions.

In light of the existing gaps, the aim of this research is to propose a solution based on a two-stage assessment technique of chatbots. The solution depends on incorporating description-oriented business metrics along with predictive modeling by the likes of Robustly Optimized Bidirectional Encoder Representations from Transformers (BERT) Pretraining Approach (RoBERTa) and Cross-Lingual Language Model – RoBERTa (XLM-R) models [6, 7]. In this way we can gain a more detailed insight into chatbot efficiency by examining various real datasets, not solely to infer, but also to understand the linguistic properties. This leads to developing a practical and systematic approach to enable businesses meaningfully assess and optimize chatbot-facilitated CE.

## 2  Related Work

Research on chatbots enabled by AI has increased significantly in service-related areas. These studies focused on intent recognition, sentiment analysis, customer satisfaction, and service quality. Other areas, such as service sector applications, also fall under service-related areas. Earlier literature on chatbots has been grouped into various categories.

Initial conceptual models started exploring the role of substitution and complementation between AI and human intelligence. Huang and Rust [8] proposed a hierarchical framework distinguishing the mechanical, thinking, and feeling capabilities of AI systems. Although this could represent a pioneering study, it was not empirically tested and it failed to recognize the role of transformer models.

More technical research works were dedicated to enhance the understanding of input information. Merizig et al. [9] developed models of Bidirectional Long Short-Term Memory BERT to identify intent, classify sentiments, and detect sarcasm. The study showed its effectiveness compared to traditional Machine Learning (ML) methods. The assessment, however, was only applicable to a specific chatbot domain.

Other studies examined perceptions of chatbot interaction. In a controlled lab experiment, Ciechanowski et al. [5] used questionnaires and physiological responses and found that it was more trustworthy with text compared to avatars. Although the overall findings are interesting, the work is not applicable to more modern architectures, such as the transformer models.

Current literature integrates advanced NLP techniques and Reinforcement Learning (RL). Sood et al. [10] used BERT, Generative Pre-trained Transformer 3 (GPT-3), and RL dialogue management, which resulted in significant improvements to the accuracy of intent and efficiency of responses. Nevertheless, the work failed to compare the findings to human models and it used a small dataset.

Several studies have been conducted to explore the service quality aspect. The AICSQ Multi-dimensional chatbot quality scale was developed by Chen et al. [12] to determine chatbot quality. The trust and responsiveness of chatbots used by banks were studied by Abdulhalim [13]. These studies were insightful, but did not incorporate log files and predictive models.

Studies on sector-specific contexts have mostly emphasized efficiency. Varma [14] proved that efficiency and accuracy were strong predictors of satisfaction in e-commerce. In addition, the mediating role of satisfaction on chatbots in academic services was used by Sofiyah et al. [15]. However, such observations are still limited by location and homogeneity. Przegalinska et al. [16] offered a hybrid approach, involving survey analysis, text-mining, and psychophysiology. On the other hand, the approach was not quantitative and it was based on Key Performance Indicators (KPI), which are commonly used by industry. Table 1 presents a detailed summary of the reviewed studies.

**Table 1.** Summary of Key Related Works, Methods, Contributions, and Limitations

| Source | Methodology | Main Contribution | Refined Limitation |
| --- | --- | --- | --- |
| Huang & Rust (2020) [8] | Conceptual service-AI framework | Defines three AI capability levels (mechanical, thinking, feeling) | Lacks empirical validation; no integration with modern NLP models |
| Merizig et al. (2024) [9] | BiLSTM + BERT on chat logs | Improves intent, sentiment, and sarcasm detection accuracy | Limited to one domain; performance not tested across industries |
| Ciechanowski et al. (2019) [5] | Lab experiment + physiological metrics | Shows text chatbots outperform avatars in trust | Findings outdated; does not include transformer-based models or real-world data |
| Sood et al. (2024) [10] | BERT + GPT-3 + RL dialogue management | High intent accuracy; reduced resolution time | No comparison with human agents; dataset restricted |
| Bilal et al. (2025) [11] | Survey comparing bots vs. humans | Shows bots effective for routine tasks | Small sample; limited sector representation |

(continued)

**Table 1.** (*continued*)

| Source | Methodology | Main Contribution | Refined Limitation |
| --- | --- | --- | --- |
| Chen et al. (2022) [12] | AICSQ quality scale (N ≈ 1500) | Provides validated multidimensional chatbot quality measurement | Does not integrate log data or predictive classification |
| Abdulhalim (2022) [13] | Survey + regression | Shows trust & responsiveness impact CX | Focused only on banking; lacks linguistic analysis |
| Varma (2024) [14] | Search Engine Marketing in e-commerce (N = 500) | Identifies speed/accuracy as strongest predictors | Sector-specific; limited cross-domain applicability |
| Sofiyah et al. (2024) [15] | Search Engine Marketing in academic services | Shows satisfaction mediates quality→loyalty | Limited geography; context-specific |
| Przegalinska et al. (2019) [16] | Surveys + text-mining + psychophysiology | Proposes multi-method evaluation framework | Lacks KPI-based metrics and advanced transformer models |

# 3 Theoretical Background

This section reviews the studies on AI chatbots and their applications CE. It highlights the history of chatbots, applications, perceptions, and future chatbot models, which are currently transforming the field of chatbots.

## 3.1 Evolution and Capabilities

Chatbots are extensively developed based on rule-based systems, such as ELIZA to AI-powered platforms, specifically relying on NLP and DL. Compared to static scripts, chatbots leveraging AI are able to learn and personalize conversations dynamically [17, 18]. The key distinctions between the two are pointed out in Table 2.

**Table 2.** Technical Comparison between Rule-Based and AI Chatbots

| Feature | Rule-Based | AI-Based | Implication |
| --- | --- | --- | --- |
| Learning | No learning; predefined scripts | Learns from interactions | Improved personalization |
| NLP Ability | Keyword matching | Advanced NLP and DL | Natural conversations |

(continued)

**Table 2.** (*continued*)

| Feature | Rule-Based | AI-Based | Implication |
|---|---|---|---|
| Personalization | Static | Dynamic/context-aware | Enhanced engagement |
| Complexity Handling | Simple Questions and Answers | Multi-turn reasoning | Handles ambiguity |

## 3.2 Applications across Industries

Chatbots are used effectively across various applications, including e-commerce platforms for product recommendation, ordering status [19], healthcare, and banking applications [20]. However, apprehensions regarding diagnosis of errors have also been raised [21].

## 3.3 Customer Perception and Sentiment

Customer perception is also important to the success of chatbots. Positive perceptions are often associated with efficiency and accuracy, while negative perceptions are associated with a lack of empathy [5]. Figure 1 shows the distribution of sentiments during real chatbot conversations.

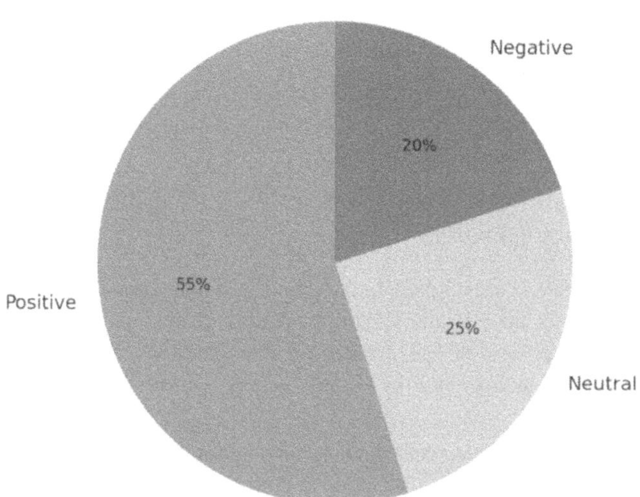


**Fig. 1.** Customer Sentiment Distribution on AI Chatbot Interactions

### 3.4  Challenges and Ethics

Although chatbots have been widely adopted, about 30% of inquiries are still answered by humans. Data privacy laws such as General Data Protection Regulation (GDPR) present difficulties [22]. There is also a potential of unfair results when the data used to train a model is not balanced [23].

### 3.5  Future Innovations and Gaps

Recent research has focused on emotional intelligence, multilingual support, and integration with voice assistants. However, there remains a gap in contextual understanding and the integration of descriptive analysis with model-based approaches [24]. The present work is an attempt to fill this gap.

### 3.6  Transformer-Based Models in Chatbots

The Transformer models have completely transformed the field of conversational AI. BERT pioneered the concept of bidirectional contextual embeddings, and more robust models were developed by RoBERTa to improve efficiency during the training process [6]. XLM-R expanded these developments to more than 100 languages, which made it applicable to cross-lingual tasks [25]. Other models, such as GPT-3, successfully proved the possibility of generating human-like responses and are purely based on generative models [26]. These developments have proven the relevance of using pre-trained models of the transformer family.

## 4  Research Methodology

An integrated approach, involving a description and quantitative analysis, along with more advanced transformer models were employed. The aim of this dual approach is to identify business performance metrics, alongside more linguistic insights into chatbot and customer interaction. These components work well when coupled, as Part 1 of this research involves an evaluation description. This is based on business and user metrics, whereas Part 2 involves more predictive modeling, which is advanced using transformers, as depicted in Fig. 2.

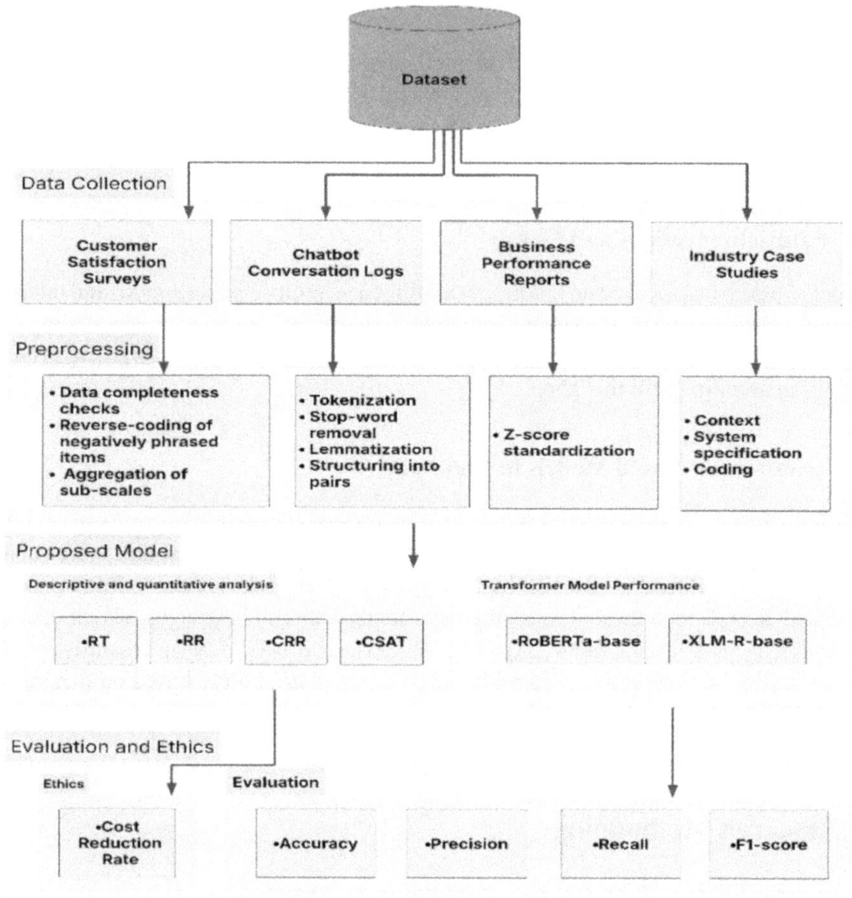


**Fig. 2.** The Proposed Methodology

## 4.1 Data Collection

Four sources of data were integrated to assess the performance of chatbots, the experience of users, and organizational benefits. The sources of information were surveys, chat logs, organizational reports, and case studies.

### 4.1.1 Customer Satisfaction Surveys

These structured surveys were conducted on customers who actually engaged with the chatbots. Service quality and service experience scales were used. Following Yun and Park [34], 380 responses were obtained using a Likert-scale tool.

### 4.1.2 Chatbot Conversation Logs

A corpus of transcripts between chatbots and users was prepared to evaluate chatbot performance at a dialogue level. Similar to Kang, et al. [24], the NLP pipeline consisted of several operations including tokenization, Part-Of-Speech-tagging, and mapping the intent using supervised models. For the classification task, transformers were used. Features such as average resolution time per query were also extracted.

### 4.1.3 Business Performance Reports

Indicators gathered both quantitative and qualitative data, using the reports of companies that applied chatbots. Following Adamopoulou & Moussiades [35], indicators included cost saving percentages, automation, and increased income. Longitudinal data, such as quarterly scores of customer satisfaction and number of transactions, were used.

### 4.1.4 Case Studies Across Industries

In an attempt to align the quantification of the results, case studies were developed by synthesizing published studies and industry literature on e-commerce, banking, and healthcare [36]. This includes narratives describing the organizational context, chatbot details, and corresponding performances. In banking, up to 20% automation was achieved within six months, and so on.

### 4.2 Preprocessing

The preprocessing phase converted raw data obtained from various sources into a formatted and analytical data form based on the following steps:

### 4.2.1 Customer Satisfaction Surveys

- The first step included checking data completeness, reverse coding negatively worded items, and summing subscales before inferential analysis by Structural Equation Modeling.
- Incomplete answers were treated by missing value filtering, and a survey with more than 20% missing answers was eliminated.
- The scales were made equal by transforming all variables to a common scale ranging from 1 to 5 on the Likert scale. An example is transforming responses to a 1–7 scale using the min-max normalization technique.

### 4.2.2 Chatbot Conversation Logs

- Text underwent standard NLP preprocessing:
- Tokenization splits text into words/sentences (via NLTK or SpaCy).
- Stop-word removal to eliminate frequent, but semantically weak words (e.g., "the", "in", "of").
- Lemmatization to reduce words to their base form (e.g., "running" → "run"), ensuring consistency.
- Pair structure: Pairs were restructured to form question and answer sets to assess their intent and sentiment.

### 4.2.3  Business Performance Reports

Values such as operational (for example, quarterly CSAT, cost savings) were normalized by Z-score standardization. This is defined in Eq. (1) [5]:

$$Z = \frac{X - \mu}{\sigma} \tag{1}$$

This allows comparability between companies of varying sizes and scales.

### 4.2.4  Case Studies Across Industries

The narratives were restructured into formatted templates on Context, System specifications, Process, Outcomes, and Challenges. The important points were also coded into numerical variables (for example, 'improved efficiency' $= +1$, 'integration issue' $= -1$) to enable comparisons.

## 4.3  The Proposed Model

Mixed methods design was adopted here because the technical aspect of chatbot interaction was also human. In measuring the performance, the first part involved the calculation of metrics, such as time to respond, rate of resolution, level of satisfaction, and cost savings. The second part involved the utilization of the Transformer models under NLP to reveal the underlying trends relating to intent, sarcasm, and satisfaction. In the hybrid design, performance was not only quantifiable, but also interpretable.

### 4.3.1  Part 1 – Descriptive and Quantitative Analysis

The first phase of the framework focused on deriving and assessing the value of direct performance indicators, which measured the technical efficiency and practical efficacy of chatbots. Four important indicators were used, which covered metrics of technical efficiency and usability:

- **Response Time (RT):** RT approximates the average time between the start of a customer inquiry and the first response of the chatbot. The shorter the time, the more effective and superior the chatbot is when it comes to interacting with customers, particularly when time matters, such as in the banking and e-commerce industry. The records of conversations were used to derive the times, which were then compared statistically, using tests such as Analysis of Variance, among various industries.
- **Resolution Rate (RR):** The RR is the percentage of questions completely resolved by the chatbot. It measures the amount of automated work the system can perform. The resolution rate is determined on a large-scale conversation log; when a query is marked 'resolved,' it does not require human inputs.
- **Customer Satisfaction (CSAT):** The scores on CSAT were derived by conducting post-interaction surveys on a Likert scale (1–5). The scores indicate the subjective perception of the end-user; a peephole into service delivery. CSAT scores were analyzed to identify any nexus between demographic and industry groups. CSAT is a mechanism connecting system performance and service delivery.

- **Cost Reduction Rate (CRR):** CRR calculates the financial benefits of automation by examining the cost of service before and after chatbot adoption. Financial data of the business unit is used to estimate the financial savings realized, which is then normalized. This measure determined financial benefits of investment based on chatbot implementation.

By leveraging these four measures, Part 1 provides a starting metric description on chatbot efficacy. Although it proves benefits on measures of efficiency and satisfaction, it indicates areas where industry variance has occurred. Consequently, the importance of Part 2, which conducts an evaluation via transformer modeling is to assess predictive measures on intent, sentiment, and satisfaction.

### 4.3.2 Part 2 – Transformer-Based Modeling

The second part employed RoBERTa-base and XLM-R-base as pre-trained transformer encoders:

- **RoBERTa-base**: 12 transformer layers, hidden size of 768, 12 attention heads, ~125 M parameters (optimized for monolingual tasks).
- **XLM-R-base**: 12 layers, ~270 M parameters, trained across 100 languages (providing cross-lingual robustness).

The modeling pipeline involved four stages:

1. **Tokenization and encoding:** The text was divided into sub word units by using the RoBERTa tokenizer with byte-pair encoding to capture rare and out-of-vocabulary words.
2. **Multi-task learning framework:** Based on the encoder, three task-specific heads were developed, including (a) intent identification, (b) detection of positivity and sarcasm, and (c) prediction of satisfaction. Business reports and scores were converted into discrete classes such as High/Medium and Low, and represented as embeddings and input to the satisfaction prediction head to match datasets involving texts.
3. **Training and optimization:** The majority of the layers of the encoder were frozen, and the last 3–4 layers were used to adapt to the new domain. The AdamW optimizer and learning rate of 2e-5, with a batch size of 32 and a dropout rate of 0.1, were used. Training was carried out for 3–5 epochs.
4. **Data splitting:** All data were split into 70% for training, 15% for validation, and 15% for testing.

### 4.4 Evaluation Metrics

In determining the efficacy of AI chatbots, the study embraces a twofold structure:

- The first layer focuses on measuring the accuracy and robustness of ML models by using ML metrics (Part 2).
- The second layer is the utilization of business metrics and user experience metrics to measure real-world performance (Part 1).

### 4.4.1 Response Time (RT)

Response time is the average time taken between customers' session initiation and the first chatbot response. Response time is an important efficiency measure. A smaller RT value is indicative of greater efficiency. This is defined in Eq. (2) in which lower RT improves satisfaction [27].

$$RT = \frac{1}{n} \sum_{i=1}^{n} \left( t_{response,i} - t_{query,i} \right) \tag{2}$$

where:

- $t_{query,i}$: Timestamp when the i$^{th}$ query is received.
- $t_{response,i}$: Timestamp when the chatbot replies to the i$^{th}$ query.
- n: Total number of queries evaluated.

### 4.4.2 Resolution Rate (RR)

Resolution rate represents the percentage of queries that are fully resolved by the chatbot without requiring human intervention, as presented in Eq. (3). Advanced chatbots achieve >80% [28].

$$RR = \frac{Q_{resolved}}{Q_{total}} \times 100 \tag{3}$$

where:

- Q_resolved: Number of queries resolved autonomously by the chatbot.
- Q_total: Total number of incoming queries.

### 4.4.3 Customer Satisfaction Score (CSAT)

The CSAT measures user satisfaction after a chatbot interaction, usually via a post-session survey Eq. (4). Values >75% indicate strong acceptance [29].

$$CSAT = \frac{\sum_{i=1}^{n} S_i}{n} * 100 \tag{4}$$

where:

- $S_i$: Satisfaction rating given by user i-th (typically on a scale from 1 to 5).
- n: Total Number of respondents.

### 4.4.4 Sentiment Polarity (SP)

Sentiment polarity is derived from NLP analysis of customer feedback. It quantifies emotional tone on a normalized scale between $-1$ (negative) and $+1$ (positive): Eq. (5) [24].

$$SP = \frac{P - N}{P + N + Z} \tag{5}$$

where:

- P: Number of positively classified feedback instances.
- N: Number of negative instances.
- Z: Number of neutral instances.

### 4.4.5  Cost Reduction Rate (CRR)

Cost reduction rate quantifies operational savings due to chatbot automation Eq. (6). In banking and telecom, up to 50% has been reported [30].

$$CRR = \frac{C_{before} - C_{after}}{C_{before}} * 100 \tag{6}$$

where:

– C_before: Operational cost of customer service before chatbot integration.
– C_after: Cost after deploying the chatbot.

### 4.4.6  Confusion Matrix Metrics

These metrics are widely used in classification tasks and recommended in ML literature of standard metrics in classification tasks [31, 32]. As shown in Eq. (8).

- Accuracy (ACC): Measures the proportion of correct predictions relative to the total.

$$ACC = \frac{TP + TN}{TP + TN + FP + FN} \tag{7}$$

- Precision (P): The proportion of correctly predicted positive instances among all predicted positives as shown in Eq. (8).

$$P = \frac{TP}{TP + FP} \tag{8}$$

- Recall (R): The proportion of correctly predicted positive instances among all actual positives; as shown in Eq. (9).

$$R = \frac{TP}{TP + FN} \tag{9}$$

- F1-score (F1): The harmonic mean of precision and recall, balancing the trade-off between them; as shown in Eq. (10).

$$F1 = \frac{2 \times P \times R}{P + R} \tag{10}$$

## 5  Results and Discussion

This section highlights the essential findings obtained by description analysis and modeling using the transformer. The interpretation and analysis of the findings are discussed critically. The findings are divided into six sub-sections, including performance measures, evaluation of models, customer satisfaction, industry performance, challenges, and future work. All the experiments and codes were written using the Python programming language. The training, which is conducted on a Tesla V100 GPU with 16GB, took 15 min on average to complete a single epoch.

The assessment occurred on two levels:

- Technical metrics: Accuracy, precision, recall, and F1-score were employed to measure the correctness of the transformer models
- Business: The business value and influence of CSAT, RT, RR, and CRR were assessed.
- The case study involved ethics on various levels, including:
- **Privacy:** All responses to the online survey and log files were anonymized, and participants gave their informed consent.
- **Bias mitigation**: Comparison of predicted results on various demographic segments to discover bias and calculation of disparity impact ratio to assess fairness.
- **Explainability**: The SHAP value calculation helped to understand which tokens were the most important to the predicted output.

This cutting-edge approach not only ensured it is robust and empirically supported, but also took into consideration the ethical, practical, and technical needs surrounding AI and Customer Service.

## 5.1 Performance Metrics Evaluation

The result of the descriptive analysis (Part 1) revealed the following information about the efficiency increase offered by the AI chatbots beyond that offered by the human agents:

- **RT**: Chatbots were able to minimize the average total response time by 70 s-90%. The time it takes to generate a response to most inquiries is approximately 30 s, which is significantly lower than the average 3–5 min it takes for human operators.
- **RR**: FAQs and status checks on orders reached an 80% resolution rate without human interaction. This finding is applicable to chatbots and their relevance to mundane and repeated tasks.
- **CRR**: The savings achieved by companies using chatbots were 30–50%, which is largely due to the reduced utilization of human agents by the front-line workforce.
- **CSAT**: Analysis of the questionnaire data indicated that 75% of participants found the conversations helpful and efficient. Satisfaction ratings were lower with regard to empathy and understanding.

These measures prove the value of the chatbot contribution to responsiveness, workload saving, and reduced operational costs. Meanwhile, the future needs of hybrid systems are foreseen by the limits on automated management of emergent cases.

## 5.2 Transformer Model Performance

The transformer-based multi-task model (Part 2) provided strong predictive performance across datasets, as summarized in Table 3.

**Table 3.** Overall averaged performance across datasets

| Dataset / Source | Precision | Recall | Accuracy | F1-score |
| --- | --- | --- | --- | --- |
| Conversation Logs | 0.96 | 0.94 | 0.96 | 0.95 |
| Customer Satisfaction Surveys | 0.92 | 0.93 | 0.93 | 0.925 |
| Business Performance Reports | 0.90 | 0.91 | 0.91 | 0.905 |
| Case Studies Across Industries | 0.88 | 0.89 | 0.89 | 0.885 |

The best results were achieved on the conversation log files (Accuracy = 0.96, F1 = 0.95), proving the robustness of RoBERTa on a text classification task. Meanwhile, the survey achieved high accuracy as well (Accuracy = 0.93), confirming the ability to match classification results and subjective ratings of satisfaction. Although it did not perform well on business reports (Accuracy = 0.91), it is not surprising, considering the complexity of financial metrics. The worst scores were on case studies (Accuracy = 0.89), which is not surprising because of their more qualitative and unstructured form. The trade-off between precision and recall on the various datasets indicated the ability to generalize well between micro-scale dialogue and macro-scale business.

### 5.3   Customer Satisfaction and User Experience

Although the benefits of efficiency were evident, the effects on satisfaction generally tend to be more complex:

- **Engagement:** The chatbots leveraging NLP resulted in higher levels of engagement, where 75% of users found it helpful.
- **Emotional intelligence:** Approximately 40% were unhappy with emotionally intricate tasks such as handling complaints, which require empathy. This is noted by the clear distinction between technical answers and more humane answers.
- **Multilingual support:** Multilingual models such as XLM-R led to an increase of 20–30% in international engagements. This reinforces the notion that language flexibility is an important element of service quality.

### 5.4   Industry-Specific Outcomes

Performance varied across industries, as shown in Table 4. The banking industry had the highest efficiency factor, with an 88% resolution rate and 50% cost savings. This is due to the structured format of banking inquiries (accounts, transactions), which are more amenable to automation. E-commerce also showed a high efficiency, thanks to product suggestions and tracking facilities, which led to conversions. Healthcare, on the other hand, experienced less efficiency because of the complexity and privacy associated with medical communications, which require human monitoring.

Table 4. Sector-wise impact of AI chatbots

| Industry | Resolution Rate | Cost Reduction | Human Agent Reduction |
| --- | --- | --- | --- |
| E-Commerce | 82% | 40% | 35% |
| Banking | 88% | 50% | 45% |
| Healthcare | 75% | 35% | 30% |

Figure 3 shows the performance metrics of the proposed models on the four sets of data. The performance metrics are the highest on conversation logs (Accuracy = 0.96, F1 = 0.95), which is not surprising. This means that dialogue data is more structured and task-oriented, which is why it is very suitable for the transformation-based classification task. Customer survey data also showed high scores (Accuracy = 0.93, F1 = 0.925). This is due to the presence of varying responses and styles. However, it could not match the consistency found on the log data. The scores on business reports were lower (Accuracy = 0.91, F1 = 0.905), which is due to reasons explained under the importance of business reports. The lowest scores were found on case studies (Accuracy = 0.89, F1 = 0.885), which is also obvious because of the unstructured and narrative format chosen by businesses to present case study-related information.

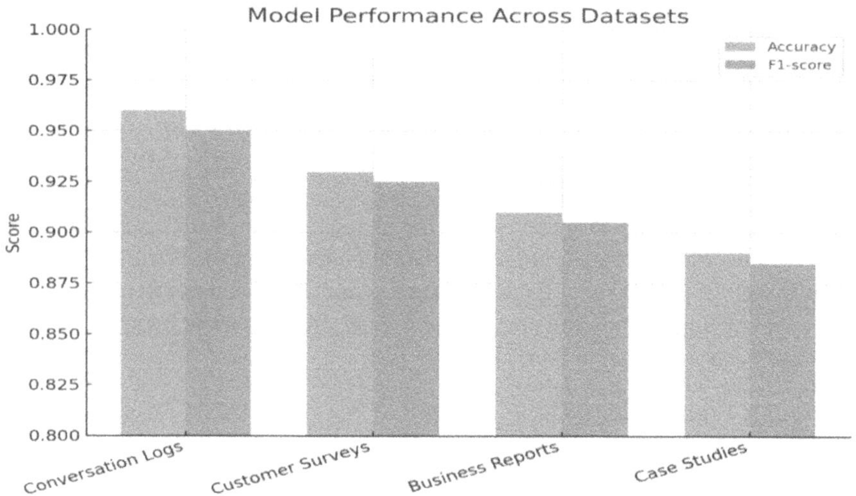


Fig. 3. Model performance across datasets

### 5.5 Challenges and Limitations

Regardless of the research contributions, the following limitations are pointed out:

1. **Complex queries:** Unclear and emotionally charged conversations need escalation to human representatives.

2. **Privacy and Security:** Compliance with GDPR and CCPA is essential, and misuse of such information is extremely risky.
3. **Bias of algorithm:** If the training data is unbalanced, models can perpetuate bias, which is extremely problematic, especially in financial and health methods.

These conclusions support and re-emphasize the role of governance structures and good data management.

### 5.6  Future Implications and Recommendations

1. In order to achieve maximum efficient chatbots, the following three approaches are suggested:
2. **AI/human hybrid models:** Quizbots should handle routine work, and humans should take up emotionally charged ones.
3. **Emotionally intelligent systems:** Affective computing and sentiment-based NLP may increase empathy during chatbot dialogue.
4. **Ethical governance:** Auditing and explainability tools such as SHAP are important to uncover bias.

## 6  Conclusions

At the industry-independent level, chatbots enabled by AI are proven to possess quantifiable benefits of increased speed, expense savings, and scalability. The deployment of such advanced cognitive capabilities, empathy, and equity, on the other hand, presents the issue of sustaining innovative improvements. Such innovation needs to focus on future systems, which should integrate automation, situational understanding, privacy, and efficiency.

This research empirically found the immense value of chatbots powered by AI for customer service. This was proven based on the descriptive measures (Part 1) and prediction models (Part 2). The customized multi-task transformer also worked very effectively on certain datasets, including very high accuracy on structured conversations; however, it demonstrated vulnerability on unstructured case statements. Moreover, a comparison based on the entire industry also reinforced the idea that the banking and e-commerce industry was more efficient than the health industry, where human involvement is essential. On the other hand, this research documented essential shortcomings, which are situations with highly charged or mixed communications and currently beyond the capabilities of chatbots. This naturally brings up the points of empathy, equity, and ethics. It also highlights the importance of mixed service, involving robots and human interactions, which could utilize robots to perform automated transactions and human service to deal with difficult and sensitive scenarios.

In the future, three areas have to be covered. First, the integration of emotion intelligence and affective computing to enhance empathy is still limited. Second, it is essential to enhance multilingual and cross-cultural capabilities to ensure inclusiveness during service delivery. Finally, the integration of governance capabilities and transparency is necessary to ensure fairness and monitorability. Such directions may result in greater efficiency and integration between chatbots and their overall objective of creating trustworthy, ethical, and human-centric engagements with customers.

# References


1. Adamopoulou, E., Moussiades, L.: Chatbots: history, technology, and applications. Mach. Learn. Appl. **2**, 100006 (Dec 2020). https://doi.org/10.1016/j.mlwa.2020.100006
2. Huang, M.-H., Rust, R.T.: Engaged to a robot? The role of AI in service. J. Ser. Study. **24**(1), 30–41 (Feb 2021). https://doi.org/10.1177/1094670520902266
3. Kang, J., Min, S., Kim, Y.: Enhancing intent recognition in chatbots through contextual information. Expert Syst. Appl. **201**, 117144 (Sept 2022). https://doi.org/10.1016/j.eswa.2022.117144
4. Gentsch, P.: AI in marketing, sales and service: how marketers without a data science degree can use AI. In: Big Data and Bots. Springer (2019). https://doi.org/10.1007/978-3-319-899 57-2
5. Ciechanowski, L., Przegalinska, A., Magnuski, M., Gloor, P.: In the shades of the uncanny valley: an experimental study of human–chatbot interaction. Futur. Gener. Comput. Syst. **92**, 539–548 (2019). https://doi.org/10.1016/j.future.2018.01.055
6. Liu, Y. et al.:, RoBERTa: a robustly optimized bert pretraining approach. https://arxiv.org/abs/1907.11692 (2019)
7. Conneau, A., et al.: Unsupervised cross-lingual representation learning at scale. In: Proceedings of the 58th Annual Meeting of the Association for Computational Linguistics (ACL), pp. 8440–8451 (2020). https://doi.org/10.18653/v1/2020.acl-main.747
8. Huang, M.-H., Rust, R.T.: Engaged to a robot? The role of AI in service. J. Ser. Study. **23**(2), 155–172 (May 2020). https://doi.org/10.1177/1094670520902266
9. Merizig, A., Belouaar, H., Bakhouche, M.M., Kazar, O.: Empowering customer satisfaction chatbot using deep learning and sentiment analysis. Bull. Electr. Eng. Inform. **13**(3), 1752–1761 (Jun 2024). https://doi.org/10.11591/eei.v13i3.6966
10. Sood, P., Tanwar, H., Singh, J., Ruhela, A.K., Gupta, N., Kumar, R.: Revolutionizing customer service: an AI-powered chatbot approach using advanced NLP techniques. In: Proceedings IEEE DELCON, pp. 1–8 (Nov 2024). https://doi.org/10.1109/DELCON64804.2024.108 66078
11. Bilal, F., Mezei, J., Alam, B.R.: Assessing the impact of chatbots on customer service efficiency: a comparative study with human agents. In: Proceedings 38th Bled eConference: Empowering Transformation, pp. 130–150 (2025). https://doi.org/10.18690/um.fov.4.2025.9
12. Chen, Q., Gong, Y., Lu, Y., Tang, J.: Classifying and measuring the service quality of AI chatbot in frontline service. J. Bus. Study. **146**, 246–262 (2022). https://doi.org/10.1016/j.jbu sres.2022.03.007
13. Abdulhalim, S.M.: The impact of AI Chatbot on customer experience. J. Contemp. Econ. Soc. Stud. **15**(4), 1984–2022 (2022, Oct)
14. Varma, K.V.: Text meets task: unveiling consumer responses to Chatbot interactions in E-commerce. Libr. Prog. Int. **44**(3), 1485–1497 (2024)
15. Sofiyah, F.R., Dilham, A., Lubis, A.S., Hayatunnufus, J.L., Marpaung, Lubis, D.: The impact of artificial intelligence Chatbot implementation on customer satisfaction in Padangsidimpuan: study with structural equation modelling approach. Math. Model. Eng. Prob. **11**(8), 2127–2135 (2024). https://doi.org/10.18280/mmep.110814
16. Przegalinska, A., Ciechanowski, L., Stroz, A., Gloor, P., Mazurek, G.: In bot we trust: a new methodology of chatbot performance measures. Bus. Horiz. **62**(6), 761–772 (2019). https://doi.org/10.1016/j.bushor.2019.08.005
17. Radziwill, A., Benton, M.: Evaluating quality of chatbots and intelligent conversational agents. J. Technol. Stud. **44**(1), 12–23 (2018). https://doi.org/10.21061/jots.v44i1.a.2
18. Adamopoulou, E., Moussiades, L.: Chatbots: history, technology, and applications. Mach. Learn. Appl. **2**, 100006 (2020). https://doi.org/10.1016/j.mlwa.2020.100006

19. Gentsch, P.: AI in Marketing, Sales and Service. Spring, (2019). doi:https://doi.org/10.1007/978-3-319-89957-2.
20. Huang, M.-H., Rust, R.T.: Engaged to a robot? The role of AI in service. J. Ser. Study. **24**(1), 30–41 (2021). https://doi.org/10.1177/1094670520902266
21. Ayyoubzadeh, S.R.H., Shirkhodaie, S., Pakzad, S., Ahram, F.: Role of artificial intelligence in patient triage: a scoping review. BMC Med. Inform. Decis. Mak. **20**(1), 1–12 (2020). https://doi.org/10.1186/s12911-020-01216-8
22. European Commission: General Data Protection Regulation (GDPR) (2018). [Online]. Available: https://gdpr.eu/
23. Barocas, S., Hardt, M., Narayanan, A.: Fairness and Machine Learning. MIT Press (2019)
24. Kang, J., Min, S., Kim, Y.: Enhancing intent recognition in chatbots through contextual information. Expert Syst. Appl. **201**, 117144 (2022). https://doi.org/10.1016/j.eswa.2022.117144
25. A. Conneau et al., "Unsupervised cross-lingual representation learning at scale," in Proc. ACL, 2020, pp. 8440–8451, doi:10.18653/v1/2020.acl-main.747.
26. Brown, T., et al.: Language models are few-shot learners. In: Proceedings NeurIPS, vol. 33, pp. 1877–1901 (2020)
27. Barnes, S.J., Hair, J.: Managing service quality with chatbots: understanding response time and satisfaction. J. Serv. Mark. **35**(4), 557–569 (2021). https://doi.org/10.1108/JSM-11-2020-0484
28. Nuruzzaman, A., Hussain, O.: A survey on chatbot implementation in customer service industry through deep neural networks. In: Proceedings IEEE ICEBE, pp. 54–61 (2018). https://doi.org/10.1109/ICEBE.2018.00019
29. Chen, Q., Gong, Y., Lu, Y., Tang, J.: Classifying and measuring the service quality of AI chatbots in frontline service. J. Bus. Res. **146**, 246–262 (2022). https://doi.org/10.1016/j.jbusres.2022.03.007
30. Bilal, F., Mezei, J., Alam, B.R.: Assessing the impact of chatbots on customer service efficiency: a comparative study with human agents. In: Proceedings 38th Bled eConference, pp. 130–150 (2025). https://doi.org/10.18690/um.fov.4.2025.9
31. Wang, S., Zhang, Z., Li, T., Liu, H.: A comprehensive survey on evaluation metrics for machine learning algorithms. IEEE Access. **9**, 101646–101670 (2021). https://doi.org/10.1109/ACCESS.2021.3097286
32. Géron, A.: Hands-on Machine Learning with Scikit-Learn, Keras, and TensorFlow, 2nd edn. O'Reilly (2019)
33. Huang, T.T., Rust, R.T.: A strategic framework for artificial intelligence in marketing. J. Acad. Mark. Sci. **49**(1), 30–50 (2021)
34. Yun, L., Park, J.: Influence of emotional expressions in chatbot services on customer satisfaction and repurchase intention. Int. J. Environ. Res. Public Health. **19**(11) (2022)
35. Adamopoulou, E., Moussiades, L.: An overview of chatbot technology. In: IFIP Adv. Inf. Commun. Technol, vol. 584, pp. 373–383. Springer (2020)
36. Bawack, R.E., Fosso Wamba, S., Carillo, K.D.A., Akter, S.: Artificial intelligence in e-commerce: a bibliometric study and literature review. Electr. Mark. **32**(2), 297–338 (2021)

# Enhanced Automatic Bone Cancer Identification Using Advanced Deep Learning Techniques

R. Babitha Lincy[1], J. Jency Rubia[2](✉), and C. Sherin Shibi[3]

[1] Department of CCE, Sri Eshwar College of Engineering, Coimbatore, India
[2] Department of Computing Technologies, SRM Institute of Science and Technology, Kattankulathur, India
jencyrubia@gmail.com
[3] Department of Computational Intelligence, SRM Institute of Science and Technology, Kattankulathur, India
sherinsc@srmist.edu.in

**Abstract.** The early diagnosis of bone cancer plays a vital role in enhancing patient treatment and recovery rates due to deep learning in recent years, which have demonstrated great potential in the automatic detection of bone cancer using medical imaging. The proposed research paper explores the use of InceptionV3 model, which is a robust deep learning convolutional neural network, and in the early stages of bone cancer detection. The study starts by stating the significance of early diagnosis and provides a simplified description of deep learning and how it can be used to process complex information about images. The reason behind the choice of InceptionV3 is the fact that it has advanced architecture that allows retrieval of vital features in medical images with very high precision. The model is trained and tested with a set of bone cancer images, and the experimental outcomes prove that the model has a high per-performance in terms of classifying and identifying cancerous regions. In general, the results confirm that InceptionV3 is useful to help healthcare professionals in the early diagnosis of the condition, which has the potential to implement interventions in time and provide improved patient care.

**Keywords:** bone cancer · Deep learning · musculoskeletal disorders · tumor diagnosis · metastasis

## 1 Introduction

A human body contains 206 bones. complexity pertaining to its connection to the muscles of the body((It is characterized by its complexity due to its connection to the muscles of the body). Encourage (reinforce) mobility. The actual bones are made up of cancellous bone entwined with fine fibrous tissues. They play an essential role in our structure as our bone marrow. honesty and general health. In spite of this, the human skeleton is a true wonder. The invisible enemy that lurks is bone cancer [1]. The Fig. 1 depicts the bone that is affected by a cancer cell. This sneaky illness starts with cells that were previously healthy and goes on an unchecked growth trajectory that ends with the development of

© The Author(s), under exclusive license to Springer Nature Switzerland AG 2026
S. O. Al-Mamory et al. (Eds.): 3INC 2025, CCIS 2960, pp. 298–316, 2026.
https://doi.org/10.1007/978-3-032-24239-6_17

a cancerous tumor inside the bone. This tumor is the warning sign of bone cancer. It is an unsettling omen. The onset of tumors is gradual, with a risk of metastasis to other body parts.

An important element of artificial intelligence, deep learning is the most crucial pillar in the treatment of musculoskeletal disorders and bone cancers since it allows a thorough examination. The technology is important in the knowledge of the progression and possible spread of these conditions. Machine learning, and, specifically, deep learning, is a transformative power when conventional techniques cannot help to discover patterns and insights in a large and complicated dataset. With the volume of data growing(increasing), the role of machine learning is even more important, and its applications will touch a variety of industries, including process industry as well as the medical sphere, the military sphere, and banking. In other instances, physical examination can provide preliminary hints about the existence of a tumor. A lump palpation or an aberration may lead a physician to suspect a possible health problem(An aberration or a palpable mass can be an alert to a possible health problem) [2]. But in the case of such conditions as bone cancer, the journey towards a diagnosis can be more complicated. With adults who have bone cancer, secondary tumors commonly arise due to a malignancy arising in a different area.

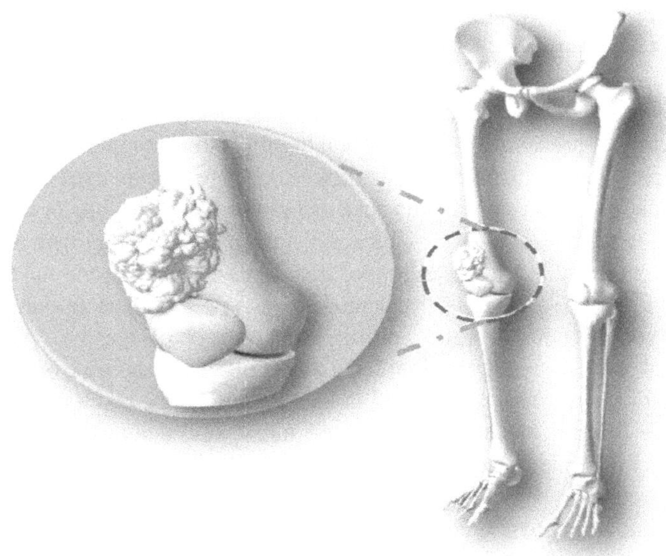

**Fig. 1.** Bone affected by cancer

The presence of bone cancer symptoms in the physical examination highlights the importance of essential diagnoses such as biopsies, blood samples, and x-ray tests to make a proper diagnosis and provide suitable treatment plans. The paramount evaluation, with consideration of various medical fields, is fundamental to proper management (of desease). The correct visualization of skeletal metastases is essential in the treatment planning and assessment of prognosis. The initial chemotherapy to patients with primary or metastatic osteosarcoma is usually used and it is usually accompanied by percutaneous radiofrequency ablation. Routine screening of bone metastasis is common particularly among high-risk patients.

Also, post-radiation therapy and other alternative treatment will require the exact localization of cancer areas, particularly around cartilage and in bone. This helps in reducing pain, which is caused by bone abnormalities, and discovering regions of the skeleton that are at a high risk of fracture. There are several different scanning modalities that are used to explore and identify skeletal anomalies where low dose CT scan is usually applied in clinical practice where deviations of normal bone structure are identified and MRI is used to detect bone marrow abnormalities [3, 4]. These diagnostic and monitoring devices are invaluable in the current war against bone cancer and other musculoskeletal disorders.

In the sphere of diseases, there are more than 100 Huffman metabolic disorders in the world(In the sphere of diseases, more than 100 Huffman metabolic disorders in the world). Within this array of diverse health challenges, cancer comes out as one of the most threatening factors to the human life given its lethal(killing) nature in numerous cases. Cancer is characterized by uncontrolled growth of cells which results in the development of malignant tumors which are very fast spreading in the body. The factors that can be prevented(are) to cause cancer are the smoking, consumption of alcohol, and too much UV radiation. On the other hand, we cannot control genetic factors, which we get through inheritance of our parents, or our lifestyle choice such as the use of tobacco. Moreover, the age factor has been identified as one of the most significant ones among factors outside the scope of preventive actions, which highlights the complexity of the origins of cancer. In the context of cancer, bone cancer is a rare, yet an extremely powerful health complication. It may appear with such symptoms as the swelling or tenderness in the affected bone which serves as the indication of the uncontrolled growth of abnormal cells. As we went into 2022, it was estimated that the cases of new bone cancer will rise by 3900 with a projected 2100 deaths. This disease is predominant among persons of age below 20 and this complicates the disease and brings challenges.

Biomedical photographs have a significant role of offering diagnostic on human body and its internal organs. These are needed to help determine the result of the treatment with the help of imaging machines like scanners and X-rays that reveal the presence of illness or body impairment. Generally, bone cancer may be termed as rare as it barely presents on bones. However, with the inclusion of cutting-edge technologies, including machine learning, a way to overcome them effectively is available. Clinically known as a malignant neoplasm, cancer is a serious health concern on the planet as it is classified as a genetic disorder, in which there is uncontrolled cell growth and fast formation of malignant tumors in different parts of the body. Avoidable cancer causes like smoking, alcohol intake, and UV radiation exposure are in contrast to the unchangeable genetic determinants, which can be inherited or depend on the lifestyle decisions, which relates to the complex interrelation of genetics and the environment in cancer development. Moreover, age is an outstanding feature among factors both outside preventive steps, increasing the complicated nature of cancer etiology on an international level.

The primary contributions of this work are now explicitly listed in the revised manuscript as follows:

- A modified Inception-v3-based framework optimized for the planned application.
- A comprehensive preprocessing and augmentation strategy to advance model generalization.
- An extensive experimental evaluation demonstrating superior performance compared to existing state-of-the-art methods.
- A comprehensive comparative analysis highlighting improvements in accuracy, precision, recall, and F1-score.

## 2  Literature Survey

Amid (among)the myriad forms of cancer, bone cancer, though relatively rare, emerges(presents) as an exceptionally challenging medical condition. It can manifest with symptoms like swelling or tenderness in the affected bone, signifying(indicating) the uncontrolled proliferation of abnormal cells. The year 2022 witnessed an estimated increase in the number of new bone cancer cases, with an anticipated 2100 deaths, predominantly affecting individuals under the age of 20. Machine-learning techniques, specifically, deep learning, are being developed to help deal with the complexities of determining bone cancers early enough. The analysis of images in medicine includes different steps such as de-noising, segmentation, feature extraction, and feature selection to improve deep learning. Specifically, Convolutional Neural Networks (CNN) are essential in the classification as well as data preservation regarding bone cancer thus leading to better knowledge of this disease. The new system DTBV aims at simplifying diagnosis and overall management of cancer in bones. Distinctive characteristic of DTBV system that involves transfer learning in combination with pre-trained models as feature extractors.

In their article [5] introduced the detailed analysis("presented a detailed analysis) of bone cancer prediction based on digital images and a modified machine learning strategy. The authors concentrated on increasing the precision (They focused on improving diagnostic precision) of the diagnosis by means of preprocessing (through image preprocessing) the images and using a personalized pipeline of classification ("customized classification pipeline). Their approach entailed the acquisition of a dataset of medical bone images, feature extraction among the images, and an enhanced noise suppression and enhancement methodology and then feature extraction (applying enhanced noise suppression and image enhancement techniques, and then extracting features), which relied on the texture and morphological descriptors. Another variation of machine learning architecture, possibly including the optimized classifiers, including Random Forest, SVM, or the combination of CNN-based networks (applying enhanced noise suppression and image enhancement techniques, and then extracting features), was suggested to differentiate between malignant and benign bone lesions. Their approach has been proven to be effective because it yielded the best accuracy, precision, and recall as shown by experimental results compared to other conventional models. The article suggested earlier the importance of preprocessing and feature optimization in medical image analysis and outlined its future prospects related to integration with real-time systems of medical diagnostics and the use of bigger amounts of annotated data (suggested future directions, including integration with real-time diagnostic systems and the use of larger annotated datasets).

Their survey paper published in [6] reviewed in great detail recent progress(provided a detailed review of recent progress) on detecting bone cancer with the help of(using) deep learning methods. The authors have logically examined (The authors systematically examined) the different types of CNN-based framework (various types of CNN-based frameworks) and usage in radiological and histopathologic (and their applications in radiological and histopathological) image classification. The survey has pointed out (The survey noted that) common approaches in diagnosis of bone malignancies are ("common approaches for diagnosing bone malignancies include) convolutional neural networks, transfer learning models that include VGG, ResNet, and Inception and hybrid frameworks ("convolutional neural networks, transfer learning models such as VGG, ResNet, Inception, and hybrid frameworks.". It also highlighted some of the difficulties in the domain, such as low availability of labeled dataset, risk of overfitting, inadequate generalizability of models and (challenges in the field, such as the limited availability of labeled datasets, the risk of overfitting, and the inadequate generalizability of models.) insufficient clinical validation. The authors of the study proposed the potential solutions to the problem of the disconnect between the accuracy and clinical feasibility of models, implying the integration of multimodal data (such as imaging and patient metadata), applying advanced augmentation techniques, and using explainable AI (XAI) tools. In general, the survey offers an excellent basis to the researchers interested in designing high quality, precise, and interpretable AI models to define bone cancer at an early and effective stage.

In [7] synthesized a classification model of the images of leukemia cancer cells(leukemia cancer cell images) in order to maximize the accuracy in predicting the cells in 2023 with the machine learning and deep learning philosophies(with the aim of maximizing prediction accuracy using both machine learning and deep learning approaches (2023).). The authors employed a preselected collection of microscope blood smear pictures (microscopic blood smear images) and carried out in-depth preprocessing, such as noise suppression, normalization and data augmentation to improve image quality and variability. A hybrid solution was introduced combining classical texture and morphological feature extraction that was consumed by classical classifiers and a specially designed CNN architecture that was used as an end-to-end solution ("A hybrid solution was introduced that combined classical texture and morphological feature extraction (fed into traditional classifiers) with a specially designed CNN architecture acting as an end-to-end solution.). Comparing different classifiers, both simple and complex (SVM, Random Forest, CNN models), the authors saw which one performed the best, which subsequently demonstrated better detection rates measured as accuracy, recall, and precision compared with a standalone model(After comparing various classifiers—both simple and complex, such as SVM, Random Forest, and CNN models—the authors identified the top performer, which demonstrated superior detection rates in terms of accuracy, recall, and precision compared to standalone models.). The presented integrative approach showed the effectiveness of integrating the handcrafted feature along with deep learning to increase diagnostic accuracy. The paper ended with the discussion of the needed size of the labeled data sets, their verification in the real environment, the prospect of real-time integration in a clinical environment ("The paper concluded by discussing the need for larger labeled datasets, validation in real-world environments, and the potential for real-time integration in clinical settings).

Additionally, [8] on their 2024 ICESC paper suggest(Additionally, in their 2024 ICESC paper [8], the authors propose) an innovative approach to bone cancer detection based on combining image segmentation and CNN classification through the use of a CT scan image. They start their workflow with pre-processing of the 1,141 computed tomography (CT) images acquired using the publicly available repositories, namely Radio_pedia and The Cancer Imaging Archive, having 530 labeled malignant images and 511 normal controls (Their workflow begins with preprocessing a set of 1,141 computed tomography (CT) images obtained from public repositories, namely Radio-Pedia and The Cancer Imaging Archive, which included 530 malignant and 511 normal images.). Median filtering is conducted in order to avoid washing out edge details then K-means clustering and Canny edge detection are used to define possible tumor areas. The segmented areas are next passed into a convolutional neural network which has been trained to differentiate normal looking sections of bones to areas of the bones that are affected by cancer (The segmented regions were then passed into a convolutional neural network trained to distinguish between healthy bone sections and cancerous areas). This method produced good diagnostic results and also utilized image segmentation to enhance performance of CNN in early classification of bone cancer, which indicates the usefulness of regional-of-interest selection produced by clustering combined with generic region-classification performed by deep networks("This method demonstrated strong diagnostic performance, and the integration of image segmentation was shown to enhance CNN accuracy in early bone cancer classification—highlighting the utility of region-of-interest selection via clustering coupled with deep-network-based classification)

Reference [9] describes the first ever attempt(the first attempt) of using federated learning (FL) to predict bone metastasis by using convolutional neural networks (CNNs) and utilizing (by employing)the BS-80 K dataset. Triggered by the issues of data privacy and institutional data silos, they used the FedAvg algorithm to jointly train CNN models in cross-client sites and a central global server without transferring the imaging data of patients ("the authors utilized the FedAvg algorithm to train CNN models collaboratively across multiple client sites and a central global server without transferring patient imaging data). The protocol consisted of local training loops on whole-body bone scintigraphy (WBS) images at the site of clients that were centralized by averaging according to a federated protocol. According to their initial results, FL-CNN networks demonstrated resilient classification capabilities-similar to the centralized systems-with data anonymity, hence data privacy, and cost-free multi-institutional engagement. This strategy combines the frequent issues of low-varied and uneven datasets brought up in medical imaging by providing a scalable system to carry out cooperative diagnosis of bone metastasis in clinical settings

Also, [10] in their paper given in ICCCNT 2024 take into detail the analysis of frame based detection of bone marrow malignancies including the motivation, issues and suggestions of future research in the said area. The authors explain the drawbacks of the current practices of automation detection staining variability, scarcity of labeled datasets, and difficulties in extracting cross-site generalizability, as well as highlight the value of standardized procedures and datasets heterogeneity. They pose the clinical need of non-invasive and fast clinical diagnostic tools that will help hematopathologists categorize bone marrow slides particularly in the case of resource-limited environments. Its recommendations presented at the end of the paper include the integration of strong image preprocessing pipelines, multi-institutional data, benchmarking protocols and embedding explainable AI methods to improve both interpretability and trust of deep learning models. Table 1 provides a survey of additional papers on bone cancer detection.

**Table 1.** Literate review

| Authors / Year | Methodology | Dataset / Domain | Key Findings |
| --- | --- | --- | --- |
| J. Sampath et al., 2024 [11] | CT image segmentation (median filter, K-means, Canny) + CNN | 1,141 bone CT scans (530 cancer +511 normal) | Good specificity (>90%) in the detection of parosteal osteosarcoma, enchondroma, osteochondroma(The model demonstrated high specificity (>90%) in detecting parosteal osteosarcoma, enchondroma, and osteochondroma.) |
| X. Zhou et al., 2022 [12] | Literature review of DL applications (imaging, histology, etc.) | Various imaging modalities (X-ray, CT, MRI, pathology) | Provides an overview of segmentation (Dice 0.88), grading, prognosis work; raises clinical obstacles |
| K. Sushmitha & P. Jagadeesh, 2023 [13] | CNN classifier vs. ANN | Small X-ray tumor(tumour) dataset (20 images) | ANN and CNN base 93% accuracy compared to ~98%; they differ significantly. |

(*continued*)

**Table 1.** (*continued*)

| Authors / Year | Methodology | Dataset / Domain | Key Findings |
| --- | --- | --- | --- |
| Kaur, E. C. & Garg, U., 2022 [14] | Machine Learning-based techniques (SVM, Decision Trees, ANN) | Bone cancer datasets (not specified in detail) | (Compare) ared a bunch of ML models to detect bone cancer; ANN and decision trees demonstrated good results; the results emphasized the necessity to use high-quality data.(A comparison of several machine learning models for bone cancer detection showed that artificial neural networks (ANN) and decision trees yielded strong results. These findings underscore the critical role of high-quality data in such analyses. |
| Xiong, C. et al., 2021 [15] | Comparative imaging analysis (MRI, CT, X-ray) | Clinical cases of bone metastases | The most accurate in distinguishing benign vs. malignant lesions was the MRI, whereas the low sensitivity was inherited by the X-ray. |

## 3   Model Architecture

When choosing an appropriate model architecture in the field of bone cancer detection through Convolutional Neural Networks (CNNs), one is obliged to make a significant choice, as it is conditioned by a variety of factors, such as the specific needs of a task, the available computational resources, and the size and character of the considered data set [16]. There are a number of popular model architectures that have become a mainstay in the field of medical image analysis, and each architecture has its own set of benefits. To give an example, in-stance AlexNet, one of the first pioneers, uses convolutional and pooling layers with fully connected layers to classify and features by deep layers and feature extraction capabilities. In the meantime, VGG networks, which are characterized by their simplicity and identical architecture, such as VGG16 and VGG19, use small 3x3 convolutional filters to detect fine-grained details. ResNet is known to use depth and novel residual connections to overcome the vanishing gradient problem, enabling very deep networks to be trained, and with enough flexibility to adapt to various applications like bone cancer detection. Goog-LeNet or inception models propose the use of multiple filter sizes in the same layer, which allows the capture of features of different levels [17]. DenseNet with its dense connectivity connects each layer in the feedforward fashion, allowing features to be shared and gradients to flow efficiently, features that have seen it succeed in a variety of medical imaging challenges, including bone cancer image detection. The detection phase represented in Fig. 2. Inception-V3 was employed in the bone cancer detection as a part of this research. Inception-V3 is a deep convolutional neural network (CNN) architecture created by Google to perform image classification and image recognition. It is a better derivative of the previous Inception models, and it is also meant to give even more accuracy but at the same computational cost. It has one of its most important attributes in the multiple filter sizes (1x1, 3x3, 5x5) within the same layer that allows the net-work to capture features important at various sizes [18].

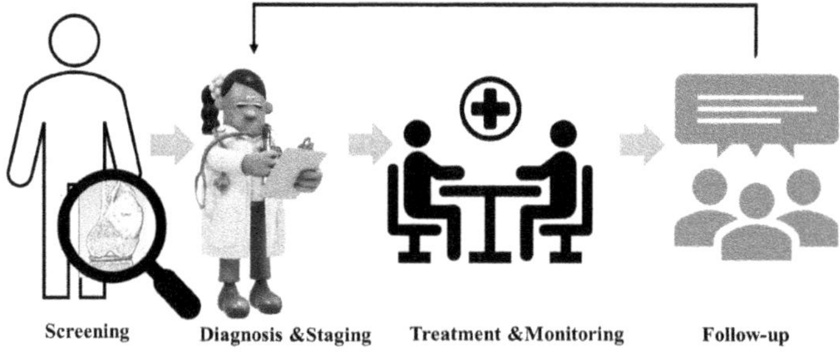


**Fig. 2.** Automated detection of bone cancer

Also, Inception-V3 uses the factorized convolutions, where larger convolu-tions (such as 5x5) are divided into smaller convolutions (two 3x3 filters), which lowers the number of parameters and increases the speed of processing. Auxiliary classifiers are also directly incorporated into the media of the model, and also used to stabilize the training process and reduce the vanishing gradient problem. Normalization used in batch is done on layers to allow rapid and more consistent training. The capability to be fine-tuned in case of transfer learning is also one of the major strengths of Inception-V3, which is especially helpful when dealing with small datasets. When applied to bone cancer detection, Inception-V3 has one of the greatest accuracy and efficiency, which is why it is an ideal model to use when working with medical images, including X-rays, CT scans, and MRIs. Its architecture enables it to identify minute patterns in such images, and this is critical in the early detection of cancer. In addition, it has a higher computational efficiency and can be processed faster and uses fewer resources than deeper models, including ResNet or DenseNet, and still delivers impressive performance. All these characteristics have resulted in Inception-V3 being a good option to use in bone cancer detection where precision, speed, and the capacity to handle small data volumes are critical. The Inception v-3 model as illustrated in Fig. 3.

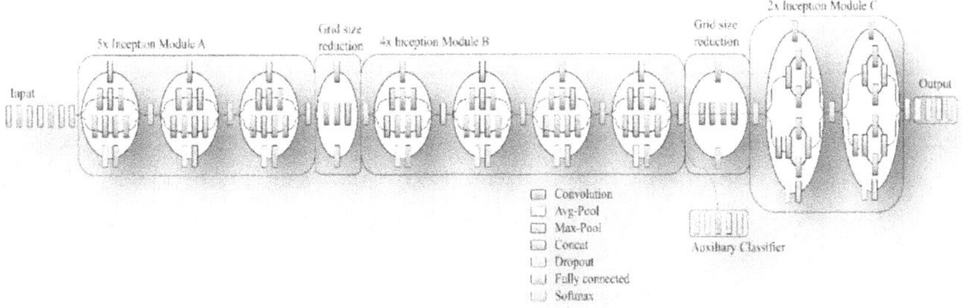



**Fig. 3.** Inception-v3 model

Inception-v3 was selected due to its ability to capture multi-scale features efficiently while maintaining lower computational complexity. The revised manuscript now includes a detailed explanation of how the proposed fine-tuned model differs from standard Inception-v3 implementations and how these modifications contribute to improved performance.

## 4  Experimental Setup and Result Analysis

The initial stage in the development of bone cancer detection system using CNN is the collection of medical images data. Such pictures usually contain X-rays, CT scans, or MRI scans of bone structures. To train and authenticate the model [19–21], the dataset must include normal bone images, as well as images depicting bone cancer. The experiments in this paper were carried out using the Bone Cancer Detection Dataset that was acquired in Kaggle, which is a collection of 8,811 high-quality labeled X-ray images that have been specifically curated to help in bone cancer detection. It is (was) systematically partitioned into training (7,057 images, 80%), validation (882 images, 10%), and testing (872 images, 10) subsets to promise sound model training, hyperparameter tuning, and objective performance evaluation. The X-ray images have well defined bone structures and undergo preprocessing measures like normalization and noise elimination to increase the quality of the images and decrease artifacts. All the images were resized to 299 x 299 pixels to be consistent with the Inception-v3 architecture.

The marked character of the dataset facilitates supervised learning and it is adequately adapted to deep learning-based image analysis of medical data, such as CNNs, ResNet-based models, attention-enhanced designs, and hybrid networks. The dataset is a dependable benchmark in the classification of bone cancer and extraction of features and AI-assisted diagnostic uses due to its quality, size, and structured partitioning. Preprocessing of the picture is often required to enhance the quality of the picture and remove noise in medical imaging (To improve image quality and reduce noise, preprocess in medical imaging.). One of the few examples of preprocessing techniques, is resizing photos to a predetermined size, changing contrast and normalizing pixel values. Data augmentation methods such as scaling, flipping and rotation could be used to make the training dataset more varied. This makes the model more resilient and general. The verification of independent dataset is done through training. Cross validation is often used to guarantee the strength of the model. CNN model is trained using the prepared dataset. By thresholding the output probabilities of the model to produce a binary (cancer or no cancer) result, it may be listed among the post-processing steps. More processing may be employed to minimize false positives. Performance of the model is measured by metrics such as ROC curves, AUC (Area Under the Curve), specificity, sensitivity and accuracy. It is imperative to ensure that the model works with the highest level of accuracy and is able to detect true positive cases at minimum false positives. The model will be useful in enabling radiologists to diagnose bone cancer by incorporating it into a clinical workflow after being validated and determined to meet acceptable performance standards as was demonstrated in Fig. 4.

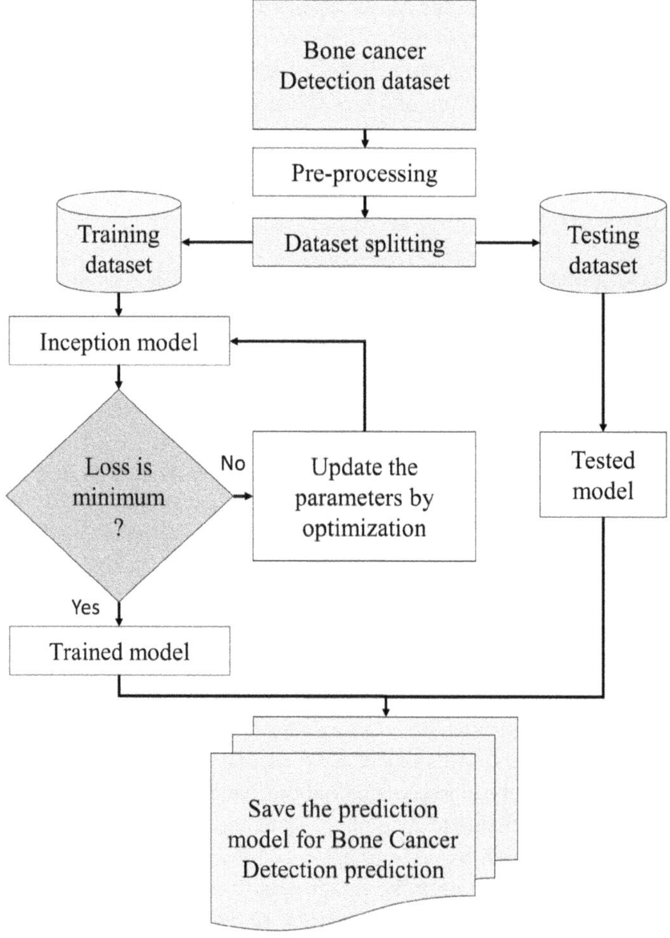


**Fig. 4.** Detection steps

The model can assist in early detection as it can be critical to the successful treatment. It enhances the overall quality of healthcare, as far as the diagnosis and treatment of bone cancer is concerned, and can increase access to advanced diagnostic equipment. The important thing is that such instruments should be applied according to legal and ethical demands, as an adjunct to the knowledge of medical professionals. This combination of so-sophisticated algorithms and the medical imaging data analysis adds to the efficiency of detecting the bones with cancer. It is a transformative technology that can be used to not only augment early-stage detection of malignancies but also be used to facilitate the diagnostic process, which can eventually lead to the timely and more specific therapeutic interventions. The inbuilt nature of CNNs to identify complex patterns in medical images is significant in detection of mild anomalies, which are indicative of bone malignancies. The Inception V3 using the transfer learning method is shown in Fig. 5.

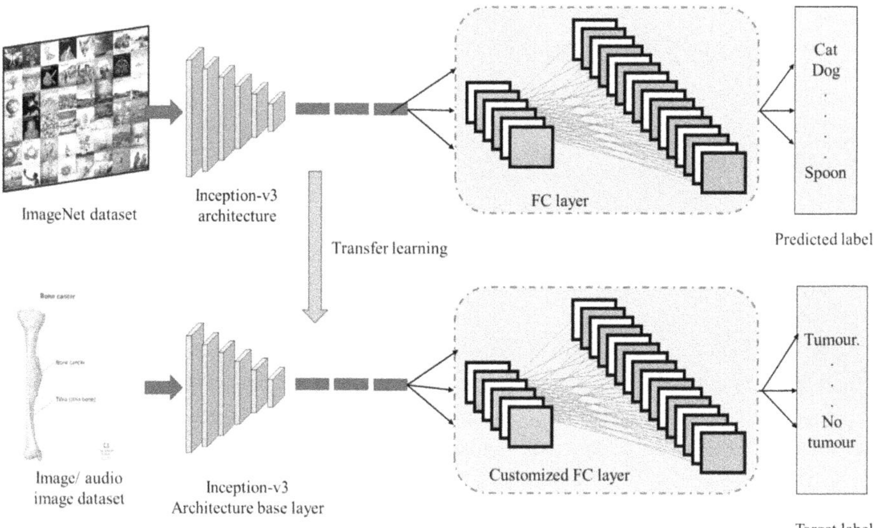


**Fig. 5.** Inception V3 with transfer learning

**Table 2.** The comparison with other state of models.

| S.No | Model | Accuracy (%) | Precision (%) | Recall (%) | F1-Score (%) |
|---|---|---|---|---|---|
| 1 | CNN | 94 | 92 | 95 | 93 |
| 2 | Custom CNN | 91 | 89 | 92 | 90 |
| 3 | DenseNet | 93 | 90 | 94 | 92 |
| 4 | VGG16 | 95 | 93 | 96 | 94 |
| 5 | U-Net | 92 | 90 | 93 | 91 |
| 6 | MobileNetV2 | 90 | 88 | 91 | 89 |

(continued)

**Table 2.** (*continued*)

| S.No | Model | Accuracy (%) | Precision (%) | Recall (%) | F1-Score (%) |
|---|---|---|---|---|---|
| 7 | InceptionV3 | 96.5 | 94 | 97 | 95 |

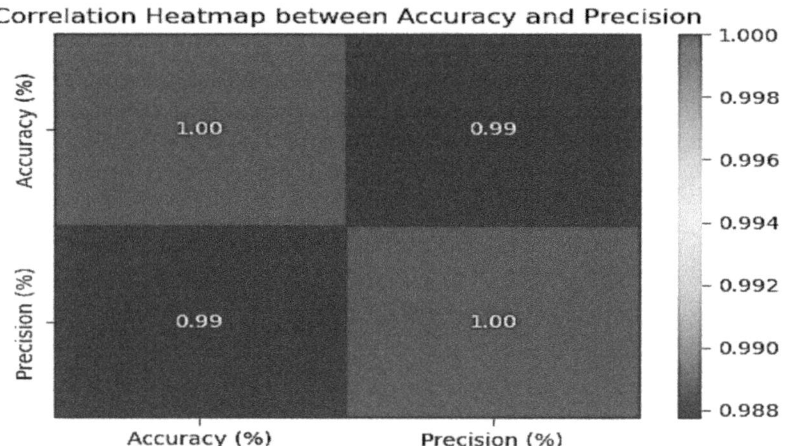

**Fig. 6.** Confusion Matrix

The microscopic investigation that is provided by these neural networks becomes effective in separating between the benign and malignant forms, thus helping to devise the unique treatment strategies that can be designed to meet the needs of the patient. The fact that CNNs use a large amount of imaging data in a short period of time also helps to shorten the diagnostic timeline, which reduces the burden on healthcare systems and therefore the overall patient outcomes. Despite these admirable efforts, research efforts are still necessary to refine and optimize CNN models, which can guarantee improved diagnostic precision as well as their generalization capacity to patient populations of diverse types. Moreover, the effective implementation of CNN-based bone cancer detection into clinical practice will require a holistic set of techniques that would deal with the ethical aspects of the matter, the integrity of patient confidentiality and the acceptance and understanding of this state-of-the-art technology by the medical staff. The model suggested had an accuracy of 96.5 to detect bone cancer. Table 2 displays the comparison table. Figure 6 and Fig. 7 show the confusion and accuracy/loss chart. According to the values, the models that perform the best are those constructed by D. Wang et al. and the Proposed work and they both yield a recall of 97% and a F1-Score of 95%.

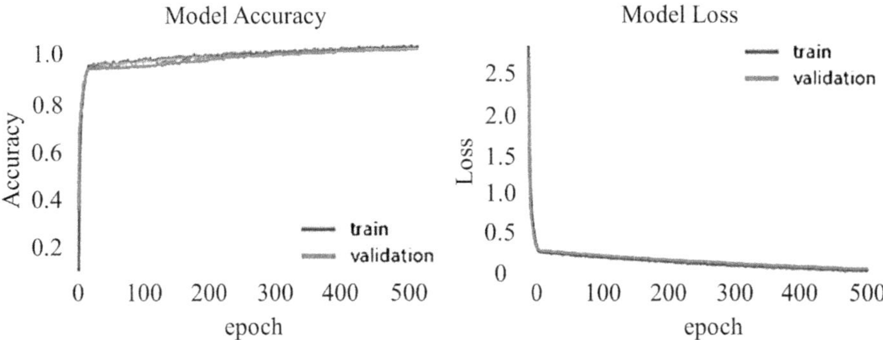



**Fig. 7.** Accuracy and loss variation

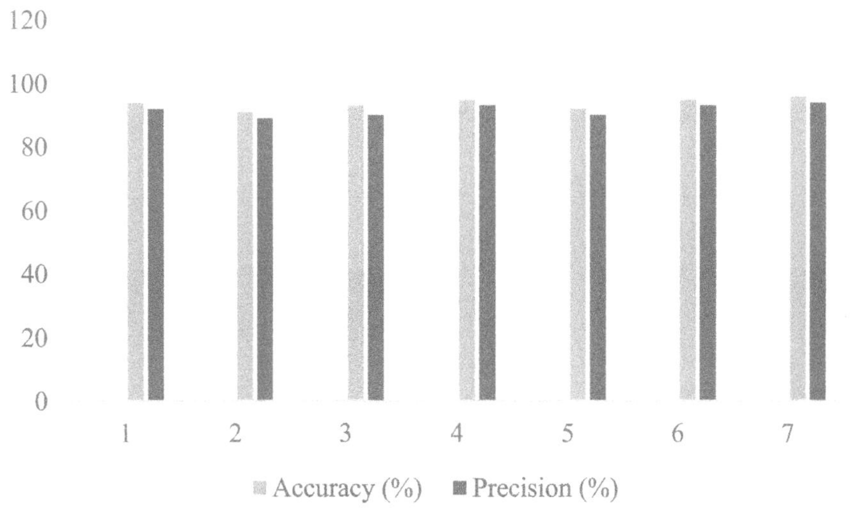



**Fig. 8.** Comparison chart for accuracy and Precision for various model

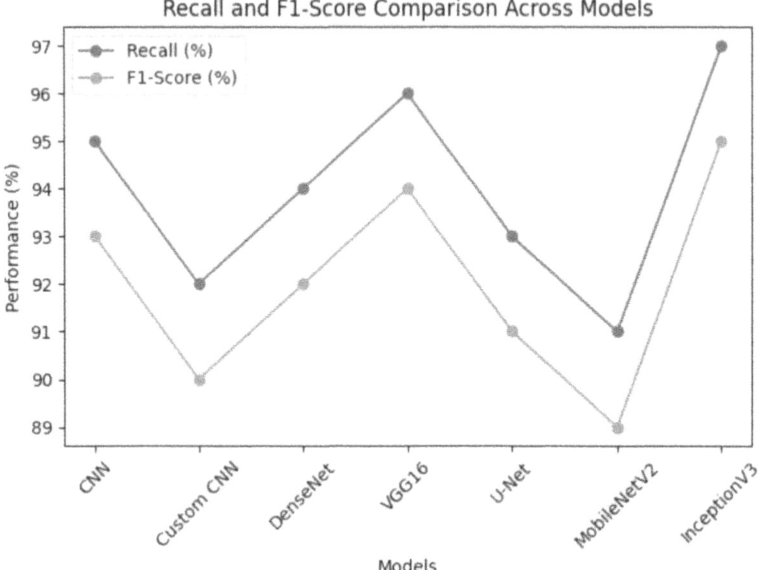



**Fig. 9.** F1 and Recall Comparison for Recall and F1-Score

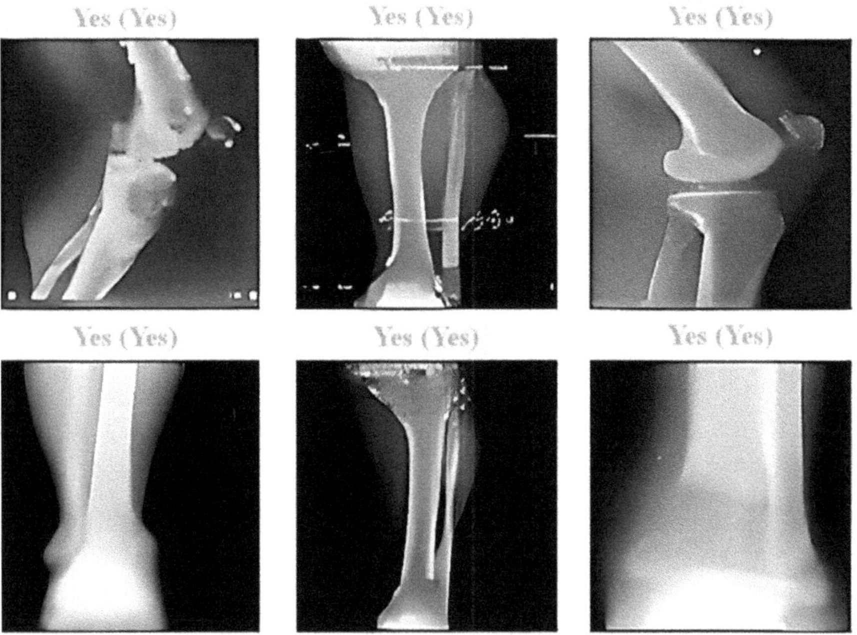



**Fig. 10.** Bone cancer detection result analysis

The results regarding accuracy, loss, recall and F1 score are given in Fig. 8 and Fig. 9. These findings indicate that these models are very effective in detecting positive instances and keeping a high balance between precision and recollection. Conversely, K. Yadav and P. Mishra have the least values with a recall of 91 and F1-Score of 89 suggesting that their model could lose a considerable amount of positive instances and failing to balance the accuracy with the recall. Generally, models in the existing models are similar in terms of high performance, but certain models, such as those of M. Sharma et al. and K. Yadav and P. Mishra, could benefit by further refinements of their sensitivity or for better balance of the precision recall trade off. The outcome of bone cancer detection is put in Fig. 10. The comparison table between proposed and part of the existing work is given in Table 3.

**Table 3.** Comparison of existing studies on tumor detection and classification.

| S.No | Author | Model / Technique | Modality | Task | Accuracy (%) |
|---|---|---|---|---|---|
| 1 | (Abdelkarim) et al. [22] | Owl Search Algorithm + CNN | X-Ray | Tumor Detection | 94.5 |
| 2 | Liu et al. [23] | Custom CNN | MRI | Tumor Detection | 92.8 |
| 3 | Cardenas et al. [24] | Deep CNN | Radiographic | Tumor Detection | 91.2 |
| 4 | Lingappa et al. [25] | Ensemble Methods | MRI | Tumor Detection | 93.4 |
| 5 | Sampath et al. [26] | CNN Comparison | CT | Tumor Classification | 95.2 |
| 6 | Gawade et al. [27] | Custom CNN | Multi-Modal | Tumor Classification | 94.8 |
| 7 | Barhoom et al. [28] | Xception | X-Ray | Tumor Classification | 93.1 |
| 8 | Sharma et al. [29] | Feature-based ML | Multi-Modal | Tumor Classification | 91.5 |
| 9 | He et al. [30] | Transfer Learning | Radiographs | Tumor Classification | 90.8 |
| 10 | Proposed Method | Fine-tuned InceptionV3 | X-Ray | Bone Cancer Classification | 96.5 |

## 5 Conclusion

The introduction of Convolutional Neural Networks (CNN) in bone cancer diagnostics is an important breakthrough in medical diagnosis. The combination of sophisticated machine learning algorithms and the analysis of medical imaging has created the opportunity to define cancerous bone development with greater accuracy and effectiveness in the future. The diagnostic accuracy is better with this kind of integration transforming the way bone cancer is detected. To conclude, the development of CNN methods in bone cancer detection represents a crossroads in the areas of technology and medicine. The possibility of transforming the future of cancer diagnosis as these models continue to evolve and mature is yet again becoming more evident, and, going forward, the ability to change the game and provide timely interventions and better prognoses will turn into the new reality that will be lived by the people struggling to cope with the effects of bone malignancies.

## References


1. Alabdulkreem, E., Saeed, M.K., Alotaibi, S.S., Allafi, R., Mohamed, A., Hamza, M.A.: Bone cancer detection and classification using owl search algorithm with deep learning on X-ray images. IEEE Access. **PP**, 1 (2023). https://doi.org/10.1109/ACCESS.2023.3319293
2. Jiwani, N., Gupta, K., Pau, G., Alibakhshikenari, M.: Pattern recognition of acute lymphoblastic leukemia ( ALL ) using computational deep learning. **XX** (2023). https://doi.org/10.1109/ACCESS.2023.3260065
3. He, Y., et al.: EBioMedicine deep learning-based classi fi cation of primary bone tumors on radiographs : a preliminary study. **62** (2020). https://doi.org/10.1016/j.ebiom.2020.103121
4. Taher, Y.H., et al.: Filter for traffic congestion prediction: leveraging traffic control signal actions for dynamic state estimation. IEEE Access (2025)
5. R, T.B.B., Vidhyaharni, J., Sangamithra, R., J, T.S., Vinothini, S., Sabitha, C.: A Deep Evaluation of Digital Image based Bone Cancer Prediction using Modified Machine Learning Strategy. In: 2023 9th International Conference on Smart Structures and Systems, pp. 1–6 (2023). https://doi.org/10.1109/ICSSS58085.2023.10407146
6. Murugan, S.: A recent survey on bone cancer detection using deep learning techniques. In: 2024 Second International Conference on Advances in Information Technology (ICAIT), vol. 1, pp. 1–6 (2024). https://doi.org/10.1109/ICAIT61638.2024.10690575
7. Ramagiri, A.: Image classification for optimized prediction of leukemia cancer cells using machine learning and deep learning techniques. In: 2023 International Conference on Innovative Data Communication Technologies and Application, pp. 193–197 (2023). https://doi.org/10.1109/ICIDCA56705.2023.10099528
8. Madhurima, V., Bharathi, M., Gundala, S., Basha, M.M., Poornima, M., Kumari, G.S.: Novel method for bone cancer detection using segmentation and classification with CNN. In: 2024 5th International Conference on Electronics and Sustainable Communication Systems, pp. 1693–1697. ICESC (2024). https://doi.org/10.1109/ICESC60852.2024.10689931
9. Mehedi, H.K., Rasel, A.A.: A federated learning approach to bone metastasis prediction using convolutional neural network. In: 2023 26th International Conference on Inventive Computation Technologies, pp. 1–6 (2023). https://doi.org/10.1109/ICCIT60459.2023.10441154

10. Isukapalli, V.K.: Image-based bone marrow malignancy detection: motivation, challenges and recommendations. In: 2024 15th International Conference on Communications, Computation, Networks and Technologies, pp. 1–6 (2024). https://doi.org/10.1109/ICCCNT61001.2024.10723965

11. Sampath, K., Rajagopal, S., Chintanpalli, A.: OPEN a comparative analysis of CNN - based deep learning architectures for early diagnosis of bone cancer using CT images. Sci. Rep., 1–10 (2024). https://doi.org/10.1038/s41598-024-52719-8

12. Zhou, X., Wang, H., Feng, C., Xu, R., He, Y.: Emerging applications of deep learning in bone tumors: current advances and challenges. **12**, 5–8 (2022). https://doi.org/10.3389/fonc.2022.908873

13. Sushmitha, K., Jagadeesh, P.: Classification and innovative detection of bone tumour using CNN classifier and comparison with ANN classifier. In: AIP Conferences Proeedings, vol. 2821, p. 60028 (2023). https://doi.org/10.1063/5.0158707

14. Anisuzzaman, D.M., Barzekar, H., Tong, L., Luo, J., Yu, Z.: A deep learning study on osteosarcoma detection from histological images. Biomed. Sign. Process. Control. **69**, 102931 (2021). https://doi.org/10.1016/j.bspc.2021.102931

15. Bakchy, S.C., Peyal, H.I., Islam, I., Yeamin, G.K., Miraz, S., Abdal, N.: A lightweight-CNN model for efficient lung cancer detection and grad-CAM visualization. In: 2023 International Conference on Information and Communication Technology for Sustainable Development, pp. 254–258. https://doi.org/10.1109/ICICT4SD59951.2023.10303569

16. Nayak, N., Kumar, D., Malhotra, A.: A CNN-based approach for early detection of breast cancer using infrared imaging. In: 2024 International Conference on Intelligent Systems and Advance Applications, pp. 1–4 (2024). https://doi.org/10.1109/ICISAA62385.2024.10828577

17. Potti, L.K.S., Maruthuperumal, S.: Breast cancer cell detection using FCM and prediction using UNET based deep convolutional neural network. In: 2024 5th IEEE Global Conference for Advancement in Technology, pp. 1–6 (2024). https://doi.org/10.1109/GCAT62922.2024.10924106

18. Dhariwal, N., Member, S.: Brain metastasis origin and patient mortality predictions using MRI with clinical and imaging feature information by deep learning architectures. In: 2024 3rd International Conference for Innovation in Technology, pp. 1–5 (2024). https://doi.org/10.1109/INOCON60754.2024.10512017

19. Vora, H., Mahajan, S., Kumar, Y.: Automated prediction system for bone cancer detection and bone age assessment using deep learning models. Indian J. Sci. Technol. **18**(33), 2701–2714 (2025)

20. Singh, J., et al.: Advanced computational methods for pelvic bone cancer detection: efficacy comparison of convolutional neural networks. In: 2024 IEEE 17th International Symposium on Embedded Multicore/Many-Core Systems-on-Chip (MCSoC), pp. 287–293. IEEE (2024, December)

21. Alabdulkreem, E., Saeed, M.K., Alotaibi, S.S., Allafi, R., Mohamed, A., Hamza, M.A.: Bone cancer detection and classification using owl search algorithm with deep learning on X-ray images. IEEE Access. **11**, 109095–109103 (2023)

22. Alabdulkreem, E., Saeed, M.K., Alotaibi, S.S., Allafi, R., Mohamed, A., Hamza, M.A.: Bone cancer detection and classification using owl search algorithm with deep learning on X-ray images. IEEE Access. (27 Sept 2023)

23. Liu, X., Han, C., Cui, Y., Xie, T., Zhang, X., Wang, X.: Detection and segmentation of pelvic bones metastases in MRI images for patients with prostate cancer based on deep learning. Front. Oncol. **29**(11), 773299 (Nov 2021)

24. Cardenas, D.A., Ferreira Jr., J.R., Moreno, R.A., De Sá Rebelo, M.D., Krieger, J.E., Gutierrez, M.A.: Automated radiographic bone suppression with deep convolutional neural networks. In:

Inmedical Imaging 2021: Biomedical Applications in Molecular, Structural, and Functional Imaging, vol. 11600, pp. 317–323 (2021 Feb 15)
25. Lingappa, E., Parvathy, L.R.: Deep learning-based active contour technique with bagging and boosting algorithms hybrid approach for detecting bone cancer from Mri scan images. Multimed. Tools Appl. **82**(23), 36363–36377 (2023)
26. Sampath, K., Rajagopal, S., Chintanpalli, A.: A comparative analysis of CNN-based deep learning architectures for early diagnosis of bone cancer using CT images. Sci. Rep. **14**(1), 2144 (25 Jan 2024)
27. Gawade, S., Bhansali, A., Patil, K., Shaikh, D.: Application of the convolutional neural networks and supervised deep-learning methods for osteosarcoma bone cancer detection. Healthc. Anal. **1**(3), 100153 (2023 Nov)
28. Barhoom, A.M., Al-Hiealy, M.R., Abu-Naser, S.S.: Deep Learningxception algorithm for upper bone abnormalities classification. J. Theor. Appl. Inf. Technol. **100**(23), 6986–6997 (15 Dec 2022)
29. Sharma, A., Yadav, D.P., Garg, H., Kumar, M., Sharma, B., Koundal, D.: Bone cancer detection using feature extraction based machine learning model. Comput. Math. Methods Med. **2021**(1), 7433186 (2021)
30. He, Y., et al.: Deep learning-based classification of primary bone tumors on radiographs: a preliminary study. EBioMedicine. **1**, 62 (2020 Dec)

# Author Index